Simians, Cyborgs, and Women

The idea that nature is constructed, not discovered – that truth is made, not found – is the keynote of recent scholarship in the history of science. Tracing the gendered roots of science in culture, Donna Haraway's writings about scientific research on monkeys and apes is arguably the finest scholarship in this tradition. She has carefully studied the publications, the papers, the correspondence, and the history of the expeditions and institutions of primate studies, uncovering the historical construction of the pedigrees for existing social relations – the naturalization of race, sex, and class. Throughout this book she is analysing accounts, narratives, and stories of the creation of nature, living organisms, and cyborgs (cybernetic organisms: systems which embrace organic and technological components). She also looks critically at the immune system as an information system, and shows how deeply our cultural assumptions penetrate into allegedly value-neutral medical research. In several of these essays she explores and develops the contested terms of reference of existing feminist scholarship; and by mapping the fate of two potent and ambiguous words – 'nature' and 'experience' – she uncovers new visions and provides the possibility of a new politics of hope.

Her recent book, *Primate Visions*, has been called 'outstanding', 'original', 'brilliant', 'important' by leading scholars in the field. *Simians, Cyborgs, and Women* contains ten essays written between 1978 and 1989. They establish her as one of the most thoughtful and challenging feminist writers today.

Donna Haraway is a historian of science and Professor at the History of Consciousness Board, University of California, Santa Cruz. She received her doctorate in biology at Yale and is the author of *Crystals, Fabrics, and Fields: Metaphors of Organicism in Twentieth-Century Developmental Biology* and *Primate Visions: Gender, Race, and Nature in the World of Modern Science*.

Simians, Cyborgs, and Women

The Reinvention of Nature

DONNA J. HARAWAY

Routledge / New York

First published in the United States of America in 1991 by
Routledge
an imprint of
Routledge, Chapman and Hall, Inc.
29 West 35 Street
New York, NY 10001

First published in Great Britain in 1991 by
Free Association Books
26 Freegrove Road
London N7 9RQ

Library of Congress Cataloging in Publication Data

Haraway, Donna Jeanne.
  Simians, cyborgs, and women: the reinvention of nature / by Donna J. Haraway.
    p. cm.
  Includes bibliographical references (p.) and index.

  ISBN 0-415-90386-6. — ISBN 0-415-90387-4 (pbk).
  1. Sociobiology. 2. Feminist criticism. 3. Primates—Behavior.
  4. Human behavior. I. Title.
GN365.9.H37 1991
304.5—dc20   90-8762
                                                       CIP

For my parents,
Dorothy Maguire Haraway (1917–1960)
and
Frank O. Haraway

Contents

Acknowledgements

Many people and many publishing practices made this book possible, beginning with the anonymous referee for *Signs* for my first published essays in feminist theory. This generous and critical person turned out to be Rayna Rapp, who has been a personal, intellectual, and political support and inspiration for me ever since. Catherine Stimpson was the editor for those papers, and her theoretical work and editorial skill have enriched my writing and that of many other contributors to contemporary feminism. Constance Clark and Stephen Cross, then graduate students at Johns Hopkins, will see their pervasive influence. Robert Young's ground-breaking writing and committed comradeship showed me that the history of science could be both political and scholarly without compromise. I owe much to his work and that of many others, especially Karl Figlio, Ludi Jordanova, and Les Levidow, associated with *Radical Science Journal*, *Science as Culture*, and Free Association Books.

Friendship, ongoing critical conversations, and published and unpublished intertextualities with Judith Butler, Elizabeth Fee, Sandra Harding, Susan Harding, Nancy Hartsock, Katie King, Diana Long, Aihwa Ong, Joan Scott, Marilyn Strathern, and Adrienne Zihlman everywhere inform these chapters. I also thank Frigga Haug and Nora Räthzel from the feminist collective of *Das Argument* and Elizabeth Weed of *differences*. Jeffrey Escofier was a persistent gadfly and gentle midwife for the Cyborg Manifesto (Chapter Eight). Scott Gilbert, Michael Hadfield, and G. Evelyn Hutchinson taught me about embryology, ecology, the immune system and much else in the culture of biology.

Extraordinary people whom I first knew through the History of Consciousness Board and graduate seminars at the University of California at Santa Cruz contributed explicitly and implicitly to this book. I am especially grateful to Gloria Anzaldúa, Bettina Aptheker, Sandra Azeredo, Faith Beckett, Elizabeth Bird, Norman O. Brown, Jim Clifford, Mary Crane, Teresa de Lauretis, Paul Edwards, Ron Eglash, Barbara Epstein, Peter Euben, Ramona Fernandez, Ruth Frankenberg, Margo Franz, Thyrza Goodeve, Deborah Gordon, Chris Gray, Val Hartouni, Mary John, Caren Kaplan, Katie King, Hilary Klein, Lisa Lowe, Carole McCann, Lata Mani, Alvina Quintana, Chela Sandoval, Zoe Sofoulis, Noel Sturgeon, Jenny Terry, Sharon Traweek, and Gloria Watkins (bell hooks).

Financial support for writing portions of this book was provided by Academic Senate Research Grants of the University of California at Santa Cruz and the Alpha Fund of the Institute for Advanced Study.

Others have offered support and inspiration in countless ways over many years. These essays especially show the imprint of living and working with Gail Coleman, Layla Krieger, Richard and Rosemarie Stith, Carolyn Hadfield, Robert Filomeno, Jaye Miller, and Rusten Hogness. Finally, I dedicate this book to my parents, Frank Haraway, a sports reporter who showed me that writing can be simultaneously pleasure and work, and Dorothy Maguire Haraway, who died in 1960 before I could know her as an adult, but who had communicated to me the trouble and strength of belief and commitment.

The following chapters have been revised from previously published essays, and are printed here with permission. Chapter One originally appeared under the title 'Animal sociology and a natural economy of the body politic, part I, a political physiology of dominance', in *Signs* 4 (1978): 21–36. Chapter Two, under the title 'Animal sociology and a natural economy of the body politic, part II, the past is the contested zone: human nature and theories of production and reproduction in primate behavior studies', in *Signs* 4 (1978): 37–60. Chapter Three, 'The biological enterprise: sex, mind, and profit from human engineering to sociobiology', in *Radical History Review* 20 (1979): 206–37. Chapter Four, 'In the beginning was the word: the genesis of biological theory', in *Signs* 6 (1981): 469–81. Chapter Five, 'The contest for primate nature: daughters of man the hunter in the field, 1960–80', in Mark Kann, ed. *The Future of American Democracy: Views from the Left* (Philadelphia: Temple University Press, 1983, pp. 175–207). Chapter Six, 'Reading Buchi Emecheta: contests for 'women's experience' in women's studies', in *Inscriptions* 3/4 (1988): 107–24. Chapter Seven, as 'Geschlecht, Gender, Genre: Sexualpolitik eines Wortes', in Kornelia Hauser, ed. *Viele Orte. Überall? Feminismus in Bewegung, Festschrift for Frigga Haug.* (Berlin: Argument-Verlag, 1987, pp. 22–41). Chapter Eight, as 'Manifesto for cyborgs: science, technology, and socialist feminism in the 1980s', *Socialist Review* 80 (1985): 65–108. Chapter Nine, as 'Situated knowledges: the science question in feminism as a site of discourse on the privilege of partial perspective', in *Feminist Studies* 14(3) (1988): 575–99. Chapter Ten, as 'The biopolitics of postmodern bodies: determinations of self in immune system discourse', in *differences: A Journal of Feminist Cultural Studies* 1(1) (1989): 3–43.

Introduction

This book should be read as a cautionary tale about the evolution of bodies, politics, and stories. Above all, it is a book about the invention and reinvention of nature – perhaps the most central arena of hope, oppression, and contestation for inhabitants of the planet earth in our times. Once upon a time, in the 1970s, the author was a proper, US socialist-feminist, white, female, hominid biologist, who became a historian of science to write about modern Western accounts of monkeys, apes, and women. She belonged to those odd categories, invisible to themselves, which are called 'unmarked' and which are dependent upon unequal power for their maintenance. But by the last essays, she has turned into a multiply marked cyborg feminist, who tried to keep her politics, as well as her other critical functions, alive in the unpromising times of the last quarter of the twentieth century. The book examines the breakup of versions of Euro-American feminist humanism in their devastating assumptions of master narratives deeply indebted to racism and colonialism. Then, adopting an illegitimate and frightening sign, the book's tale turns to the possibilities of a 'cyborg' feminism that is perhaps more able to remain attuned to specific historical and political positionings and permanent partialities without abandoning the search for potent connections.

A cyborg is a hybrid creature, composed of organism and machine. But, cyborgs are compounded of special kinds of machines and special kinds of organisms appropriate to the late twentieth century. Cyborgs are post-Second World War hybrid entities made of, first, ourselves and other organic creatures in our unchosen 'high-technological' guise as information systems, texts, and ergonomically controlled labouring, desiring, and reproducing systems. The second essential ingredient in cyborgs is machines in their guise, also, as communications systems, texts, and self-acting, ergonomically designed apparatuses.

The chapters comprising Part One of this book examine feminist struggles over the modes of producing knowledge about, and the meanings of, the behaviour and the social lives of monkeys and apes. Part Two explores contests for the power to determine stories about 'nature' and 'experience' – two of the most potent and ambiguous words in English. Part Three focuses on cyborg embodiment, the fate of various feminist concepts of gender, reappropriations of metaphors of vision for feminist ethical and epistemological purposes, and the immune system as a biopolitical map of the chief systems of 'difference' in a postmodern world. Throughout these diverse contents, this book treats constructions of nature as a crucial cultural process for people who need and hope to live in a world less riddled by the dominations of race, colonialism, class, gender, and sexuality.

Inhabiting these pages are odd boundary creatures – simians, cyborgs, and women – all of which have had a destabilizing place in the great Western evolutionary, technological, and biological narratives. These boundary creatures are, literally, *monsters*, a word that shares more than its root with the word, to *demonstrate*. Monsters signify. *Simians, Cyborgs, and Women* interrogates the multi-faceted biopolitical, biotechnological, and feminist theoretical stories of the situated knowledges by and about these promising and non-innocent monsters. The power-differentiated and highly contested modes of being of these monsters may be signs of possible worlds – and they are surely signs of worlds for which we are responsible.

Simians, Cyborgs, and Women collects essays written from 1978 through 1989, a period of complicated political, cultural, and epistemological foment within the many feminisms which have appeared in the last decades. Focusing on the biopolitical narratives of the sciences of monkeys and apes, the earliest essays were written from within US Eurocentric socialist-feminism. They treat the deep constitution of nature in modern biology as a system of production and reproduction, that is, as a labouring system, with all the ambiguities and dominations inherent in that metaphor. How did nature for a dominant cultural group with immense power to make its stories into reality become a system of work, ruled by the hierarchical division of labour, where the inequities of race, sex, and class could be naturalized in functioning systems of exploitation? What were the consequences for views of the lives of animals and people?

The middle set of chapters examines contests for narrative forms and strategies among feminists, as the heteroglossia and power inequities within modern feminism and among contemporary women became inescapable. The section concludes with an examination of ways of reading a modern Nigerian-British author, Buchi Emecheta, as an example of contests among differently situated African, Afro-American, and Euro-American critics over what will count as women's experience in the pedagogical context of a women's studies classroom. What kind of accountability, coalition, opposition, constituencies, and publishing practices structure particular readings of such an author on such a topic?

Part Three, 'Differential Politics for Inappropriate/d Others', contains four essays. The phrase, 'inappropriate/d others', is borrowed from the Vietnamese film-maker and feminist theorist, Trinh T. Minh-ha. She used the term to suggest the historical positioning of those who refuse to adopt the mask of either 'self' or 'other' offered by dominant narratives of identity and politics. Her metaphors suggest a geometry for considering the relations of difference other than hierarchical domination, incorporation of 'parts' into 'wholes', or antagonistic opposition. But her metaphors also suggest the hard intellectual, cultural, and political work these new geometries will require, if not from simians, at least from cyborgs and women.

The essays show the contradictory matrices of their composition. The examination of the recent history of the term sex/gender, written for a German Marxist dictionary, exemplifies the textual politics embedded in producing standard reference-work accounts of complicated struggles. The Cyborg Manifesto was written to find political direction in the 1980s in the face of the hybrids 'we' seemed to have become world-wide. The examination of the debates about 'scientific objectivity' in feminist theory argues for a transformation of the despised metaphors of organic and technological vision in order to foreground specific positioning, multiple mediation, partial perspective, and therefore a possible allegory for feminist scientific and political knowledge.

Nature emerges from this exercise as 'coyote'. This potent trickster can show us that historically specific human relations with 'nature' must somehow – linguistically, ethically, scientifically, politically, technologically, and epistemologically – be imagined as genuinely social and actively relational; and yet the partners remain utterly inhomogeneous. 'Our' relations with 'nature' might be imagined as a social engagement with a being who is neither 'it', 'you', 'thou', 'he', 'she', nor 'they' in relation to 'us'. The pronouns embedded in sentences about contestations for what may count as nature are themselves political tools, expressing hopes, fears, and contradictory histories. Grammar is politics by other means. What narrative possibilities might lie in monstrous linguistic figures for relations with 'nature' for ecofeminist work? Curiously, as for people before us in Western discourses, efforts to come to linguistic terms with the non-representability, historical contingency, artefactuality, and yet spontaneity, necessity, fragility, and stunning profusions of 'nature' can help us refigure the kind of persons we might be. These persons can no longer be, if they ever were, master subjects, nor alienated subjects, but – just possibly – multiply heterogeneous, inhomogeneous, accountable, and connected human agents. But we must never again connect as parts to wholes, as marked beings incorporated into unmarked ones, as unitary and complementary subjects serving the one Subject of monotheism and its secular heresies. We must have agency – or agencies – without defended subjects.

Finally, the mapping of the biopolitical body considered from the perspective of contemporary immune system discourse probes again for ways to refigure multiplicities outside the geometry of part/whole constraints. How can our 'natural' bodies be reimagined – and relived – in ways that transform the relations of same and different, self and other, inner and outer, recognition and misrecognition into guiding maps for inappropriate/d others? And inescapably, these refigurings must acknowledge the permanent condition of our fragility, mortality, and finitude.

Throughout these essays, I have tried to look again at some feminist discards from the Western deck of cards, to look for the trickster figures that might turn a stacked deck into a potent set of wild cards for refiguring possible worlds. Can cyborgs, or binary oppositions, or technological vision hint at ways that the things many feminists have feared most can and must be refigured and put back to work for life and not death? Located in the belly of the monster, the 'First World' in the 1980s and after, how can we develop reading and writing practices, as well as other kinds of political work, to continue to contest for the material shapes and meanings of nature and experience? How might an appreciation of the constructed, artefactual, historically contingent nature of simians, cyborgs, and women lead from an impossible but all too present reality to a possible but all too absent elsewhere? As monsters, can we demonstrate another order of signification? Cyborgs for earthly survival!

Part One

Nature as a System of Production and Reproduction

Chapter One

Animal Sociology and a Natural Economy of the Body Politic: A Political Physiology of Dominance

I want to do something very important. Like fly into the past and make it come out right.
Marge Piercy, Woman on the Edge of Time

T he concept of the body politic is not new. Elaborate organic images for human society were richly developed by the Greeks. They conceived the citizen, the city, and the cosmos to be built according to the same principles. To perceive the body politic as an organism, as fundamentally alive and as part of a large cosmic organism, was central for them (Collingwood, 1945). To see the structure of human groups as a mirror of natural forms has remained imaginatively and intellectually powerful. Throughout the early period of the industrial revolution, a particularly important development of the theory of the body politic linked the natural and political economy on multiple levels. Adam Smith's theory of the market and of the division of labour as keystones of future capitalist economic thought, with Thomas Malthus's supposed law of the relation of population and resources, together symbolize the junction of natural forces and economic progress in the formative years of capitalist industrialism. The permeation of Darwin's evolutionary theory with this form of political economy has been a subject of considerable analysis from the nineteenth century to the present (Young, 1969). Without question, the modern evolutionary concept of a population, as the fundamental natural group, owes much to classical ideas of the body politic, which in turn are inextricably interwoven with the social relationships of production and reproduction.

The union of the political and physiological is the focus of this chapter. That union has been a major source of ancient and modern justifications of domination, especially of domination based on differences seen as natural, given, inescapable, and therefore moral. It has also been transformed by the modern biobehavioural sciences in ways we must understand if we are to work effectively for societies free from domination. The degree to which the principle of domination is deeply embedded in our natural sciences, especially in those disciplines that seek to explain social groups and behaviour, must not be underestimated. In evading the importance of dominance as a part of the theory and practice of contemporary sciences, we bypass the crucial and difficult examination of the *content* as well as the social function of science. We leave this central, legitimating body of skill and knowledge to undermine our efforts, to render them utopian in the worst sense. Nor must we lightly accept the damaging distinction between pure and applied science, between use and abuse of science, and even between nature and culture. All are versions of the philosophy of science that exploits the rupture between subject and object to justify the double ideology of firm scientific objectivity and mere personal subjectivity. This anti-liberation core of knowledge and practice in our sciences is an important buttress of social control.[1]

Recognition of that fact has been a major contribution by feminist theorists. Women know very well that knowledge from the natural sciences has been used in the interests of our domination and not our liberation, birth control propagandists notwithstanding. Moreover, general exclusion from science has only made our exploitation more acute. We have learned that both the exclusion and the exploitation are fruits of our position in the social division of labour and not of natural incapacities.[2] But if we have not often underestimated the principle of domination in the sciences, if we have been less mesmerized than many by the claims to value-free truth by scientists as we most frequently encounter them – in the medical marketplace (Gordon, 1976; Reed, 1978) – we have allowed our distance from science and technology to lead us to misunderstand the status and function of natural knowledge. We have accepted at face value the traditional liberal ideology of social scientists in the twentieth century that maintains a deep and necessary split between nature and culture and between the forms of knowledge relating to these two putatively irreconcilable realms. We have allowed the theory of the body politic to be split in such a way that natural knowledge is reincorporated covertly into techniques of social control instead of being transformed into sciences of liberation. We have challenged our traditional assignment to the status of natural objects by becoming anti-natural in our ideology in a way which leaves the life sciences untouched by feminist needs.[3] We have granted science the role of a fetish, an object human beings make only to forget their role in creating it, no longer responsive to the dialectical interplay of human beings with the surrounding world in the satisfaction of social and organic needs. We have perversely worshipped science as a reified fetish in two complementary ways: (1) by completely rejecting scientific and technical discipline and developing feminist social theory totally apart from the natural sciences, and (2) by agreeing that 'nature' is our enemy and that we must control our 'natural' bodies (by techniques given to us by biomedical science) at all costs to enter the hallowed kingdom of the cultural body politic as defined by liberal (and radical) theorists of political economy, instead of by ourselves. This cultural body politic was clearly identified by Marx: the marketplace that remakes all things and people into commodities.

A concrete example may help explain what I see as our dangerous misunderstanding, an example which takes us back to the point of union of the political and physiological. In *Civilization and Its Discontents*, Freud (1962) developed a theory of the body politic that based human social development on progressive domination of nature, particularly of human sexual energies. Sex as danger and as nature are central to Freud's system, which repeats rather than initiates the traditional reduction of the body politic to physiological starting points. The body politic is in the first instance seen to be founded on natural individuals whose instincts must be conquered to make possible the cultural group. Two recent neo-Freudian and neo-Marxist theorists have ironically reworked Freud's position in illuminating ways for the thesis of this essay: one is Norman O. Brown, the other Shulamith Firestone. Freud, Brown, and Firestone are useful tools in a dissection of the theories of the political and physiological organs of the body politic because they all begin their explanations with sexuality, add a dynamic of cultural repression, and then attempt to liberate again the personal and collective body.

Brown (1966), in *Love's Body*, developed an elaborate metaphorical play between individual and political bodies to show the extraordinary patriarchal and authoritarian structure of our conceptions and experiences of both. The phallus, the head; the body, the state; the brothers, the rebellious overthrow of kingship only to establish the tyranny of the fraternal liberal market – these are Brown's themes. If only the father was head, only the brothers could be citizens. The only escape from the domination that Brown explored was through fantasy and ecstasy, leaving the body politic unchallenged in its fundamental male supremacy and in its reduction to the dynamic of repression of nature. Brown rejected civilization (the body politic) in order to save the body; the solution was necessitated by his root acceptance of Freudian sexual reductionism and the ensuing logic of domination. He turned nature into a fetish worshipped by a total return to it (polymorphous perversity). He betrayed the socialist possibilities of a dialectical theory of the body politic that neither worships nor rejects natural science, that refuses to make nature and its knowledge into a fetish.

Firestone (1970), in the *Dialectic of Sex*, also faces the implications of Freud's biopolitical theory of patriarchy and repression but tries to transform it to yield a feminist and socialist theory of liberation. She has been immensely important to feminists in this task. I think, however, that she committed the same mistake that Brown did, that of 'physiological reduction of the body politic to sex', which fundamentally blocks a liberating socialism that neither fatalistically exploits the techniques given by sciences (while despairing of transforming their content) nor rejects a technical knowledge altogether for fantasy. Firestone located the flaw in women's position in the body politic in our own bodies, in our subservience to the organic demands of reproduction. In that critical sense she accepted a historical materialism based on reproduction and lost the possibility for a feminist-socialist theory of the body politic that would not see our personal bodies as the ultimate enemy. In that step she prepared for the logic of the domination of technology – the total control of now alienated bodies in a machine-determined future. She made the basic mistake of reducing social relations to natural objects, with the logical consequence of seeing technical control as a solution. She certainly did not underestimate the principle of domination in the biobehavioural sciences, but she did misunderstand the status of scientific knowledge and practice. That is, she accepted that there are natural objects (bodies) separate from social relations. In that context, liberation remains subject to supposedly natural determinism, which can only be avoided in an escalating logic of counterdomination.

I think it is possible to build a socialist-feminist theory of the body politic that avoids physiological reductionism in both its forms: (1) capitulating to theories of biological determinism of our social position, and (2) adopting the basically capitalist ideology of culture against nature and thereby denying our responsibility to rebuild the life sciences. I understand Marxist humanism to mean that the fundamental position of the human being in the world is the dialectical relation with the surrounding world involved in the satisfaction of needs and thus in the creation of use values. The labour process constitutes the fundamental human condition. Through labour, we make ourselves individually and collectively in a constant interaction with all that has not yet been humanized. Neither our personal bodies nor our social bodies may be seen as natural, in the sense of existing outside the self-creating process called human labour. What we experience and theorize as nature and as culture are transformed by our work. All we touch and therefore know, including our organic and our social bodies, is made possible for us through labour. Therefore, culture does not dominate nature, nor is nature an enemy. The dialectic must not be made into a dynamic of growing domination.[4] This position, a historical materialism based on production, contrasts fundamentally with the ironically named historical materialism based on reproduction that I have tried to outline above.

One area of the biobehavioural sciences has been unusually important in the construction of oppressive theories of the body political: animal sociology, or the science of animal groups. To reappropriate the biosocial sciences for new practices and theories, a critical history of the physiological politics based on domination that have been central in animal sociology is important. The biosocial sciences have not simply been sexist mirrors of our own social world. They have also been tools in the reproduction of that world, both in supplying legitimating ideologies and in enhancing material power. There are three main reasons for choosing to focus on the science of animal, especially primate, groups.

First, its subject and procedures developed so as to span the nature–culture split at precisely the same time in American intellectual history, between 1920 and 1940, when the ideology of the autonomy of the social sciences had at last gained acceptance, that is, when the liberal theory of society (based on functionalism and hierarchical systems theories) was being established in the universities. Intrinsic to the new liberal relations of natural and social disciplines was the project of human engineering – that is, the project of design and management of human material for efficient, rational functioning in a scientifically ordered society. Animals played an important role in this project. On the one hand, they were plastic raw material of knowledge, subject to exact laboratory discipline. They could be used to construct and test model systems for both human physiology and politics. A model system of, for example, menstrual physiology or socialization processes did not necessarily imply reductionism. It was precisely direct reduction of human to natural sciences that the post-Spencerian, post-evolutionary naturalist, new ordering of knowledge forbade. The management sciences of the 1930s and after have been strict on that point. It is part of the nature–culture split. On the other hand, animals have continued to have a special status as natural objects that can show people their origin, and therefore their pre-rational, pre-management, pre-cultural essence. That is, animals have been ominously ambiguous in their place in the doctrine of autonomy of the human and natural sciences. So, despite the claims of anthropology to be able to understand human beings solely with the concept of culture, and of sociology to need nothing but the idea of the human social group, animal societies have been extensively employed in rationalization and naturalization of the oppressive orders of domination in the human body politic.[5] They have provided the point of union of the physiological and political for modern liberal theorists while they continue to accept the ideology of the split between nature and culture.

Second, animal sociology has been central in the development of the most thorough naturalization of the patriarchal division of authority in the body politic and in the reduction of the body politic to sexual physiology. Thus this area of the natural sciences is one we need to understand thoroughly and transform completely to produce a science that might express the social relations of liberation without committing the vulgar Marxist mistake of deriving directly the substance of knowledge from material conditions. We need to understand how and why animal groups have been used in theories of the evolutionary origin of human beings, of 'mental illness', of the natural basis of cultural co-operation and competition, of language and other forms of communication, of technology, and especially of the origin and role of human forms of sex and the family. In short, we need to know the animal science of the body politic as it has been and might be.[6] I believe the result of a liberating science of animal groups would better express who the animals are as well; we might free nature in freeing ourselves.

Third, the levels at which domination has formed an analytical principle in animal sociology allow a critique of the embodiment of social relations in the content and basic procedures of a natural science in such a way as to expose the fallacies of the claim to objectivity, but not in such a way as to permit facile rejection of scientific discipline in our knowledge of animals. We cannot dismiss the layers of domination in the science of animal groups as a film of unfortunate bias or ideology that can be peeled off the healthy objective strata of knowledge below. Neither can we think just anything we please about animals and their meaning for us. We come face to face with the necessity of a dialectical understanding of scientific labour in producing for us our knowledge of nature.

I will restrict my analysis primarily to a few years around the Second World War and to work on a single group of animals – the primates, in particular, the rhesus monkey, native to Asia but present in droves in scientific laboratories and research stations world-wide. I will focus principally on the work of one person, Clarence Ray Carpenter, who helped found the first major research station for free-ranging monkeys as part of the school of tropical medicine affiliated with Columbia University off Puerto Rico on the tiny island, Cayo Santiago, in the late 1930s. These monkeys and their descendants have been central actors in dramatic reconstructions of natural society. Their affiliation with tropical medicine in a neo-colonial holding of the United States, which has been so extensively used as an experiment station for capitalist fertility management policies, adds an ironic backdrop appropriate to our subject.

Men like Carpenter moved within a complex scientific world in which it would be incorrect to label most individuals or theories as sexist or whatever. It is not to attach simplistic labels but to unwind the specific social and theoretical structures of an area of life science that we need to examine the interconnections of laboratory heads, students, funding agencies, research stations, experimental designs, and historical setting. Carpenter earned his PhD at Stanford for a study of the effects on sexual behaviour of the removal of the gonads of male pigeons in mated pairs. He then received a National Research Council Fellowship in 1931 to study social behaviour of primates under the direction of Robert M. Yerkes of the Laboratories of Comparative Psychobiology at Yale University. Yerkes had recently established the first comprehensive research institution for the psychobiological study of anthropoid apes in the world. For Yerkes, apes were perfect models of human beings. They played a major part in his sense of mission to promote scientific management of every phase of society, an idea typical of his generation.

> It has always been a feature for the use of the chimpanzee as an experimental animal to shape it intelligently to specification instead of trying to preserve its natural characteristics. We have believed it important to convert the animal into as nearly ideal a subject for biological research as is practicable. And with this intent has been associated the hope that eventual success might serve as an effective demonstration of the possibility of re-creating man himself in the image of a generally acceptable ideal. (Yerkes, 1943, p. 10)[7]

He, then, designed primates as scientific objects in relation to his ideal of human progress through human engineering.

Yerkes was interested in the apes in two main regards – their intelligence and their social-sexual life. For him intelligence was the perfect expression of evolutionary position. He saw every living object in terms of the outstanding problem of experimental comparative psychology in America since its inception around 1900: the intelligence test. Species, racial, and individual qualities were fundamentally tied to the central index of intelligence, revealed on the one hand through behaviour-testing and on the other through the neural sciences. He had designed the army intelligence tests administered to recruits in the First World War, tests seen to provide a rational basis for assignment and promotion, to indicate natural merit fitting men for command (Yerkes, 1920; Kevles, 1968).[8] His role in the war was entirely compatible with his role as an entrepreneur in primate studies. In both cases he saw himself and his scientific peers working to foster a rational society based on science and preserved from old ignorance, embodied especially in religion and politics.

The social-sexual life of primates was for Yerkes thoroughly intertwined with their intelligence. Mind would order and rule lower functions to create society. In a classic study of the origin of the body politic, Yerkes (1939) observed that female chimpanzees who were sexually receptive were allowed by the dominant males to have food and 'privileges' to which they were ordinarily not entitled. Primate intelligence allowed sexual states to stimulate the beginnings of human concepts of social right and privilege. The sexual reductionism hardly needs emphasis. His study linking sex and power was typical of work in the 1930s, and hardly different from much to this day. In an early feminist critique, Ruth Herschberger (1948) marvellously imagined the perspective of Josie, the female chimpanzee whose psychosexual life was of such concern to Yerkes. Josie seems not to have seen her world in terms of trading sex for 'privilege', but to Yerkes that economic link of physiology and politics seemed to have been scientifically confirmed to lie at the organic base of civilization.

In addition to direct investigation of physiological sex and social behaviour in human beings' closest relatives, Yerkes exercised, along with his peers, a tremendous influence on the overall direction of the scientific study of sex in this country. He was for twenty-five years chairman of the Rockefeller Foundation-funded National Research Council Committee for Research on Problems of Sex (CRPS). This committee, from 1922 until well after the Second World War when federal funding became massively available for science, provided the financial base for the transformation of human sex into a scientific problem. Fundamental work on hormones and behaviour, sex-linked differences in mental and emotional qualities, marital happiness, and finally the Kinsey studies were all funded by the Committee for Research on Problems of Sex. It played a key role in opening up sexual topics for polite discussion and respectable investigation in an era of undoubted prurience and ignorance.[9]

However, the opening was double edged; the committee, in its practice and ideological expressions, was structured on several levels according to the principle of the primacy of sex in organic and social processes. To make sex a scientific problem also made it an object for medical therapy for all kinds of sexual 'illness', most certainly including homosexuality and unhappy marriages. The biochemical and physiological basis of the therapeutic claims immensely strengthened the legitimating power of scientific managers over women's lives. The committee closed the escape holes for those who rejected the American Freud's kind of sexual reductionism: whether from the psychoanalytic or physical-chemical directions, sex was safely in the care of scientific-medical managers. Monkeys and apes were enlisted in this task in central roles; as natural objects unobscured by culture, they would show most plainly the organic base in relation to which culture emerged. That these 'natural objects' were thoroughly designed according to the many-levelled meanings of an ideal of human engineering has hardly been noticed.

Carpenter arrived at Yale's primate laboratories already enmeshed in the web of funding and practice represented by the CRPS. His PhD work had been funded by the committee, his post-doctoral fellowship granted by essentially the same men, and his host, Yerkes, was the central figure in a very important network of scientific assumptions and practices. Those scientific networks crucially determined who did science and what science was considered good. From his education, funding, and social environment, there was little reason for Carpenter to reject the basic assumptions that identified reproduction and dominance based on sex with the fundamental organizing principles of a natural body politic. What Carpenter added, however, was significant. Methodologically, he established the demanding skill of naturalistic observation of wild primates in two extraordinarily careful field studies, one on New World howler monkeys and one on Asian gibbons. These studies are worthy of note because they are simultaneously excellent, commanding work and fully reflective of social relations based on dominance in the human world of scientists.[10] Theoretically, Carpenter tied the interpretations of the laboratory disciplines of comparative psychology and sexual physiology to evolutionary and ecological field biology centred on the concepts of population and community. In short, he started to link the elements of natural and political economy in new and important ways. The classic Darwinian conception of natural political economy of populations began to be integrated with the physiological and psychological sciences that greatly flourished in the early twentieth century. The integration would be complete only after the Second World War, when Sherwood Washburn and his students transformed physical anthropology and primate studies by systematically exploiting the evolutionary functionalism of the neo-Darwinian synthesis and the social functionalism of Bronislaw Malinowski's theory of culture.

In addition to linking levels of psychobiological analysis to modern evolutionary theory, Carpenter analysed primate groups with the tools of early systems theory that were simultaneously providing the technical base for the claim to scientific maturity of the social sciences based on concepts of culture and social group. Carpenter's early social functionalism – with all its remaining ties to an older comparative psychology and to developmental physiology (experimental embryology) – is crucial for examining the connecting chains from physiology to politics, from animal to human. Carpenter himself did not work within the doctrine of autonomy of natural and social sciences. Neither did he permit direct reduction of social to physiological or of human to animal. He elaborated analytical links between levels that were shared by both adherents and opponents of the crucial nature–culture distinction. Indeed, his primate sociology is a useful place to begin to unravel the many varieties of functionalism emerging within biological and social sciences between the two world wars, all based on principles of hierarchical order of the body and body politic. The functionalist disciplines underlay strong ideologies of social control and techniques of medical, educational, and industrial management.

A single experimental manipulation embodies in miniature all the layers of significance of the principle of dominance in Carpenter's seminal work on the animal body politic. In 1938 he collected about 400 rhesus monkeys in Asia and freed them on Cayo Santiago. After a period of social chaos, they organized themselves into six groups containing both sexes and ranging in size from three to 147 animals. The monkeys were allowed to range freely over the thirty-seven-acre island and to divide space and other resources with little outside interference. The first major study undertaken of them was of their sexual behaviour, including periodicity of oestrus, homosexual, autoerotic, and 'nonconformist' behaviour. Carpenter's conclusions noted that intragroup dominance by males was strongly correlated with sexual activity, and so presumably with evolutionary advantage. All the sexist interpretations with which we have become monotonously familiar were present in the analysis of the study, including such renderings of animal activities as, 'Homosexual females who play masculine roles attack females who play the feminine role prior to the formation of a female–female consort relation' (Carpenter, 1964, p. 339).

In harmony with the guiding notion of the ties of sex and dominance in the fundamental organization of the rhesus groups, Carpenter performed what on the surface is a very simple experiment, but one which represents the whole complex of layered explanation of the natural body politic from the physiological to the political. After watching the undisturbed group for one week as a control, he removed the 'alpha male' (the animal judged most dominant on the basis of priority access to food, sex, and so on) named Diablo, from his group. Carpenter then observed the remaining animals for one week, removed the number 2 male, waited another week, removed the number 3 male, waited, restored all three males to the group, and again observed the social behaviour. He noted that removal of Diablo resulted in immediate restriction of the territorial range of the group on the island relative to other groups. Social order was seriously disrupted. 'The group organization became more fluid and there was an increase in *intra-group conflict* and fights . . . After a marked disruption lasting three weeks, the group was suddenly restructured when the dominant males were released' (1964, p. 362). Social order was restored, and the group regained its prior favourable position relative to other groups.

Several questions immediately arise. Why did Carpenter not use as a control the removal of other than dominant males from the group to test his organizing hypothesis about the source of social order? Literally, he removed the putative head from the collective animal body. What did this field experiment, this decapitation, mean to Carpenter?

First, it must be examined on a physiological level. Carpenter relied on biological concepts for understanding social bodies. He drew from theories of embryological development that tried to explain the formation of complex whole animals from simpler starting materials of fertilized eggs. One important embryological theory used the concept of fields organized by axes of activity called dominance gradients. A field was a spatial whole formed by the complex interaction of gradients. A gradient was conceived, in this theory, to consist of an ordered series of processes from low to high levels of activity measured, for example, by differential oxygen consumption. Note that at this basic level dominance was conceived as a purely physiological property that could be objectively measured. The slope of a gradient could be shallow or steep. Several gradients making up a field would be organized around a principal axis of greatest slope, the organization centre. An organism grew in complexity through integrated multiplication of dominance systems. An appropriate experimental system within developmental physiology designed to test theories of fields, gradients, physiological dominance, and organization centres was the simple hydra. It had only one axis or possible gradient: head to tail. One could cut off the polyp's head, observe temporary disorganization of remaining tissue, and see ultimate re-establishment of a new head from among the physiologically 'competing' cells. Further, one could remove much or little from the head portion of the activity gradient and test the extent of ensuing organic disorganization.[11]

Carpenter conceived social space to be like the organic space of a developing organism, and so he looked for gradients that organized the social field through time. He found such a physiological gradient of activity in the dominance hierarchy of the males of the social group. He performed the theoretically based experiment of head removal and 'observed' ensuing physiological competition among cells or organs (i.e., other points – animals – on the activity–dominance gradient) to re-establish a chief organization centre (achieve alpha male status) and restore social harmony. Several consequences flow from these identifications.

First, other groups of animals in the society could be ordered on activity axes as well; females, for example, were found to have a dominance hierarchy of less steepness or lower slope. Young animals had unstable dominance gradients; the observation underlying that interpretation was that ordinary dominance behaviour could not be reliably seen and that immature animals did not show constant dominance relations to one another. As unseen 'observations' became just as important as evidence as seen ones, a concept of latent dominance followed readily. From this point, it is an easy step to judgements about the amount of dominance that functions to organize social space (call that quantity leadership) and the amount that causes social disruption (call that pathological aggression). Throughout the period around the Second World War, similar studies of the authoritarian personality in human beings abounded; true social order must rest on a balance of dominance, interpreted as the foundation of co-operation. Competitive aggression became the chief form that organized other forms of social integration. Far from competition and co-operation being mutual opposites, the former is the precondition of the latter – on physiological grounds. If the most active (dominant) regions, the organization centres, of an organism are removed, other gradient systems compete to re-establish organic order: a period of fights and fluidity ensues within the body politic. The chief point is that without an organizing dominance hierarchy, social order supposedly is seen to break down into individualistic, unproductive competition. The control experiment of removing other animals than the dominant males was not done because it did not make sense within the whole complex of theory, analogies to individual organisms, and unexamined assumptions.

The authoritarian personality studies bring us to the second level of explanation of the body politic implicit in Carpenter's experiment: the psychological. The idea of a dominance hierarchy was derived in the first instance from study of 'pecking orders' in domestic chickens and other birds initiated by the Norwegian Thorlief Schjelderup-Ebbe (1935) as early as 1913, but not incorporated into American comparative psychology in any important way until the 1930s. Then animal sociology and psychology, as well as human branches of the disciplines, focused great attention on ideas of competition and co-operation. Society was derived from complex interactions of pairs of individuals, understood and measured by psychological techniques, which constituted the social field space. One looked for axes of dominance as organizing principles on both the physiological and psychological levels.

The third and last level implicit in Carpenter's manipulation is that of natural political economy. The group that loses its alpha male loses in the competitive struggle with other organized organic societies. The result would be reflected in less food, higher infant mortality, fewer offspring, and thus evolutionary disadvantage or even extinction. The market competition implicit in organic evolutionary theory surfaces here. The theory of the function of male dominance nicely joins the political economy aspect of the study of animal behaviour and evolution (competitive, division of labour, resource allocation model) with the social integration aspect (co-operative co-ordination through leadership and social position) and with the purely physiological understandings of reproductive and embryological phenomena. All three perspectives link functionalist equilibrium social models – established in the social sciences of the period – to explicit ideological, political concerns with competition and co-operation (in labour struggles, for example). Since animal societies are seen to have in simpler form all the characteristics of human societies and cultures, one may legitimately learn from them the base of supposedly natural, integrated community for humanity. Elton Mayo (1933) – the influential Harvard, anti-labour union, industrial psychologist-sociologist of the same period – called such a community the 'Garden of Industry'.[12]

The political principle of domination has been transformed here into the legitimating scientific principle of dominance as a natural property with a physical-chemical base. Manipulations, concepts, organizing principles – the entire range of tools of the science – must be seen to be penetrated by the principle of domination. Science cannot be reclaimed for liberating purposes by simply reinterpreting observations or changing terminology, a crass ideological exercise in any case, which denies a dialectical interaction with the animals in the project of self-creation through scientific labour. But the difficult process of remaking the biosocial and biobehavioural sciences for liberation has begun. Not surprisingly, one of the first steps has been to switch the focus from primates as models of human beings to a deeper look at the animals themselves – how they live and relate to their environments in ways that may have little to do with us and that will surely reform our sense of relation to nature in our theories of the body politic. These 'revisionist' scientific theories and practices deserve serious attention. Of them, 'feminist' perspectives in physical anthropology and primatology have stressed principles of organization for bodies and societies that do not depend on dominance hierarchies. Dominance structures are still seen and examined, but cease to be used as causal explanations of functional organization. Rather, the revisionists have stressed matrifocal groups, long-term social co-operation rather than short-term spectacular aggression, flexible process rather than strict structure, and so on. The scientific and ideological issues are complex; the emerging work is justly controversial.

In our search for an understanding of a feminist body politic, we need the discipline of the natural and social sciences, just as we need every creative form of theory and practice. These sciences will have liberating functions in so far as we build them on social relations not based on domination. A corollary of that requirement is the rejection of all forms of the ideological claims for pure objectivity rooted in the subject–object split that has legitimated our logics of domination of nature and ourselves. If our experience is of domination, we will theorize our lives according to principles of dominance. As we transform the foundations of our lives, we will know how to build natural sciences to underpin new relations with the world. We, like Dawn in Marge Piercy's *Woman on the Edge of Time*, want to fly into nature, as well as into the past, to make it come out all right. But the sciences are collective expressions and cannot be remade individually. Like Luciente and Hawk, in the same novel, feminists have been clear that 'Nobody can *make* things come out right'; that 'It isn't bad to want to help, to want to work, to seize history . . . but to want to do it alone is less good. To hand history to someone like a cake you baked' (Piercy, 1976, pp. 188–9).

Chapter Two

The Past Is the Contested Zone: Human Nature and Theories of Production and Reproduction in Primate Behaviour Studies

People like to look at animals, even to learn from them about human beings and human society. People in the twentieth century have been no exception. We find the themes of modern America reflected in detail in the bodies and lives of animals. We polish an animal mirror to look for ourselves. The biological sciences' focus on monkeys and apes has sought to make visible both the form and the history of our personal and social bodies. Biology has been pre-eminently a science of visible form, the dissection of visible shape, and the acceptance and construction of visible order. The science of non-human primates, primatology, may be a source of insight or a source of illusion. The issue rests on our skill in the construction of mirrors.

Primatology has focused on two major themes in interpreting the significance of animals for understanding human life – sex and economics, reproduction and production. The crucial transitions from a natural to a political economy and from biological social groups to the order of human kinship categories and systems of exchange have been basic concerns. These are old questions with complex relations to technical and ideological dimensions of biosocial science. Our understandings of both reproduction and production have double-edged possibilities. On the one hand, we may reinforce our vision of the natural and cultural necessity of domination; on the other, we may learn to practise our sciences so as to show more clearly the now fragmentary possibilities of producing and reproducing our lives without overwhelming reliance on the theoretical categories and concrete practices of control and enmity.

Theories of animal and human society based on sex and reproduction have been powerful in legitimating beliefs in the natural necessity of aggression, competition, and hierarchy. In the 1920s, primate studies began to claim that all primates differ from other mammals in the nature of their reproductive physiology: primates possess the menstrual cycle. That physiology was asserted to be fraught with consequences, often expressed in the fantasy-inspiring 'fact' of constant female 'receptivity'. Perhaps, many have thought and some have hoped, the key to the extraordinary sociability of the primate order rests on a sexual foundation of society, in a family rooted in the glands and the genes. Natural kinship was then seen to be transformed by the specifically human, language-mediated categories that gave rational order to nature in the birth of culture. Through classifying by naming, by creating kinds, culture would then be the logical domination of a necessary but dangerous instinctual nature. Perhaps human beings found the key to control of sex, the source of and threat to all other kinds of order, in the categories of kinship. We learned that in naming our kind, we could control our kin. Only recently and tentatively have primatologists seriously challenged the indispensability of these sorts of explanations of nature and culture.

Biosocial theories focusing on production rest on a fundamental premise: humankind is self-made in the most literal sense. Our bodies are the product of the tool-using adaptation which predates the genus *Homo*. We actively determined our design through tools that mediate the human exchange with nature. This condition of our existence may be visualized in two contradictory ways. Gazing at the tools themselves, we may choose to forget that they only mediate our labour. From that perspective, we see our brains and our other products impelling us on a historical course of escalating technological domination; that is, we build an alienated relation to nature. We see our specific historical edifice as both inevitable human nature and technical necessity. This logic leads to the superiority of the machine and its products and ensures the obsolescence of the body and the legitimacy of human engineering. Or, we may focus on the labour process itself and reconstruct our sense of nature, origins, and the past so that the human future is in our hands. We may return from the tool to the body, in its personal and social forms. This chapter is about efforts to know the body in the biosocial conditions of production and reproduction. Our bodies, ourselves.

More particularly, this chapter is about the debate since approximately 1930 in primate studies and physical anthropology about human nature – in male bodies and female ones. The debate has been bounded by the rules of ordinary scientific discourse. This highly regulated space makes room for technical papers; grant applications; informal networks of students, teachers, and laboratories; official symposia to promote methods and interpretations; and finally, textbooks to socialize new scientists. The space considered in this chapter does not provide room for outsiders and amateurs. One of the peculiar characteristics of science is thought to be that by knowing past regularities and processes we can predict events and thereby control them. That is, with our sciences – historical, disciplined forms of theorizing about our experience – we both understand and construct our place in the world and develop strategies for shaping the future.

How can feminism, a political position about love and power, have anything to do with science as I have described it? Feminism, I suggest, can draw from a basic insight of critical theory. The starting point of critical theory – as we have learned it from Marx, the Frankfurt school, and others – is that the social and economic means of human liberation are within our grasp. Nevertheless, we continue to live out relations of domination and scarcity. There is the possibility of overturning that order of things. The study of this contradiction may be applied to all our knowledge, including natural science. The critical tradition insists that we analyse relations of dominance in consciousness as well as material interests, that we see domination as a derivative of theory, not of nature. A feminist history of science, which must be a collective achievement, could examine that part of biosocial science in which our alleged evolutionary biology is traced and supposedly inevitable patterns of order based on domination are legitimated. The examination should play seriously with the rich ambiguity and metaphorical possibilities of both technical and ordinary words. Feminists reappropriate science in order to discover and to define what is 'natural' for ourselves.[1] A human past and future would be placed in our hands. This avowedly interested approach to science promises to take seriously the rules of scientific discourse without worshipping the fetish of scientific objectivity.

My focus will be four sets of theories that emphasize the categories of reproduction and production in the tangled web of the reconstruction of human nature and evolution. The first, centring on reproduction, was the work of Sir Solly Zuckerman. Born in 1904 in South Africa, he studied anatomy at the University of Cape Town, then earned his MD and BS at University College Hospital, London. He combined in complex and illuminating ways research interests in human palaeontology and physical anthropology, reproductive physiology and the primate menstrual cycle, and broad zoological and taxonomic questions focused on primates. His social base included zoological gardens and research laboratories in British universities and medical schools; his training and career reflect intersections of the perspectives of anatomist, biochemist, anthropologist, clinician, administrator, and government science adviser.[2] He has been the architect of an extremely influential theory that sexual physiology is the foundation of primate social order. He also offered a variation of the theory of the origin of human culture in the hunting adaption, which delineated crucial conse-quences for the division of labour by sex and the universal institution of the human family. In focusing on the sexual biology of monkeys, Zuckerman constructed a logic for setting the boundaries of human nature. In effect, Zuckerman claimed, the only universal for all the primates is the menstrual cycle. Therefore, only on that basis may we make valid comparisons of human and non-human ways of life.

A second set of theories stressing reproduction is that of Thelma Rowell, now at the University of California at Berkeley. She earned her doctorate in the early 1960s under Robert Hinde of Cambridge, the man who also supervised Jane Goodall's dissertation on chimpanzees. That period saw the beginning of a still continuing acceleration of publication based on long-term field observations of wild primates. Rowell's training was in zoology and ethology. Her first intention was to write her thesis on mammalian (hamster) communication, using the ethological approach worked out particularly by Niko Tinbergen at Oxford. Because Tinbergen then felt the methodology to be inappropriate to the non-stereotypical social communication of mammals, Rowell pursued her ideas at Cambridge under Hinde, a major synthesizer of American comparative psychology and Continental ethology. Rowell's research (1966a, 1966b, 1970), which has used both traditions, has been concerned with primate communication, the baboon menstrual cycle, comparison of the naturalistic behaviour of monkeys with their behaviour in captivity and in laboratory experimental situations, and mother–infant socialization systems. An outspoken critic of the pervasive dominance concept, she has made social role and stress her overriding theoretical concerns.

Yet both Zuckerman and Rowell, who are very different, adopt varieties of biological and sociological functionalism that set limits on permitted explanations of the body and body politic. The most important is the functionalist requirement of an ultimate explanation in terms of equilibrium, stability, balance. Functionalism has been developed on a foundation of organismic metaphors, in which diverse physiological parts or subsystems are co-ordinated into a harmonious, hierarchical whole. Conflict is subordinated to a teleology of common interests.[3] Both Zuckerman's and Rowell's explanations also reflect the ideological concerns of their society in complex ways, which can instruct feminist efforts to deal with biological and social theories.

The third and fourth sets of theories are reconstructions of human evolution. Both claim to reveal the meaning of crucial adaptations, both focus on production. They see adaptation as a concept relating to the interpretation of functional complexes, of ways of life in which behaviour and structure mutually inform each other. If both Rowell and Zuckerman restrict themselves (almost) to talking about monkeys, Sherwood Washburn of the University of California at Berkeley, his former student Adrienne Zihlman, and her colleague at the University of California at Santa Cruz, Nancy Tanner, argue about the connection of physical and social anthropology. Telling scientific tales about human nature, they are unapologetic about the place of speculative reconstruction in the study of evolution. There can be no hiding behind mechanistic or purely structural explanations in evolutionary biology and anthropology. But since function is still pre-eminent, the resulting scientific approach may be called evolutionary functionalism.

The central figure in the third set of theories, Washburn, is most immediately associated with the modern man-the-hunter hypothesis. This maintains that the hunting adaptation has been the fundamental functional complex which set the rules for nearly all the history of the genus *Homo* until the very recent past. He has also generated the theory of tool use as the motor of evolution of the human body, including the brain and its power of language. His influential vision of the self-made species has earned him praise from such Marxist feminists as Eleanor Leacock (1972) and such Freudian feminists as Dorothy Dinnerstein (1977). He has also been an arch-villain of the piece because of the overwhelming concentration on males as practically the only active sort of human being. Washburn is, in my opinion, both more complicated and more important than either approach reveals. By developing functional anatomy as part of the synthetic theory of evolution and then extending the approach to the social behaviour of living primates, he has integrated sophisticated genetic theory and disciplined field and experimental methodology into the practice of evolutionary reconstruction.

Authors of the fourth set of theories, Zihlman and Tanner, have produced an excellent critique of Washburn's scientific sexism with the use of his own tools. They could not have thought as they do without the functional physical anthropology Washburn has advanced. Tanner and Zihlman have also added a new twist to feminist, scientific evolutionary reconstruction: the use of sociobiological concepts. The pleasure and irony of their approach is that the ideas of some of the most explicitly sexist theories have been enlisted to tell another story. Yet at this level, the feminist debate is still about the nature and existence of human universals. Theories of origins quickly become theories of essences and limits (see Figure 1).

The 1930s was a decade of exciting advance in the study of sexual endocrinology. Early in the decade Solly Zuckerman produced a powerful theory of the physiological basis of mammalian society in general and primate society in particular. He repeatedly asserted that he intended only to adopt a zoologist's perspective on animal sociology and to avoid extrapolation to human, cultural, language-mediated behaviour. Yet his work informed investigations into the origin of human organization and the use of primates in studies of it. He gave the concept of dominance an up-to-date scientific legitimation, for example, connecting it to the new endocrinology. Dominance was closely linked, in his theory, to male competition for control of resources (females). Females then emerged as natural raw material for the

FIGURE 1: RELATIONS OF MAJOR FIGURES

focus on Reproduction		focus on Production	
Zuckerman ⟶ Rowell		Washburn ⟶ Tanner and Zihlman	
1 physiological functionalism	1 social functionalism	1 hunting adaptation	1 gathering adaptation
2 analysis of individual	2 analysis of group	2 neo-Darwinian synthesis genetic tools	2 sociobiological genetic tools

common themes	common themes
1 restrict analysis to animals	1 basic interest in hominid line
2 global expalantory concept Z — dominance R — stress	2 evolutionary functionalism + social functionalism
3 primary identification as biologists, primatologists	3 primary identification as anthropologists
4 study of menstrual cycle	4 study of fossil structures as clue to social behaviour (function)

The categories in this figure do not indicate rigid separations, but emphases found in the writings of each worker.
⟶ = some direct debt.

imposition of male order through the consequences of reproductive physiology. The human innovation was the practice of control of the natural physiological economy. In brief, domination changed levels with culture.

Zuckerman's starting point for considering the causes of primate sociability was twofold: (1) debate in the anthropological community – represented by Malinowski's *Sex and Repression in Savage Society* and Freud's *Totem and Taboo* and *Civilization and Its Discontents* – on the cultural domination of instinct in the formation of the human level of organization; and (2) a new biological discipline, relating hormones and behaviour, rooted in neural and reproductive physiology and comparative and behaviourist psychology. Zuckerman adopted a firm physiological and medical orientation in both areas. He criticized all existing theories of animal organization for their anthropomorphic and teleological overtones. For the older evolutionary meaning of functional adaptation, Zuckerman substituted a physiological approach, which rested on studies of particular mechanisms in anatomical and biochemical terms. Function meant mechanism. Behaviour and society were to be related to mechanistic physiology, and taxonomy was to be reformed on that basis as well. The taxonomic project was undertaken in the book, *Functional Affinities of Man, Monkeys, and Apes* (1933). Here, Zuckerman constructed his 'hunting hypothesis' to account for the transition from nature to culture.

But first we must look at his general theory of non-human primate society, found in *The Social Life of Monkeys and Apes* (1932). Zuckerman imposed an important limit on primatology. He did not recognize a ladder of perfection of living primates representing stages of mental function and corresponding degrees of social co-operation (which always meant hierarchical organization) through which human beings must have passed. Thus, 'Only the behavior common to all apes and monkeys can be regarded as representing a social level through which man once passed in the prehuman stages of his development' (1932, p. 26). Only one thing met this requirement: 'When all questions of its applications to human behavior are laid aside, and when teleological speculation is disregarded, the chief subject matter of a scientific mammalian sociology is seen to be ecology, reproductive physiology, and those influences which can be classed together as due to the variations of the individual' (1932, p. 28). That nod to ecology is the last we hear of it until a precipitating cause was later required to fire the cultural answer (hunting) to primate sexuality. Individual variation explained details, 'But social behavior – the interrelation of individuals within a group – is determined primarily by the mechanisms of reproductive physiology' (p. 29).

Zuckerman had already told the reader that his excursion into mammalian sociology had begun in response to the urgings of anthropologists; he aimed to replace anecdotal accounts of animal societies with hard physiology. He simply assumed that the important bone of contention was the nature and origin of the human family, itself the origin of society. At this point, Zuckerman turned to the writings of the American mammologist, G. S. Miller, who had criticized Malinowski's contention that the human family was unique, that kinship represented the crucial human–animal break. Malinowski regarded the human physiology on which the institution of kinship (i.e., fatherhood) was imposed as unique. In contrast, Miller and Zuckerman agreed that one found all the biological essentials of the human family (namely, constant female receptivity) in mammalian reproductive association. Zuckerman simply developed that viewpoint into an analysis of consequent social forms among primates. Freud's story of the origin of civilization in repression was prefigured on the prehuman level. Zuckerman's story was based on the comparative physiological anatomy of the different primate groups informed by his recent discovery of the baboon menstrual cycle and on the behaviour of a colony of Hamadryas baboons on Monkey Hill in the London Zoo since 1925. The zoo behavioural observations were supplemented by nine days of field study of a different species (the chacma baboon) in South Africa during an excursion to collect anatomical material for the study of reproduction.

The logic of his story, though exquisitely simple, influenced a whole domain of advanced research and provided the logical ground for the new science of hormones and behaviour to encompass the study of social order. Animals, except when they come together to reproduce, are solitary because the basic model of life is competition for scarce resources. Reproductive association is fraught with danger because here competitive success requires the co-operation of other animals. Males fight to obtain the maximum number of reproductive opportunities. These elements Zuckerman retained from Darwin. They did not appear teleological to him in the same way as discussions of animal altruism and co-operation. Males dominate females to preclude another source of competitive insubordination. After the bare essentials of reproduction are accounted for, animals separate to avoid further inevitable injuries from sexual battles. Sexual periodicity (seasonality) evolved to protect the animal atoms from each other during the rest of the year. Mother–young groups hardly constitute society. In any case, these groups are general to mammals and cannot explain primate societies. Different degrees of long-term heterosexual association were rigorously related to requirements of reproduction in the particular ecological environments available to the animals. Males compete to accumulate the means of (re)production, through which alone they can increase their genetic capital in evolution. Females are the means of evolutionary production and the source of surplus value. As dominance became the universal medium of exchange among males and the measure of value, the political and natural economy of Hobbes's *Leviathan* has found its twentieth-century biological expression. The economic order is exclusively physiological in all but human beings, where cultural ownership of females and property is also to be found.

To Zuckerman, the main event in social evolution had been the elimination of extreme seasonality and the introduction of year-long association based on the continuous sexual 'receptivity' of females. First the oestrus and then the menstrual cycle introduced regular repeating bouts of sexual intercourse. Monthly cycles replaced seasonal ones, and a social revolution ensued. Continuous association required strong control mechanisms if the animals were to survive it. So developed the 'harem', exemplified by the London Hamadryas which Zuckerman observed personally during 1929–30 and for which he had records dating to the establishment of the colony in 1925. Especially since the London Hamadryas did not survive on Monkey Hill – nearly all were killed in brutal fights and only one infant was reared successfully – it was important for Zuckerman to establish that captive baboons in extreme conditions of sexual imbalance and crowding still revealed the essential structure of primate society in nature. The traditional physiological argument was used: extreme circumstances are the best windows to the normal because they highlight basic mechanisms which would otherwise be obscured. Hierarchy and deadly competition were crucial regulators of primate society, not creations of human captors. It was also important for him to convince his readers that variations in social form among primates, none of whom had been studied in other than a casual way in the wild, were only details imposed upon the fundamental physiologically determined family. Within the pattern of dominance, such behaviour as female 'prostitution' (which Zuckerman and Miller defined as presenting for non-sexual reasons) was explained as the beginning of the trading of sexual favours for otherwise competitively unobtainable goods. Grooming, feeding order, vocal and gestural expression, allotment of social space, and many other aspects of social behaviour were all derived from the physiologically determined harem organization of primates. Zuckerman was unequivocal:

> The argument outlined above goes far toward explaining the broad basis of subhuman primate society. The main factor that determines social grouping in subhuman primates is sexual attraction . . . The limit to the number of females held by any single male is determined by his degree of dominance, which will again depend not only on his own potency, but also upon his relationship with his fellow males. (Zuckerman, 1932, p. 31)

Of course, human beings share with other primates 'a smooth and uninterrupted sexual and reproductive life' (p. 51); yet human beings and their families exist in the realm of culture, buffered, if not exempt, from the physiologist's gonadectomies and injections. How did the physiologist re-enter the kingdom of culture with his medical tools for producing family health and behavioural adjustment within social hierarchy defined as co-operation? Through hunting, through the taste for meat. Returning to *Functional Affinities*, we meet Zuckerman in his guise as physical anthropologist who unites the physiological to the ecological in order to generate a large-brained hunting animal who needs more complex forms of male co-operation and female fidelity in order to feed the family. The reproductive unit remains on the throne as the fundamental core of social association in the cultural form of kinship, the basic object of the social science of cultural anthropology. Again, Zuckerman's logic is elegantly simple. Some unknown ecological changes produced selection pressure for prehumans to exploit new sources of food, to rework the age-old unspecialized feeding patterns, and to introduce sexual division of labour as a necessary consequence of the requirements of large-scale meat-eating. Food-sharing necessitated the human form of the family, which for Zuckerman meant selection pressure for 'overt monogamy' and conceptual recognition of significant social relations (ownership of women) even when no one was

around to enforce them. The passivity of females in such major transformations was an unexamined assumption. So developed marriage and the
hunting band of males, with all the startling consequences for the brain and
its products of speech and culture.

Zuckerman hinted at the later form of the hunting hypothesis that
emphasized the tool-using adaptation in the origin of the self-made species.
But more important was the fact that the all-male band – the human form of
co-operation signalling the divorce of culture from nature – became a
scientific, even a physiological, object in Zuckerman's hands. The valuable
female continued to pose the threat of disorder through sexuality. Co-
operation came to mean conscious male regulation of previously natural
hierarchy and competition, which in turn had been the fruits of permanent
female sexuality. These themes were not new with Zuckerman, but the way
he integrated them into modern physiological disciplines was. Further, his
biological ideology did not violate, but actually reinforced, the important
doctrine of the autonomy of biological and social science, of animal and
human order. Zuckerman left full room for functionalist social anthropology.
He only reformed Malinowski's physiology.

Zuckerman's importance in the development of primate behaviour studies
themselves has not been his scant empirical observations, but his provision of
a theory that met the needs of rapidly advancing new disciplines. At the same
time, he rescientized conventional prejudices with the liberal ideology that
claimed that culture was autonomous from previous forms of biological
determinism. That same liberal ideology legitimated a logic of scientific
control over 'nature', now rationalized as a material given reduced either to
pre-rational danger or ordered resource. The alienating core of this is not
obscure. Zuckerman set questions for workers to follow that even in their
asking reinforced scientific beliefs about natural male competition and
dangerous female sexuality. His tie of sexuality to dominance in ways
acceptable to the physiological and behavioural sciences of the 1930s helped
establish the status of dominance as a trait or fact rather than a concept.
Primatologists have continued to ask about the selective advantage of
dominance behaviour and have tended to assume, rather than test, a
correlation of breeding advantage with an entity called dominance. Not until
1965, with a paper by two of Sherwood Washburn's students, was his theory
of the origin of primate society in year-round female sexuality convincingly
laid to rest.[4] Zuckerman's mode of blending covert Freudianism, biochemical mechanisms, and studies of social behaviour has had a long and
influential life.

At first glance, the only comparisons of Thelma Rowell with Zuckerman
must be in contrast. Though she praised Zuckerman for his ground-
breaking work on the baboon menstrual cycle and refrained from very severe

criticism of him in her historical paper on the dominance concept, her whole work seems to have been in opposition to his ideas and his methods. She does not claim scientific purity for a language bathed in multiple waves of meaning in the common tongue as well as in scientific tradition. Her arguments have been zoological and explicitly sociological rather than an extrapolation from reproductive physiology. She is known for her care in dividing cage space for captive monkeys to permit more naturalistic behaviour, and for excellent field studies, rather than for physiological arguments about provoked extreme behaviour as the window to the normal. Rather than emphasizing primate universals, Rowell's papers are permeated by particularism, by counsels to notice complexity, by insistence on variability in a manner reminiscent of early proponents of the culture concept and cultural particularism. Moreover, Rowell is working in very different scientific and ideological circumstances. She benefits from and contributes to the now extensive literature based on direct field studies of primates, studies which themselves referred back to Zuckerman but went beyond that to which he had access. This body of literature has tended to reject Zuckerman's doctrines on sex but to retain focus on dominance. Finally, Rowell writes to an audience sensitized to the feminist implications of biosocial theory. It is not an accident that she emphasizes female behaviour and active social roles and finds dominance to be, at best, a convenient expression for predicting the frequency of some learned behaviours.

But it would be a dangerous mistake to see Rowell's work as simply exemplifying normal scientific progress in rooting out unnecessary prejudice while accumulating better data. Nor does her work simply substitute more satisfying (to me) female prejudices for Zuckerman's infuriating male consciousness. In fact, Rowell and Zuckerman are like each other in a crucial way, which I believe indicates part of the nature of the ideological function of impeccable work in perfectly controlled laboratory science. In 'stress', Rowell does have a global category of explanation corresponding to Zuckerman's sexual physiology. Like sex or dominance, stress is a category that incorporates general social belief into the extracts in the biochemist's test-tube. Stress may be studied on the level of adrenal function, on the level of mental illness, or on the level of 'explanation' of life in modern capitalism. If dominance was the crucial concept in the 1930s, in a context of extraordinary scientific and popular concern for the foundation of social co-operation and competition in a time of world crisis, then stress has been the favourite concept, in the guise of a thing, in more recent times of serious threat to privileged social order. Dominance is not dead, but stress is really more useful in social theory. It has a further referent, namely, to the concept of a social system and to structural functionalism as the principal mode of sociological explanation. The physical metaphors of systems theories – like tolerance, stress, balance, and equilibrium – lead us to many levels of meaning. One which we must note is that of the idea of 'obsolescence' of certain biological systems and the medical function of relieving stressed, perhaps obsolescent, behaviour patterns. A second level of meaning implicit in systems functionalism is the imperative of 'reproduction' of the system as a social whole and as a breeding population. Behaviour can be explained, then, ultimately in terms of system maintenance or pathological failure to achieve such stability.

In 1974, Rowell summarized the arguments against use of the dominance concept to understand social structure. She gave two major lines of approach: (1) presenting all putative dominance behaviours as learned responses easily accounted for by current theories in animal psychology; and (2) removing the basis for considering dominance as a trait or adaptive complex subject to selection pressures. That is, so-called dominance behaviours do not. seem to relate to reproductive success. In addition to amusing points about the slippery nature of concepts like 'latent dominance', which enter arguments to fill gaps in observation, Rowell asserts that conditions of observation introduce the determinants in which one should expect social animals to learn responses called dominance. Hierarchy for Rowell is primarily an artefact of methods of observation. Reinforcing this position is the discovery that different measures of dominance do not correlate highly with each other, and hierarchies worked out by different measures do not reveal the same social structure. Thus it is hard to see what observed behaviours related to dominance have to do with evolution, which requires a genetic basis for selection. In Rowell's words, 'the function of *dominance* becomes a non-question' (1974, p. 151; italics altered).

But function does remain the essential question, the grail that unifies the actors in this chapter. For Rowell, function must be seen in terms of the concept of social system. Communication analysis, studies of mother–young interactions, role change in relation to age and sex class, social subsystems based on matrilines (kinship), territory and hierarchy as spatial order, and variation of social structure in response to environmental variables: these become the areas of interest, the analytical objects that bear on the structural-functional explanation of system in terms of function. Rowell's theoretical stance is most plain in her very useful, linguistically sophisticated book, *Social Behaviour of Monkeys* (1972). The problem of the social system is the problem of multiple-variable analysis in fluid structures in dynamic equilibrium through time and space. The debt of animal sociology to human sociology and anthropology from Bronislaw Malinowski, L. J. Henderson, and Talcott Parsons has hardly begun to be noticed, much less critically examined.

How does stress relate to the social system? Ironically, through the concept of subordination hierarchies. Animals would be compared to each other on a scale of susceptibility to stress. Very sensitive animals would be easily roused to fear, flight, or cringing postures. Such sensitivity would reasonably be associated with high levels of adrenal-stimulating hormones. So the capacity to produce ACTH in 'stressful' situations would be reasonably postulated to have a genetic foundation. These are testable propositions, at least in principle. Calm animals might be called 'dominant' by observers simply because they move freely in social space and take freely from available resources, while their nervous comrades cringe or move away. Rowell would see the poor huddling beast as the stimulus or cause of the resulting 'hierarchy'. Such a social scheme should be called a subordination order. A variety of response thresholds to stressful situations would be adaptive in the social group in nature. Both nervous and calm animals would have a role in efficiently monitoring the environment for danger or for maintaining intragroup peace. The genetic diversity in the population underlying the differences in response stress would be kept in evolution. One must note how functionalist notions of social role for overall system balance, genetic concepts for biochemical and hormonal function, and psychological approaches to dominance–subordination all converge in the central idea of stress.

Stress as a global, multi-layered concept embedded in functionalist explanation provides the critical tie between Thelma Rowell and Sherwood Washburn. The tie is represented by David Hamburg, later president of the Institute of Medicine of the National Academy of Sciences, in the 1960s chairman of the Department of Psychiatry at the Stanford School of Medicine, and collaborator with Sherwood Washburn in building primate studies around modern medical and evolutionary questions. In Hamburg's and Washburn's work, the darker side of functionalist explanation is starkly revealed; the metaphoric structure surrounding stress ceases to be more congenial than dominance. Hamburg has been a principal figure in evolutionary theories of emotional adaptive configuration, which lead to the notion of our obsolescent biology. Medical management of emotions maladaptive in 'modern society' seems justified to relieve pathological stress and maintain the social system. 'Modern society' itself seems given by some sort of technological imperative laid over our limiting biological heritage. Primate studies are motivated by, and in turn legitimate, the management needs of a stressed society. The animals model our limitations (adaptive breakdowns) and our innovations (tool use).

Social functionalism and evolutionary functionalism come together in the study of selection for behaviours and emotional patterns that maintain societies as successful breeding populations over time. The imperative is reproduction – of the social system and of the organisms who are its member-role actors. In general, animals have to like to do what they must do to survive in their evolutionary history. Evolutionary theory here joins a sociology of systems and a psychology of personality and emotion in modern versions of a pleasure calculus connected to the organic, motivational base of learning theory. Rowell summarizes:

> A zoologist, however, must always return to the question of selective advantages ... It is so very obvious that monkeys enjoy being together that we take it for granted. But pleasure like every other phenomenon of life is subject to, and the result of, evolutionary pressure – we enjoy a thing because our ancestors survived better and left more viable offspring than their relations who did not enjoy (and so seek) comparable stimuli ... This is speculation; but it is by research which examines the function of social systems of monkeys and other animals that we shall be able to understand fully their mechanisms. (1972, pp. 174, 180)

Washburn and Hamburg have shared the same analysis, but have applied it to another concept, again often perceived as a thing, in the vocabulary of meaning-laden scientific words: aggression, especially male aggression. Through this concept we must make a transition from explanations based on theories of reproduction to those based on production in human evolution and primate behaviour studies. Clearly, reproduction and production are complements, not opposites. But we must see how Washburn reached a 'man-the-hunter' theory from consideration of the economic functions of the species, while Zuckerman traced primate order through reproductive physiology, and Rowell led us to understand the junction of sociological and evolutionary notions of reproducing systems.

Washburn and Hamburg (1968) developed themes initiated in their collaboration in 1957, when Washburn spent a year as a fellow at the Stanford Center for Advanced Study in the Behavioral Sciences, and furthered in 1962–63 when Washburn and Hamburg organized at the centre a full year of conferences and collaboration among the new, exciting, world-wide community of primatologists. In 'Aggressive behavior in Old World monkeys and apes', the two collaborators introduced their work as part of the study of the forces that produced humankind. They wished to pay attention to unique human biology and unique conditions of human evolution. They saw aggression as a fundamental adaptation or functional complex common to the entire primate order, including human beings. 'Order within most primate groups is maintained by a hierarchy, which depends ultimately primarily on the power of males ... Aggressive individuals are essential actors in the social system and competition between groups is necessary for species dispersal and control of local populations' (1968, p. 282). The biology of aggression has been extensively studied and seems, they argue, to rest on similar hormonal and neural mechanisms, modified in primates, and especially in humans, by new brain complexes and extensive learning. In non-human primates, aggression is constantly rewarded, and, the authors maintain, aggressive individuals (males) leave more offspring. So they argue for selection of a system of co-adapted genes involving complex feedback among motor anatomy, gestural anatomy, hormones, brain elements, and behaviour. Presumably, all parts of the aggressive complex evolve. The functions requiring aggression did not abate for humankind, Hamburg and Washburn believe. Protection, policing, and finally hunting all required a continued selection for male organisms who easily learned and enjoyed regulated fighting, torturing, and killing:

> Throughout most of human history societies have depended on young adult males to hunt, to fight, and to maintain the social order with violence. Even when the individual was cooperating, his social role could be executed only by extremely aggressive action that was learned in play, was socially approved, and was presumably gratifying. (1968, p. 291)

But with the advance of civilization, this biology has become a problem. It is now often maladaptive because of our accelerating technological progress. Our bodies, with the old genetic transmission, have not kept pace with the new language-produced cultural transmission of technology. So now, when social control breaks down, we must expect to see pathological destruction. Hamburg and Washburn's examples here are Nazi Germany, the Congo, Algeria, and Vietnam! The lesson is that we must face our *nature* in order to control it. 'There is a fundamental difficulty in the fact that contemporary human groups are led by primates whose evolutionary history dictates, through both biological and social transmission, a strong dominance orientation' (1968, p. 295). This logic has been developed to posit a need for scientifically informed, rational controls to replace pre-scientific customs: 'But an aggressive species living by prescientific customs in a scientifically advanced world will pay a tremendous price in interindividual conflict and international war' (p. 296). The lesson here, the liberal scientist argues, is not to favour a particular social order – those are political and value questions – but to establish the preconditions for all advanced society, namely, scientific management of now inefficient, maladaptive, obsolescent biology. We are only one product, and one subject to considerable breakdown. On the personal level, psychiatric therapy is a species of repair work; on the social level, scientific policy dictates we use our skill to update our biology through social control. Our system of production has transcended us; we need quality control.

But before despairing that society is doomed to hierarchies and dominance relations regulated by scientific management, let us ask more closely what convinces Washburn and Hamburg that we, or at least males, have a woefully aggressive nature. After all, human males do not have the so-called fighting anatomy of many primate males – the dagger-like canines, associated threat gestures so appropriate for ethological analysis, great difference in male and female body size, or extra structures such as a mane to enhance one's threatening aspect. Nor do we have appeasement gestures to placate aggressors. Why argue that we do have an aggressive, authority-requiring brain? The line leading to the genus *Homo*, Washburn judges, was bipedal and tool-using very early. Selection pressures favoured increased tool use, which in turn made possible the hunting way of life, evolution of a big brain, and language. Human males no longer fought with teeth and gestures but with words and handmade weapons. We lack big canines because we make knives and hurl insults. The selection pressures requiring aggression did not abate, but the structural basis for the function evolved in harmony with the whole adaptational complex of a new way of life. This argument itself relates to Washburn's basic reformulation of physical anthropology, beginning in the 1940s, as part of the synthetic theory of evolution, and to his successful efforts to promote primate behaviour studies in the study of human evolution.

Washburn earned his PhD in physical anthropology at Harvard in 1940. His training was in traditional anthropometric methods and primate anatomy, and he taught medical anatomy at Columbia College of Physicians and Surgeons until 1947, when he moved to the University of Chicago. He had accompanied the 1937 Asia Primate Expedition, from which C.R. Carpenter produced the first monograph on gibbon behaviour and social system. But Washburn felt Carpenter then had little sense of the exciting possibilities of the concept of social system. His own task on the expedition was anatomical collecting, that is, shooting specimens. By the mid-1940s Washburn was practising physical anthropology as an experimental science; by 1950 he was developing a powerful programme for reinterpreting the basic concepts and methods of his field in harmony with the new population genetics, systematics, and palaeontology of Dobzhansky, Mayr, and Simpson. By 1958, he had a Ford Foundation grant to study the evolution of human behaviour in a complex manner, including provision for field studies of baboons in East Africa. A year later, now at Berkeley, he developed funding for one of the first experimental primate field stations in the United States. From the beginning of his career, he lectured, wrote popular texts, made pedagogical films, reformed curricula on all educational levels, and promoted successful careers of now well-known figures in evolution and primatology.

This is not the place to explore the origins of Washburn's ideas, nor his organization of a very large research and education programme, but only to note essential features in relation to the hunting thesis and primate behaviour.[5] The purpose is to begin to recognize how Washburn's career as a careful, experimental scientist has been part of the scientific and social controversies on human nature as the foundation for the human future. We must understand how Washburn could simultaneously be the co-author of the article on evolution of aggression, an opponent of sociobiology, alternately a hero and villain for Robert Ardrey, a favourite of some Marxist feminists, and the teacher of both sociobiological feminist Adrienne Zihlman and of sociobiological sexist Irven DeVore. He is rightly all these things and unusually consistent and unified in his methods, theories, and practices. Perhaps the key to Washburn is that he has produced a fundamental theory with tremendous implications for the practice of many sciences and for the rules of speculative evolutionary reconstruction. In Kuhnian terms, Washburn seems to have something basic to do with scientific paradigms. In Marxist terms, he has to do with alienated theorizing of the established disorder.

Washburn's fundamental innovation in physical anthropology was evident in the publication of his widely reprinted papers, 'The new physical anthropology' (1951a) and 'The analysis of primate evolution with particular reference to man' (1951b). He applied the new population genetics to the study of primate evolution. For Washburn population genetics meant that the process of evolution was the crucial problem, not the fossil results. Therefore, selection and adaptation were his central concepts. Adaptive traits could only be interpreted by understanding conditions or forces capable of producing the traits. The first problem that confronted the physical anthropologist was how to identify a 'trait'. Washburn practised a new kind of theoretical and practical dissection of the body into 'functional complexes', whose meaning had to be sought in their action during life. For example, instead of measuring the nose, he analysed the forces in the central region of the face from chewing and growth. That task required model experimental systems of living animals. Instead of setting up scales of evolution based on brain enlargement, he analysed regions of the body involved in adaptive transformations related to locomotion, eating, and similar functions. In sum, 'The anatomy of life, of integrated functions, does not know the artificial boundaries which still govern the dissection of a corpse' (1951a, p. 303).

Washburn was part of a larger revolution in physical anthropology accompanied by the discovery of new fossils, dating techniques, experimental possibilities, and more recently, molecular taxonomy. One of the revolution's central objects was the small-brained South African human-ape, *Australopithecus*. 'The discovery of the South African man-like apes, or small-brained men, has made it possible to outline the basic adaptation which is the foundation of the human radiation' (1951b, p. 70). The origin of the

human radiation was like any other mammalian group's, though its consequences were decidedly novel. 'But the use of tools brings in a set of factors
which progressively modifies the evolutionary picture. It is particularly the
task of the anthropologist to assess the way the development of culture
affected physical evolution' (1951b, p. 71). Evolutionary and social functionalism again come together; both, for Washburn, are analyses of the meaning
of living systems, of action, of ways of life. From the 1950s Washburn
maintained that functional anatomy and the synthetic theory of evolution
laid to rest for ever the old conflicts of physical and social anthropology.

In 1958, Washburn and his former student, Virginia Avis, contributed a
paper to a symposium on behaviour and evolution, which had been
organized, beginning in 1953, to effect a synthesis of comparative psychology
and the synthetic theory. Washburn's emphasis on the importance of
behaviour made his interest in the psychological consequences of evolutionary adaptation natural. In that paper, 'The evolution of human behavior',
Washburn and Avis (1958) developed the consequences of the hunting
adaptation, including enlarged curiosity and mobility, pleasure in the hunt
and kill, and new ideas about our relation to other animals. Perhaps most
important, 'Hunting not only necessitated new activities and new kinds of
cooperation but changed the role of the adult male in the group . . . The very
same actions which caused man to be feared by other animals led to more
cooperation, food sharing, and economic interdependence within the group'
(pp. 433–4). The human way of life had begun.

From seeing behaviour first as motor activity and then as psychological
orientations, it was a short, logical step to looking at behaviour as social
system. Beginning in 1955, almost casually, Washburn investigated not only
actions of individual organisms but of social systems. The baboon studies of
Washburn and Irven DeVore, with all their emphasis on male roles in
protection and policing as models of pre-adaptations to a human social
system, were appropriate outgrowths of evolutionary functional anatomy.
Differences between human and monkey society were always highlighted;
Washburn never engaged in chain-of-being reconstructions. He looked at
animal social systems the same way as he looked at forces determining
growth in kitten skulls – as model systems for particular problems in
interpreting skull formation in fossils. His was an experimental, comparative
biological science based on function. But the baboon model system drove
home a lesson: troop structure came from dominance hierarchies of males.
Hunting transformed such structures but only to produce the special roles of
the co-operating male band. The reproductive function of females, and the
social continuity of matrilines, remained a conservative pattern reinforced by
bigger-headed, more dependent infants.

The classic paper which brings together the anatomical, psychological, and social consequences of hunting in setting the rules for culture based on human nature is 'The evolution of hunting', by Washburn and C. S. Lancaster (1968). This paper has earned Washburn his poor reputation in socialist and feminist circles. Its appearance in a symposium emphasizing the hunting nature of man in the midst of years of challenge to sexual, economic, and political power is part of the social situation of contemporary evolutionary reconstruction. Washburn is not an ideologue; he is a scientist and educator. That is the point. Interpreting human nature is a central scientific question for evolutionary functionalism. The past sets the rules for possible futures in the 'limited' sense of showing us a biology created in conditions supposedly favouring aggressive male roles, female dependence, and stable social systems appropriately analysed with functional concepts. Telling stories of the human past is a rule-governed activity. Washburn's science changed the rules of the game to require argument from the conditions of production.

In 'Women in evolution. Part I: innovation and selection in human origins', Nancy Tanner and Adrienne Zihlman (1976)[6] play by the new rules but tell of a different human nature, of different universals. They focus less on tools as such and more on the labour process, that is, on a new productive adaptation – gathering. They immediately place themselves within the recent population genetic developments of sociobiology. Their study explores a natural economy in terms of investment strategies for the increase of genetic capital. Yet Tanner and Zihlman deliberately appropriate sociobiology for feminist ends. They no more make themselves ideologues than Washburn has, but their practice of science is controversial both for internal reasons of debated evidence and argument, and for political reasons. They do not, at any point, leave the traditional social space of science. They can stay there, in part, because sociobiology is not necessarily sexist in the sense that Irven DeVore or Robert Trivers (1972) have made it, any more than the concept of stress necessarily leads to Hamburg's particular ideas on aggression and human obsolescence. Further, it is not easy to imagine what evolutionary theory would be like in any language other than classical capitalist political economy.[7] No simple translation into other metaphors is possible or necessarily desirable. Tanner and Zihlman bring us face to face with fundamental questions that have barely been phrased, much less answered. How should we theorize our experience of the past and of 'nature' in new ways to build adequate concepts for scientific practice and social transformation? This question stands in a complicated relation with the internal craft rules for working within the natural sciences.

Tanner and Zihlman begin by announcing the goal of understanding human nature in terms of processes 'which shaped our physical, emotional, and cognitive characteristics' (1976, p. 585). They note the obvious fact that the hunting thesis has largely ignored the behaviour and social activity of one of the two sexes, and is therefore deficient by ordinary criteria of evolutionary functionalism. Behaviour does not fossilize for either sex, so the problem is one of rational reconstruction, of choosing hypotheses.

> Specifically, we hypothesize the development of gathering [both plant and animal material] as a dietary specialization of savanna living, promoted by natural selection of appropriate tool using and bipedal behavior. We suggest how this interrelates with the roles of maternal socialization in kin selection and of female choice in sexual selection. We emphasize the connections among savanna living, technology, diet, social organization, and selective processes to account for the transition from a primate ancestor to the emergent human species. (Tanner and Zihlman, 1976, p. 586)

This paper is clearly a normal outgrowth for Zihlman of her 1966 presentation on bipedal behaviour, in the context of hunting, to a Washburn-organized symposium of the American Anthropological Association. Titled 'Design for Man', the session included Hamburg on emotions as adaptational complexes and the problem of maladaptive, obsolete patterns.

Like Washburn, Tanner and Zihlman argue from animal model systems and from the most recent genetic theory applied to populations. They see chimpanzees as the most closely similar of all living animals to the stem population that probably gave rise to apes and hominids. So chimpanzees make better mirrors, or models, than baboons do for glimpses of the evolution of the human way of life. The authors add to the traditional genetic parameters of the synthetic theory (drift, migration, and so on), the sociobiological genetic concepts of inclusive fitness, kin selection, sexual selection, and parental investment. Understanding changes in gene frequencies of populations from selection pressures operating on individuals remains the goal. They note lots of tool use by chimpanzees, with a sex difference in the behaviour. Females make and use tools more often, although the males seem to hunt more readily. Rigid dominance hierarchies do not occur, although the concepts of high ranks and influence seem useful. The social structure is flexible, but not random. Social continuity seems to flow through continuing associations of females, their young, and associates.

The transitional population to hominids is imagined to have moved into the savannah, a new adaptive zone. 'A new way of life is initiated by a change in behavior; the anatomical changes follow' (Tanner and Zihlman, 1976, p. 586). The new behaviour was greatly enlarged dietary choice accompanied by tool use. Gathering was the early critical invention of hominids. Food-sharing with ordinary social groups of females and offspring (including male sharing with these groups) resulted. Digging sticks, containers for food, and above all, carrying devices for babies were extremely likely early technological innovations related to the new diet and sharing habits.

Knowledge of a wide range of plants and animals, as well as their seasons and habits, became important. Selection pressure for symbolic communication increased. The predation dangers of the savannah were probably dealt with by cunning not fighting, so hominids reduced the need for baboon-like dominance and male fighting anatomy. The flexible chimp social structure probably became even more opportunistic, allowing better understanding of the basis for human cultural diversity. Like Rowell, Tanner and Zihlman take every opportunity to emphasize human possibility and variety. Gathering of plants and animals was unlikely to maintain much selection pressure for an aggressive biology. Cognitive processes, on the other hand, were greatly elaborated in the new productive mode.

At this point, Tanner and Zihlman make use of mother-centred units to introduce kin and sexual selection and parental investment. New selection pressures put a premium on great sociability and co-operation. Babies were harder to raise, and bisexual co-operation would be useful. Males learned the friendly interaction patterns, even with strangers, which became crucial to the human way of life based on linguistic communities, small bands, and frequent outbreeding. But maintenance of a fighting anatomy including big canines and stereotyped threat gestures would be incompatible with the new functional behaviours. Females would mate more readily with friendly, non-threatening males. Female sexual choice has been shown to be general in mammalian groups, and the hominid stem was not likely to have been an exception. Two things leap at the reader who has followed Zuckerman's and Washburn's hunting arguments. First, female receptivity has been renamed female choice, with large genetic consequences. Second, the anatomy of the reduced canines is reinterpreted when different behaviour and different functions are postulated.

Tanner and Zihlman believe anthropology as a whole is better served by their different reconstruction, based on similar evidence.

> Observers usually begin from their own perspective, and so inadvertently the question usually has been: how did the capacity and propensity for adult Western male behaviors evolve? This viewpoint offers scant preparation for comprehending the wide range of variability in women's roles in non-Western societies or for analyzing the changes in the roles of men and women which are currently occurring in the West. (Tanner and Zihlman, 1976, p. 608)

In other words, evolutionary reconstructions condition understanding of contemporary events and future possibilities. Tanner and Zihlman, in their interpretation of the tool-using adaptation, avoid telling a tale of obsolescence of the human body caught in a hunting past. The open future rests on a new past.

Focusing on the categories of reproduction and production, I have traced four major positions on human history and human nature. All were argued strictly within the boundaries of modern physiology, genetics, and social theory. All four hinged on the concept of function and recognized the 'liberal' doctrine of the autonomy of nature and culture. It has been against the rules to argue from a position of biological reductionism. But the goal of each tale has been a picture of human universals, of human nature as the foundation for culture. Ironically, reconstructions of human nature useful to feminists were derived from two of the theories most despised by socialist-feminist thought: functionalism and sociobiology. They have been criticized as ideological justifications of unjust economic and political structures, as rationalizations for the reproduction of present relations of the body and body politic. Obviously, as Rowell, Tanner, and Zihlman show, these theories can be deployed for other ends: to stress human and animal variability, complexity, capacity for change. Feminists can engage seriously, then, in the biosocial debate from within the sciences.

We must, however, be acutely aware of the dangers of using old rules to tell new tales. This is compatible with a larger refusal to pretend that science is either only discovery, which erects a fetish of objectivity, or only invention, which rests on crass idealism. We both learn about and create nature and ourselves. We must also see the biosocial sciences from the point of view of the process of resolving the contradiction between, or the gap between, human reality and human possibility in history. The purpose of the sciences of function is to produce both understanding of meaning and predictive means of control. They show both the given and the possible in a dialectic between the past and the future. Often, the future is given by the possibility of a past. Sciences also act as legitimating meta-languages that produce homologies between social and symbolic systems. That is acutely true for the sciences of the body and the body politic. In a strict sense, science is our myth. That claim does not in any way vitiate the discipline scientific practitioners impose on each other to study the world. We can both know that our bodies, other animals, fossils, and what have you are proper objects for scientific investigation, and remember how historically determined is our part in the construction of the object. It is not an accident of nature that our social and evolutionary knowledge of animals, hominids, and ourselves has been developed in functionalist and capitalist economic terms.[8] Feminists must not expect even arguments that answer clear sexist bias within the sciences to produce adequate final theories of production and reproduction as well. Such theories still elude us, because we are now engaged in a political-scientific struggle to formulate the rules through which we will articulate them. The terrain of primatology is the contested zone. The future is the issue.

Chapter Three

The Biological Enterprise: Sex, Mind, and Profit from Human Engineering to Sociobiology

Life can be moulded into any conceivable form. Draw up your specifications for a dog, or a man ... and if you will give me control of the environment, and time enough, I will clothe your dreams in flesh and blood ... A sensible industrial system will seek to put men, as well as timber, stone, and iron, in the places for which their natures fit them, and to polish them for efficient service with at least as much care as is bestowed upon clocks, electric dynamos, or locomotives.

Frank Parsons, Human Engineer, 1894

Now they swarm in large colonies, safe inside gigantic, lumbering robots, sealed off from the outside world, communicating with it by remote control. They are in you and me; they created us, body and mind; and their preservation is the ultimate rationale for our existence. They have come a long way, those replicators. Now they go by the name of genes, and we are their survival machines.

Richard Dawkins, Sociobiologist, 1976

Part of remaking ourselves as socialist-feminist human beings is remaking the sciences which construct the category of 'nature' and empower its definitions in technology. Science is about knowledge and power. In our time, natural science defines the human being's place in nature and history and provides the instruments of domination of the body and the community. By constructing the category nature, natural science imposes limits on history and self-formation. So science is part of the struggle over the nature of our lives. I would like to investigate how the field of modern biology constructs theories about the body and community as capitalist and patriarchal machine and market: the machine for production, the market for exchange, and both machine and market for reproduction. I would like to explore biology as an aspect of the reproduction of capitalist social relations, dealing with the imperative of biological reproduction. That is, I want to show how sociobiology is the science of capitalist reproduction.

TABLE 1: TRANSFORMATIONS IN LIFE SCIENCE IN THE TWENTIETH CENTURY

Pre-Second World War Represented by R.M. Yerkes	Post-Second World War Represented by E.O. Wilson
psychobiology	sociobiology
human engineering	communication control
organism	cybernetic machine
physiology	systems theory
intelligence	information
person	gene
personality sciences	population genetics and ecology
sex and mind	genes and survival machines
instinct and engineering	constraints and choice or redesign of trajectories
time–motion studies	ergonomics
human relations management	sociotechnical systems management
adaptivity	optimization
eugenics for race hygiene	sexual investment strategies for genetic profit
nervous system for integration	sensory channels and processing centres for environmental tracking
endocrine system for integration	chemical communication for environmental tracking
homoeostasis	feedback and other control system mechanisms
superorganism	population

All items in the left-hand list are appropriate to a bioscience of organisms, in which the model of scientific intervention is medical and clinical. The nature of analysis is organic functionalism, and ideological appeals are to the fulfilment of the 'person'. All the items in the right-hand list are appropriate to an engineering science of automated technological devices, in which the model of scientific intervention is technical and 'systematic'. The nature of analysis is technological functionalism, and ideological appeals are to alleviation of stress and other signs of human obsolescence.

Between the First World War and the present, biology has been transformed from a science centred on the organism, understood in functionalist terms, to a science studying automated technological devices, understood in terms of cybernetic systems. Organic form, with its hierarchical and physiological co-operation and competition based on 'natural' domination and division of labour, gave way to systems theory with its control schemes based on communications networks and a logical technology in which human beings become potentially outmoded symbol-using devices. Life science moved from physiology to systems theory, from scientific medicine to investment management, from Taylorite scientific management and human engineering of the person to modern ergonomics and population control, from psychobiology to sociobiology.

This fundamental change in life science did not occur in a historical vacuum; it accompanied changes in the nature and technology of power, within a continuing dynamic of capitalist reproduction. This chapter sketches those changes in an effort to investigate the historical connection between the content of science and its social context. The larger question informing this critique is how to develop a socialist-feminist life science.[1]

Because science is part of the process of realizing and elaborating our own nature, of constituting the category of nature in the first place, our responsibility for a feminist and socialist science is complex. We are far from understanding precisely what our biology might be, but we are beginning to know that its promise is rooted in our actual lives, that we have the science we make historically. As Marx showed for the science of wealth, our reappropriation of knowledge is a revolutionary reappropriation of a means by which we produce and reproduce our lives. We must be interested in this task.

This chapter compares and contrasts the biologies of Robert Mearns Yerkes and E.O. Wilson to show the transformation of biology from a science of sexual organisms to one of reproducing genetic assemblages. Throughout I focus on the machine and market as organizing ideas in life science. Table 1 outlines the categories of comparison. It is important to note that this chapter does not claim that Yerkes and Wilson singly built intellectual systems with conscious relations to the needs of patriarchal capital; rather it examines them as representing important formations, so as to give an idea where to continue a critical reading of classical biology in the process of formulating another biology.[2]

Yerkes was committed to development of personality sciences based on the model of physiology and scientific medicine.[3] As the goal of scientific management in industry in that period was the microcontrol of individual workers, establishment of co-operative hierarchies, and clear separation of control functions from manual work, Yerkes' psychobiology was founded on the individual organism and hierarchies of intelligence and adaptivity that were appropriate to the creation of rationally managed, modern societies. He built a complex evolutionary picture of the relation of sex and mind, raw material and engineering, instinct and rational control, that was appropriate to a genuinely usable capitalist science.

But by the end of his career around 1940, Yerkes' science was already outmoded. It was being replaced by a different engineering perspective, based not on physiology, but on the physical sciences' analysis of information and energy in statistical assemblages.[4] The physiology of sexual organisms gave way to biochemistry, structural analysis, and molecular genetics of information machines: integrons, replicators, self-assembling biological subsystems such as viruses and cell organelles and populations – the new books of nature to be read by mathematics. It is not an accident that modern genetics is pursued as a linguistic science, with attention to signs, punctuation, syntax, semiotics, machine read-out, directional information flow, codons, transcription, and so on (Jacob, 1974; Watson, 1976). The social goal of the new life science was clearly statistical control of the mass through sophisticated communications systems. Similarly, the damping and control of variation, prediction of large-scale pattern, and development of optimization techniques in every kind of system became a basic strategy of social institutions. Further, everything has become a system. The search has been for evolutionary stable strategies for maximizing profit. In life science, sociobiology is a mature fruit of this approach; it is genuinely a new synthesis that makes many distinctions between natural and social science outmoded.[5]

Robert Mearns Yerkes (1876–1956), in a lifetime of committed work in psychobiological research and science promotion and management, established the first comprehensive permanent laboratory for the study of anthropoid apes as models for human 'eings. Between 1924 and 1942, through Yale University and the Rockefeller Foundation, Yerkes assembled the funding, animals, researchers, buildings, maintenance staff, and publications which have made it possible to breed, rear, and study chimpanzees in captivity. He also made the first field studies of wild primate behaviour possible (Hilgard, 1965). On a wider level, Yerkes worked to establish the utility of primates for interpreting the place of human beings in scientifically managed corporate capitalism – called nature. His investigations in mental and sexual psychobiology included designing tests for all aspects of mental functions in organisms ranging from daphnia and dancing mice to psychopaths, soldiers, and corporate managers. Yerkes also examined natural dominance and co-operation in the evolutionary interrelation of sexual instinct and rational mind.[6] This work was a central part of his explicit project of scientific engineering as a proper replacement for the irrationalities of received culture.[7]

Yerkes had no interest in rationalizing conservative social forms. Science has constructed nature as a category facilitating redesign of natural objects, including society. Yerkes saw nature and society in managed capitalist terms. Nature was a problem in test design. Adaptivity meant solving the problem of the rational control of nature on the level of individual organisms and their social analogues – families, labour groups, and other superorganisms.[8] The scientific frameworks for interpreting primate behaviour and biology have changed radically since the early years of Yerkes' work before the First World War. Knowledge of primates has corresponded to general developments in biology, psychology, and sociology, as well as to political conflict. The ways arguments have been constructed for relating primate science to human needs have also changed. But a constant dimension of primate studies has been the naturalization of human history; that is, making human nature the *raw material* rather than the *product* of history. Engineering is the guiding logic of life science in the twentieth century.

Human engineering sought to construct a control hierarchy, modelled on the individual organism with the nervous system on top. This organismic model facilitated the conception of society as a harmonious, balanced whole with proper distribution of function. The interrelations of nervous and reproductive systems, the two main integrative mechanisms of the organism, provided a microcosm of life, including social life (superorganism). The principal scientific goal was a biological theory of co-operation based on management hierarchies. What had to be managed were organic life, instinct, sex. At the top of the organism-pyramid was mind, permitting altruism to mitigate the excesses of competition. Psychobiology, as sociobiology later, was faced with rationalizing altruism in a competitive world – without threatening the basic structure of domination.

ROBERT YERKES: THE PRIMATE LABORATORY AS PILOT PLANT FOR HUMAN ENGINEERING

> *It has always been a feature of our plan for the use of the chimpanzee as an experimental animal to shape it intelligently to specification instead of trying to preserve its natural characteristics. We have believed it important to convert the animal into as nearly ideal a subject for biological research as is practicable. And with this intent has been associated the hope that eventual success might serve as an effective demonstration of the possibility of re-creating man himself in the image of a generally acceptable ideal.*
>
> *Robert Yerkes*, Chimpanzees, A Laboratory Colony

By the 1930s, human engineering in the form of personnel management integrated the methods of the physical, biological, and social sciences in order to produce harmony, team work, adjustment. The structure of co-operation involved the entire complex division of labour and authority in capitalist production and reproduction. Co-operation most certainly included rational organization of hand and head, of subordination and dominance, of instinct and mind. Motivation of co-operation was a management problem (Mayo, 1933; Baritz, 1960; Bravermann, 1974).

It was also a biomedical problem, necessitating detailed physiological knowledge of the 'irrationalities', which could become pathological – instinct, personality, and culture. These three were closely tied to organic sex, and led to the proliferation of scientific disciplines such as endocrinology, gender-differentiated personality studies, Freudian psychotherapy, anthropology based on personality and culture, eugenic doctrines of race hygiene, and sexual counselling through the birth control movement.[9] Despite controversies among all these approaches, they shared a grounding in organic functionalism based on sexuality. Engineering meant rational placement and modification of human raw material – in the common interest of organism, family, culture, society, and industry. Human engineering was a kind of medical encouragement of natural homoeostatic mechanisms of intelligent integration. The life sciences which studied organic capacity and variation from a physiological viewpoint provided the scientific underpinnings for the application of human engineering. Yerkes helped build those sciences.

Yerkes received his PhD at Harvard in 1902. Before the First World War, his research in Cambridge and Boston concerned the sensory psychophysiology and mental capacity of a wide range of organisms. Sensory physiology was intimately related to modes of 'adaptivity', or learning, in both individual and evolutionary frameworks. Early in his career Yerkes was interested in extending his work to primates, and envisaged a comprehensive primate research station which would include physiology, learning, and social behaviour. Yerkes worked within the framework of comparative psychology, which studied evolution of animal behaviour as a chain of being, a series of increasingly complex physiological organizations, best shown in growth of intelligence. Having defined intelligence as problem-solving behaviour, Yerkes relied on the construction of testing apparatus for comparing learning strategies of different species and individuals within species. The relation to a hierarchically conceived physiology as the model for this psychology cannot be overstressed. As scientific medicine was based on experimental physiology, so too psychological therapies relied on experimental psychology (Yerkes, 1913, 1921).

In studying adaptivity of primates, Yerkes (1927b, 1928) developed the notion of three stages of complexity, which he actually called monkeying, aping, and thinking. His pre-war ideational studies of the orangutan Julius and of patients in the Boston Psychopathetic Hospital were part of the development of tests applicable to all sorts of problems of organic inventory. The First World War supplied an opportunity for demonstrating the utility of this psychophysiological natural science. Yerkes is well known for helping devise the intelligence tests for conscripts; these test results were frequently used for immigration restriction and other racist purposes during and after the war. It is less well known that Yerkes designed his tests under the auspices of the army surgeon general and conceived the work as part of the medical management of society (Kevles, 1968; Ann Arbor Science for the People, 1977, pp. 21–57; Cravens, 1978, pp. 80–5, 181–8).

After the war, Yerkes remained in Washington, DC, forming an economic and political base for his lifelong goal of a primate research station. From 1919 until accepting a professorship in Yale University's new Institute of Psychology in 1924, he worked within the National Research Council of the National Academy of Sciences.

Two committees formed under the auspices of the National Research Council (NRC) are relevant to the themes of this chapter: the Committee on Scientific Aspects of Human Migration (CSAHM) and the Committee for Research on Problems of Sex (CRPS). Yerkes was chairman of both, the CSAHM from 1922 to 1924 and the CRPS from 1922 to 1947. Both committees were set up to study human variability for purposes of rational social management policy. Neither committee worked from a population perspective, but rather from a physiological model of organic capacity, variation, and health. Widespread population genetic and ecology approaches to demography and to sexuality only emerged after the Second World War and were related to the elaboration of communications technology and information sciences.

The Committee for Research on Problems of Sex grew out of efforts by the New York City Bureau of Social Hygiene to establish a structure of pure research for enlightened social policy on matters such as sex education, family counselling, eugenics, venereal disease, divorce, and birth control.[10] The NRC committee was part of an effort to relate medical-physiological research to social issues. The committee sponsored work in four categories, *not* including direct action agencies:[11] (1) biology of sex (systematic, genetic, and physiological aspects); (2) physiology of reproduction; (3) infrahuman psychobiology of sex; and (4) human psychobiology of sex, including anthropological and social-psychological approaches. Two assumptions stand out in the records of the sex committee. First, social practice had to be based on basic research conducted and controlled by independent specialists; the parent philanthropy had no direct say about funding once the committee was established. Second, the sex instinct was perceived to underlie the whole pyramid of life and human sciences and to be the key to understanding culture and personality. The CRPS did not conceive of science as rationalizing sexual repression. Quite the opposite: the committee in large measure played a liberalizing role.[12] It was committed to facilitating rational social engineering. Animal models for human organic capacity and variation allowed human engineering to be an experimental natural science. In that sense, Yerkes built his primate laboratory as a pilot plant for human engineering.

In consultation with a powerful old friend and colleague, Yale University President James Rowland Angell, Yerkes planned the Institute of Psychology at Yale as the home for his primate research. The Institute housed a range of graduate research on general problems of adaptation; its staff was made up of former members of the Committee on Scientific Aspects of Human Migration.[13] These men brought with them a commitment to the scientific management of race, sex, and class, based on sciences of heredity, drives, learning, and environment, all in a biomedical context grounded in physiology. In 1924, Yerkes moved to New Haven. His early facilities consisted of his farm in New Hampshire and a converted old building at Yale, where four young chimpanzees grew up in full view of modern science. Their psychosexual and ideational development were the primary concerns. Mind and sex were a natural pair (Bingham, 1928).

In 1929, Yerkes achieved his dream, a $500,000 grant from the Rockefeller Foundation for a permanent, large research facility on great apes. Grant proposals and Foundation correspondence were full of the relevance of the project to human social and psychological issues.[14] No other goal could justify the large expense of using chimpanzees as research animals. The resulting Yale Laboratories of Primate Biology existed in three parts: (1) special laboratories for short-term work in New Haven needing special apparatus, with close co-operation with John Fulton's Department of Physiology in the Medical School; (2) a breeding colony of thirty to forty animals in Orange Park, Florida, where long-term sexual and ideational psychobiological observation and experimentation would be possible; and (3) special provision for studies of wild primates in their natural habitat, to provide base line information on the natural social physiology of the organisms.[15] Research centred on the idea of evolution, and all but ignored the idea of populations. Animal behaviour was not a genetic science in Yerkes' and his contemporaries' hands. Or rather, the comparative psychologists used the word *genetic* always in the sense of the genesis of individual capacities. All this would change with the post-Second World War synthesis of ethology, neural biology, and population genetics and ecology. Figure 2 shows the picture of life science that Yerkes knew around 1930.

FIGURE 2

LIFE SCIENCES

AGE OF BIOLOGY
(unifying science and ideology)

NATURE	MEDIATORS	CULTURE
(autonomous)		(autonomous)

		Psychology		
	drives			
Physiology	reflexes	BEHAVIOUR	SOCIAL RELATIONS	Anthropology
(experimental)	genes			
	hormones			
Evolution		animal: human		Sociology
(comparative)		(personality)		
Environmental Sciences				Mental and Social Hygiene
		Psychobiology		

experimental medicine	*experimental sociology*
reproductive system	family
nervous system	social group
health	management
	adjustment

HUMAN ENGINEERING

PSYCHIATRY
(unifying technologies)

The life sciences focused on organisms, personalities, and cultures, around 1930. Both sides of the figure are rooted in organismic, functionalist doctrines; both involve differentiated roles for basic and applied sciences, modelled on experimental medicine.

People associated with the primate laboratories at Yale maintained two organizing ideas rooted in organismic physiology. The first was domination, which included brain region dominance, dominance in competitive interactions between individuals, dominance as a personality trait related to leadership, and dominance hierarchies as social structure. Dominance was perceived as inherent to individual organisms; it was probably inheritable, just like eye colour or IQ. The second idea was co-operation – from homoeostatic mechanisms at all levels, to deliberate modification of dominance in the interests of higher organization, to everyday rules for running the laboratory. Co-operation and dominance were closely connected on an organic level as forms of integration.

A choice opportunity presented itself for the experimental investigation of dominance in the context of family-centred experimental sociology. The experiment tested co-ordination of sexual drive, status hunger, masculine and feminine personality types, and evolutionary transformation to higher forms of social control. This study carried noteworthy implications for counselling and human social services by relating drive and personality to social order.

In the course of tests for delayed response and representational processes, as part of the study of the phylogeny of language, Yerkes observed that sexual periodicity and dominance–subordination appeared to influence which animal of a caged pair would come to the food chute to be examined. Yerkes (1939) then conducted competitive food experiments on four kinds of caged companions: mates, two mature females, mature with immature females, and two immature females. Pieces of banana were presented one at a time in a series of ten through a chute in the cage. Along with other information, the observer recorded which animal of the pair would take the piece. Results were correlated with sexual status of the females in terms of dominance–subordination and response by 'right or privilege'. Right or privilege meant that in the period of maximum genital swelling of the female, that is, when the female was on heat, the ordinarily dominant male granted her the privilege of taking the banana, although dominance itself was not seen to reverse. Yet the female acted as if by right. Yerkes recognized various problems with the data: for example, observations were made in only one case for an entire cycle, and variation of the response pattern virtually swamped the postulated regularities. Tests of statistical significance were not reported. In female pairs, sexual swelling affected performance on the food priority test, but the animal offering sexual favours would be either the previously 'dominant' or previously 'subordinate' chimp. The sexual market among females was disorderly. Even among 'mates', it seemed presence or absence of prior 'friendship' greatly affected the results. But Yerkes spent most of the paper describing in detail a pair which showed clear substitution of right and privilege for dominance. The tone was simultaneously tentative and expectant that these observations were the beginning of very important studies. Yerkes' experimental social physiology, which explored the sexual market as fundamental to the origin of human cultural co-operation in the institution of marriage (and marriage's 'pathological' form – prostitution) has a long history (Herschberger, 1948, pp. 5–14).

Dominance as a drive was not sex specific, in Yerkes' opinion. It was the organism's basic hunger for social status. 'Assuming that dominance is hereditary and that inheritance is independent of sex, men and women might be expected to become creative leaders with approximately equal frequency' (Yerkes, 1939, pp. 133–4). Culture accounted for actual observed predominance of male leaders. But the association of 'leadership' and biological dominance was considered natural. Yerkes was liberal-to-moderate on the sex role controversies of the day and made clear his opinion that human females should have greater 'opportunity' than allowed by tradition. The issue here is not whether Yerkes or other spokespeople for comparative psychobiology were or were not liberals in their own time, but the logic of naturalization of the issues in terms of hierarchy from instincts to rational control, through personality and associated educational and medical therapies. With the weakening of religion, comparative life science became the new bedrock for value decisions, the more evolutionarily adaptive ground for judgement. With respect to the division of labour in the family, which was the model for the division of labour in all of society, the logic of naturalization provided a cornerstone of historical explanation based on reproduction. The dynamic was management, *not* repression.

To make the above point concrete, let us follow Yerkes through his analysis of the implications of the interweaving of sex hungers with dominance drives. First, Yerkes put the entire investigation of sex drive and dominance–subordination explicitly in the context of pressing contemporary debates. Yerkes assumed that feminism was equivalent to the proposition that males and females were biologically 'equal'; that is to say, he assumed that the concept of rights in political philosophy was properly rooted in natural economy. On 'scientific grounds', Yerkes firmly rejected the proposition that males were mentally superior, or, for that matter, naturally dominant. Males and females had the same psychological (ideation) and drive (motivation) structure. But as a consequence of hormonal structures there were differences in expression of drives. The result was personality. Life science required a physical marker for the internal state. Yerkes' work articulated the relation of psychobiology to contemporary biology and physiology of sex, the first two categories of the Committee for Research on Problems of Sex's promotional programme. If the division of labour in society could be correlated with the differences in drive expression, then the feminists of Yerkes' time were misguided (Yerkes, 1943, p. 69).

'Many clear-cut sex contrasts appear in the varied and complex expressions of dominance and subordination, leadership and control, aggression and defense. To these,' Yerkes (1943, p. 71) wrote, 'as uniquely important in the further description of masculinity and femininity, attention is especially invited.' In the context of discussing differentiated techniques of social control adopted by males and females, Yerkes described biologically determined differences in drive expression. The existence of chimpanzee differences in 'techniques of social control' suggested that human modes were also psychobiologically legitimated and inevitable.

> In a word, the masculine behavior is predominantly self-distracting; the feminine, primarily favor-currying and priority-seeking ... To the observer the male seems often to be trying hard to blot out awareness of his subordination; the female, by contrast, to be hopefully trying to induce the male to give place to her at the chute ... As for the females, wiles, trickery, or deceitful cunning, which are conspicuous by their absence in the male list, are favorite resources. But even more so are sexual allure and varied forms of solicitation ... That the female is, chameleon-like, a creature of multiple personality, is clear from our observations. (Yerkes, 1943, p. 83)

Yerkes based these 'observations' on the experimental sociology of the food chute test. He did not leave the lesson for the *limits* of cultural formation of personality, and therefore of possible social change, to the imagination:

> I am impressed by the contrasted attitudes and activities revealed by the competitive food situation, and I offer them as evidence that male and female chimpanzees differ as definitely and significantly in behavioral traits as in physique. I am not convinced that by reversal of cultural influences the pictures characteristic of masculinity and femininity can be reversed. (Yerkes, 1943, p. 85)

This opinion should be evaluated in light of Yerkes' extraordinary belief in human malleability and perfectibility through engineering. 'Personality differences' should be managed, not foolishly denied.

Yerkes believed the personality studies using anthropoid material were especially favourable because of the absence of social taboos and personal inhibitions.

> Therefore, I submit that such observational items as appear in this report, and in related studies of the psychology of sex in the anthropoid apes, should have exceptional value for those who concern themselves with problems of social behavior, and, especially at this juncture, for those psychopathologists who are intent on appraising, perfecting, and using psychoanalytical methods of observation and interpretation. (Yerkes, 1939, p. 130)

Though less differentiated than in the human species, personality 'clearly' existed among chimpanzees 'as the unit of social organization'. Personality meant the functional whole, 'the product of integration of all the psycho-biological traits and capacities of the organism'. In a normal personality, inherited characteristics and basic organic drives were integrated with the conscious self. In sum, personality was an absolutely central scientific object for life and human science. To have a masculine or feminine personality was not a minor matter; on its proper development hinged the adjustment and happiness of the individual and the body politic. Yerkes did not want to underestimate diversity and variability. Comparative science was designed precisely to deal scientifically with variability. For drives as central as sex and dominance and for expressions as consequential as masculinity and feminin-ity, nurture of personality was a matter for responsible scientific service. The possibility of prescription of social role on rational grounds was at stake. If drives and personality could be measured early, proper treatment could be initiated. Yerkes was cautious, but hopeful.

> If in man dominance as personality trait is highly correlated positively with leadership, as it evidently is in chimpanzee; if it is a condition of or markedly favorable to individual initiative, inquiringness, inventiveness, and creativeness; and if, further, it should prove to be reliably measurable during childhood, it may very well come to possess conspicuous value as indicator of vocational aptitudes and social usefulness and therefore also as the basis for differential educational treatment and occupational choice. Even marital advice might be affected by it, for congeniality or social fitness may depend appreciably upon similarity or the reverse in dominance as personality trait of mates or companions. (Yerkes, 1939, p. 133).

It is significant that the culture concept depended on personality in the anthropology of the 1930s. We have moved with Yerkes from instinct, through personality, to culture, to human engineering. Scientists themselves interwove sex, mind, and society in a vocation of scientific service estab-lishing a promising new life science of comparative primate psychobiology, reaching from learning through motivation to experimental sociology. Primatology served as a mediator between life and human sciences in a critical period of reformulation of the doctrines of nature and culture. Yerkes ordered his life in the belief this science would serve to foster a higher state of individual and social consciousness, the ideological goal of liberal humanism.

Before developing the second major section of this chapter, sociobiology, it is worth returning from Yerkes' mature positions in the late 1930s on

drive and personality in primates as models for humans, to his involvement
in the early 1920s with industrial personnel research.

In his capacity as temporary chairman at the 1920 annual meeting of the
Personnel Research Federation, Yerkes developed themes which permeated
his work for human engineering. He began with a call to 'look confidently to
disinterested research to guide our race to a wise solution' of the problem of
whether 'the industrial system and its products [shall] be treated as ends or
means to human welfare' (Yerkes, 1922, p. 56). He saw personnel research,
the study of the human factor of production, as the key discipline of the new
era. 'There is every reason to believe that human engineering will shortly
take its place among the important forms of practical endeavor' (p. 57).
Yerkes believed that industrial systems had evolved from slavery, to the wage
system, to the present system based on co-operation and that only now could
the value of the person be realized. Because personnel research took the
person as the proper unit of production, that discipline led the way to the
scientific nurture of intelligent co-operation to replace class strife between
labour and maladaptive, evolutionarily out-moded *laissez-faire* capitalism.
Yerkes and his liberal peers advocated studying traits of the body, mind,
spirit, and character in order to fit 'the person' perfectly into the proper place
in industry. Equality clearly did not mean organic sameness; therefore it
must mean that 'in the United States of America, within limits set by age,
sex, and race, persons are equal under the law and may claim as their right as
citizens like opportunities for human service and responsibility' (Yerkes,
1922, p. 58).

By Yerkes' logic, equality was everyone's right to occupy one's natural
place determined by disinterested science. *Differences* were the essential
subject for the new science. Personnel research would provide reliable
information for the employment manager and proper vocational counselling
for the 'person'. The 'vocations' themselves were regarded as neutral
products of industrial progress so that the problem was simply one of human
inventory in a democracy. The unit of analysis was the person, transformed
by the scientific concept of personality which tied physiology, medicine,
psychology, anthropology, and sociology into the service of management.
Further, 'the person', and 'personality', retained a strong anti-materialist
meaning at the same time that the associated ideology permitted scientific
reduction by objective methods – like intelligence testing, motivational
research, and sexual psychobiology. The wedding of philosophical idealism
and natural science produced well-behaved modern children in the factory
and the home. In short, '[I]ndustry now has abundant opportunity to develop
suitable methods of measuring persons with respect to qualities of character,
mind, and body, and to make this information immediately available in

connection with placement, vocational choice, and guidance' (Yerkes, 1922, p. 60).

Although the person should be the *object* of scientific management – an essential structure of domination in the science of co-operation – the ideology of self-expression was also intrinsic to Yerkes' exposition. The harmony of self and social management hinged on capitalist doctrines of personality. Satisfaction of basic instincts, themselves known through science, was the essence of self-expression in this model. Science, not class conflict, could provide for further human adaptive evolution. To be socially useful the drive had to be a kind of organic instinct compatible with the biological evolution of co-operation that was at last finding adequate industrial development. Yerkes logically collapsed the scientific object of personality into the spiritual value of the person: 'It now remains for personnel research to effect a still more significant and beneficial revolution or reformation [than the invention of machines] by making available adequate knowledge of man in all his essential aspects and relations, and by bringing into clear relief the supreme value of the person' (1922, p. 63). In rationalizing the market exchange of marriage and the productive machine of industry, comparative psychobiology took its place among the life and human sciences theorizing nature and humanity according to the logic of capitalist patriarchy.

SYSTEMS ENGINEERING AND SCIENCES OF INVESTMENT MANAGEMENT: SOCIOBIOLOGY

> *Sex is an antisocial force in evolution ... When sexual reproduction is introduced, members of the group become genetically dissimilar ... The inevitable result is a conflict of interest ... The outcomes of these conflicts of interest are tension and strict limits on the extent of altruism and the division of labor.*
> E.O. Wilson, Sociobiology: The New Synthesis

Organic engineering based on the person is not the dominant form of life science in the late twentieth century. It can even be argued that biology has ceased to exist and that the organism has been replaced by cybernetic systems, which have radically changed the connections of physical, life, and the human sciences.[16] Such claims are made by sociobiologists, and I think they have a strong case. How did it happen? What is the result, especially for the relations of sex, mind, and profit? This chapter can explore only a fraction of the revolution in biology that has resulted in molecular biology, population genetics and ecology of ecosystems, and sociobiology. By the mid-1930s, Yerkes' psychobiology, as well as the research programmes of many of his peers, was in trouble at the Rockefeller Foundation. Warren Weaver, the new head of the Division of Natural Sciences, had quite a different vision of the future of biology and of engineering as a life science. Weaver was both an instrument and a sign of much larger forces.[17] By the early 1960s, the communications revolution was established in power; its effects can be followed in biology in four revealing, collective, authoritative texts, culminating in a well-published, state-of-the-art introductory biology text by E. O. Wilson and his colleagues.[18] The themes of machine and market in the constitution of capitalist life science recur in the work of Wilson (born 1929, PhD from Harvard 1955) and his many peers. Sociobiology is a communications science, with a logic of control appropriate to the historical conditions of post-Second World War capitalism.

The communications revolution changed the strategy of control from organism to system, from eugenics to population management, from personnel management to organization structures (sociotechnical systems and ergonomics) based on operations research (Lilienfeld, 1978, ch. 4). A communications revolution means a re-theorizing of natural objects as technological devices properly understood in terms of mechanisms of production, transfer, and storage of information. Changes in the technology of actual communications systems provided part of the material foundation of fundamental scientific reformulations. War and problems of military management encouraged new developments in science. Operations research began with the Second World War and efforts to co-ordinate radar devices and information about enemy position in a total or systems way, which conceived of the human operator and the physical machinery as the unified object of analysis. Statistical models were increasingly applied to problems of simulation and prediction for making key decisions. After the war, the explosive development of electronics industries and communications technology was increasingly tied to strategies of social and military planning to devise and manage stable systems organized around several axes of variation.[19] Knowledge about range of variation and interaction effects among classes of variables replaced concern for individual states. The computer, a communications machine, both effected and symbolized new strategies of control.

Let us grant that communication means control – but for what? And does that particular goal really allow the labelling of whole scientific structures as capitalist in any deep way? Without suggesting a final answer to the second question, let us look at the first. Complex stable configurations, stable evolutionary strategies, were essential to realization of profit in immensely complex economic and political circumstances. The problem which systems theory addressed was the maintenance and maximization of profit in crisis-ridden post-Second World War capitalism. The range of intermediate structures between extraction of surplus value and realization of profit required a whole set of discourses and technologies that constituted the communications revolution.

No natural or human science has been unaffected by these technical and theoretical transformations. Precisely how each scientific discourse relates to these historical changes is a matter for detailed study; it is certain the connections will not often be direct or simple.[20] But it is a striking fact that the formal theory of nature embodied in sociobiology is structurally like advanced capitalist theories of investment management, control systems for labour, and insurance practices based on population disciplines. Furthermore, sociobiology, like all modern biologies, studies a control machine as its central object. Nature is structured as a series of interlocking cybernetic systems, which are theorized as communications problems. Nature has been systematically constituted in terms of the capitalist machine and market. Let us look first at the market.

The market is best approached in terms of the history of the concept of natural selection. Contemporaries realized that a Darwinian natural economy, the competitive struggle of all against all for profit, suggested troubling parallels to political economy. Darwin himself realized his debt to Thomas Malthus; scarcity was the motor of nature as well as of history (Malthus, 1798, pp. 26–30, 73–5, 98). Biological populations increased at a rate that guaranteed permanent scarcity, as well as permanent technical improvement in the means of production. Progress and scarcity were the twin forces in capitalist development.[21] Reproduction of biological organisms seemed the basic process in both nature and history, and reproduction was inherently competitive. Scarcity seemed inevitably linked to a natural process, and not to a historical limiting form of appropriation of the product of human production. Reproduction, not production, seemed the proper focus for a natural science of society. Similarly, as Marx noted, bourgeois political economists focused on equal and competitive exchange in the market, while obscuring the relations of domination in production. Those relations were enforced by particular mechanisms (including technology) which were designed to transfer the locus of control away from the worker. All of this is familiar. From this point of view, sociobiology is merely an extension and development of the theory of natural selection.

Sociobiology (Wilson, 1975, p. 10) is a biological understanding of *groups* – societies and populations. As for all capitalist science, the fundamental problem needing explanation is the combination of individuals for the common good. From a starting point of atomic individualism, reproduced in Darwin's theory of natural selection, *altruism* needed explanation; it seemed an irrationality for a consistent theory of selection. Altruism in sociobiology is defined as 'self-destructive behavior performed for the benefit of others' (Wilson, 1975, p. 578). How could individuals profit in the long run, if they wasted time and courted danger in self-destructive generosity? The problem seemed particularly acute in the most advanced natural societies – social insects and non-human primates, not to mention human orders. Sociobiology's solution is the quantitatively sophisticated extension of natural selection and population genetics, producing the notion of 'inclusive fitness: the sum of an individual's own fitness plus all its influence on fitness in its relatives other than direct descendants; hence the total effect of kin selection with reference to an individual' (Wilson, 1975, p. 586).

The ideas related to inclusive fitness – kin selection, sexual selection, parental investment – permitted a refocusing of an old argument; that is to say, at what level can selection occur (Wynne-Edwards, 1962; Trivers, 1971, 1972)? In particular, can the social group be the locus of selection? If so, is the group a kind of superorganism, physiologically as well as genetically analogous to an individual? The answer for sociobiology is no.[22] Or rather, those suggestions no longer make sense. The genetic calculus of sociobiology concerns maximization strategies of genes and combinations of genes. All sorts of phenomenal orders are possible, from asexual individuals to cast-structured insect societies with only one reproductive pair, to role-diversified societies with many reproducing members. None of these orders is the central object of concern. That noumenal object is the gene, called by Richard Dawkins the 'replicator', within the gene pool. Sociobiology analyses all behaviour in terms of the ultimate level of explanation, the genetic market place.

Bodies and societies are only the replicators' strategies for maximizing their own reproductive profit. Apparent co-operation of individuals may be a perfectly rational strategy, if long-term cost-benefit analyses are made at the level of the genes. Such analyses call for the development and application of mathematical tools directly related to political economy and the technical demands made by that science. The novel dimension in late twentieth-century political and natural economy is the shared problem of understanding very complex forms of combination, which obscure the competitive bedrock of capitalism with phenomena like altruism and liberal corporate responsibility in transnational enterprises.

In 'nature' profit is measured in the currency of genes, and reproduction or replication is the natural imperative. But reproduction is not sex. In fact, sex is a dangerous modern innovation, one so challenging to older logics of individual profit-making as to require considerable attention. Like any other capitalist system, natural replication systems are compelled to make radical innovations all the time, or be outclassed by the dynamic competition. Sex is such an advance. Societies can be rationalized by probing the consequences of individual advantage and inclusive fitness, but the most highly integrated societies, the insects, minimize the disruptive effects of sex. Sex is a constraint on the formation of societies because sexually reproducing individuals are not identical genetically. They therefore compete with different investment strategies (Wilson, 1975, p. 314 ff).

So why risk dangerous investment strategies? Because they speed innovation – the rapid production of new genotypes which can respond to environmental changes or other contingencies. Such diversification maximizes the chances of long-term success. Through *speedy* production of new genotypes, not primarily dependent on mutation, reproducers secure a competitive advantage. Naturally, sociobiology argues, there will be some circumstances in which the dangers of sexual competition outweigh the advantages of rapid diversification. Sociobiology aims at a quantitative assessment of appropriate strategies. If sex ceases to provide an edge, it will have to go. But any society with most of its members engaging in sexual reproduction cannot hope for real peace. The best to be anticipated is a harmonious management of competing investment strategies, in such a way that the system as a whole (natural evolution) is preserved.

A consequence of this analysis of sex is the attention given to competing interests of males and females in reproduction. Some of the best work on parental investment strategies has been done on birds, allowing an understanding of such issues as clutch size and male and female differences in behaviour (especially readiness to mate).[23] The claim has been made that sociobiology establishes the ultimate equality of males and females by showing that they compete equally – if by different strategies – in the only game that counts, amassing genetic profit. The different strategies are a function of the different energetic commitment to reproduction that the sexes make. Mates must regard each other as means of capital accumulation not reliably under control. The sex which commits huge energy resources to incubating and nurturing will develop coy behaviour and adopt a sceptical stance towards errant mates. These fundamental behaviours would almost certainly be genetically mandated and constrained (Dawkins, 1976).

In advertising Sarah Blaffer Hrdy's book on langur behaviour, in which she emphasized competitive reproductive strategies of males and females, Harvard University Press referred to that kind of natural history as feminist (Ford, 1976; Hrdy, 1977). It would be hard to find a more market-limited rationale for feminist political theory. Much of the application of sociobiology to human beings centres around sexual competition (Weinrich, 1977).

But let us leave the market, despite its wealth of unexplicated topics, and look at sociobiology's theorizing of nature as a communications or control machine. Again, I focus not on the application of sociobiology to human life, but on the fundamental concepts of the science. The genes must make stable mediating devices; that is, they must produce machines *embodying* evolutionary stable strategies, just as capital requires capitalist institutions. Without mechanisms for transmission and replication, the genes are like hoarded money. The market demands a technology of production consistent with its own imperatives. Here we leave the realm of competition and exchange and enter the factories of life. What kind of mediating machines do the genes inform? Naturally, cybernetic systems.

Sociobiology studies two fundamental sorts of systems: populations and societies. Both are studied in terms of boundaries of information and energy flow. Information and energy are different faces of a common coin, a realization made possible by thermodynamics and information sciences. Populations are measured in terms of boundaries of gene flow over time; genes are materializations of information. Sociobiology studies societies in terms of zones of communication and exchange of information (Wilson, 1971, p. 224 ff; 1975, ch. 1). Individuals are systems common to sociobiology and other areas of life science. Individuals also are studied as part of structured flows of information and energy, interacting with other individuals; higher levels of order (societies, populations) result. Individuals are intermediate structures constructed, or rather instructed, by the genes.

What the genes really make are behaving machines. Thus behaviour becomes a central concern of sociobiology. Behaviour is the evolutionary pacemaker; it determines the rate of system change by its capacity to track and respond to variables. Dawkins, in his chapter 'The Gene Machine', discusses behaviour in terms of motion timed and controlled by a biological computer whose least element is the neurone (Dawkins, 1976, pp. 49–70). Genes are like programs for chess-playing computers; that is, genes build brains, effector organs, and sensory channels. Brains are processing devices with logical programs. Terms like 'imagination' (all mentalistic language) refer to forms of simulation made possible by advanced brains. The task of brains is the prediction of interlocking system contingencies, including the environment, and control of rate of motion. The system goal is maximization of genetic profit, necessitating the structuring of specific forms of control. Speed and capacity of processing are the basic parameters of the brain as control device.

Wilson (1975, ch. 7) calls social behaviour a tracking device for changes in the environment. He elaborates the concept of multi-level, hierarchically designed tracking systems. Relating the appropriate tracking mechanisms to the appropriate time scale, he works 'down' from levels of evolutionary adaptation (including morphogenetic changes and a hierarchy of organismic 'responses', from instinct-reflex systems to generalized learning systems) to individual adaptations (including learning, socialization, and play). Nothing is as silly as arguing about nature and nurture. The question is which level of tracking device one is considering.

> The important point to keep in mind is that such phenomena as the hormonal mediation of behavior, ontogenetic development of behavior, and motivation . . . are really only sets of adaptations keyed to environmental change of different durations. They are not fundamental properties of organisms around which the species must shape its biology . . . The phenomena cannot be generally explained by searching for limiting features in the adrenal cortex, vertebrate mid-brain, or other controlling organs, for the reason that these organs have themselves evolved to serve the requirements of special multiple tracking systems posessed by particular species. (Wilson, 1975, p. 145)

So, physiology is subordinate to another level of analysis, that of operations research directed at biological tracking devices much more sensitive than radar. This approach to behaviour, adaptation, and the brain, in operations terms analogous to those studied in the Second World War, stands in sharp contrast to Yerkes' psychobiological doctrines of mind, brain, and society. Biological inventory and personnel management have been superseded. The distance is large between persons or superorganisms (the mind co-ordinates sexual instinct to produce co-operation) on the one hand, and multiple tracking systems (with mind as the strategy of genes) on the other hand.

Communications theory is closely related to the sociobiological treatment of behaviour. From operations research to information sciences is a short step. Communication is sending and receiving meaningful signals, resulting in changed probabilities of behaviour. According to Wilson (1975, p. 201) a task of his science is to construct 'zoosemiotics'; that is, the study of general properties of communication.[24] Basic to that task is an analysis of *modes* of communication, which necessitates attention to sensory channels, whether auditory, tactile, acoustical, or chemical.

> It is therefore legitimate to analyze advantages and disadvantages of the several sensory modalities as though they were competing in an open marketplace for the privilege of carrying messages. Put another, more familiar way, we can reasonably hypothesize that species evolve toward the mix of sensory cues that maximizes either energetic or informational efficiency, or both. (Wilson, 1975, p. 231)

It is in this context that we should consider one of Wilson's most important research contributions to sociobiology: a study of insect chemical communication mediated by pheromones. Pheromones are chemical substances, usually glandular in origin. 'One individual releases the material as a signal and another responds after tasting or smelling it' (1975, p. 591). Social insects make extensive use of this mode. In about 1958, Wilson (1962; 1971, chs 12–14) adapted a mathematical technique to measure the amount of information transmitted by the fire ant odour trails and to compare it with the amount transmitted by the waggle dance of the honey bee. The general project was the translation of behaviour of all sorts into bits which could be treated by conventional information theory relating energy, capacity, noise, ambiguity, and so on. Wilson's goal was to understand communication as part of hierarchically graded evolutionary stable strategies, differentiated by time scale and material modality, in the interest of genetic fitness or maximization of genetic profit.

Territoriality and dominance systems are modes of communication which maintain stable configurations over intermediate time spans (Wilson, 1975, chs 12–13). Aggression, a form of competition, is basically a type of communication which must be analysed in terms of functional content and energetic efficiency. In principle, if found wanting by the evolutionary engineer, aggression, like sex, is dispensable. This is very unlikely; but outmoded expressions of aggression should be expected, providing models for social and psychological therapy in human orders. Obsolescence is a central theme in the biology of automated technological devices. The contrast with Yerkes' organismic psychobiology culminating in the person is evident. For a sociobiologist, dominance is not a trait, nor even an individual organismic predisposition, but a system property. The type of engineering intervention appropriate to sociobiology is systems analysis and design, not clinical diagnosis based on an analogy to physiology and scientific medicine. But both forms of engineering argue for a special role for the scientific expert in designing history (systems) on the human level.

The point of systems design is optimization. Optimization does not mean perfection. A system has to be good enough to survive under given conditions. Nature can be lazy, and seems to have abandoned a natural theological project of adaptive perfection. Yerkes sought to find perfection in adaptivity, but not the sociobiologists. Optimization does not mean maximum productive efficiency at all times. Insects in optimized societies can be lazy as well as industrious; it has been precisely measured. Crucial to system optimization are the *mass* effects of many variables, not perfection of the individual worker ant. So, Taylorite scientific management is inappropriate as an analogue to modern scientific study of the natural economy.

In the early 1960s, Wilson drew on the systems science of ergonomics that had been developed in human sociology of capitalist production.[25] Ergonomics is the quantitative study of the distribution of work, performance, and efficiency; it must take account of the history of systems because that history results in limits on available materials and in other constraints. In natural systems, those constraints would likely be built into the genetic programmes. Existing systems of production in both natural and political economy are compromises; the engineer determines the best choice of possible trajectories, with no apologies to the utopian activist. Wilson applied ergonomic analysis to the problem of number, type, and timing of production of various castes in insect societies, in order 'to analyze optimality'. Such an analysis should reveal when and how many sexually reproducing forms will be found under particular environmental conditions for a given species.

> First, consider the concept of cost in colony reproduction . . . The mature colony, on reaching its predetermined size, can be expected to contain caste ratios that approximate the *optimal mix*. This mix is simply the ratio of castes that can achieve the maximum rate of production of virgin queens and males while the colony is at or near its maximum size. It is helpful to think of a colony of social insects as operating somewhat like a factory constructed inside a fortress . . . [the] colony must send foragers out to gather food while converting the secured food inside the nest into virgin queens and males as rapidly and efficiently as possible. The rate of production of the sexual forms is an important, but not an exclusive, component of colony fitness. (Wilson, 1971, p. 342)

It would be hard to find a clearer example of an analysis of biological objects in terms of the systems sciences rooted in military combat, competitive sexuality, and capitalist production. Wilson's science of sociobiology no longer sees sex in terms of the problem of personality and personnel sciences applied to family, education, and industry. Yerkes' terms of reference have no place in the new biology of optimized communications systems assessed by a design engineer. The disquieting aspect of all this is that sociobiologists can and have correctly predicted insect caste distributions with these analyses.

Wilson concluded the chapter in *Sociobiology* on origins and evolution of communications by drawing attention to the central aspect of biology as an engineering science; that is, a science that studies systems design, with an eye to human-mediated improvement of potentially outmoded natural control systems. 'If the theory of natural selection is really correct, an evolving species can be metaphorized as a communications engineer who tries to assemble as perfect a transmission device as the materials at hand permit' (1975, p. 240). Phylogenetic constraints on the evolution of natural systems could, in the human case, be studied and perhaps redesigned. There would, however, be limits to design, limits crucial from a human political perspective that denies a natural necessity for hierarchical control systems and other modes of domination, for example, socialist-feminism.

The theoretical view of nature underlying genetic engineering and bioethics as a kind of quality control industry appears clearly in sociobiology.

On Human Nature emphasizes constraints and deeply established trajectories, but there is no logical, much less moral, barrier to a full engineering approach to outmoded systems.[26] In that sense, the status quo rationalizations of the book, though extensive and explicitly sexist, racist, and classist, are on the surface. The foundation of sociobiology is a capitalist and

TABLE 2
LIFE SCIENCE IN AND FOR CAPITALISM AND PATRIARCHY

Biology as an Engineering Science

Machine (production)	Control	Engineering
machine as organism	functionalism	adjustment, inventory, and normalization of diversity
machine as cybernetic system	communication, information	expanded integration, redesign

Key biologies: physiology, cell and developmental biology, molecular biology
Key machine subsystems: nervous system, reproductive system (mind and sex, culture and nature, intelligence and instinct)
Basic metaphors: balance, equilibrium, stress
Model for breakdown: obsolescence, defect, noise or disorder
Basic ethics: bioethics as quality control
Basic processes permitting an engineering perspective: breakdown and assembly, re-assembly, self-assembly (e.g., viruses, membranes, visual system, organelles); regulation and control (linguistics, new logics, electronics industries and sciences providing basic biological categories)

Biology as an Investment Science

Market (exchange)	Management of Portfolio

Key biologies: genetics, population biology, ecology and evolution
Strategy: individual self-interest, maximization of profit, accumulation, diversification
Basic scandal: altruism
Basic ethics: contract compliance and opportunism
Basic processes permitting an investment perspective: competition and co-operation both as forms of maximization strategy, game strategies, contract and exchange at the origin of all society (key industries providing biological categories: insurance, consulting, advertising)

patriarchal analysis of nature, which requires domination, but is very innovative about its forms. The limits to engineering redesign in sociobiology are set by the capitalist dynamic of private appropriation of value and the consequent need for a precise teleology of domination. The fundamental sexism is less in rationalization of sex roles as genetically predisposed, than in the basic engineering logic of 'human' domination of 'nature'. The humanism of sociobiology, which Wilson correctly cites in his defence, is precisely the core of his science's sexism.[27] In addition of course, sociobiological reasoning applied to human societies easily glides into facile naturalization of job segregation, dominance hierarchies, racial chauvinism, and the 'necessity' of domination in sexually based societies to control the nastier aspects of genetic competition. But, ironically, sociobiology is probably *less* tied to explicit sexism and racism than psychobiology and other organic functionalist biologies were. Sociobiology is a radical engineering science which can readily cleanse its objects of obsolescent flaws in natural design. The deities of the organic body are not sacred to the new designers of evolutionary stable strategies. It is no wonder that Wilson (1978, p. 209) ends *On Human Nature* with a rejection of Pandora and an appeal to renew worship of Prometheus, the titan who symbolizes human liberation through domination. In Greek, *Prometheus* means *forethought*, an optimal result for a communications science.

CONCLUSION: IS FEMINIST-SOCIALIST SCIENCE POSSIBLE?

> *Nature is, above all, profligate ... [Its schemes] are the brainchild of a deranged manic-depressive with limitless capital. Extravagance. Nature will try anything once. That is what the form of the insect says. No form is too gruesome, no behavior too grotesque. If you're dealing with organic compounds, then let them combine. If it works, if it quickens, set it clacking in the grass; there's always room for one more; you ain't so handsome yourself. This is a spendthrift economy; though nothing is lost, all is spent.*
>
> *Annie Dillard,* Pilgrim at Tinker Creek

We have seen two varieties of biology as an engineering science in relation to the knowledge and practices of patriarchal capitalism. There has been no clear distinction between objective science and abusive ideology because the relations of knowledge and historical determinants require more complex concepts. In an important sense, science, like capital, has been progressive. The computer is not just a machine built according to laws of domination related to labour and war. Communications sciences, including sociobiology, are human achievements in interaction with the world. But the construction of a natural economy according to capitalist relations, and its appropriation for purposes of reproducing domination, is deep. It is at the level of fundamental theory and practice, not at the level of good guys and bad guys.

A socialist-feminist science will have to be developed in the process of constructing different lives in interaction with the world. Only material struggle can end the logic of domination. Marx insisted that one must not leap too fast, or one will end in a fantastic utopia, impotent and ignorant. Abundance matters. In fact, abundance is essential to the full discovery and historical possibility of human nature. It matters whether we make ourselves in plenty or in unfulfilled need, including need for genuine knowledge and meaning. But natural history – and its offspring, the biological sciences – has been a discipline based on scarcity. Nature, including human nature, has been theorized and constructed on the basis of scarcity and competition. Moreover, our nature has been theorized and developed through the construction of life science in and for capitalism and patriarchy. That is part of the maintenance of scarcity in the specific form of appropriation of abundance for private and not common good. It is also part of the maintenance of domination in the form of escalating logics and technologies of command-control systems fundamental to patriarchy. To the extent that these practices inform our theorizing of nature, we are still ignorant and *must* engage in the practice of science. It is a matter for struggle. I do not know what life science would be like if the historical structure of our lives minimized domination. I do know that the history of biology convinces me that basic knowledge would reflect and reproduce the new world, just as it has participated in maintaining an old one.

Part Two

Contested Readings: Narrative Natures

Chapter Four

In the Beginning Was the Word: The Genesis of Biological Theory

'When I use a word,' Humpty Dumpty said, in rather a scornful tone, 'it means exactly what I choose it to mean – neither more nor less.'

'The question is,' said Alice, 'whether you can make words mean so many different things.'

'The question is,' said Humpty Dumpty, 'which is to be master – that's all.'

Lewis Carroll, Through the Looking Glass

Master – *a person with the ability or power to use, control, or dispose of something; male head of a household; a victor or conqueror; a man eminently skilled in something; one holding this title.*

Random House Dictionary of the English Language

Do feminists have anything distinctive to say about the natural sciences? Should feminists concentrate on criticizing sexist science and the conditions of its production? Or should feminists be laying the foundation for an epistemological revolution illuminating all facets of scientific knowledge? Is there a specifically feminist theory of knowledge growing today which is analogous in its implications to theories which are the heritage of Greek science and of the Scientific Revolution of the seventeenth century? Would a feminist epistemology informing scientific enquiry be a family member to existing theories of representation and philosophical realism? Or should feminists adopt a radical form of epistemology that denies the possibility of access to a real world and an objective standpoint? Would feminist standards of knowledge genuinely end the dilemma of the cleavage between subject and object or between non-invasive knowing and prediction and control? Does feminism offer insight into the connections between science and humanism? Do feminists have anything new to say about the vexed relations of knowledge and power? Would feminist authority and the power to name give the world a new identity, a new story? Can feminists master science?

These large questions may be usefully broached in a meditation on four recent books addressed to one little corner of contemporary natural science – the debate about biological determinism and human nature. One thing is undeniable about biology since its early formulations in the late eighteenth and early nineteenth centuries: biology tells tales about origins, about genesis, and about nature. Further, modern feminists have inherited our story in a patriarchal voice. Biology is the science of life, conceived and authored by a word from the father. Feminists have inherited knowledge through the paternal line. The word was Aristotle's, Galileo's, Bacon's, Newton's, Linnaeus's, Darwin's; the flesh was woman's.[1] And the word was made flesh, naturally. We have been engendered. Sandra Gilbert and Susan Gubar (1979), in their study of nineteenth-century women writers, discuss women's travail to construct a voice, to have authority, to author a text, to tell a story, to give birth to the word. To author is to have the power to originate, to name. Women who seek to produce natural knowledge, like our sisters who learned to write and speak, also must decipher a text, the book of nature, authored legitimately by men.

Gilbert and Gubar, analysing the extraordinary influence of Milton's justification of the ways of God on nineteenth-century female writers seeking to tell stories, suggest that all of us begin in some sense as Milton's daughters, forced to read a book in a language that signifies our lack, our difference. *The Madwoman in the Attic* asserts that Milton's literary daughters adopted two main strategies for gaining authority: they either reinterpreted the origin story to get it right the second time, or they rebelliously proclaimed a totally new story. In deep similarity, feminists taking responsibility for modern origin stories – that is, for biology – may try to get the story right, to clean up shoddy science about evolution and brains and hormones, to show how biology really comes out right with no conflict between reason and authority. Or feminists may more boldly announce a completely new birth. In both cases, feminists are contesting for a voice. And so rhetorical strategies, the contest to set the terms of speech, are at the centre of feminist struggles in natural science. The four books discussed in this chapter may be read primarily as entries in the contest of rhetorical strategies for setting the terms that define good science. How should we know whom to believe? After examining these four books, the stories they tell, and the modes of telling they adopt in their attempt to prove authority, we may return to the questions of the opening paragraph with a new ear.

Let us begin at the beginning. David Barash (1977), zoologist-sociobiologist at the University of Washington, did probing research on rape in mallards and wrote the authoritative textbook *Sociobiology and Behavior*. In

The Whisperings Within, Barash (1979) intends to reveal to the popular audience the inner voice of biology, the cake of nature under the icing of culture, the biogrammar of genes structuring the message of the organism – all so that modern people might come to know themselves and fulfil their potential. Barash maintains that biology is the most powerful tool in the humanist project to know and achieve the self.[2] Barash makes unbridled use of the literary devices and thematic structure of Genesis and its commentators. Harper & Row actually marketed *Whisperings* in a dust jacket picturing a blond, blue-eyed, young white male and a brown-haired, blue-eyed, young white woman standing, genitals hidden, in a garden of vegetables dominated by sword plants that could have come only from Lewis/Luis's nursery in Marge Piercy's *Woman on the Edge of Time*. Barash invited his packaging: his first quote is from Pius XII on natural law and reproductive sex in marriage; the first sentence of Chapter 2 is, 'In the beginning was the gene' (p. 16). Milton might not have liked these new children's stories or recognized his Adam and Eve in Barash's original partnerships in which male and female are 'co-shareholders in any offspring' engaged in the 'eternal evolutionary struggle to get ahead'; but the lineage is intact (Barash, 1979, pp. 123, 126).[3] Milton's fierce determinism has been translated into Barash's doctrine of people as 'temporary, skin-encapsulated egos, serving as complex tools by means of which their potentially immortal genes replicate themselves' (p.2).

Indeed, Barash's concern for lineages is his central rhetorical strategy. He calls on the authority of the father and names it scientific knowledge. Most important, Barash wishes to establish that Darwin begat sociobiology through his sons, especially men like himself, Robert Trivers, and W. D. Hamilton. Introducing experts to validate sociobiological reasoning, Barash rarely lets a name or argument stand alone. His authorities are Harvard biologist X, the great physicist Y, the leading evolutionary biologist Z, and so on (pp. 29, 34, 91, 133, 135, 166, 221, 240). In Chapter 1 – a pious homily before Chapter 2's genesis story of the gene and its great drama of endless replication, sexual reproduction, and the titanic market struggles among its thralls – Barash calls sociobiology the child of Copernicus and the Scientific Revolution. The promise of science – to know man – will at last be fulfilled. 'Sociobiology, in the same tradition, may help us discover our own nature and allow us to eavesdrop on the whispers of biology within us all' (p. 9). The true scientist in the legitimate lineage must face the scorn of scoffers, of those who prefer untruth because it is comfortable.[4] Like Darwin, the brilliant and courageous truth-teller will gain honour in the end. And sociobiology promises more than knowledge of the self; it also promises, like all humanisms, human unity, a real togetherness of nature beneath the merely verbal icing of culture. The lonely hero, the true child, will take us back to the garden of ourselves.[5]

So, attention to patrilineages is Barash's first fictive strategy for producing facts. His second is the legitimation of sociobiology's authority and power to achieve the promises of humanism. Sociobiology is fundamentally a scientific humanism which makes self-fulfilment possible by revealing the common coin, the medium of exchange, the equivalent that defines reality, the generator of meaning. At first glance, Barash's skin-encapsulated egos who serve the replicative ends of the prolix code-gene-coin-word within seem part of a strategy of reduction and objectification deeply opposed to humanism and human subjectivity, self-definition, and freedom. On the surface, Barash offers a doctrine of necessary biological determinism of all the chief forms of domination which are especially driven by the motors of ruthless competition and male dominance. In the beginning was the gene. And the gene was hungry; to live was to multiply. But the 'ultimate message' of sociobiology is quite different: it is the identification of the proper expert who has authority to exercise effective power over nature through knowledge of the word, control of the coin, cracking the code of nature's secret voice. Barash's message is the technology of power. He disavows the 'naturalistic fallacy'; 'is' is *not* 'ought' for him.[6] Knowing how to read the word, how to assess the value of the coin, gives the power of determination to those who use those tools. Of course, freedom and necessity come together as they must for humanists – in the end freedom is doing what we *really* want to do, and that is revealed by listening to the voice within, interpreted in the patriline of sociobiology. But we can change what we want; humanist power is radical. Power and authorship fabricate reality. The patriarchal voice of sociobiology is less the effusive sexism that ripples over the whole plane of the text than it is the logic of domination embedded in fashioning the tool of the word. Science and humanism have always been bedfellows. Their arguments are the wrangling of the two made into one flesh. Subject and object need each other. Their union gives birth to the patriarchal authorial voice.

A nagging question persists when one reads sociobiological texts: does anyone listen to these stories? An affirmative answer emerges from reading the seventeen essays in Gregory *et al.*'s collection, *Sociobiology and Human Nature* (1978). Ironically, the editors based this book on a symposium held under the very official auspices of the Science-Humanities Convergence Program (NEXA) funded by the National Endowment for the Humanities to explore 'humanistic implications of sociobiological inquiry ... NEXA provided a setting in which biologists, sociobiologists, anthropologists, psychologists, physicists, economists, and humanists could combine their efforts to understand the import of the questions currently being raised in sociobiological research' (p. x). The experts, then, were assembled to mediate and interpet the marital squabble between science and humanism and to show their higher unity. And they spoke – individually, authoritatively, joined in debate by the power of editors and panel moderators – in the rhetoric to which we have become accustomed. Each speaker seemed especially anxious to have his version of the history of science adopted, so that the legitimate lineage could be established. (The one woman who was invited – a senior scholar, Marjorie Greene – was assigned the task of discussing sociobiological implications for a philosophy of *mind*! The patriarchal voice is sometimes flatly funny.) This collection does contain some well-reasoned and very interesting essays, but this discussion will do them the injustice of limited analysis in order to keep to the theme of rhetorical strategies important for feminist mastery of scientific discourse.

E. O. Wilson, the arch-scientist of the moment, introduces the volume with the rhetoric of the innocent seeker for truth, the eternally young scientist surprised by all the *furor* (Gregory *et al.*, 1978, p. 1). He reiterates that sociobiology aims only to provide perspective for formulating the highest social goals, for bridging the two cultures, science and humanities. David Barash, his authority to speak acknowledged by his invitation to this expensive, taxpayer-supported forum, provides a manifesto for a scientific revolution and exclaims over the 'epiphantic insights' of the cost-benefit theorists in the history of sociobiology (p. 11). Sociobiologist Pierre L. van den Berghe preaches to the derelict social sciences and argues that only a return to the pastures of biology will reroot the human sciences in the soil of truth; history of science shows it. Sherwood Washburn scathingly chastises sociobiology for ruining social science by biologizing; his history of science shows the necessity of social explanation for social facts.[7] Physicist and historian of the physical sciences Gerald Holton, whose authority to speak must derive from his association with the most real of sciences (he notes in the first paragraph that he checked his pronouncements about biology with the relevant experts), praises sociobiology because it 'takes risks' and 'throws down the challenge' (pp. 75, 79). In short, sociobiology has proper male attributes. Holton proceeds to talk about the lineage of Ernst Haeckel, Jacques Loeb, Lucretius, and, of course, Newton. The point is to assess whether sociobiology measures up to the standards of a new synthesis. Animal psychologist Frank Beach argues persuasively that real science has more to say about proximate mechanisms and detailed empirical investigation and eschews easy ultimate claims and premature risky theory. Comparing the history of evolutionary biology and phrenology, historian-philosopher David Hull disclaims any pronouncements on the truth of scientific theories and points out that judgements of history have to do with success – who marshals resources to stay in the game and so by definition practises good science. In short, he adapts sociobiological standards to a cynical, agnostic history of science which has the virtue of showing that historically science *is* produced through struggles over power. Garrett Hardin, famed in the United States for the ethics of sinking lifeboats and desecrated commons, adopts a rhetoric of simple red-baiting. Those who oppose the truth of a selfish world are self-deceiving Marxists. Joseph Alper speaks for Science for the People, summing up the critique of ideologies of objectivity and demonstrating the false political neutrality of sociobiology.

The last article in this expert collection is actually a pronouncement by a Nobel Prize winner on the human condition! George Wald, a good friend of science radicals, insists immodestly that 'A scientist should not just study nature but should take care of humanity, life, and our planet' (p. 282). The text has moved from innocent to innocent, Wilson to Wald. After this pious ending, the editors' voices re-enter to sum it all up: Wilson speaking for the sociobiologists has turned our attention (as if it had wavered!) to the quest for 'our humanity'. 'We have no recourse but to accept his challenge. And paradoxically, he deserves our thanks for having cast it in so extreme a form' (p. 294). *Deo gratias.*

Let us now turn to Milton's scientific daughters who are taking stock of this rhetorical inheritance. We have not set the original terms of discourse; that fact determines our texts. What are the degrees of freedom for feminist reshaping of the production of science? Again, let us approach our question by exploring rhetorical strategies presented in the texts at hand. *Genes and Gender* (Hubbard and Lowe, 1979) unabashedly puns on the central problematic of genesis in biology; the title of *Women Look at Biology Looking at Women* (Hubbard et al., 1979) could hardly be more explicit about the mirror theme in the fictive scientific production of reality. Between the covers of these works, explicit commentary on the productive and reproductive power of the word continues. Language is a principal preoccupation of nearly every author in both books of collected essays. Susan Leigh Star makes the pervasive theme explicit in *Genes and Gender*: power to determine the language of discourse is the power to make flesh, to

> somatize our oppression . . . We have no language at present that does not reflect a Cartesian nature/nurture dichotomy for discussing sex differences. It is difficult to resist the urge to ask, 'But what, *underneath it all,* really *are* the differences between men and women.' *What we must begin to give voice to as scientists and feminists is that there is no such thing, or place, as underneath it all.* Literally, empirically, physiologically, anatomically, neurologically . . . the only accurate locus for research about us who speak to each other is the changing, moving, complex web of our interactions, in light of the language, power structures, natural environments (internal and external), and beliefs that weave it in time. (Hubbard and Lowe, 1979, p. 116)

Star writes this in a book that sets as its task the re-establishment of standards of research on all aspects of sex differences. *Genes and Gender* concludes that such research is now impossible – it simply cannot measure up to standards of scientific knowledge. This group of feminists has set out to name the rules of enquiry. And Star speaks in this group not as a Nobel Prize winner or as a tenured sociobiologist at a major university claiming Darwin's mantle, if not Newton's. She speaks as an editor of poetry for *Sinister Wisdom* and as a graduate student in geriatrics who studied research on brain asymmetry in an undergraduate seminar at Radcliffe, an institution that has led many women to authority. The authors in *Genes and Gender* try to persuade researchers to accept new standards, indeed, to abandon their field, in a way analogous to a physicist's telling biologists that anything they cannot quantify does not qualify as the matter of science. It remains a question whether natural selection and evolutionary biology itself would not have to abandon the field in the face of enforcement of that standard. What leads the authors in *Genes and Gender* to reach their nihilistic conclusion?

First, they cite the ubiquity of 'bad science' in the field of sex differences.[8] This strategy emerges from the historical necessity for feminists to begin with the heritage of names in a patriarchal voice. We are obliged to comment on the received texts. After all, one does not start from scratch when John Money has the gender clinic, E. O. Wilson the professorship at the Museum of Comparative Zoology, and so on. Milton's feminist daughters are as concerned about lineages as Barash, Holton, or Hardin. The strategy of reinterpretation of received stories is widely used by the authors in this book. In the 'begats' as presented by these authors, Darwin and Galileo become anti-heroes who either scientized Victorian social prejudice or alienated the subject from the object in a doctrine of the primacy of quantifiable qualities (pp. 15–17). The critique of bad science leads directly to an analysis of the material conditions of the production of knowledge and to a personal identification of the objective voice behind the 'pure, unadulterated facts'. Reality has an author. The author always has a proper name, but it has a way of disappearing into declarative sentences or even graphs embedded in published papers issuing from well-funded laboratories.[9]

Through these kinds of analyses, the authors in *Genes and Gender* want to persuade us that the bad science did not emerge accidentally, but systematically – and further, *must* continue to emerge, no matter how much individual scientists try to do good science on sex and gender. Facts are theory-laden; theories are value-laden; values are history-laden. And the history in this case makes it impossible for any researcher to step far enough away from daily, lived dominations of gender to study gender with any authority. Indeed, the very constitution of gender and sex as objects of study is part of the reproduction of the problem – the problem of genesis and origin. The historical project of humanism and its associated life and human sciences is the search for and fulfilment of the self. The constitution of sex and gender as privileged objects of knowledge is a tool in the search for the self. This construction regenerates the infinite regress of the search for the illusive subject that paradoxically ends regularly in the discovery of the totalitarian object – nature, the gene, the word.

These are strong words, and their difficulty is revealed when the feminists of *Genes and Gender* want to emerge from agnosticism and say what *is* the case with sex and gender. Feminists want also to adopt the second strategy of Milton's literary daughters and tell truly new stories with authority. But the critique of bad science that glides into a radical doctrine that all scientific statements are historical fictions made facts through the exercise of power produces trouble when feminists want to talk about producing *feminist* science which is more *true*, not just better at predicting and controlling the body of the world. David Hull's success story in the NEXA volume (that science becomes official through opportunistic survival) will not do for feminists because they do not wish to adopt the mask of having no position, mere spectators on the sidelines of the history of science. Corrosive scepticism cannot be midwife to new stories. Naomi Weisstein puts the matter well in *Woman Look at Biology* when she says, '[E]vidence became a hero of mine' (Hubbard *et al.*, 1979, p. 187).[10]

The process of exposing bad science, showing the fictive character of all science, and then proposing the real facts results in repeated unexamined contradictions in the feminist essays in both books.[11] These contradictions are important; they also bring us back to the opening questions of this chapter. Ruth Hubbard, a kind of scientific mother in the production of both *Genes and Gender* and *Women Look at Biology*, provides a sophisticated analysis of the issues and also shows clearly some of the contradictions in extant feminist analysis of biology.

In 'Have only men evolved', Hubbard begins with a thorough critique of theories of representation and ideologies of objectivity in science in general.

> For humans, language plays a major role in generating reality ...
> However, all acts of naming happen against a backdrop of what is socially accepted as real. The question is *who* has social sanction to define the larger reality into which one's everyday experiences must fit in order that one be reckoned sane and responsible ... At present science is the most respectable legitimator of new realities. (Hubbard *et al.*, 1979, pp. 8–9)[12]

Language *generates* reality in the inescapable context of power; it does not *stand for* or *point to* a knowable world hiding somewhere outside the ever-receding boundaries of particular social-historical enquiries. Yet somehow the task of the scientist as Sisyphus is to try to produce a picture of the world that is 'more than a reflection of various aspects of ourselves and of our social arrangements' (p. 11). Next Hubbard provides a nuanced reading of male-'engendered' origin stories of human evolution. But then, in the midst of discussing the difficulty of reconstructing the past, she puts in a little sentence that categorically asserts a fact: 'Since the time when we and the apes diverged some fifteen million years ago, the main features of human evolution that one can read from the palaeontological finds are the upright stance, reduction in the size of the teeth, and increase in brain size' (p. 29) Maybe, but what are the rules of interpretation that make this story unequivocally readable, and how do they differ from the rules for reading social and behavioural evolution? The main difference seems to be that there is *now* a *non*-gender-linked agreement about upright stance, so the reading is uncontested. But does the end of controversy mean that a story has achieved the status of fact, has escaped social determination, and has become objective? So suggests an innocent declarative sentence in the midst of scathing deconstruction. Yet upright stance and times of divergence between ape and hominid lines have been arenas of mortal combat in evolutionary theory more than once.

These problems become acute in the conclusion of the article when Hubbard suggests tasks for feminists as they take responsibility for the production of science. In particular, the hidden link between theories of representation and the humanist projects of self-discovery causes trouble. Hubbard cautions that women should not produce mirror-image 'estrocentric' stories, except perhaps as joke and parody. We should sift through current work to find raw data. But how, when we have also been told *all* facts are laden with theory and thus with value and history? We should demythologize masculinist science; and, able to 'think beyond it, [we] must do the necessary work in the field, in the laboratories, and in the libraries and come up with ways of seeing the facts and of interpreting them' (p. 32). 'False facts' and 'androcentric science' have endured too long, and a feminist science is necessary for finding ourselves, for getting our true inheritance. 'To see our alternatives is essential if we are to acquire the space in which to explore who we are, where we have come from, and where we want to go' (p. 32). In short, feminism is a *true* humanism based on *true* knowledge or at least on true interpretation. But all of the epistemological and political problems of humanism and realism are latent – or patent – here.

Feminists want some theory of representation to avoid the problem of epistemological anarchism. An epistemology that justifies not taking a stand on the nature of things is of little use to women trying to build a shared politics.[13] But feminists also know that the power of naming a thing is the power of objectifying, of totalizing. The *other* is simultaneously produced and located *outside* the *more real* in the twin discourses of life and human sciences, of natural science and humanism. This is the creation of difference that plagues 'Western' knowledge; it is the patriarchal voice in the production of discourse that can name only by subordinating within legitimate lineages.

Nancy Hartsock and Sandra Harding try to overcome this dilemma by arguing in slightly different ways that, because of our historical *position*, women can have a theory of objectivity, of the radical material-social production of knowledge, and of the possible end of dominating by naming. We have nothing to hide, so the self will not play its usual tricks and recede while substituting a fetish.[14] Subject and object can cohabit without the master–slave domination. Harding and Hartsock work from the Marxist premise that those suffering oppression have no interest in appearances passing for reality and so can really show how things work. Life and human sciences have merely been obscured by the position of the knowers – on top. I find this approach promising but not fully convincing. That argument must wait. What becomes very clear, however, is that feminists have now entered the debates on the nature and power of scientific knowledge with authority: we do have something to say. The only remaining problem is what, and here we are speaking in many voices. One voice for beginning again is offered by the epilogue of *Women Look at Biology*:

> The man–nature antithesis was invented by men. Our job is to reinvent a relationship that will realize (in the literal sense of making real) the unity of humankind with nature and will try to understand its workings from the inside ... Science is a human construct that came about under a particular set of historical conditions when *men's* domination of nature seemed a positive and worthy goal. The conditions have changed and we know now that the path we are travelling is more likely to destroy nature than to explain or improve it. Women have recognized more often than men that we are part of nature and that its fate is in human hands that have not cared for it well. We must now act on that knowledge. (Hubbard *et al.*, 1979, p. 209)

That is a feminist voice; is it also a humanist whisper?

Chapter Five

The Contest for Primate Nature: Daughters of Man-the-Hunter in the Field, 1960–80

For these things passed as arguments
With the anthropoidal apes.
> *Charlotte Perkins Gilman, 'Similar Cases'*

L anguage is not innocent in our primate order. Indeed, it is said that language is the tool of human self-construction, that which cuts us off from the garden of mute and dumb animals and leads us to name things, to force meanings, to create oppositions, and so craft human culture. Even those who dismiss such radical talk must acknowledge that major reforms of public life and public knowledge are coupled with projects for the purification of language. In the history of science, the fathers of things have been first of all fathers of words – or so the story is told to students of the discipline. Aristotle named beings and thereby constructed the rules of logic; Bacon denounced Aristotle in a project for the reform of language so as to permit, at last, true knowledge. Bacon also needed a new logic appropriate to his correct names. Linnaeus legitimated the kinship of human beings with animals in 1758 in the order he named, Primates. Linnaeus's taxonomy was a logic, a tool, a scheme for ordering the relations of things through their names. Linnaeus may have known himself as the eye of God, the second Adam who built science, trustworthy knowledge, by announcing at last the correct names for things.[1] And even in our time, when such giants and fathers are dead, scientific debate is a contest for the language to announce what will count as public knowledge. Scientific debate about monkeys, apes, and human beings, that is, about primates, is a social process of producing stories, important stories that constitute public meanings. Science is our myth. This chapter is a story about part of that myth, in particular aspects of recent efforts to document the lives of Asian leaf-eating monkeys called langurs.

This chapter is not innocent; it is an interested story searching for clues about how to ask feminist questions concerning public scientific meanings in an area of the life sciences so crucial to tales about human nature and human possibility. Feminism is, in part, a project for the reconstruction of public life and public meanings; feminism is therefore a search for new stories, and so for a language which names a new vision of possibilities and limits. That is, feminism, like science, is a myth, a contest for public knowledge. Can feminists and scientists contest together for stories about primates, without reducing both political meanings and scientific meanings to babble?

I would like to explore the writings of four primatologists linked together in a particular social network in physical anthropology, primatologists who are also all Euro-American women, in order to probe some aspects of these issues. In particular, does the practice of their science by these women in a field of modern biology-anthropology substantially structure discourse in ways intriguing to feminists? Should we expect anything different from women than from men? What are the right questions to ask about the place of sex and gender in the social structuring of scientific meanings in the areas of scientific work under investigation: animal behaviour and evolutionary theory? What questions seem most unhelpful? We will return to look at these questions after following the careers of some of our primate kin, US white primatologists and langurs.

Why look through the window of words and stories? Isn't the essence of a science elsewhere, perhaps in the construction of testable propositions about nature? But what can count as an object of study? What is a biological object? Why do these objects change so radically historically? Such debates are complicated; here I would only like to establish the fruitfulness of paying close attention to stories in biology and anthropology, to the common structures of myths and scientific stories and political theories, in such a way as to take all these forms seriously. Stories are a core aspect of the constitution of an object of scientific knowledge. I do not wish to reduce natural scientific practice to political practice, or the reverse, but to watch the weaving of multi-layered meanings in the social working out of what may count as explanation in an area of biology-anthropology where sex and gender seem to matter a great deal.

The student of the history of primatology is immediately confronted with a rich tapestry of images and stories. For a person formed by a Judaeo-Christian mythological inheritance, the extraordinary persistence of the Genesis story in scientific reconstructions of human evolution demands attention, and not just in the flourish of popular presentations. Equally prominent are secular origin stories.[2] The history of the relations of science and religion is represented on the primate stage, for example, in the contest in the early twentieth century for medical rather than moral definitions of sexual behaviour, using animal models (Yerkes, 1943). One of the first book-length treatments of the organization of wild primate societies can only be understood in the line of Thomas Hobbes and the social Leviathan (Zuckerman, 1932). Stories of the origin of the family, of language, of technology, of co-operation and sharing, and of social domination all demand sensitivity to echoes of significance embedded in available metaphor and in the rules for telling meaningful stories in particular historical conditions. It is impossible not to suspect that multi-levelled stories are at the core of things when, without ever necessarily speaking about human primates, contemporary primatologists must speak seriously about harems, dual-career mothering, social signalling as a cybernetic communication control system, troop takeovers and infanticide, rapid social change, time–energy budgets, reproductive strategies and genetic investments, conflicts of interest and cost-benefit analyses, nature and frequency of orgasm in non-human animal females, female sexual choice, male overlords and leadership, social roles, and division of labour.[3]

But why explore the weaving of multiple meanings in the practice of primatology by looking at the obscure Asian leaf-eating monkeys, the langurs?[4] Langurs are a major group of monkeys, familiar to primatologists, but virtually unknown until very recently to a wider public which would not fail to recognize a gorilla, a rare mammal indeed. Surely the apes, especially chimpanzees, and cercopithecines, especially baboons and rhesus monkeys, have most often and most importantly been at the centre of debates about human evolution, legitimate and illegitimate ways of arguing an animal model for any human dimension, the nature and significance of primate social organization, and the impact of gender on the social construction of facts and theories (Fedigan, 1982)? Perhaps this was true, until the question of infanticide emerged at the centre of the debate about langur social life and evolution (Ford, 1976). Why and when do langur males kill langur babies? What should these acts be called? What should the rules be for reliable observation of such acts? Do they really occur? What shall have the social status of fact and of scientific explanation? These are the questions internal to a little corner of primatology which provoked the focus of this chapter. Why and how did these questions come to be crucial to technical discourse by the late 1970s? A response to that question will lead us back to an exploration of scientific practice as the social production of important public stories.

First, however, let us remember that evolutionary biology in the nineteenth and twentieth centuries is part of the public debate about the human place in nature – that is, about the nature of politics and society. Primate social behaviour is studied inescapably as part of the complex struggle in liberal Western democracies to name who is a mature, healthy citizen and why. Argument about human politics from a state of nature is a hoary tradition in Western political discourse; its modern form is the interweaving of stories in natural and political economy, in biology, and in social sciences. Further, I want to argue that primate stories, popular and scientific, echo and rest on the material social processes of production and reproduction of human life. In particular, primate bioanthropology from the 1920s has figured prominently in contests in ideology and practice for who will control the human means of reproduction, as well as in contests over the causes and controls of human war, and struggles over technical ingenuity and co-operative capacities in family and factory. These generalizations, I believe, are true whether or not particular primate scientists intend their work to be part of such struggles; their stories are part of the public resource in the contests. And primatologists tell stories remarkably appropriate to their times, places, genders, races, classes – as well as to their animals.

A series of quick illustrations must suffice for the longer argument, if we are to get on to the missing, maybe murdered, langur babies and to the Euro-American women who watch monkeys professionally. During the 1920s, in the hands of psychobiologists, comparative psychologists, and reproductive and neural physiologists, primates in laboratories figured prominently in debates about human mental function and sexual organization. Marriage counselling, immigration policy, and the testing industry all are directly indebted to primates and primatologists, who in Robert Yerkes' words were 'servants of science'. Primates seemed models of natural co-operation unobscured by language and culture. During the 1930s, in early field work on wild primates, the sexual physiology of natural co-operation (in the forms of dominance of males over females and of troop demographic structure) emerged in arguments about human social therapeutics for social disorder – like labour strikes and divorce. Primate models of nuclear families and of fathering in the suburbs, as well as of the doleful results of absent mothers, appeared in public debates about US social problems throughout the 1950s and 1960s. Primate models for human depression have been avidly sought, and a great deal of technical ingenuity has gone into reliably producing psychoses in monkeys. Population policy and questions about population regulation drew on primate studies, as did psychiatry (even proposed telemetric control) of stressed, perhaps black male human primates in riotous cities in the 1960s. The pressing question of 'man's' naturally co-operative or warlike nature was argued in symposia and classrooms throughout the Vietnam war, with constant debts to developing new theories of human evolution based on recent fossils from South and East Africa, new field studies of living primates, and the anthropology of modern gatherer-hunters. Primatologists could be found on most sides of most debates, including the 'side' of not wanting to be part of any explicit political attitude. From the point of view of practising primatologists, perhaps the most pressing direct political questions involve the rapid destruction of non-human primates all over their range. But that worry quickly embroils the most apolitical scientist in international politics profoundly determined by the history of imperialism.

It should surprise no one that langur bioanthropology began to interest a wide US public in the 1970s and 1980s, when questions about domestic violence (specifically beaten women and children); reproductive freedom (or often coercion); abortion; parenting (a euphemism for mothering and an ambivalent look at fathering); and 'autonomous' women who are not primarily defined in terms of a social (that is, family) group are prominent. Is mothering itself 'selfish'? One cannot but be struck by the plethora of feminist and anti-feminist, biological and homiletic, subtle and blatant publishing on human and non-human mothering and on female reproductive strategies. It is not easy to disentangle the technical and popular threads in the langur story in this context, and that disentanglement is in any case a certain ideological move in the interests of saving the purity of science. Perhaps for the moment it is more intriguing, even more responsible, to leave the weaving tangled and try to sort out the principal arguments about infanticide among the sacred Hanuman monkeys of India.

PATRILINEAL PRIMATOLOGY: A WAY OF LIFE
It is appropriate in biology to begin with descent, with modification, and in anthropology with the social object of kinship; so let us approach the subjects of this chapter through the fiction of a patriline – that of a very visible father in the primate order, Sherwood Washburn. All the women whose work will be examined (Phyllis Jay [later, Dolhinow], Suzanne Ripley, Sarah Blaffer Hrdy, and Jane Bogess) are academic 'daughters' or granddaughters in an important network of primatologists in the United States after the Second World War. It is directly through the Washburn lineage that the langur students of this story inherited core elements of their fictive strategies, their allowable stories, and their tools with which to craft the outlines of a different story. Primatology has been a collective historical production, not the offspring of an omnipotent father. But the analyses, entrepreneurial activities, and institutional power of Washburn have grafted primate science as a branch of physical anthropology on to roots of modern neo-Darwinian evolutionary theory and structural-functional social anthropology. The rules of these root sciences must be sketched to follow the debates about langur babies.

All the women discussed in this paper have experienced multiple influences on their work; the fiction of a patriline should connote neither unique influence nor necessary harmony. In fact, families should be expected to be scenes of intense conflict. But the patriline, and language of daughters and sons, does connote both public identification of people as present or former students of a prominent figure and common discussion of academic 'begats' among biologists and anthropologists. The language itself is charged with questions of independence and indebtedness, of individual achievement and ascribed identities. Part of women's struggle against patriarchy has been to insist on being named independently of fathers. My use of family language is intended to suggest problems and tensions, as well as to note an ambivalent starting point in present scientific social relations historically ordered by male-dominant hierarchies. I think there is little question that Washburn's professional power has had profound effects for his female and male students. Like any family name, the academic patronymic is a social fiction. The language of a patriline does not tell the natural history of an academic family; it names a lineage of struggles, mutual concerns, and inheritance of tools and public social identities.

The chief intellectual legacy of the patriline of Washburn's physical anthropology was the imperative to reconstruct not fixed structures, but ways of life – to turn fossils into the underpinnings of living animals and to interpret living primates in carefully rule-bound ways as models for aspects of human ways of life. Adaptation, function, and action were the real scientific objects, not frozen structures or hierarchical, natural scales of perfection or complexity. By developing functional comparative anatomy as part of the synthetic theory of evolution and extending the approach to the social behaviour of living primates, Washburn and his students integrated genetic selection theory and disciplined field and experimental methodology into the practice of evolutionary reconstruction.

The best-known product of practice in the Washburn patriline was the 'man-the-hunter' hypothesis of the 1960s. This hypothesis suggested that the crucial evolutionary adaptations making possible a human way of life in the hominid line in its likely ecological setting were those associated with a new food-getting strategy, a subsistence innovation carrying the implications of a human future based on social co-operation, learned technical skill, nuclear families, and eventually fully symbolic language. It is important to stress from the beginning that the fundamental elements of the man-the-hunter hypothesis guiding much of primate field study for well over a decade were co-operation and the social group as the principal adaptations. Phenomena such as aggression, competition, and dominance structures were seen primarily as mechanisms of social co-operation, as axes of ordered group life, as prerequisites of organization. And of course, the man-the-hunter hypothesis was pre-eminently about male ways of life as the motors of the human past and future. Hunting was a male innovation and speciality, the story insisted. And what was not hunting had always been. Hunting was the principle of change; the rest was a base line or a support system.[5]

So Washburn's daughters entered the field as part of a complex social family of life scientists practising at the disputed boundaries of biology and anthropology, arguing about the meanings of long-disputed objects of knowledge called primates, and constructing origin and action stories about disputed visions of past constraint and future possibility. Field and laboratory studies of living primates developed exponentially from modest pre-war levels nearly simultaneously and internationally after the Second World War for complex reasons, such as polio research, new fossil hominid finds in Africa, Japanese development of longitudinal studies of primate societies as part of comparative anthropology, and searches for animal model systems for human emotional disorders and social disorganization within a cybernetic control model of social management. But these reasons take us beyond the concerns of this essay. Washburn was one of perhaps a dozen key actors in developments rooted in large historical determinations like war, new technologies for international travel and tropical disease control, modern medical research institutionalization, and international conservation organization in decolonialized but contested neo-imperialist world orders.[6]

Washburn earned his doctorate in physical anthropology at Harvard in 1940. His training reflected the medical heritage and colonial racist social basis of physical anthropology and primatology. Schooled in traditional anthropomorphic methods and primate anatomy, he taught medical anatomy at Columbia College of Physicians and Surgeons until 1947, when he moved to the University of Chicago, where he worked with his first important graduate students in social behaviour (as opposed to strict functional comparative anatomy), including Phyllis Jay. Washburn belonged to the generation of physical anthropologists who disavowed the practice of their science to construct racial hierarchies, a practice of comparative life science based on premises of increasing complexity and perfection in evolution with implicit and explicit teleological standards of white, male, professional, bourgeois social organization. Washburn actively contested to move physical anthropology away from part of this heritage, primarily by crafting rules for telling evolutionary stories that did not easily yield racist meanings.[7] He did not see or challenge similar scientific frameworks for knowing and for producing hierarchically ordered gender – not because of personal ill-will, but because world struggles challenging racism were ending colonialism and making visible many of its rules for generating public knowledge, including the life sciences. The women's movement of the 1970s made different scientific constructions of gender possible, not the insight of genius in the heads of either men or women. But specific women and men did produce transformed debates about sex and gender in scientific contests grounded in changed social possibility. These primate scientists had no more of a direct relationship to various feminisms and other dimensions of revolutionized social relations of women and men than Washburn did to African, Asian, and United States liberation struggles. But neither did Washburn and his academic children have direct relations to the social lives of baboons and langurs. The mediations of public stories are multiple. However, we are moving ahead of our story and asserting what must be told.

By the mid-1940s Washburn was practising physical anthropology as an experimental science; by 1950 he was developing a powerful programme for reinterpreting the basic concepts and methods of his field in harmony with the recent population genetics, systematics, and palaeontology of Theodosius Dobzhansky, Ernst Mayr, and George Gaylord Simpson. By 1958 he had a Ford Foundation grant to study the evolution of human behaviour from multiple points of view, including initial provision for field studies of baboons in East Africa. This work was done in collaboration with his student, Irven DeVore; it grounds the first development of the baboon comparative model for interpreting hominid evolution from the viewpoint of man-the-hunter. In a subsequent National Science Foundation grant proposal ('Analysis of Primate Behavior', 1961), DeVore and Washburn were principal investigators, although the grant supported others' work as well. Acknowledging differences from baboon data and interpretations, the final report to the foundation paid considerable attention to Jay's langur investigations. Those early grant proposals cited the relevance of the baboon social behaviour studies to human psychology and psychiatry. Psychiatrist David Hamburg from NIH and comparative psychologist Harry Harlow from the University of Wisconsin were among the consultants named in the proposals. In 1959, at Berkeley, Washburn developed funding for one of the first primate field stations in the United States. From the beginning of his career, he lectured, wrote popular texts, made pedagogical films, reformed curricula on all educational levels, and helped determine the careers of prominent figures in evolution and primatology.[8]

I am including in the Washburn patriline primate behaviour and evolution students at the Universities of Chicago and California who earned their PhDs after about 1958. Included also are many students of students and people who earned degrees elsewhere. For example, Jane Bogess (1976) was the doctoral student of Phyllis Jay/Dolhinow (1963), who earned her doctorate with Washburn; and Sarah Blaffer Hrdy (1975) was the PhD student of Irven DeVore (1962) of Harvard, who earned his degree with Washburn. One should not expect harmony in a family; and, indeed, we will see the emergence of major debates among the Washburn siblings, as well as major deviations from the father's stories. DeVore and Washburn have been in conflict from the late 1970s over sociobiology; Jay/Dolhinow and Bogess share positions in opposition to Ripley and Hrdy. All of these oppositions centre on reproductive strategies and their meanings. We will also see a field of common discourse and transformations of inherited stories which have the result of centring debates about sex and gender in ways not possible before the 1970s.

A preliminary survey of the direct (Universities of Chicago and California, Berkeley) Washburn lineage shows at least 40 doctoral students, of whom about 15 are active professional women. These figures should be placed in the context of very rough preliminary statistics for primatology as a whole. There are three major professional associations to which primate behaviour and evolution scientists belong: (1) The International Primatological Society (founded 1966) has a membership of about 750, of whom 380 are from the United States, and 120 (16 per cent) of whom are women. Judged by professional address, about 130 IPS members consider themselves anthropologists; only 17 per cent of these are women. (2) The American Society of Primatologists (founded 1977) has a membership of about 445, of whom 23 are foreign, mostly Canadian. About 30 per cent, or 131, are women, and about 16 per cent (70) of the membership have an address in an anthropological institutional division. (No specialty, not even medicine [16 per cent] or psychology [13 per cent], has a larger representation.) There are about 30 women anthropologists (45 per cent of members who are anthropologists) listed in the ASP, 7 of whom are originally PhDs from the University of California at Berkeley. The Washburn lineage is remembered by several of its members from its beginning to have included atypically large numbers, for the profession, of women graduate students. It is certainly true that prominent women in primate debates are in the Washburn lineage, but these statistics indicate that by 1980 women generally practised primatology in the United States within the specialty of anthropology in large numbers compared to the total international figures and compared to other primate-related specialties in the United States. (3) The American Association of Physical Anthropology has a membership of about 1,200, about 26 per cent of whom are women. None of these figures gives an accurate sense of how many people study primate behaviour and evolution, as opposed to many other aspects of primatology, and deciding the specialty of a practitioner is often fairly arbitrary: where does anthropology end and comparative psychology begin? Moreover, addresses are sometimes ambiguous. But even these rough figures indicate the collective and international nature of primate studies, the significant participation of women in the field, especially in the United States, and the visible presence of members of the Washburn lineage.[9]

What are the social mechanisms for passing on rules for telling stories? How did the Washburn lineage work in giving the daughters of man-the-hunter tools for modifying their inheritance in the scientific construction of sex and gender as both objects and conditions of study? We have already glanced at the logical skeleton of evolutionary stories told by Washburn. The principal rule was to weave stories about function and action, about ways of life. It remains to glance equally quickly at what might be called his 'plan' for establishing authoritative stories about primates. The main element in the 'plan' was making space for his students to speak, initially covered by his substantial social authority, but ultimately with their own professional bases. Another principal component in Washburn's training was insistence on what was in 1960 an unusual structure of course and field-lab work for physical anthropology. Washburn students, whatever their final concentration, ideally studied functional comparative anatomy, social-cultural theory in social anthropology, and field investigations of living primates. Some students did not actually study all three elements, but the ideal was stressed in Washburn grant proposals and other descriptions of his projects for the reform of physical anthropology. Fossils, modern hunter-gatherers, and living primates were all necessary to Washburn's programme that produced the synthetic man-the-hunter hypothesis guiding research and informing explanatory stories. His students were equipped for leadership roles in an emerging discipline. This was a father who knew how to ground an inheritance materially.

Washburn's primatology patriline may be said to have been born with the 1957–58 University of Chicago seminar 'Origins of Human Behaviour'. Members of this group, including Phyllis Jay and Irven DeVore, became formative figures in evolving primate field studies; and the knowledge of the Japanese language of another participant, the Jesuit, John Frisch, permitted a fuller initial conception of the contemporary work of Japanese colleagues.

Washburn students were not members of a particularly authoritarian laboratory; they chose their own topics. They also opposed Washburn in several ways and worked independently of his ideas and support. But several report the sense in retrospect that the intellectual excitement of a new synthesis in physical anthropology and Washburn's nurturance of students' choices and opportunities (as well as indifference to other choices) suggest the existence of a more explicit plan. For example, since functional anatomy appropriate to a hunting way of life was an essential part of the story, it should not be surprising to find students in the 1960s working out new anatomical adaptational complexes made visible by the man-the-hunter hypothesis. Different students could be found studying the hand, vertebral column, foot, communication, range and diet, maternal behaviour, and so on.

Two special sessions in the 1960s at the American Anthropological Association (AAA) meetings were typical of the social mechanisms which Washburn made available to his students and associates and which grounded the man-the-hunter hypothesis firmly in the discipline. In 1963, an all-day symposium featured fifteen Washburn students, six of them women. Adrienne Zihlman spoke on range and behaviour; she would do her doctorate on bipedalism within the framework of the hunting hypothesis. Later she would be a central figure in challenging this explanatory framework and in proposing a major synthetic alternative. Her colleague for part of this task, Nancy Tanner (died 1989), was a social anthropologist who worked as a teaching assistant for Washburn while she was a graduate student. Judith Shirek spoke on diet and behaviour; her PhD concerned visual communication in a macaque species. Phyllis Jay spoke on dominance in 1963; her doctorate treated langur monkey social organization. Suzanne Chevalier gave a paper on mother–infant behaviour; her later research brought questions and methods from Masters and Johnson into consideration of non-human primate female orgasm, within the context of the widespread challenge to notions of the primary importance of male sexual activity. Suzanne Ripley communicated results from her study of maternal behaviour in langurs, the species at the heart of her dissertation and later work. Jane Lancaster spoke about primate annual reproductive cycles, an early presentation of what became a major new point of view for studying primate reproduction outside the laboratory. Her dissertation was on primate communication; her later work would be an important part of the daughters' revolt against the man-the-hunter synthesis. Washburn's male graduate students similarly spoke on aspects of the hunting hypothesis in its three-part plot of anatomy, primate behaviour, and social anthropology. The 1966 AAA session was called 'Design for Man'; all the components of the male-centred hunting story were then in place, including approaches to psychological and emotional adaptational complexes, within the context of the ideology of stress proposed within modern psychiatry.

Washburn summarized the talks of the session in a brief, pointed talk on 'The Hunting Way of Life'.[10] The lessons for the discipline of physical anthropology would have been hard to miss. And whatever meanings individual students attached to their own work at the time of their graduate training, it seems very likely that in the 1960s the public meanings of presentations from the University of California, Berkeley, framed by Washburn's interpretations – and sometimes more active direction – included: (1) the primacy of the baboon model for a comparative functional understanding of hominid evolution; (2) the crucial role of the social group (and a much lesser role of sexual bonds) as the key behavioural adaptation of primates; and (3) the central drama of a male subsistence innovation – hunting – in the human origin story, which included bipedalism, tools, language, and social co-operation. Again, male dominance hierarchies were a key mechanism of this promising co-operation.

THE LANGUR CONNECTION

It should be clear that the daughters of the Washburn patriline were raised to speak in public, to have authority, to author stories. They also often got teaching jobs which permitted time for research and publication. A lengthy story deserves to be told about these primate students, their brothers, and their tribe (troop?). But here let us turn to only one set of stories authored by man-the-hunter's daughters in the field, the langur saga.[11] In looking more closely at part of just one complex tale, perhaps we can clarify how stories with public meanings change within the life sciences.

One conclusion of this idiosyncratic exegesis should be announced in advance: the langur story with all its multiple public meanings is not a mechanical reflection of ideology and social forces outside physical anthropology-primatology; nor is it the product of diligent objective science ever improving its own methods of finally seeing nothing but Ur-monkeys. The natural sciences are neither so tame nor so mystifying. Both these points of view caricature the production of science as myth, that is, as meaning-laden public knowledge. But both poles of the caricature contain a suggestion of what I find to be true and what makes the process of crafting science interesting to a person who wonders how new kinds of stories can be given birth. Natural scientific stories are supposed to be fruitful; they regularly lead people who practise science to see things they did not know about before, to find the unexpected. Scientific stories have an intriguing rule of construction: in spite of the best precautions, they force an observer to see what one cannot expect and probably does not want to see. The tools to craft this vision are quite material, even mundane. For example, primatologists over decades have developed and progressively enforced on each other quite explicit criteria for collecting data worthy of respect: number of hours in the field, physical position of observer, ability to recognize animals, inter-observer similarity in naming and counting 'units' of behaviour, form of data sheets and storage of data, sampling procedures to counter observer preferences to watch what is *already* interesting, and so on. Washburn's patriline provided the children with tools to force provocative vision in a historical environment which structured the possibility of different stories. The chief problem with arguing this position from the point of view of social forces determining scientific stories from the 'outside' versus painstaking scientific practice clearing out bias from the 'inside' is that inside and outside are the wrong metaphors. Social forces and daily scientific practice both exist inside. Both are part of the process of producing public knowledge, and neither is a source of purity or pollution. Indeed, daily scientific practice is a very important social force. But such practice can only make visible what people can historically learn to see. All stories are multiply mediated (Latour and Woolgar, 1979).

A cautionary word is necessary: no attempt is made in this chapter to describe, much less explain, the whole career, publication record, or historical influences for Dolhinow, Ripley, Hrdy, or Bogess. Particular moments in the history of modern primatology and particular papers come into focus here in order to highlight public debates about female human nature and about parenting and violence. These debates raise political-historical questions about scientific origin stories and lead to contests for naming meanings and possibilities, in the context of current US struggles to define and judge human female and male co-operation and competition, domestic violence, abortion and political reproductive freedoms and con-straints, social pathology and stress, and sociobiological arguments about inherited tendencies in human social behaviour, including sex roles. These concerns are traditional in the history of evolutionary biology and physical anthropology. Primates are privileged objects in specific historical contests to name the unmarked human place in nature, as well as to describe the equally unmarked nature of human society.

SOCIAL GROUPS IN SICKNESS AND IN HEALTH: A QUESTION OF MODELS

Phyllis Jay, today Phyllis Dolhinow, a full professor in the University of California, Berkeley's Department of Anthropology and dissertation adviser to another of the daughters of this story, Jane Bogess, was one of Washburn's first graduate students to study social behaviour and a member of the Chicago seminar on the origins of human behaviour. She conducted observations on langur monkeys (*Presbytis entellus*) in central and north India for 850 hours over 18 months in 1958–60, work that formed the core of her dissertation, 'The social behavior of the langur monkey' (1963a), and several other publications (Jay, 1962, 1963b, 1965; Dolhinow, 1972). Jay was the first post-Second World War systematic observer of these monkeys in the field; her study was followed quickly by those of a team of observers from the Japan Monkey Center with Indian colleagues, working in south India from 1961 to 1963, and of her fellow Washburn graduate student, Suzanne Ripley, who completed a one-year study in 1963 of grey langurs in Ceylon. Jay's story was complex; but I should like to isolate a few elements for closer analysis: the question of how to establish a model for an aspect of ways of life of early hominids, the structure of argument about the organized social group as an evolutionary adaptation, the criteria for establishing social behaviour as pathological or healthy, the shifting of positions of phenomena within an observer's field of vision and the strategy for explanation of these shifts, and the transformation of meanings of stories when such shifts occur. The focus here will be on Phyllis Jay's early publications, based on field study done as a graduate student in the first years of re-awakened, post-Second World War interest in naturalistic primate behaviour. In many ways primatology was structurally different in the early 1960s from what it was around 1980, when Hrdy and Bogess did their first field work and publishing. The size of related literatures, standardization of field procedure, dynamics of career social networks and professional possibilities, and relations to other debates in biology (for example, within ecology and population biology) and anthropology (for example, about sociobiology applied to human groups) have all changed. A thesis of this chapter is that some of these changes have been a function of, and have in turn contributed to, major political struggles over the social relations of human reproduction and over the political place of all primate females in nature.

At the same time that Jay was in the field watching langurs, her fellow graduate student was watching baboons in Africa. Washburn and Irven DeVore conducted a 12-month, 1,200-hour study of baboons in Kenya in 1959, following up a 200-hour preliminary study conducted by Washburn in 1955, as an almost accidental opportunity at a pan-African conference on human evolution. The baboon field work explored the power of a scientific model for certain aspects of reconstructed hominid behavioural adaptational complexes, postulated to be associated with savannah living and the hunting innovation. Modelling in the Washburn school did not mean searching for a simpler version of a supposedly more complex human behaviour, much less searching for a species considered as a whole to be a simpler version of hominids. Scales of complexity were not objects of knowledge here. Other primate species could be models for quite specific aspects of adaptational complexes, such as range or diet or correlation of intensity of dominance hierarchies with predation pressure. Such models, like any other biological model systems, should be subject to observation and experimental manipulation in field and laboratory. Logically, primate model systems had the same status as *in vitro* or even totally synthetic cell membrane subsystems in studying cell movement. Baboons seemed like promising models in the study of human evolution because they were ground-living primates dependent on a structured social group for survival. Behaviour, ecology, functional anatomy – all had to be correlated in any explanatory story. Models could be illuminating as contrasts as well as comparisons; model building was part of construction of a *comparative* evolutionary science. Indeed, Washburn and DeVore (1961) concluded that the differences between baboons and hominids were *most* significant. But there was an explicit centre to all the comparisons: *Homo sapiens*. In its beginning, the Washburn school did not pose the questions of zoologists, but of students of the human way of life. And baboons emerged early as privileged model systems determining meanings for other species studied by Washburn students, for example, vervet monkeys and langurs. Baboons seemed the correct model system for discussions of male–male co-operation, male dominance hierarchies as a form of adaptive social organization, and male indispensability in troop defence for a savannah-living potential hominid.

Did this baboon centre structure the meanings of Jay's story about langurs? Jay's early papers are replete with references to DeVore's story about baboons, a story with a strong plot turning on the life of males, especially in their supposed role as troop protectors, internal peace-keepers, and organizers through the mechanism of their dominance hierarchy. DeVore literally saw a male-centred baboon troop structure, containing a core of allied dominant males immensely attractive to females and children, with other males on the periphery when the troop was stationary or following behind as special guards when the troop seemed threatened by danger. This tableau proved hard for anyone else to see physically, but symbolically it has been repeated in multiple variations, including textbook illustrations.[12] If male dominance were the mechanism of troop organization, then variations in male dominance should be the object of attention to generate comparative stories. An implicit corollary was that degrees of social organization were correlated to fullness of development of that key adaptational mechanism for life in a social group, stable male hierarchies, the germ of co-operation. The logical link to medical-psychiatric therapeutics of social groups should be clear: social disorder implies a breakdown of central adaptational mechanisms. Stressed males would engage in inappropriate (excessive or deficient) dominance behaviours – at the expense of troop organization and even survival.

Both DeVore and Jay saw the organized social group as the basic adaptive unit of the species. This was not necessarily a group selectionist claim, and this issue was hardly raised until sociobiological challenges to (or extensions of?) neo-Darwinian selection theory emerged in the 1970s. Social roles were basic objects of study because they structured groups. Social bonds maintained troop unity, and male dominance relations were hardly the only kind of social bond for either observer. But in DeVore's explanations, they were the bonds that ultimately made a group possible; and groups made primates possible, as well as the human way of life, the pre-eminent object of knowledge in the Washburn patriline. Note that the important level of explanation is mechanisms and adaptational complexes. Jay's early papers showed a series of fascinating oppositions to this story structure, because her langurs failed to act like good baboons, but still had very stable groups.

The bulk of Jay's papers on overall langur life was about infants and mothers. Her approach to social organization was longitudinal and develop-mental, in contrast to DeVore's topical plot with dominant adult male central actors on a savannah stage set for hominid possibilities. I read Jay's early work as substantively more biologically and ecologically complex and multi-centred than DeVore's. Jay published separate papers on infants and mothers as well. In spite of their frequent publications on the theme, some female former graduate students recall trying to avoid too much identification with the topic of females and infants – too much attention to females pollutes the observer, labels the *observer* as peripheral. In any case, Jay was repeatedly requested to write papers on that subject for early collected volumes on primates. Again, whatever her sense of the overall biology of langurs, she was publicly associated with a story *not* named as the comparative centre for hominid innovation. Baboons were the privileged model system; and that meant, in the hands of DeVore, male activity. Although DeVore knew infants were centres of attraction, and all observers recorded infant socialization in describing the genesis of group structure, the *explanation* of a group could not rest on the activity of mothers and infants. Jay explicitly saw the infant as a key centre of attraction in langur troop structure; but that subplot was not a major component of her story *conclusions*. She described the passage of infants among females, relative male lack of interest in infants, sex differences in infant development, the lack of well-defined dominance hierarchies among adult females, temporary alliances of adult females in conflict with other females (no female–female organizations were seen as stable or primary by Westerners until well after 1960, and matrilines continued to be about ranks of *sons* for even longer), low incidences of aggression in the troops, and generally looser troop organization than DeVore's baboons had. She argued that the mother–infant relationship was the most intense of a langur's life, maintaining as well that all dominance structures were exceedingly complex and subtle and not very important in daily existence. In short, she literally, physically saw what almost could not figure in her major conclusions because another story ordered what counted as ultimate explanation. Washburn's physical anthropology of man-the-hunter required comparative primate social behaviour studies, but the not-so-silent centre of comparison lived on the African savannah and yawned a dominant threat at other story structures and conclusions. All comparisons are not equal when the scientific goal is to know 'man's' place in nature.

When possible, Jay conducted her observations physically from *within* the troop; she acted like a troop subordinate, averting her eyes from direct glances to avoid any provocation. Although most langur troops Jay watched could not be observed from within because, for example, they were high in trees overhead, Jay's only explicit methodological comment in her early papers about her own physical relation as an observer named herself explicitly *within* the troop, and *neither* dominant nor intervening to provoke the animals' dominance among themselves. In contrast, DeVore watched from the periphery, protected by a landrover, partly because of the presence of lions in the region; daily life therefore looked different. DeVore also experimentally provoked the male–male dominance interactions that had to be seen to signify central meanings, called observations. Jay, on the other hand, spent much less space describing male activities than those of females and infants and had a hard time specifying exactly what males did that mattered in daily troop life. However, she explicitly concluded, 'Adult males maintain internal troop stability by establishing and asserting a stable male dominance hierarchy that structures the relationships of adult males within the troop' (Dolhinow, 1972, p. 230). Males were leaders who co-ordinated troop unity and stability, despite the observation structure of her papers. It was the generation of Washburn daughters after Jay who turned the constant observations of matrifocal groups into an *explanation* of troop structure and into privileged models for hominid evolution.[13]

Although females and infants were very visible to Jay, she did not see something which other observers elsewhere began to report in dramatic terms: males killing infants after they moved into a troop, ousting the previous resident male or males. For example, Yukimaru Sugiyama from the Laboratory of Physical Anthropology at Kyoto University, and part of the team from the Japan Monkey Center that studied langurs at Dharwar from 1961 to 1963, told a story of animals for whom, 'Apart from the fact that one large adult male leads the troop, there is no other evident social differenti-ation.' He observed what he called 'social change' in troops, including 'reconstruction' through successful attack of a bisexual troop by an all-male group. Subsequently, all but one of the usurping males were ousted. In the next two months the remaining male apparently bit a juvenile female and all five troop infants, none of whom survived. But it seems Sugiyama did *not* see the male killing the infants. The same observer also experimentally provoked troop social change by removing the sole male (called 'the dominant male overlord who had protected and led the troop') in another bisexual group. Ultimately a male entering this troop killed four infants; these events appear to have been witnessed directly. In these studies the important experimental manipulations of troops, that is, of model systems for studying social organization, were *always* of high-status males, presumed points of organic vitality and 'social change'.[14]

It was not that Jay could not record such a drastic event; none occurred during her study or in her region of India. But she did comment on others' observations of infant deaths in noting the extraordinary variability of habitat and behaviour characteristic of langurs and the need for more study correlating ecology and social behaviour. It is here that the criteria for deciding the significance of male troop takeover and infanticide began to be enunciated. For Jay, such 'rapid social change' occurred in the context of a high population density of langurs, which produced stress that in turn yielded social pathology. The infanticide did not *explain* anything. In any case, these events occupied the periphery of a stage set to represent the success of social groups as primate adaptations. That stage was necessary to man-the-hunter as harbinger of human, male-based co-operation expressed through healthy dominance relations. Jay noted the observations of infanticide, but her story did not alter because of them.

Let us now turn to a major effort to wreck that stage in the confrontation of sociobiological explanation with the rules for meaning that had given birth to the Washburn line. Then we will return to the question of key event in explanatory stories versus accidental occurrence or social pathology. For Sarah Blaffer Hrdy the social group emphasis seemed to obscure, ironically, female equality – equality in reproductive strategies, that is. But reproductive strategies lie close to the heart of contests for political meanings in the 1970s and 1980s, including full human female citizenship in the United States based on reproductive autonomy, 'ownership of one's own body'. Reproductive strategies concern the body's investments. Remember that at least since Thomas Hobbes and seventeenth-century debates in England about sovereignty, citizenship, and suffrage, property in the self – the right and ability to dispose of one's investment, one's incorporation – was argued to ground legitimate political action, particularly the formation of civil society in contrast to a supposedly natural reproductive family. The sociobiological logic of feminism we are about to glance at draws from the theoretical wellsprings of Western political democracy. Pollution of the waters does not date from E. O. Wilson's sociobiological publications on human nature. Biology's logic of reproductive competition is merely one common, early form of argument in our inherited capitalist political economy and political theory. Biology has intrinsically been a branch of political discourse, not a compendium of objective truth. Further, simply noting such a connection between biological and political/economic discourse is *not* a good argument for dismissing such biological argument as bad science or mere ideology. It should not be surprising that the contest over langur infanticide touches raw political and scientific nerves.

A LANGUR ODYSSEY: HEROES, SEX, AND INVESTMENT MANAGEMENT

In Sarah Blaffer Hrdy's version of langur life, infanticide and male troop takeovers became the key to the meaning of langur social behaviour. And Hrdy's (1977) work was heralded with meanings Jay/Dolhinow never claimed: the dust jacket to her Harvard University Pressbook announces *'The Langurs of Abu* (subtitle: *Female and Male Strategies of Reproduction*) is the first book to analyze behavior of wild primates from the standpoint of both sexes. It is also a poignant and sophisticated exploration of primate behavior patterns from a feminist point of view.' Hrdy, the former graduate student of Irven DeVore at Harvard, also worked closely with Robert Trivers and E.O. Wilson. These three men are fundamental sociobiological theorists. DeVore, in root opposition to Washburn, has reinterpreted the social anthropology of human hunter-gatherers in terms of the behavioural systems emerging from a genetic kinship calculus of interest. For Hrdy, the primate social group became one possible result of the strategies of individual reproducers to maximize their genetic fitness, to capitalize on their genetic investments. The social origin story of pure liberal, utilitarian political economy ruled; individual competition produced all the forms of combination of the efficient animal machine. Social life was a market where investments were made and tested in the only currency that counts: genetic increase.

Infanticide in certain circumstances became a rational reproductive strategy of langur males, opposed to a rational extent by langur females, whose reproductive interests were certainly not the same as the males'. Indeed, root sexual conflict from a sociobiological viewpoint is a necessary consequence of sexual reproduction. Any genetic difference introduces some degree of conflict, even if expressed in coalition. The pattern here is the reverse of seeing dominance hierarchies as mechanisms of co-ordination for the chief adaptational complex, the social group. Sociobiologists might still view dominance hierarchies as patterns co-ordinating a social group, but the basic logic is different. All biological structures are expressions of a genetic calculus of interest, that is, the best possible (not perfect) resolutions of fundamental conflict when all the elements in a system need each other for their own reproductive success. Note that the crucial level of explanation is not mechanism, function, or way of life, but pared-down fitness maximization strategy. Explanation is game theory. The dust jacket of Hrdy's book could call her use of this logic 'feminist' because she paid systematic attention to female activity in their reproductive interest and did not explain individual behaviour in terms of roles for co-ordinating elements for group survival. Where Jay/Dolhinow speaks of adaptation, Hrdy speaks of selection. It is only in a situation of direct controversy that all the differences in meaning of these two apparently harmonious evolutionary terms emerge.

Although Hrdy did not, probably, write her own dust jacket, it still frames her story for readers. She did, however, write her dedication and acknowledgements, both marvellous icons, or stories in miniature, suggesting public meanings that open a book replete with the language of heroic struggle and Odyssean voyages to preserve the products of genetic investment in dangerous times. The book, dedicated to her mother, opened with 'a catalogue of heroes'. Hrdy continued, 'I first learned of langurs accidentally, while satisfying a distribution requirement in one of Harvard's most popular undergraduate courses, primate behavior, starring Irven DeVore.' Her teaching assistant in that course was Trivers. Later, 'In the voyage that followed, Professors DeVore and Trivers, together with a synthesizing omnipotent, Edward O. Wilson, introduced me to a realm of theory that transformed my view of the social world.' The mundane nature of scientific socialization again shows clearly. After acknowledging langurs themselves, animals named after gods and heroes in Hindu and Roman mythology (Hanuman, the Hindu monkey god, and Entellus, a boxing champion in the *Aeneid*), Hrdy concluded, 'Anyone heroic enough to read on to the end of this book will learn why the identification of langurs with warriors was an appropriate taxonomic choice, and why the final salute must be to the prescience of the nineteenth-century British naturalists who first went out to study the Hanuman (1977, pp. v–x). A salute to the naturalist-imperialist ventures of Britain at the height of its bourgeois triumph, ideologized as a fruit of unrestrained capitalism, could not be more appropriate for the logic of the story that followed.

Hrdy's book is a sustained polemic against what she sees as group selection arguments and structural-functional social system theory. Dolhinow and her students are Hrdy's principal antagonists in a 'heroic' struggle for correct vision. The purpose, like the purpose of the stories in the orthodox Washburn lineage, is to illuminate the logic of the human way of life by telling scientific stories, thereby producing public meanings. As Hrdy put it:

> Not surprisingly, when we first began to intensively study our closest non-human relatives, the monkeys and apes, an idealization of our own society was extended to theirs: thus, according to the first primatological reports, monkeys, like humans, maintain complex social systems geared towards ensuring the group's survival. It is this particular misconception about ourselves, and about primates, that lends the history of langur studies its significance. By revealing our misconceptions about other primates, the langur saga may unmask misconceptions about ourselves. (1977, p. 11)

In the language of command, control, war, adultery, property and investment strategies, and dramatic soap opera about power struggles, Hrdy tells a story that is fundamentally a political history of troops dominated by male combat and female and male conflicting reproductive calculations. She argues for the hypothesis that langur males have several possible reproductive strategies given the design constraints of a leaf-eating monkey body and their ecological niche possibilities. For a male outside a troop, one of those strategies is to invade and oust the resident male, kill his putative offspring, and provoke females into an earlier oestrus so that they will mate with the usurper as quickly as possible, before he too is deposed. His children must have the best chance to reach maturity; a few months' difference would matter if the frequency of troop takeovers (rapid social change?) is that calculated from Hrdy's and others' observations. Females clearly have an interest in preserving former genetic investments, but only to a point short of damage to their overall best possible reproductive chances. Females have counterstrategies for male patterns, as well as patterns of reproductive conflict of interest with each other – and with their own offspring. The point is that any explanatory bind in the story is undone by an appeal to profit calculations under conditions of the market (species biology and habitat). The degree to which these calculations are rooted in 'observations', or simply follow from the plot, is highly controversial – a point to which we will return in the discussion of the work of Dolhinow's student, Jane Bogess, which contains scathing critiques of Hrdy's self-styled soap opera. The rules of observation themselves are very much contested by the daughters of the Washburn lineage. But most of all, the stories are contested – which 'idealizations' about primate life, human and non-human, will have the status of scientific knowledge.[15]

REPRODUCTIVE RIGHTS AMONG OPPORTUNISTS: LANGURS AND PEOPLE AS ECOLOGICAL GENERALISTS

But before looking at the responses to the deviant daughter within the direct (legitimate?) Washburn lineage, let us look at the langur story of Jay/Dolhinow's near contemporary among graduate students at Berkeley, Suzanne Ripley. Ripley also enters in the contest for primate nature a candidate for a model for human possibility within inherited constraint. Her model turns on the logic of mechanisms for population regulation and calls on the language of women's contemporary struggles for reproductive rights, as well as the language of ecological stress and population catastrophes. *Stress* is a basic determinant of the story's plot. Stress has been a common theme in the Washburn lineage. It is linked to stories of past adaptation and the threat of present human obsolescence. And as Jay had published 'The Female Primate' in a book entitled *The Potential of Women* and Zihlman had published 'Motherhood in Transition' in a conference organized around human psychiatric and therapeutic concerns for the family, resulting in the book *The First Child and Family Formation*, Ripley published in a socially charged context in a very scientifically respectable setting: an interdisciplinary symposium on crowding, density dependence, and population regulation in 1978. The proceedings were published by Yale University Press.

Ripley's (1980) argument also contested for the logic of models for the human way of life; hers, like those of many Washburn daughters, centred on female activity. The problem she set herself was to look at human infanticide 'from the perspective of another primate species' (p. 350). She asked if widespread *human* infanticide is pathological or adaptive. Unlike Dolhinow, Bogess, and Hrdy, she did not here contest for what counts as an observation; she accepted the 'facts' of troop takeover and infanticide as established. She compared both human beings and langurs as foraging generalists with exceptionally wide ranges of habitat compared to the habitats of their near relatives with similar design constraints set by their respective basic biology (colobines and apes). How do langurs and humans survive as generalists within the parameters of their biology? Flexible social systems and learned behavioural plasticity turning on reproductive practices are the answer. Sex is at the centre of the explanation, hardly a novel aspect of explanation in life science. Sex is the principle of increase (vitality) in biological stories, and biology has been from its birth in the late eighteenth century a discourse about productive systems or, better, modes of production. Sex is also especially prone to stress and pathology. Finally, to connect reproduction and production has been the key theoretical desideratum of both natural and political economy for 200 years.

Ripley's story contends that generalists exploit marginal habitats all the time, avoiding specialization and its confining consequences. A cost of this life strategy is periodic population crashes, when marginality turns into disaster; a need then is for a reproductive-behavioural system that can re-establish populations quickly. That property entails the inevitability of periodic population excesses when conditions are easy. So in turn some feedback population regulation mechanism should be expected in successful species, and infanticide is a perfectly good candidate. Note the general cybernetic model of the animal machine; this aspect of models is typical of post-Second World War stories. Steam engines and telephone exchanges belong to an earlier era of biology.

The best feedback device should operate close to the steps tying reproductive and subsistence subsystems of species life strategies together. So for humans, female-controlled infanticide in gatherer-hunter groups would be an excellent mechanism for maintaining population regulation, that is, a close fit of subsistence opportunities and numbers. Ripley assumes the demotion of hunting and the requirement to consider female activity in hominid subsistence innovations. That she can so quietly assume this major change in stories in physical anthropology in 1980 is the result of work by others, many in the Washburn lineage, in the context of an 'external' women's movement.

In langurs, infanticide is male-controlled; but that is a minor point. Langurs also need some mechanism for ensuring outbreeding in the face of their rather closed troop structure. Male aggression and troop takeover habits in crowded conditions ensure just that good. Humans have evolved culture-kinship systems, so langurs are no model here for Ripley.

Although there is little fundamental disagreement, Ripley contests with Hrdy for the level of final biological explanation. For all the story-tellers in this paper, real explanation is evolutionary, a plot in which the past both constrains and enables the future and contains its germ of change, even progress. But for Ripley, infanticide is a mechanism, one possible, rather interesting enabling strategy for obligate generalists. Male langur reproductive strategies are proximate causes; final causes ('ultimate biological value') are retention of polymorphism of genotypes in *populations* for an ecological generalist within a social structure that otherwise produces inbreeding. Hrdy's final causes are strategies of least units of reproduction: genes or individuals. Ripley is not arguing for group selection, but for the genetic conditions of continued system persistence.

In her conclusions, Ripley focuses on questions of adaptation, pathology, stress, obsolescence, and the limits of models. Facing an analogous evolutionary dilemma, langurs and humans, though phylogenetically remote, are related in modelling a jointly experienced opposition of fundamental conditions for continued existence. Human population dilemmas are not new, from this point of view, but are an aspect of our basic evolutionary history for which people found a learned behavioural solution (female-regulated infanticide) in small-group societies. Modern humans, though, do introduce a troubling novelty. They have uncoupled decisions about reproduction and production. The ability to make decisions about future ecosystem-carrying capacity does not lie with reproducing units, and rapid feedback regulation could hardly be expected. What is a simple achievement in small-scale societies is nearly impossible in modern conditions. The threat of obsolescence in the face of such stresses suggests solutions: small is beautiful, and women should make decisions about productive and reproductive links in the human life system. Of course, biological value is not social value; but still Ripley concludes pregnantly:

> It seems that the possibility of adaptive infanticide is an inevitable accompaniment of the status of an ecologically generalist species and is simply a price our species had to pay in the process of becoming, and remaining, human. It is the interplay of carrying capacity ... and combinations of evolutionary strategies (generalist or specialist ...) that determines the biological value of infanticide in *both* human and non-human primate species problems. (1980, pp. 383–4)

Here, medical appropriation of moral-political stories about human behaviour, which characterized arguments about sex in primatology earlier, yields pride of place to biological cost-benefit analysis. Economics and biology are logically one. Hrdy and Ripley are both well within the boundaries of their technical discourse in crafting these public stories. It is all a question of becoming and remaining human, a stressful problem.

WHO SAW WHAT: THE DESTABILIZATION OF FACTS

Of course, Ripley and Hrdy may simply be wrong; at least that conclusion is argued in still another version of the langur story, that of Jane Bogess of the University of California, Berkeley. Bogess argues that Hrdy and others who advance the language of troop takeover and goal-directed infant-killing by males fundamentally have not fulfilled the necessary conditions for convincing their peers they know what they claim. Bogess works to establish that Hrdy and others extrapolated on the basis of the logic of their stories, and that the best observational foundations lead to different stories, those closely related to Dolhinow's original ones, but with greater explicit emphasis on the workings of natural selection. The core meaning of the Bogess tale is again social health and pathology (Bogess, 1979, 1980).

Bogess insists on naming putative troop 'takeover' as 'rapid social change' (also Jay's terminology), to avoid the teleology of the sociobiological investment argument. She looks at males in troop structure in terms of the concept of 'male social instability' because of frequent changes in male troop membership. She does not remark on this intriguing transformation in language about males and the determinants of troop organization. She says easily, without comment, what twenty years ago no one saw or said. Bogess can even say such things without further comment in a paper totally about *male* behaviour. Female behaviour in 1980 is an implicit centre partly ruling the story's plot. Almost the opposite was true for Jay in 1960. What intervened was more than monkeys – and more than primatology. Bogess argues that changes in male troop membership usually occur in staggered introductions and exclusions, not dramatic takeovers. Moreover, infant-killing was in fact rarely directly observed; and even when it was, ascribed paternity important to the logic of Hrdy's sociobiological story is very doubtful. A second look at the reports suggests to Bogess that attacks may have been against the females of troops in stressed circumstances and, furthermore, may have been in keeping with a particular aspect of langur biology (low tolerance, especially by females, of strangers). Hrdy's takeovers and infanticide become, in the view of Bogess, 'sudden and complete replacement in adult male membership and attendant infant mortality' (1979, p. 88).

Stress was likely to be a human-mediated condition resulting from recent habitat disruption. Behaviour resulting from modern human impacts on habitat could hardly be given centre stage in the evolutionary story of langurs. Infant-killing would then be either the sign of social pathology resulting from the unnatural human element or an 'accident'. Bogess argues that there is precious little observational evidence for goal-directed infant-killing, and the logic of her story demotes the incidents she agrees were seen. Bogess is quite explicit about standards for calling specific social behaviour pathological, rather than calling it the key to genetic investment strategies. If the behaviours in question, infant-killing and uncontrolled male social instability, harm the reproductive success of both sexes, call them pathological, maladaptive.

> In certain populations, where there is social crowding and artificially high densities and where adult males live outside bisexual troops, the species-typical characteristic male social instability can operate against the reproductive success of all troop members, including the new male residents. (Bogess, 1979, p. 104)

Bogess values explanation at the level of mechanisms; like Dolhinow she is committed to structural-functionalism and neo-Darwinian evolutionary theory. She is interested in the social system as a behavioural adaptation, and she focuses on environmental variables and range of flexibility in the social system.

But Bogess does enter the argument about genetic fitness maximization strategies; such an argument is required in contemporary evolutionary discourse. She is within the received logics of this argument in focusing on inter-male dominance competition as the primary male strategy for maximizing male reproductive success, but not for troop organization itself. She carefully documents exactly what she means by male dominance competition. Rates and forms of competition are here contested more than the logic of explanation. But perhaps the most fundamental challenge of Bogess's paper to other langur students is from her standards of field work and dissection of what can count as data. She has inherited and crafted high standards for pursuing her stories.

UNRAVELLING AND WEAVING: CONTESTS FOR MEANING

I cannot tell a story about who is weaving the best langur tales, though I have my favourites. I have neither the scientific authority to name the facts, nor is that my purpose in this chapter. On the other hand, I am certainly not arguing that the women whose work I have squeezed for my meanings have been unscientific in modelling human life or have imported in some illegitimate way the pollutions of women's interests into scientific discourse. Nor have they purified science by importing women's 'natural' insights. I do find some intriguing meanings for feminist reflection in this tale of the transformation of stories, meanings that bear on the nature of feminist responsibility for crafting science as public myth in the present and future.

It is my opinion that forbidding comparative stories about people and animals would impoverish public discourse, assuming any individual or group could enforce such draconian restrictions on stories people tell about themselves and other beings in Western traditions. But no class of these stories can be seen as innocent, free of determination by historically specific social relations and daily practice in producing and reproducing daily life. Surely scientific stories are not innocent in that sense. It is equally true that no class of tales can be free of rules for narrating a proper story within a particular genre, in this case the discourse of life science. Demystifying those rules seems important to me. Nature is constructed, constituted historically, not discovered naked in a fossil bed or a tropical forest. Nature is contested, and women have enthusiastically entered the fray. Some women have the social authority to author scientific stories.

That fact is fairly new. Before the Second World War, indeed before the birth of the daughters of the Washburn patriline, women did not directly contest for primate nature; men did. That point mattered, as even a sceptical glance at the work of the leaders in primatology (for example, Robert Yerkes or Solly Zuckerman) will show. Many primatologists, including women, claim gender does not materially determine the contents of natural science; if it does, the result is called poor science. I think the evidence supports a different interpretation. At the least, gender is an unavoidable condition of observation. So also are class, race, and nation.

It is also new to look at a group of women constituting the major authoritative contestants in a publicly important debate. There are several men who study langurs, but with a little qualification, exclusive focus on Euro-American women does not leave out the generative centres of debate about the species. I do not think these white women are the major figures in langur sagas merely because langurs appeal to their nature somehow. White women exist in primatology in substantial numbers; they occupy nearly every position possible in various controversies, and they have collectively changed the rules for explicit and implicit logics of stories. It is no longer acceptably scientific to argue about animal models for a human way of life without considering female and infant activity as well as male. That result seems complexly the product both of a historical world-wide women's movement and of phenomena made visible by field and laboratory practice in primatology by culturally specific men and women. It has not just been the women whose scientific practice has responded to recent history. What would the stories be in a genuinely multi-racial field of practice?

Women scientists do not produce nicer, much less more natural, stories than men do; they produce their stories in the rule-guided public social practice of science. They help make the rules; it is a mundane affair requiring the trained energy of women's concrete lives. Responsibility for the quality of scientific stories, for the meaning of comparative tales, for the status of models is multi-faceted, non-mystical, and potentially open to ordinary women 'in' and 'out' of science. To ignore, to fail to engage in the social process of making science, and to attend only to use and abuse of the results of scientific work is irresponsible. I believe it is even less responsible in present historical conditions to pursue anti-scientific tales about nature that idealize women, nurturing, or some other entity argued to be free of male war-tainted pollution. Scientific stories have too much power as public myth to effect meanings in our lives. Besides, scientific stories are interesting.

My moral is that feminists across the cultural field of differences should contest to tell stories and to set the historical conditions for imagining plots. It should be clear that the nature of feminism is no less at issue than langur social habits. There seems a grain of truth in the dust jacket statement of Harvard University Press that simply putting females at an explanatory centre is in some sense feminist. But not just any story will do. Hrdy's sense of our illusions about our social life is not mine. The differences matter.

Explanations of human female sexual physiology provide good examples of stories that have centred on females, but the stories remain profoundly male supremacist. Loss of oestrus in the hominid line has been part of the explanation of primate society for a long time. Or rather, loss of oestrus by females needed explaining, as differences generally do in our narratives. An important father in primatology, Solly Zuckerman, followed the example of his fathers from Aristotle through the nineteenth-century naturalists eulogized by Hrdy: the female sexual pattern was *for* male control of women. Zuckerman gave a functional biological explanation. So for him, and everybody else in these narrative communities until very recently, female human non-oestrus menstrual cycles enabled males to count on female sexual fidelity, that is, on women unpossessed by cycles of sexual insatiability when the owner-male was out making culture by co-operating with other males. In 1967 a son in the Washburn patriline, Donald Lindberg, emphasized the fact, known since Darwin, of female sexual selection; that is, animal females generally determine with whom they will mate. Lindberg put this principle in the context of debates about primate physiology and evolution. A few years later a daughter, Adrienne Zihlman, took Lindberg's element and wove it into a story about the physiological conditions for evolution of the human way of life – a way of life that depended on greater female control of her own sexuality, in the context of gathering-and-sharing subsistence innovations and altered reproductive practices that had the effect of selecting males who knew how to co-operate with stable female-centred social groups basic to human evolution.[16] I like that new story; I also suggest that it changed the rules of what can count in scientific debate about oestrus. At the very least there is a widely published story told by someone possessing the authority to author and working by the rules of scientific discourse. Another daughter in the Washburn lineage, Jane Lancaster (1978), embodied the new story about female sexual self-determination in a widely read popular article in *Human Nature*; stories spread.[17]

This chapter has argued that Jay's (and DeVore's) stories about the social group as the principal primate adaptation, Hrdy's sociobiological challenges based on game theory, strict liberal political economy, and Hobbesian origin stories, Ripley's curious rendering of reproductive rights in stressed conditions, and Bogess's destabilization of what counts as fact are all important scientific products of ordinary good scientific practice judged by standards applicable at publication. That tradition of practice has been symbolized by the fictional device of controversies in a patriline. I have argued that all the examined scientific stories were also shaped materially by contemporary political struggles, in particular conflict over the reproductive social behaviour of women in the last quarter-century. The main point has been to insist on demystifying the emergence of scientific meanings in public discourse. People in particular historical settings make the meanings; it is in the nature of primates.

Plates

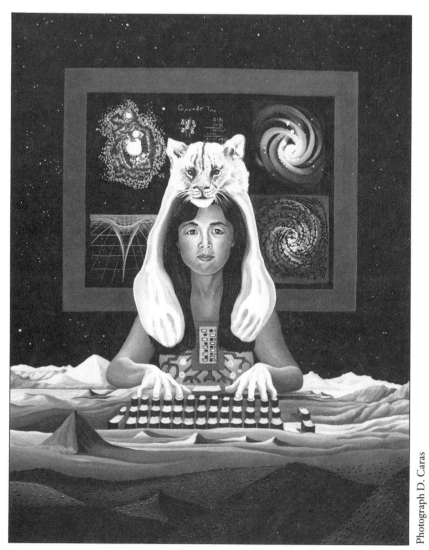

Plate 1

Cyborg, 1989, oil on canvas, 36″ × 28″ by Lynn Randolph ©

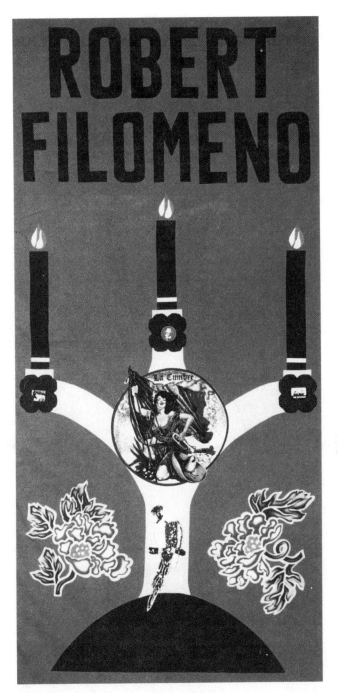

Plate 2

This panel was made for the Names Project's AIDS memorial quilt by Robert's lover and life partner, Jaye Miller, and their friends, Debra Martin, Rusten Hogness, and Donna Haraway.

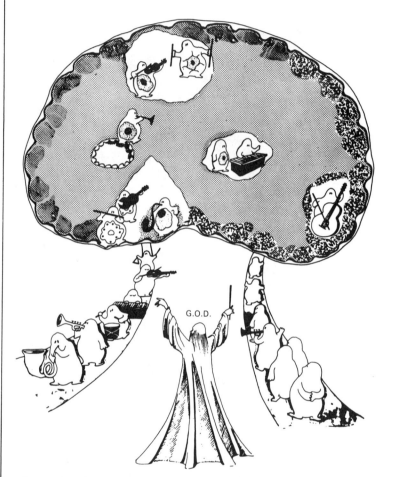

GERSHON'S IMMUNOLOGICAL ORCHESTRA

The immunological orchestra in 1968. The focus was on cell cooperation. The players are B cells, T cells, and macrophages conducted by the generator of diversity (G.O.D.).

Plate 3

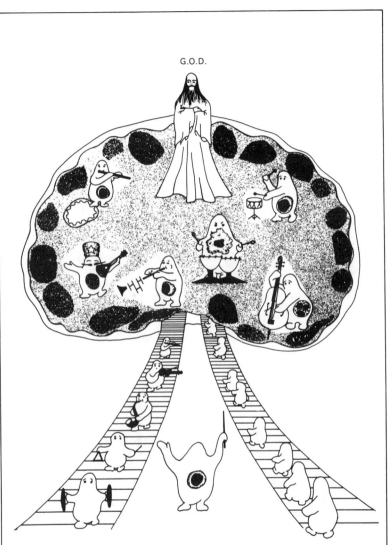

The immunological orchestra in 1974. The role of the thymus as helper, cytotoxic, and suppressor cell is known and Gershon has made the T cell the conductor.

Plate 4

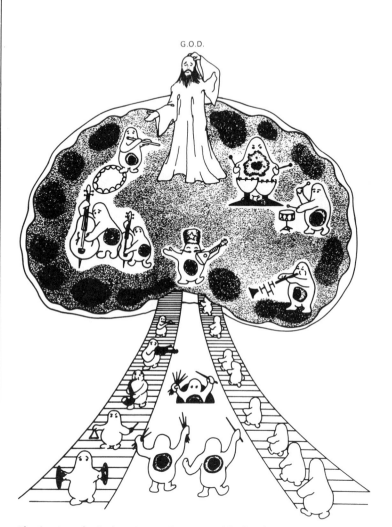

The immunological orchestra in 1977. With the discovery of subsets of T cells Ly 1 and Ly 2,3 cells become joint conductors and Ly 1,2,3 becomes the prompter. This complicated situation clearly has distressed the generator of diversity.

Plate 5

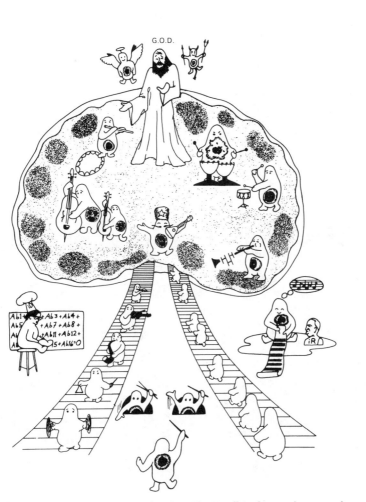

The immunological orchestra in 1982. The T cell is the conductor and the Lyt 1^+ (helper) and Lyt 2^+ (suppressor) cells are prompters, each urging its own interpretation. The generator of diversity seems resigned to the conflicting calls of the angels of help and suppression. At the sides sit the idiotype network and Ir gene (as impresarios?). The caricatures are of Niels Jerne and Baruj Benacerraf.

Plate 6

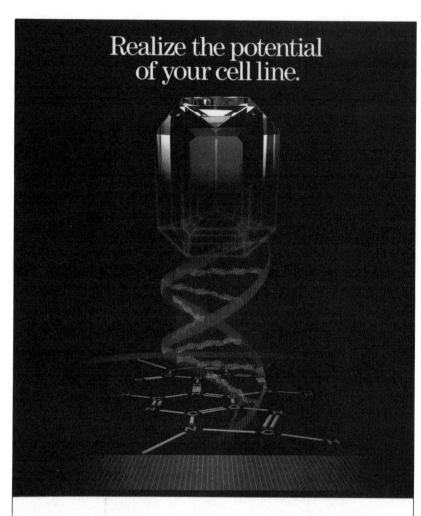

Plate 7

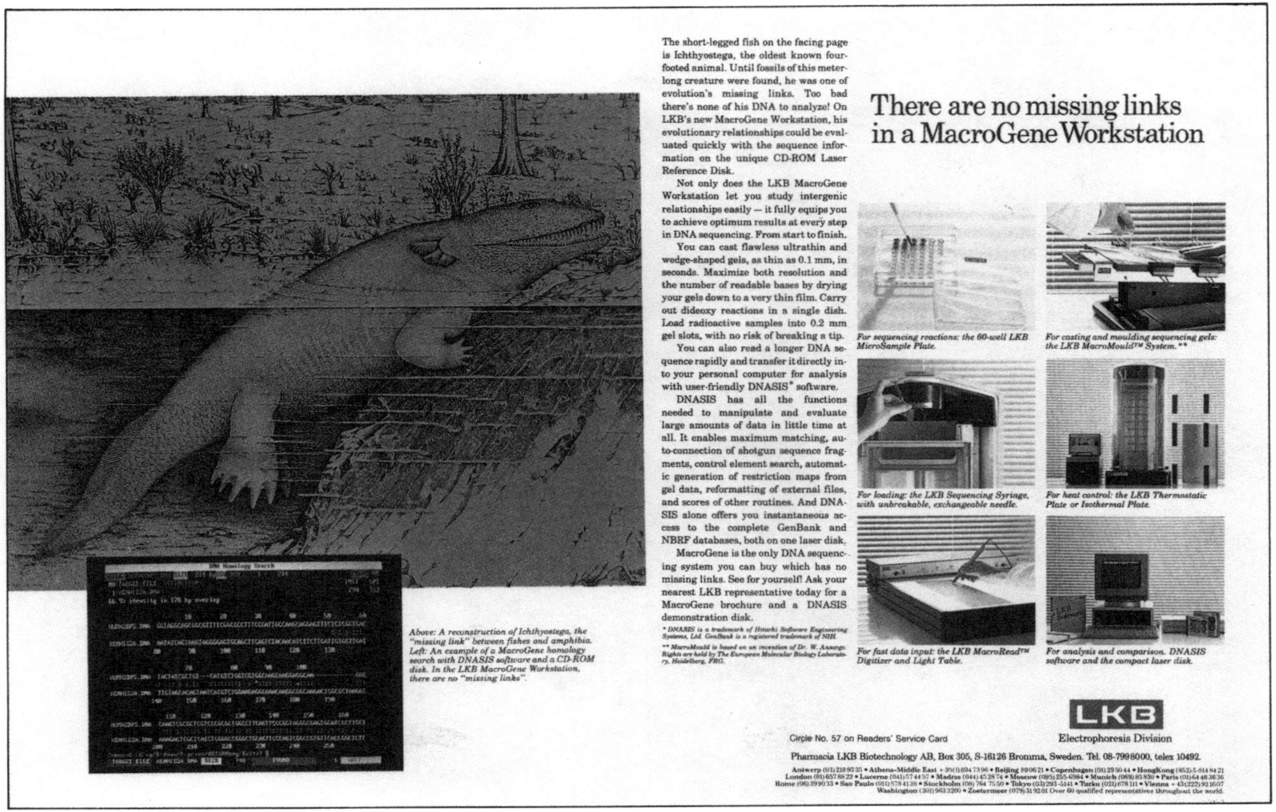

Courtesy of the Electrophoresis Division, Pharmacia LKB Biotechnology Inc.

Plate 8

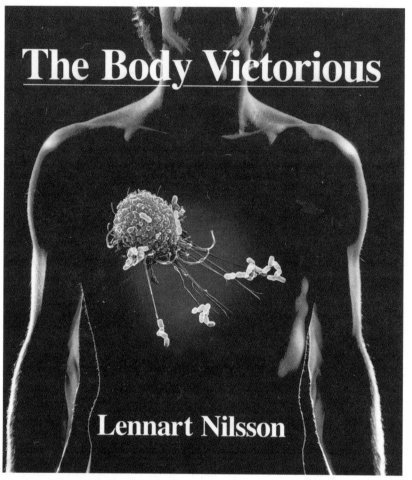

The Body Victorious

Lennart Nilsson

Plate 9

Contents

7

Plate 10

Evolution of recognition systems

UNICELLULAR → MULTICELLULAR → COELOMATE → VERTEBRATE

PROTOZOA
phagocytosis

BACTERIA
enzymes

graft rejection
"non self-
recognition"

CORALS

phagocytic cells
graft memory
agglutinins

ECHINODERMS

SPONGES
specific
aggregation
"self-
recognition"

TUNICATES
stem cells, MHC
lymphocytes ?

WORMS
specialised
cells
opsonins
lysins
agglutinins

ARTHROPODS
complement ?

MOLLUSCS
? no graft rejection

JAWLESS FISHES
lymphocytic foci
antibody response

CARTILAGINOUS FISHES
spleen, thymus, Ig + T cells
plasma cells, IgM (18S,7S)

BONY FISHES
T - B cooperation
Ig + T cells

AMPHIBIANS
lymph nodes, Ig + T cells
MLR ?IR genes
IgM, IgG

MAMMALS
Ig - T cells
IgM, IgG, IgA, IgE, IgD

REPTILES
Ig - T cells, IgM, IgG

BIRDS
bursa
Ig - T cells, IgM, IgG, IgA

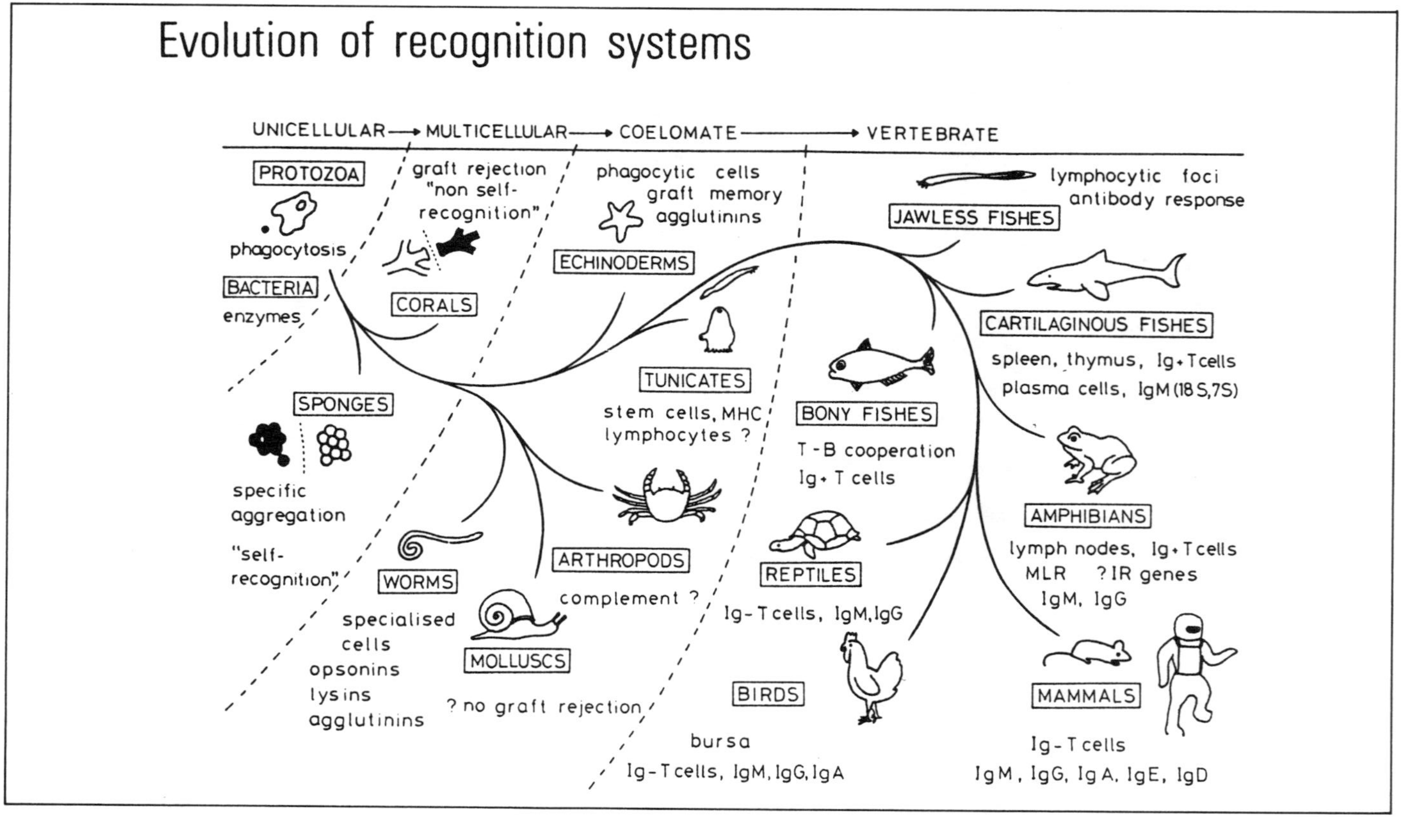

Courtesy of Blackwell Scientific Publications

Plate 11

Chapter Six

Reading Buchi Emecheta: Contests for 'Women's Experience' in Women's Studies[1]

Teaching in women's studies classrooms is a historically specific activity. Such teaching inherits, constructs, and transmits particular reading and writing practices that are politically complex. These material practices are part of the apparatus for producing what will count as 'experience' on personal and collective levels in women's movement.[2] It is crucial to be accountable for the politics of experience in the *institution* of women's studies. Such accountability is not easy, nor is it obvious what forms it might take, nor how struggles over different articulations of experience and different positionings for making these articulations should be addressed. Nor can experience be allowed simply to appear as endlessly plural and unchallengeable, as if self-evident, readily available when we look 'inside' ourselves, and only one's own, or only one's group's. Experience is a crucial *product* and *means* of women's movement; we must struggle over the terms of its articulation. Women do not find 'experience' ready to hand any more than they/we find 'nature' or the 'body' preformed, always innocent and waiting outside the violations of language and culture. Just as nature is one of culture's most startling and non-innocent products, so is experience one of the least innocent, least self-evident aspects of historical, embodied movement.

Through the politically explosive terrain of linked experience feminists make connection and enter into movement. Complexity, heterogeneity, specific positioning, and power-charged difference are not the same thing as liberal pluralism. Experience is a semiosis, an embodying of meanings (de Lauretis, 1984, pp. 158–86). The politics of difference that feminists need to articulate must be rooted in a politics of experience that searches for specificity, heterogeneity, and connection *through struggle*, not through psychologistic, liberal appeals to each her own endless difference. Feminism is collective; and difference is political, that is, about power, accountability, and hope. Experience, like difference, is about contradictory and necessary connection.

I am writing here as a Euro-American, professional, tenured, feminist, middle-class woman in her forties, who works with both undergraduate and graduate students on a campus with a lively feminist culture. It is not the same thing to teach women's studies at the University of California at Santa Cruz in 1989 as it was at the University of Hawaii in 1970. The University of Hawaii was in important respects obviously a colonial institution, located at the periphery of educational privilege in the US. Many of the students in my women's studies classes were women and men of colour, majoring in hotel management and other tourist industry subjects. Feminism as a word was hardly used, and the Women's Liberation Movement seemed to me and many of those I knew in women's movement to be very new, very radical, and unproblematically singular. We were wrong about many of those judgements. UCSC is a relatively left-wing, feminist, and – what ought to be an oxymoron – largely white campus within the most privileged sector of the state higher educational system in a period of acute racism, class antagonism, language chauvinism, sexism, homophobia, and political reaction of many kinds in the state of California and in the nation. It is also a period of tremendous transformation in the racial and ethnic composition and power relations in the state and the nation. And it is a period of exhilarating multi-cultural production; the last quarter of the twentieth century is a time of a many-coloured cultural and political, local, and global renaissance. The days of white hegemony – a power consolidation perhaps more dangerous now than ever – seem visibly numbered. These matters profoundly affect the constructions of 'women's experience' in the classroom.

In these circumstances, I am regularly responsible for teaching 'Methodological Issues in the Study of Women', a required course in a women's studies major. In the present potent political moment, the intense intersections and co-constructions of feminist theory, the critique of colonial discourse, and anti-racist theory have fundamentally restructured individually and collectively the always contested meanings of what counts as 'women's experience'. What may count as 'women's experience' has shifted in the discursive practices of feminism over its history. Showing how teaching arrangements are themselves theoretical practice, those of us teaching women's studies need to come to terms with these issues in our pedagogical approaches for beginning students. Women's studies pedagogy is a theoretical practice through which 'women's experience' is constructed and mobilized as an object of knowledge and action. In this chapter I want to inspect a small part of the apparatus for the discursive production of women's experience in the women's studies classrooms which I inhabit and for which I am accountable to and with others in the circuits of women's movement.

A typical class might begin with the serious logical joke that, especially for the complex category and even more complex people called 'women', *A* and *not-A* are likely to be simultaneously true. This correct exaggeration insists that even the simplest matters in feminist analysis require contradictory moments and a wariness of their resolution, dialectically or otherwise. 'Situated knowledges' is a shorthand term for this insistence. Situated knowledges build in accountability.[3] Being situated in an ungraspable middle space characterizes actors whose worlds might be described by branching bushes like the map or bush of consciousness I have drawn in Figure 3.[4] Situated knowledges are particularly powerful tools to produce maps of consciousness for people who have been inscribed within the marked categories of race and sex that have been so exuberantly produced in the histories of masculinist, racist, and colonialist dominations. Situated knowledges are always *marked* knowledges; they are re-markings, reorientatings, of the great maps that globalized the heterogeneous body of the world in the history of masculinist capitalism and colonialism.

The 'bush of women's consciousness' or the 'bush of women's experience' is a simple diagramatic model for indicating how feminist theory and the critical study of colonial discourse intersect with each other in terms of two crucial binary pairs – that is, *local/global* and *personal/political*. While the tones of personal/political sound most strongly in feminist discourse, and local/global in the critical theory of colonial discourse, both binaries are tools essential to the construction of each. Also, of course, each term of the binary constructs its opposite. I have put the pair 'local/global' at the top of the diagram. To begin, drawing from a particular descriptive practice (which can never simply be innocently available; descriptions are *produced*), place an account of 'women's experience' or 'women's consciousness' at the top. The simple 'dichotomizing machine' immediately bifurcates the experience into two aspects, 'local/global' or 'personal/political'. Wherever one begins, each term in turn bifurcates: the 'local' into 'personal/\political' and the 'global' into 'personal/\political'. Similarly, continuing indefinitely, every instance of the analytical pair 'personal/political' splits on each side into 'local/global'.

This noisy little analytical engine works almost like the dichotomous systems of European Renaissance rhetoricians, such as Peter Ramus, to persuade, teach, and taxonomize simultaneously by means of an analytical technology that palpably makes its objects simultaneously with bisecting them. Referring to the European Renaissance should also alert us to the particular Western history of binary analysis in general and of the pairs adopted here in particular. Other binary pairs that might well appear in my bush are 'liberatory/oppositional' or 'resistance/revolution', pairs deeply embedded in particular Western histories (Ong, 1988). Noting this tradition does not invalidate its use; it *locates* its use and insists on its partiality and accountability. The difference is important. Binaries, rather suspect for the feminists I know, can turn out to be nice little tools from time to time.

FIGURE 3
'BUSH' OR 'MAP' OF WOMEN'S CONSCIOUSNESS/
EXPERIENCE

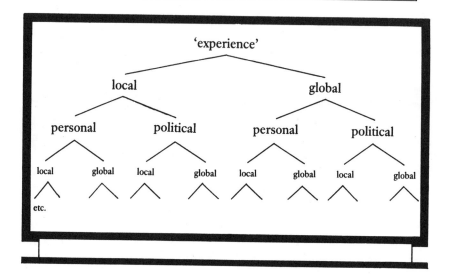

Indeed, the noisiness of the analytical engine is part of its usefulness for feminist accountability; it is difficult to mistake the representation for an innocent, noumenal, transcendent reality. The representational technology makes too much clatter.

The bush plainly does not guarantee unmediated access to some unfixable referent of 'women's experience'. However, the bush does guarantee an open, branching discourse with a high likelihood of reflexivity about its own interpretative and productive technology. Its very arbitrariness and its inescapable encrustings within the traditions of Western rhetoric and semantics are virtues for feminist projects that simultaneously construct the potent object, 'women's experience', and insist on the webs of accountability and politics inherent in the specific form that this artefact takes on.

I suggest that this simple little diagram-machine is a beginning geometry for sketching some of the multiple ways that anti-colonial and feminist discourses speak to each other and require each other for their own analytical progress. One can work one's way through the analytical/descriptive bush, making decisions to *exclude* certain regions of the map, for example, by concentrating only on the global dimension of a political aspect of a particular local experience. But the rest of the bush is implicitly present, providing a resonant echo chamber for any particular tracing through the bush of 'women's experience'.

What should be plain from this way of analysing is that what counts as 'experience' is never prior to the particular social occasions, the discourses, and other practices through which experience becomes *articulated* in itself and *able to be articulated* with other accounts, enabling the construction of an account of *collective* experience, a potent and often mystified operation. 'Women's experience' does not pre-exist as a kind of prior resource, ready simply to be appropriated into one or another description. What may count as 'women's experience' is structured within multiple and often inharmonious agendas. 'Experience', like 'consciousness', is an intentional construction, an artefact of the first importance. Experience may also be *re*-constructed, re-membered, re-articulated. One powerful means to do so is the reading and re-reading of fiction in such a way as to create the effect of having access to another's life and consciousness, whether that other is an individual or a collective person with the lifetime called history. These readings exist in a field of resonating readings, in which each version adds tones and shapes to the others, in both cacophonous and consonant waves.

Claims about 'women's experience' are particularly liable to derive from and contribute to what Wendy Rose, in a poem about appropriations of Native American experience, aptly called 'the tourism of the soul'. Women's studies must negotiate the very fine line between appropriation of another's (never innocent) experience and the delicate construction of the just-barely-possible affinities, the just-barely-possible connections that might actually make a difference in local and global histories. Feminist discourse and anti-colonial discourse are engaged in this very subtle and delicate effort to build connections and affinities, and not to produce one's own or another's experience as a resource for a closed narrative. These are difficult issues, and 'we' fail frequently. It is easy to find feminist, anti-racist, and anti-colonial discourses reproducing others and selves as resources for closed narratives, not knowing how to build affinities, knowing instead how to build oppositions. But 'our' writing is also full of hope that we will learn how to structure affinities instead of identities.

The construction of 'women's experience' through the reading of fiction in women's studies classrooms and women's studies publishing is the practice I wish to examine in this chapter. My focus is on particularly non-innocent objects at this moment in 'our' history in Santa Cruz and in the world: 'African' women's fiction; contending readings of this fiction; and the field of constructions of women's consciousness and experience in the 'African diaspora' as an allegorical figure for many political constituencies, local and global. The novels I attend to were written in English; the genre, the language, and the modes of circulation all mark histories full of colonial and post-colonial contradiction and struggle. The contradictions and the struggles are all the sharper for women's writing and reading of these potent fictions. As Lata Mani (1987) has made clear from her study of eighteenth-century colonial discourse on suttee in India, constructions of women's experience can be fundamental to the invention of 'tradition', 'culture', and 'religion'. Women are a privileged 'site of discourse'. On this terrain, taxation, labour migration policies, or family law have been and still can be legitimated or resisted. Women's 'self-constructions' of experience, history, and consciousness will be no less the ground of material practice – including 'our' own. (Watch how 'experience', 'history', and 'consciousness' are all complex European-derived terms with particular resonances in many US cultures, including Euro-American ethnophilosophies important in academic and activist contexts.)[5]

Reading fiction has had a potent place in women's studies practice. Fiction may be appropriated in many ways. What will count as fiction is itself a contentious matter, resolved partly by market considerations, linguistic and semiotic practices, writing technologies, and circuits of readers. It is possible to foreground or to obscure the publishing practices that make some fiction particularly visible or particularly unavailable in women's studies markets. The material object, the book itself, may be made to seem invisible and transparent or to provide a physical clue to circulations of meanings and power. These points have been made forcefully in Katie King's (1988) reading of the 'genre' of biomythography in Audre Lorde's (1982) *Zami*. Readings may function as technologies for constructing what may count as women's experience and for mapping connections and separations among women and the social movements which they build and in which they participate in local/global worlds. Fiction may be mobilized to provoke identifications as well as oppositions, divergences, and convergences in maps of consciousness. Fictions may also be read to produce connections *without* identifications. The fictions published by and about 'women of colour' occupy a particularly potent node in women's studies practice at the present historical moment in many locations. Appropriations through particular reading practices of these fictions are far from innocent, regardless of the locations in the intersecting fields of race, class, and gender of any reader.

Readings must be engaged and produced; they do not flow naturally from the text. The most straightforward readings of any text are also situated arguments about fields of meanings and fields of power. Any reading is also a guide to possible maps of consciousness, coalition, and action. Perhaps these points are especially true when fiction appears to offer the problematic truths of personal autobiography, collective history, and/or cautionary allegory. These are the textual effects that invite identification, comparison, and moral discourse – all inescapable and problematic dimensions of women's studies discourse. Contesting critically for readings is a fundamental women's studies practice that simultaneously insists on the constructed quality of politics and meanings and holds the readers responsible for their constructions as ways of making and unmaking the potent and polysemic category, 'women'. In this category feminist, colonizing, anti-colonial, and womanist discourses converge and diverge powerfully. Partially allied and partially contending, differently situated women's readings of the fiction published by a 'Third World woman of colour', who personally and textually also inhabits the 'First World', foreground the issues I am trying to sketch. The readers themselves are tied and separated by multiple histories and locations, including race, sexuality, nationality, access to reading publics, and access to the fictions themselves. How are these readings maps of possible modes of affinity and difference on the post-colonial terrain of women's liberatory discourses? How do the figures of the unity of women in the African diaspora enter into nationalist, feminist, womanist, postmodernist, black, multi-cultural, white, First World, Third World, and other political locations?

So, risking falling into the 'tourism of the soul' that Wendy Rose warned against, I will outline three different readings of a popular author, most of whose readers probably have no interest in women's studies, but whose fiction appears in women's studies courses and is also an object of contention in womanist/feminist literary criticism and politics. Before engaging with these three readings, consider a short construction of the text of the author's life, a text that will become part of my stakes in reading her fiction. The author is Buchi Emecheta, born in Nigeria in 1944 of Ibuza background. Emecheta married in 1962 and went to London with her husband, who had a student fellowship. In England, the couple had five children in difficult circumstances, and the marriage ended painfully. Emecheta found herself a single mother in London, black, immigrant, on welfare, living in council housing, and going to college for a degree in library science and then for a PhD in sociology.[6]

Emecheta also became a writer. Her becoming a writer was constituted from those webs of 'experience' implicit in the biographical text in the last paragraph. She was a mother, an immigrant, an independent woman, an African, an Ibo, an activist, a 'been to', a writer. It is said that her husband destroyed her first manuscript because he could not bear the idea that his wife was thinking and acting for herself (Schipper, 1985, p. 44). She published a series of novels that are simultaneously pedagogical, popular, historical, political, autobiographical, romantic – and contentious.

Let us study the dust jackets and reference library texts on Emecheta's life a little further. Besides learning about the academic degrees, a job as a sociologist, and her habit of rising to write in the early hours of the day, we learn that in addition to children's novels she has written eight other novels, including *The Joys of Motherhood* (1979), available in the prestigious African Writers Series, whose founding editor was Chinua Achebe, author of *Things Fall Apart* and other internationally renowned fiction. In the UK, Emecheta's work is published by Allen & Unwin and by Allison & Busby, in the US by Braziller, and in Nigeria by Ogwugwu Afor. Until recently, it was easier to purchase Emecheta's fiction in England or the US than in Nigeria. Emecheta's writing is read as mass-market paperbacks on trains and buses in Britain more than it is read in classrooms. Her work is now published simultaneously in Africa and the West, and it is part of debates among African anglophone readers. In part because of its treatment of African women's issues by an expatriate identified with feminism, Emecheta's writing is controversial, perhaps especially in Nigeria and especially among political academics everywhere it is read.

The Dutch critic, Mineke Schipper (1985, p. 46), claimed that 'Emecheta's novels are extremely popular in Nigeria and elsewhere, but they have some-times been coolly received or even ignored by African critics.' Emecheta's relations to feminism, and the relations of her readers to feminism, are very much at the heart of this matter. Adopting a perspective that bell hooks in the United States named intrinsic to feminist movement, in an interview in 1979 Emecheta's account of her writing explicitly refused to restrict her attention to women:

> The main themes of my novels are African society and family: the historical, social, and political life in Africa as seen by a woman through events. I always try to show that the African male is oppressed and he too oppresses the African women ... I have not committed myself to the cause of African women only, I write about Africa as a whole. (Bruner, 1983, p. 49)

The Joys of Motherhood, set roughly in the 1920s and 1930s in Nigeria, treated the conflicts and multi-layered contradictions in the life of a young married woman who was unable to conceive a child. The woman subse-quently conceived all too many children, but only after she lost access to her own trading networks and so lost her own income. The mother moved from village to city; and her children emigrated to Canada, the United States, and Australia. Although she had many sons, she died childless in an extraordin-arily painful story of the confrontation of urban and village realities for women in early twentieth-century Nigeria.

But, as for Achebe, for Emecheta also there is no moment of innocence in Africa's history before the fall into the conflict between 'tradition' and 'modernity'. Much of Emecheta's fiction is set in Ibuza early in the twentieth century, where the great patterns of cultural syncretism in Africa were the matrix of the characters' lives. In *The Bride Price* (1976) and *The Slave Girl* (1977), Emecheta explored fundamental issues around marriage, control of one's life from different women's points of view, and the contradictory positions, especially for her Ibuza women characters, in every location on the African cultural map, whether marked foreign or indigenous. Life in Europe was no less the locus of struggle for Emecheta's characters. *Second Class Citizen* (1974) explored the breakup of the protagonist's marriage in London. *In the Ditch* (1972, 1979) followed the main character as a single mother into residence in British council housing and her solidarity with white and coloured, working-class, British women's and feminist organizations challenging the terms of the welfare state. *The Double Yoke* (1983a) returned to Nigeria in the late twentieth century to take up again Emecheta's interrogation of the terms of women's struggles in the local and global webs of the African diaspora, viewed from a fictional reconstruction of the paths of travel from and to a minority region in Nigeria.[7]

In my course called 'Methodological Issues in the Study of Women', the students read politically engaged essays by two literary theorists who placed Emecheta in their paradigms of women's fiction and women's unity in the African diaspora. One was by Barbara Christian, a professor of Afro-American Studies at the University of California at Berkeley and a pioneer of black feminist literary criticism, and the other was by Chikwenye Okonjo Ogunyemi, a professor teaching Afro-American and African literature in the English Department at the University of Ibadan in Nigeria. With women from Ibadan and Ife, Ogunyemi participated in 1988 in a group developing women's studies in Nigeria (Tola Olu Pearce, personal communcation). She has published on Emecheta's fiction elsewhere (Ogunyemi, 1983); but in the text we read in class, it was Ogunyemi's explicit marginalization of Emecheta that organized our reading of her essay in its particular publishing context and in other political aspects. Barbara Christian published *Black Feminist Criticism* (1985) in the Athena series of Pergamon Press, a major feminist series in British and US women's studies publishing. The third reading was my own, developed from the perspectives of a Euro-American women's studies teacher in a largely white state university in the United States and first delivered in a conference co-constructing the critical study of colonial discourse and feminist theory. I wanted my women's studies undergraduate students to read, mis-read, re-read, and so reflect on the field of possible readings of a particular contested author, including the discursive constructions of her life on the literal surfaces of the published novels themselves. These readings were directed to fictions in which we all had considerable stakes – the publishers', Emecheta's, Ogunyemi's, Christian's, mine, each of the students', and those of anonymous readers of thousands of paperbacks in several nations. I wanted us to watch how those stakes locate readers in a map of women's self-consciously liberatory discourses, including constructions, such as 'womanism', that place 'feminism' under erasure and propose a different normative genealogy for women's movement. The goal was to make these critically reflexive readings open up the complexities of location and affinities in partially allied, partially oppositional drawings of maps of women's consciousness in the local/global, personal/political webs of situated knowledges.

First, let us examine how Ogunyemi (1985, pp. 66–7) read – or declined to read – Emecheta in an essay published for a largely non-African audience in *Signs: Journal of Women in Culture and Society*, a major scholarly organ of feminist theory in the US. Out of seventeen international correspondents for *Signs*, one was from Africa in 1987 – Achola Pala of Kenya. Many *Signs* essays are assigned in women's studies courses, where most, but by no means all, of the students would be Euro-Americans. Ogunyemi's essay was an argument to distance herself from the label 'feminist' and to associate herself with the marker 'womanist'. She argued that she had independently developed that term and then found Alice Walker's working of it. Ogunyemi produced an archaeology or mapping of African and Afro-American anglophone women's literature since the end of colonization, roughly from the 1960s. The map led to a place of political hope, called womanism. Ogunyemi used the word to designate a woman committed to the survival and the wholeness of the 'entire people', men and women, Africa and the people of its diaspora. She located her discourse on Emecheta in the diaspora's joining of Afro-Caribbean, Afro-American, and African anglophone literatures. Ogunyemi argued that a womanist represents a particular moment of maturity that affirms the unity of the whole people through a multi-layered exploration of the experiences of women as 'mothers of the people'. The mother binding up the wounds of a scattered people was an important image, potent for womanist movement away from both black male chauvinism and feminist negativism, iconoclasm, and immaturity.

But Ogunyemi's principal image was somewhat oblique to that of the mother; it was a *married woman*. Ogunyemi read the fiction since the 1960s in order to construct the relationships of women in the diaspora as 'amicable co-wives with an invisible husband' (1985, p. 74). In her archaeology of anglophone African and African-American literature that finds the traces of womanism in black foremothers-as-writers, Ogunyemi rejected Emecheta. Her fiction did not affirm marriage as the image of full maturity that could represent the unity of black people internationally. Quite the opposite, Emecheta's explorations frequently involved an account of the failure of marriage. In particular, far from recuperating polygamy as an image for liberatory women's movement, Emecheta regarded the practice as a 'decaying institution' that would disappear 'as women became more and more educated and free to decide for themselves' (Bruner, 1983, p. 49). Emecheta's fiction has a sharp edge on marriage throughout, even where it is most affirmed, as in *The Double Yoke*. Seeing the novelist's characters as merely rebellious, Ogunyemi treated Emecheta's fictional and personal relation to marriage harshly, even scornfully, stating that she started to write 'after a marital fiasco', that her writing feminizes black men, and that she finally kills off her heroines in childbirth, enslavement in marriage, insanity, or abandonment by their children. Ogunyemi went so far as to claim, 'Emecheta's destruction of her heroines is a feminist trait that can be partly attributed to narcissism on the part of the writer' (1985, p. 67).

Emecheta in political action allied herself with Irish and British feminists and developed an international discourse quite different from Ogunyemi's account of womanism. In addition to criticizing Emecheta's discourse on and history in relation to marriage, Ogunyemi highlighted Emecheta's exile status. Having lived abroad for twenty years, Emecheta returned to Nigeria to teach in 1980–81 as a senior research fellow at the University of Calabar. On this specific publishing occasion, Ogunyemi problematized Emecheta's 'authenticity' as a returned emigrant writer. In Ogunyemi's archaeology of African anglophone literature, socialism, feminism, and lesbianism all stood explicitly for an immature moment, perhaps recuperable later, but for the moment not incorporable within the voices of the 'co-wives', who figured a normative kind of black women's unity. Womanism meant that the demands of 'culture' take precedence over those of 'sexual politics'. Because of that relationship, for the womanist writer who still does not forget the inequities of patriarchy, 'the matrilineal and polygynous societies in Africa are dynamic sources for the womanist novel' (1985, p. 76). Ogunyemi proposed a logic of inclusion and exclusion in an emerging literary canon as part of a politics about nationalism, gender, and internationalism, argued through the central images of polygynous African marriage.

Barbara Christian had very different stakes in reading Emecheta. In *Black Feminist Criticism* Christian read *The Joys of Motherhood* (1979) in close relation with Alice Walker's *Meridian* (1976), in order specifically to reclaim a matrilineal tradition around the images of a particular feminism that Christian's text foregrounds. Christian located this discourse on matrilineal connection and mothering in these two important novels of the 1970s in order to discuss the simultaneous exaltation and disruption/destruction of mothering for black women in African traditions, in Afro-American slavery, and in post-slavery and post-civil rights movement contexts in the US.[8] She uncovered the contradictions and complexities of mothering, reflecting on the many ways in which it is both enjoyed, celebrated, enforced, and turned into a double bind for women in all of those historical locations. So while Christian sounded a faint note of a lost utopian moment of mothering before the 'invaders' came, the invaders were not only the white slave traders. Rather the invaders seemed to be coeval with mothering; the world is always already fallen apart.

But the mother was no more Christian's fundamental image for the unity of women in the African diaspora through time and space than it was for Ogunyemi. Christian read *Meridian* and *The Joys of Motherhood* in delicate echo with each other in order to foreground a particular kind of feminism that also carried with it an agenda of affirming lesbianism within black feminism and within the model of the inheritance from Africa of the tie between mother and daughter, caring for each other in the impossible conditions of a world that constantly disrupts the caring. Barbara Christian was committed to forbidding the marginalization of lesbianism in feminist discourse by women of colour, and she subtly enlisted Emecheta as one of her texts, for precisely the same reasons that Ogunyemi excluded Emecheta from her genealogy of womanism in the African diaspora. But like Ogunyemi, Christian proposed a narrative of maturation in the history of the writing of her literary foremothers. The trajectory of maturation for each theorist provided a specific model of the growth of selfhood and community for the women of the diaspora. Ogunyemi schematized the history of West African women writers' consciousness since national independence movements in terms of an initial 'flirtation' with feminism and socialism, culminating in a mature womanism organized around the trope of the community of women as mothers, healers, and writers centred in the image of 'co-wives with an absent husband'. That last image could not avoid being a stark reminder of the labour migration realities for many rural women in colonial and post-colonial Africa, even as it invoked the positive self-sufficiency of married women, in contrast to the Western stereotyped figure of the (hetero)sexualized white bourgeois couple with its dependent and isolated wife and her consequent negative 'feminist' politics of protest.

Christian's narrative schematized the history of Afro-American women writers' consciousness in terms of a chronology with suggestive similarities to and differences from Ogunyemi's. Christian argued that, before about 1950, American black women wrote for audiences that largely excluded themselves. Christian characterized the fiction as other-directed, rather than inward searching, in response to the dominating white society's racist definitions of black women. Zora Neale Hurston was the exception to the pattern. Christian traced a process of initial self-definition in the 1950s and the emergence of attention to the ordinary dark-skinned black women. Roughly, the 1960s was a decade of finding unity in shared blackness, the 1970s a period of exposure of sexism in the black community, and the 1980s a time of emergence of a diverse culture of black women engaged in finding selfhood and forming connections among women that promised to transcend race and class in a world-wide community patterned on the ties of mother and daughter. In the 1980s, the terrain for the growing understanding of the personhood of black women, figured in the fictions of the diaspora, was world-wide.

I will conclude by suggesting a third non-innocent reading of Emecheta's fiction – my own, as a Euro-American, middle-class, university-based feminist, who produced this reading as part of a pedagogical practice in US women's studies in the 1980s, in a class in which white students greatly outnumbered students of colour and women greatly outnumbered men. Enmeshed in the debates about postmodernism, the multiplicity of women's self-crafted and imposed social subjectivities, and questions about the possibility of feminist politics in late twentieth-century global and local worlds, my own stakes were in the potent ambiguities of Emecheta's fiction and of the fictions of her life. My reading valorized her heterogeneous statuses as exile, Nigerian, Ibo, Irish-British feminist, black woman, writer canonized in the African Writers Series, popular writer published in cheap paperback books and children's literature, librarian, mother on welfare, sociologist, single woman, reinventor of African tradition, deconstructor of African tradition, member of the Advisory Council to the British Home Secretary on race and equality, subject of contention among committed multi-racial womanist and feminist theorists, and international figure. As for Ogunyemi and Christian, there was a utopian moment nestled in my reading, one that hoped for a space for political accountability and for cherishing ambiguities, multiplicities, and affinities without freezing identities. These risk being the pleasures of the eternal tourist of experience in devastated postmodern terrains. But I wanted to stay with affinities that refused to resolve into identities or searches for a true self. My reading naturalized precisely the moments of ambiguity, the exile status and the dilemma of a 'been-to' for whom the time of origins and returns is inaccessible. Contradiction held in tension with the crafting of accountability was my image of the hoped-for unity of women across the holocaust of imperialism, racism, and masculinist supremacy. This was a feminist image that figured not mothers and daughters, co-wives, sisters, or lesbian lovers, but adopted families and imperfect intentional communities, based not so much on 'choice' as on hope and memory of the always already fallen apart structure of the world. I valued in Emecheta the similarities to the post-holocaust reinvented 'families' in the fiction of Afro-American SF writer, Octavia Butler, as tropes to guide 'us' through the ravages of gender, class, imperialism, racism, and nuclear exterminist global culture.

My reading of Emecheta drew on *The Double Yoke* (1983a), in which the incoherent demands on and possibilities for women in the collision of 'tradition' and 'modernity' are interrogated. At the same time, what counts as 'traditional' or 'modern' emerges as highly problematic. The fictions important to the intersection of postmodernism, feminism, and post-colonial local/global webs begin with the book as a material object and the biographical fragments inscribed on it that construct the author's life for international anglophone audiences. In the prose of the dust jacket, the author metamorphosed from the earlier book jackets' accounts of the woman with five children, on welfare and simultaneously going to college, who rose at 4.00 a.m. in order to write her first six novels, into a senior research fellow at Nigeria's University of Calabar and a member of the Arts Council of Great Britain. There are many Emechetas on the different dust jackets, but all of these texts insist on joining the images of a mother, writer, and émigré Nigerian in London.

A short synopsis must serve to highlight the multiply criss-crossing worlds of ethnicity, region, gender, religion, 'tradition' and 'modernity', social class, and professional status in which Emecheta's characters reinvent their senses of self and their commitments and connections to each other. In *The Double Yoke*, a 'been-to', Miss Bulewao, taught creative writing to a group of mainly young men at the University of Calabar. Framed by Miss Bulewao's assignment to the students and her response to the moral dilemmas posed in one man's story, the core of the novel was the essay submitted by Ete Kamba, who had fallen in love with a young woman, Nko, who lived a mile from his village. Nko, a young Efik woman, came from a different ethnic group from Ete Kamba, an Ikikio. Hoping to marry, both were at the university on scholarships and both had complicated obligations to parents as well as ambitions of their own. But gender made their situations far from symmetrical. In a narrative that cannot but refer the reader to Aihwa Ong's (1987) account of young Malay factory workers in Japanese multinationals in Malaysia, Emecheta sketched the University of Calabar as a microcosm of the contending forces within post-independence Nigeria, including the New Christian Movement, Islamic identities, demands of ethnic groups, economic constraints from both family and national locations in the global economy, contradictions between village and university, and controversy over 'foreign' ideologies such as feminism.

All of these structured the consequences of the love between Ete Kamba and Nko. The pair had intercourse one night outside the village, and afterwards he was consumed with worry over whether Nko was or was not still a virgin, since they had had intercourse with their clothes on and standing up. It was crucial to him that she was still a virgin if he was to marry her. Nko refused to answer his obsessive questions about her virginity. Instead of images of matrilineality linking mother and daughter or of the community of women as co-wives as emblems of collective unity, a deconstruction of 'virginity' structures this novel's arguments about origins, authenticity, and women's positions in constructing the potent unit called 'the people' in the heterogeneous worlds of post-independence Nigeria. The young man went for advice to an elder of Nko's village, who was also a faculty member and a leader of the American-inspired, revivalist, New Christian Movement at the university. The professor, religious leader, and model family man had been sexually harassing Nko, who was also his student; and following Ete Kamba's visit, the older man forced her into a sexual relationship in which she became pregnant.

Nko told Ete Kamba that whether he called her 'virgin', 'prostitute', or 'wife', those were all his names. She came to the university to get a degree by the fruits of her own study. If she were forced to get her degree through negotiating the tightening webs of sexualization drawn around her, she would still not flatten into the blank sheet on which would be written the text of post-colonial 'woman'. She would not allow the local/global and personal/political contradictions figured in Ete Kamba's need for her to be an impossible symbol of non-contradiction and purity to define who she – and they – might be. Perhaps Emecheta's fiction should be read to argue that women like Nko struggle to prevent post-colonial discourse being written by others on the terrain of their bodies, as so much of colonial discourse was. Perhaps Emecheta is arguing that African women will no longer be figures for any of the great images of Woman, whether voiced by the colonizer or by the indigenous nationalist – virgin, whore, mother, sister, or co-wife. Something else is happening for which names have hardly been uttered in any region of the great anglophone diaspora. Perhaps part of this process will mean that, locally and globally, women's part in the building of persons, families, and communities cannot be fixed in any of the names of Woman and her functions.

Ete Kamba related his dilemma and Nko's story in his assigned essay for Miss Bulewao, who called him in to talk. In a wonderful depiction of a faculty–student meeting where the personal, political and academic are profoundly interwined, Miss Bulewao advised Ete Kamba to marry the woman he loved. The young man was absent when the papers were passed back; he had gone to join Nko, who had returned to her village to bury her father. Their marriage was left open.

Ogunyemi's, Christian's, and my readings of Emecheta are all grounded in the texts of the published fiction; and all are part of a contemporary struggle to articulate sensitively specific and powerfully collective women's liberatory discourses. Inclusions and exclusions are not determined in advance by fixed categories of race, gender, sexuality, or nationality. 'We' are accountable for the inclusions and exclusions, identifications and separations, produced in the highly political practices called reading fiction. *To whom* we are accountable is part of what is produced in the readings themselves. All readings are also mis-readings, re-readings, partial readings, imposed readings, and imagined readings of a text that is originally and finally never simply there. Just as the world is *originally* fallen apart, the text is always already enmeshed in contending practices and hopes. From our very specific, non-innocent positions in the local/global and personal/political terrain of contemporary mappings of women's consciousness, each of these readings is a pedagogic practice, working through the naming of the power-charged differences, specificities, and affinities that structure the potent, world-changing artefacts called 'women's experience'. In difference is the irretrievable loss of the illusion of the one.

Part Three

Differential Politics for Inappropriate/d Others

Chapter Seven

'Gender' for a Marxist Dictionary: The Sexual Politics of a Word

In 1983, Nora Räthzel from the autonomous women's collective of the West German independent Marxist journal, *Das Argument*, wrote to ask me to write a 'keyword' entry for a new Marxist dictionary. An editorial group from *Das Argument* had undertaken an ambitious project to translate the multi-volume *Dictionnaire Critique du Marxism* (Labica and Benussen, 1985) into German and also to prepare a separate German supplement that brought in especially the new social movements that were not treated in the French edition.[1] These movements have produced a revolution in critical social theory internationally in the last twenty years. They have also produced – and been partly produced by – revolutions in political language in the same period. As Räthzel expressed it, 'We, that is the women's editorial group, are going to suggest some keywords which are missing, and we want some others rewritten because the women do not appear where they should' (personal communication, 2 December 1983). This gentle understatement identified a major arena of feminist struggle – the canonization of language, politics, and historical narratives in publishing practices, including standard reference works.

'The women do not appear where they should.' The ambiguities of the statement were potent and tempting. Here was an opportunity to participate in producing a reference text. I had up to five typed pages for my assignment: sex/gender. Foolhardy, I wrote to accept the task.

There was an immediate problem: I am anglophone, with variously workable but troubled German, French, and Spanish. This crippled language accomplishment reflects my political location in a social world distorted by US hegemonic projects and the culpable ignorance of white, especially, US citizens. English, especially American English, distinguishes between sex and gender. That distinction has cost blood in struggle in many social arenas, as the reader will see in the discussion that follows. German has a single word, *Geschlecht*, which is not really the same as either the English *sex* or *gender*. Further, the dictionary project, translating foreign contributors' entries into German, proposed to give each keyword in German, Chinese (both ideogram and transcription), English, French, Russian (in transcription only), and Spanish. The commingled histories of

Marxism and of imperialism loomed large in that list. Each keyword would inherit those histories.

At least I knew that what was happening to *sex* and *gender* in English was not the same as what was going on with *género*, *genre*, and *Geschlecht*. The specific histories of women's movement in the vast global areas where these languages were part of living politics were principal reasons for the differences. The old hegemonic grammarians – including the sexologists – had lost control of gender and its proliferating siblings. Europe and North America could not begin to discipline the twentieth-century fate of its imperializing languages. However, I did not have a clue what to make of my sex/gender problem in Russian or Chinese. Progressively, it became clear to me that I had rather few clues what to make of sex/gender in *English*, even in the United States, much less in the anglophone world. There are so many Englishes in the United States alone, and all of them suddenly seemed germane to this promised five-page text for a German Marxist dictionary that was splitting off from its French parent in order to pay attention to new social movements. My English was marked by race, generation, gender (!), region, class, education, and political history. How could *that* English be my matrix for sex/gender *in general?* Was there any such thing, even as words, much less as anything else, as 'sex/gender in general'? Obviously not. These were not new problems for contributors to dictionaries, but I felt, well, chicken, *politically* chicken. But the presses roll on, and a due date was approaching. It was time to pluck out a feather and write. In the late twentieth century, after all, we are ourselves literally embodied writing technologies. That is part of the implosion of gender in sex and language, in biology and syntax, enabled by Western technoscience.

In 1985 I was moderately cheered to learn that the editorial group really wanted an entry on the sex/gender *system*. That helped; there was a specific textual locus for the first use of the term – Gayle Rubin's (1975) stunning essay written when she was a graduate student at the University of Michigan, 'The traffic in women: notes on the political economy of sex'. I could just trace the fate of the 'sex/gender system' in the explosion of socialist and Marxist feminist writing indebted to Rubin. That thought provided very brief consolation. First, the editors directed that each keyword had to locate itself in relation to the corpus of Marx and Engels, whether or not they used the precise words. I think Marx would have been amused at the dead hand guiding the living cursor on the video display terminal. Second, those who adopted Rubin's formulation did so out of many histories, including academic and political interests. US white socialist feminists generated the most obvious body of writing for tracing the 'sex/gender system' narrowly considered. That fact itself was a complex problem, not a solution. Much of the most provocative feminist theory in the last twenty years has insisted on the ties of sex and *race* in ways that problematized the birth pangs of the sex/gender system in a discourse more focused on the interweaving of gender and *class*.[2] It has seemed very rare for feminist theory to hold race, sex/gender, and class analytically together – all the best intentions, hues of authors, and remarks in prefaces notwithstanding. In addition, there is as much reason for feminists to argue for a race/gender system as for a sex/gender system, and the two are not the same *kind* of analytical move. And, again, what happened to class? The evidence is building of a need for a theory of 'difference' whose geometries, paradigms, and logics break out of binaries, dialectics, and nature/culture models of any kind. Otherwise, threes will always reduce to twos, which quickly become lonely ones in the vanguard. And no one learns to count to four. These things matter politically.

Also, even though Marx and Engels – or Gayle Rubin, for that matter – had not ventured into sexology, medicine, or biology for their discussions of sex/gender or the woman question, I knew I would have to do so. At the same time, it was clear that other BIG currents of modern feminist writing on sex, sexuality, and gender interlaced constantly with even the most modest interpretation of my assignment. *Most* of those, perhaps especially the French and British feminist psychoanalytic and literary currents, do not appear in my entry on *Geschlecht*. In general, the entry below focuses on writing by US feminists. That is not a trivial scandal.[3]

So, what follows shows the odd jumps of continual reconstructions over six years. The gaps and rough edges, as well as the generic form of an encyclopaedia entry, should all call attention to the political and conventional processes of standardization. Probably the smooth passages are the most revealing of all; they truly paper over a very contentious field. Perhaps only I needed a concrete lesson in how problematic an entry on any 'keyword' must be. But I suspect my sisters and other comrades also have at times tended simply to believe what they looked up in a reference work, instead of remembering that this form of writing is one more process for inhabiting possible worlds – tentatively, hopefully, polyvocally, and finitely. Finally, the keyword entry exceeded five typed pages, and the chicken was plucked bare. The body had become all text, and the instrument for the inscription was not a feather, but a mouse. The new genitalia of writing will supply the analyst with her metaphors, as the sex/gender system transmogrifies into other worlds of consequential, power-charged difference.

KEYWORD

Gender (English), Geschlecht (German), Genre (French), Género (Spanish)

[The root of the English, French, and Spanish words is the Latin verb, *generare*, to beget, and the Latin stem *gener-*, race or kind. An obsolete English meaning of 'to gender' is 'to copulate' (*Oxford English Dictionary*). The substantives 'Geschlecht', 'gender', 'genre', and 'género' refer to the notion of sort, kind, and class. In English, 'gender' has been used in this 'generic' sense continuously since at least the fourteenth century. In French, German, Spanish, and English, words for 'gender' refer to grammatical and literary categories. The modern English and German words, 'gender' and 'Geschlecht', adhere closely to concepts of sex, sexuality, sexual difference, generation, engendering, and so on, while the French and Spanish seem not to carry those meanings as readily. Words close to 'gender' are implicated in concepts of kinship, race, biological taxonomy, language, and nationality. The substantive 'Geschlecht' carries the meanings of sex, stock, race, and family, while the adjectival form 'geschlechtlich' means in English translation both sexual and generic. 'Gender' is at the heart of constructions and classifications of systems of difference. Complex differentiation and merging of terms for 'sex' and 'gender' are part of the political history of the words. Medical meanings related to 'sex' accrue to 'gender' in English progressively through the twentieth century. Medical, zoological, grammatical, and literary meanings have all been contested in modern feminisms. The shared categorical racial and sexual meanings of gender point to the interwoven modern histories of colonial, racist, and sexual oppressions in systems of bodily production and inscription and their consequent liberatory and oppositional discourses. The difficulty of accommodating racial and sexual oppressions in Marxist theories of class is paralleled in the history of the words themselves. This background is essential to understanding the resonances of the theoretical concept of the 'sex-gender system' constructed by Western anglophone feminists in the 1970s.[4] In all their versions, feminist gender theories attempt to articulate the specificity of the oppressions of women in the context of cultures which make a distinction between sex and gender salient. That salience depends on a related system of meanings clustered around a family of binary pairs: nature/culture, nature/history, natural/human, resource/product. This interdependence on a key Western political-philosophical field of binary oppositions – whether understood functionally, dialectically, structurally, or psychoanalytically – problematizes claims to the universal applicability of the concepts around sex and gender; this issue is part of the current debate about the cross-cultural relevance of Euro-American versions of feminist theory (Strathern, 1988). The value of an analytical category is not necessarily annulled by critical consciousness of its historical specificity and cultural limits. But feminist concepts of gender raise sharply the problems of cultural comparison, linguistic translation, and political solidarity.]

History

Articulation of the problem area in the writings of Marx and Engels In a critical, political sense, the concept of gender was articulated and progressively contested and theorized in the context of the post-Second World War, feminist women's movements. The modern feminist concept for gender is not found in the writings of Marx and Engels, although their writings and other practice, and those of others in the Marxist tradition, have provided crucial tools for, as well as barriers against, the later politicization and theorization of gender. Despite important differences, all the modern feminist meanings of gender have roots in Simone de Beauvoir's claim that 'one is not born a woman' (de Beauvoir, 1949; 1952, p. 249) and in post-Second World War social conditions that have enabled constructions of women as a collective historical subject-in-process. Gender is a concept developed to contest the naturalization of sexual difference in multiple arenas of struggle. Feminist theory and practice around gender seek to explain and change historical systems of sexual difference, whereby 'men' and 'women' are socially constituted and positioned in relations of hierarchy and antagonism. Since the concept of gender is so closely related to the Western distinction between nature and society or nature and history, via the distinction between sex and gender, the relation of feminist gender theories to Marxism is tied to the fate of the concepts of nature and labour in the Marxist canon and in Western philosophy more broadly.

Traditional Marxist approaches did not lead to a political concept of gender for two major reasons: first, women, as well as 'tribal' peoples, existed unstably at the boundary of the natural and social in the seminal writings of Marx and Engels, such that their efforts to account for the subordinate position of women were undercut by the category of the natural sexual division of labour, with its ground in an unexaminable natural heterosexuality; and second, Marx and Engels theorized the economic property relation as the ground of the oppression of women in marriage, such that women's subordination could be examined in terms of the capitalist relations of class, but not in terms of a specific sexual politics between men and women. The classical location of this argument is Engels' *The Origins of the Family, Private Property and the State* (1884). Engels' analytic priority of the family as a mediating formation between classes and the state 'subsumed any separate consideration of the division of the sexes as an antagonistic division' (Coward, 1983, p. 160).[5] Despite their insistence on the historical variability of family forms and the importance of the question of the subordination of women, Marx and Engels could not historicize sex and gender from a base of natural heterosexuality.

The German Ideology (Part I, Theses on Feuerbach) is the major locus for

Marx and Engels' naturalization of the sexual division of labour, in their assumption of a pre-social division of labour in the sex act (heterosexual intercourse), its supposed natural corollaries in the reproductive activities of men and women in the family, and the consequent inability to place women in their relations to men unambiguously on the side of history and of the fully social. In *The Economic and Philosophic Manuscripts of 1844*, Marx refers to the relation of man and woman as the 'most natural relation of human being to human being' (Marx, 1964b, p. 134). This assumption persists in volume one of *Capital* (Marx, 1964a, p. 351). This inability fully to historicize women's labour is paradoxical in view of the purpose of *The German Ideology* and subsequent work to place the family centrally in history as the place where social divisions arise. The root difficulty was an inability to historicize sex itself; like nature, sex functioned analytically as a prime matter or raw material for the work of history. Relying on Marx's research on ethnographic writings (1972), Engels' *Origins* (1884) systematized Marx's views about the linked transitions of family, forms of property, the organization of the division of labour, and the state. Engels almost laid a basis for theorizing the specific oppressions of women in his brief assertion that a fully materialist analysis of the production and reproduction of immediate life reveals a twofold character: the production of the means of existence and '*the production of human beings themselves*' (1884; 1972, p. 71). An exploration of this latter character has been the starting point for many Euro-American Marxist-feminists in their theories of the sex/gender division of labour.[6]

The 'woman question' was widely debated in the many European Marxist parties in the late nineteenth and early twentieth centuries. In the context of the German Social Democratic Party the other of the two most influential Marxist treatments of the position of women was written, August Bebel's *Woman under Socialism* (1883; orig. *Women in the Past, Present and Future*, 1878). Alexandra Kollontai drew on Bebel in her struggles for women's emancipation in Russia and the Soviet Union; and within German social democracy, Clara Zetkin, a leader of the International Socialist Women's Movement, developed Bebel's position in her 1889 'The Question of Women Workers and Women at the Present Time'.[7]

Current Problematic

The gender identity paradigm The story of the political reformulations of gender by post-1960s Western feminists must pass through the construction of meanings and technologies of sex and gender in normalizing, liberal, interventionist-therapeutic, empiricist, and functionalist life sciences, principally in the United States, including psychology, psychoanalysis, medicine, biology, and sociology. Gender was located firmly in an individualist problematic within the broad 'incitement to discourse' (Foucault, 1976) on sexuality characteristic of bourgeois, male-dominant, and racist society. The concepts and technologies of 'gender identity' were crafted from several components: an instinctualist reading of Freud; the focus on sexual somatic- and psychopathology by the great nineteenth-century sexologists (Krafft-Ebing, Havelock Ellis) and their followers; the ongoing development of biochemical and physiological endocrinology from the 1920s; the psycho-biology of sex differences growing out of comparative psychology; proliferating hypotheses of hormonal, chromosomal, and neural sexual dimorphism converging in the 1950s; and the first gender reassignment surgeries around 1960 (Linden, 1981). 'Second-wave' feminist politics around 'biological determinism' vs. 'social constructionism' and the biopolitics of sex/gender differences occur within discursive fields pre-structured by the gender identity paradigm crystallized in the 1950s and 60s. The gender identity paradigm was a functionalist and essentializing version of Simone de Beauvoir's 1940s insight that one is not born a woman. Significantly, the construction of what could count as a woman (or a man) became a problem for bourgeois functionalists and pre-feminist existentialists in the same historical post-war period in which the social foundations of women's lives in a world capitalist, male-dominant system were undergoing basic reformulations.

In 1958, the Gender Identity Research Project was established at the University of California at Los Angeles (UCLA) medical center for the study of intersexuals and transexuals. The psychoanalyst Robert Stoller's work (1968, 1976) discussed and generalized the findings of the UCLA project. Stoller (1964) introduced the term 'gender identity' to the International Psychoanalytic Congress at Stockholm in 1963. He formulated the concept of gender identity within the framework of the biology/culture distinction, such that sex was related to biology (hormones, genes, nervous system, morphology) and gender was related to culture (psychology, sociology). The product of culture's working of biology was the core, achieved, gendered person – a man or a woman. Beginning in the 1950s, the psychoendocrinologist, John Money, ultimately from the institutional base of the Johns Hopkins Medical School's Gender Identity Clinic (established 1965), with his colleague, Anke Ehrhardt, developed and popularized the interactionist version of the gender identity paradigm, in which the functionalist mix of biological and social causations made room for a myriad of 'sex/gender differences' research and therapeutic programmes, including surgery, counselling, pedagogy, social services, and so on. Money and Ehrhardt's (1972) *Man and Woman, Boy and Girl* became a widely used college and university textbook.

The version of the nature/culture distinction in the gender identity paradigm was part of a broad liberal reformulation of life and social sciences in the post-Second World War, Western, professional and governing élites' divestment of pre-war renditions of biological racism. These reformulations failed to interrogate the political-social history of binary categories like nature/culture, and so sex/gender, in colonialist Western discourse. This discourse structured the world as an object of knowledge in terms of the appropriation by culture of the resources of nature. Many recent opposition-al, liberatory literatures have criticized this ethnocentric epistemological and linguistic dimension of the domination of those inhabiting 'natural' categor-ies or living at the mediating boundaries of the binarisms (women, people of colour, animals, the non-human environment) (Harding, 1986, pp. 163–96; Fee, 1986). Second-wave feminists early criticized the binary logics of the nature/culture pair, including dialectical versions of the Marxist-humanist story of the domination, appropriation, or mediation of 'nature' by 'man' through 'labour'. But these efforts hesitated to extend their criticism fully to the derivative sex/gender distinction. That distinction was too useful in combating the pervasive biological determinisms constantly deployed against feminists in urgent 'sex differences' political struggles in schools, publishing houses, clinics, and so on. Fatally, in this constrained political climate, these early critiques did not focus on historicizing and culturally relativizing the 'passive' categories of sex or nature. Thus, formulations of an essential identity as a woman or a man were left analytically untouched and politically dangerous.

In the political and epistemological effort to remove women from the category of nature and to place them in culture as constructed and self-constructing social subjects in history, the concept of gender has tended to be quarantined from the infections of biological sex. Consequently, the ongoing constructions of what counts as sex or as female have been hard to theorize, except as 'bad science' where the female emerges as naturally subordinate. 'Biology' has tended to denote the body itself, rather than a social discourse open to intervention. Thus, feminists have argued against 'biological determinism' and for 'social constructionism' and in the process have been less powerful in deconstructing how bodies, including sexualized and racialized bodies, appear as objects of knowledge and sites of interven-tion in 'biology'. Alternatively, feminists have sometimes affirmed the categories of nature and the body as sites of resistance to the dominations of history, but the affirmations have tended to obscure the *categorical* and overdetermined aspect of 'nature' or the 'female body' as an oppositional ideological resource. Instead, nature has seemed simply there, a reserve to be preserved from the violations of civilization in general. Rather than marking a categorically determined pole, 'nature' or 'woman's body' too easily then means the saving core of reality distinguishable from the social impositions of patriarchy, imperialism, capitalism, racism, history, language. That repression of the *construction* of the category 'nature' can be and has been both used by and used against feminist efforts to theorize women's agency and status as social subjects.

Judith Butler (1989) argued that gender identity discourse is intrinsic to the fictions of heterosexual coherence, and that feminists need to learn to produce narrative legitimacy for a whole array of non-coherent genders. Gender identity discourse is also intrinsic to feminist racism, which insists on the non-reducibility and antagonistic relation of coherent women and men. The task is to 'disqualify' the analytic categories, like sex or nature, that lead to univocity. This move would expose the illusion of an interior organizing gender core and produce a field of race and gender difference open to resignification. Many feminists have resisted moves like those Butler recommends, for fear of losing a concept of agency for women as the concept of the subject withers under the attack on core identities and their constitutive fictions. Butler, however, argued that agency is an instituted practice in a field of enabling constraints. A concept of a coherent inner self, achieved (cultural) or innate (biological), is a regulatory fiction that is unnecessary – indeed, inhibitory – for feminist projects of producing and affirming complex agency and responsibility.

A related 'regulatory fiction' basic to Western concepts of gender insists that motherhood is natural and fatherhood is cultural: mothers make babies naturally, biologically. Motherhood is known on sight; fatherhood is inferred. Analysing gender concepts and practices among Melanesians, Strathern (1988, pp. 311–39) went to great pains to show both the ethnocentric quality of the self-evident Western assertion that 'women make babies' and the inferential character of *all* vision. She showed the productionist core of the belief that women make babies (and its pair, that man makes himself), which is intrinsic to Western formulations of sex and gender. Strathern argued that Hagen men and women do not exist in permanent states as subjects and objects within Aristotelian, Hegelian, Marxist, or Freudian frames. Hagen agency has a different dynamic and geometry. For Westerners, it is a central consequence of concepts of gender difference that a person may be turned by another person into an object and robbed of her or his status as subject. The proper state for a Western person is to have ownership of the self, to have and hold a core identity as if it were a possession. That possession may be made from various raw materials over time, that is, it may be a cultural production, or one may be born with it. Gender identity is such a possession. Not to have property in the self is not to be a subject, and so not to have agency. Agency follows different pathways for the Hagen, who as persons 'are composed of multiple gendered parts, or multiple gendered persons, who are interacting with one another as donors and recipients in maintaining the flow of elements through the body' (Douglas, 1989, p. 17). Sexist domination between persons can and does systematically occur, but it cannot be traced or addressed by the same analytical moves that would be appropriate for many Western social fields of meaning (Strathern, 1988, pp. 334–9). Butler could – cautiously – use Strathern's ethnographic arguments to illustrate one way to disperse the coherence of gender without losing the power of agency.

So, the ongoing tactical usefulness of the sex/gender distinction in life and social sciences has had dire consequences for much feminist theory, tying it to a liberal and functionalist paradigm despite repeated efforts to transcend those limits in a fully politicized and historicized concept of gender. The failure lay partly in not historicizing and relativizing sex and the historical-epistemological roots of the logic of analysis implied in the sex/gender distinction and in each member of the pair. At this level, the modern feminist limitation in theorizing and struggling for the empirical life and social sciences is similar to Marx and Engels' inability to extricate themselves from the natural sexual division of labour in heterosexuality despite their admirable project of historicizing the family.

Sex/gender differences discourse exploded in US sociological and psychological literature in the 1970s and 80s. (This is shown, for example, in the occurrence of the word *gender* as a keyword in the abstracts for articles indexed in *Sociological Abstracts* [from 0 entries between 1966 and 1970, to 724 entries between 1981 and 1985], and in *Psychological Abstracts* [from 50 keyword abstract entries from 1966 to 1970, to 1326 such entries from 1981 to 1985].) The explosion is part of a vigorous political and scientific contestation over the construction of sex and gender, as categories and as emergent historical realities, in which feminist writing becomes prominent about the mid-1970s, primarily in criticisms of 'biological determinism' and of sexist science and technology, especially biology and medicine. Set up within the epistemological binary framework of nature/culture and sex/gender, many feminists (including socialist and Marxist feminists) appropriated the sex/gender distinction and the interactionist paradigm to argue for the primacy of culture-gender over biology-sex in a panoply of debates in Europe and the United States. These debates have ranged from genetic differences in mathematics ability of boys and girls, the presence and significance of sex differences in neural organization, the relevance of animal research to human behaviour, the causes of male dominance in the organization of scientific research, sexist structures and use patterns in language, sociobiology debates, struggles over the meanings of sex chromosomal abnormalities, to the similarities of racism and sexism. By the mid-1980s, a growing suspicion of the category of gender and the binarism sex/gender entered the feminist literature in these debates. That scepticism was partly an outgrowth of challenges to racism in the Euro-American women's movements, such that some of the colonial and racist roots of the framework became clearer.[8]

The sex-gender system Another stream of feminist sex/gender theory and politics came through appropriations of Marx and Freud read through Lacan and Lévi-Strauss in an influential formulation by Gayle Rubin (1975) of the 'sex-gender system'. Her paper appeared in the first anthology of socialist/ Marxist feminist anthropology in the United States. Rubin and those indebted to her theorization adopted a version of the nature/culture distinction, but one flowing less out of US empiricist life and social science, and more from French psychoanalysis and structuralism. Rubin examined the 'domestication of women', in which human females were the raw materials for the social production of women, through the exchange systems of kinship controlled by men in the institution of human culture. She defined the sex-gender system as the system of social relations that transformed biological sexuality into products of human activity and in which the resulting historically specific sexual needs are met. She then called for a Marxian analysis of sex/gender systems as products of human activity which are changeable through political struggle. Rubin viewed the sexual division of labour and the psychological construction of desire (especially the oedipal formation) as the foundations of a system of production of human beings vesting men with rights in women which they do not have in themselves. To survive materially where men and women cannot perform the other's work and to satisfy deep structures of desire in the sex/gender system in which men exchange women, heterosexuality is obligatory. Obligatory heterosexuality is therefore central to the oppression of women.

> If the sexual property system were reorganized in such a way that men did not have overriding rights in women (if there was no exchange of women) and if there were no gender, the entire Oedipal drama would be a relic. In short, feminism must call for a revolution in kinship. (Rubin, 1975, p. 199)

Adrienne Rich (1980) also theorized compulsory heterosexuality to be at the root of the oppression of women. Rich figured 'the lesbian continuum' as a potent metaphor for grounding a new sisterhood. For Rich, marriage resistance in a cross-historical sweep was a defining practice constituting the lesbian continuum. Monique Wittig (1981) developed an independent argument that also foregrounded the centrality of obligatory heterosexuality in the oppression of women. In a formulation which its authors saw as the explanation for the decisive break with traditional Marxism of the Movement pour la Libération des Femmes (MLF) in France, the group associated with

Wittig argued that all women belong to a class constituted by the hierarchical social relation of sexual difference that gives men ideological, political and economic power over women (Editors of *Questions féministes*, 1980).[9] What *makes* a woman is a specific relation of appropriation by a man. Like race, sex is an 'imaginary' formation of the kind that produces reality, including bodies then perceived as prior to all construction. 'Woman' only exists as this kind of imaginary being, while women are the product of a social relation of appropriation, naturalized as sex. A feminist is one who fights for women as a class and for the disappearance of that class. The key struggle is for the destruction of the social system of heterosexuality, because 'sex' is the naturalized political category that founds society as heterosexual. All the social sciences based on the category of 'sex' (most of them) must be overthrown. In this view, lesbians are not 'women' because they are outside the political economy of heterosexuality. Lesbian society destroys women as a natural group (Wittig, 1981).

Thus, theorized in three different frames, withdrawal from marriage was central to Rubin's, Rich's, and Wittig's political visions in the 1970s and early 80s. Marriage encapsulated and reproduced the antagonistic relation of the two coherent social groups, men and women. In all three formulations both the binary of nature/culture and the dynamic of productionism enabled the further analysis. Withdrawal of women from the marriage economy was a potent figure and politics for withdrawal from men, and therefore for the self-constitution of women as personal and historical subjects outside the institution of culture by men in the exchange and appropriation of the products (including babies) of women. To be a subject in the Western sense meant reconstituting women outside the relations of objectification (as gift, commodity, object of desire) and appropriation (of babies, sex, services). The category-defining relation of men and women in objectification, exchange, and appropriation, which was the theoretical key to the category 'gender' in major bodies of feminist theory by white women in this period, was one of the moves that made an understanding of the race/gender or race/sex system and the barriers to cross-racial 'sisterhood' hard for white feminists analytically to grasp.

However, these formulations had the powerful virtue of foregrounding and legitimating lesbianism at the heart of feminism. The figure of the lesbian has been repeatedly at the contentious, generative centre of feminist debate (King, 1986). Audre Lorde put the black lesbian at the heart of her understanding of the 'house of difference':

> Being women together was not enough. We were different. Being gay-girls together was not enough. We were different. Being Black together was not enough. We were different. Being Black women

together was not enough. We were different. Being Black dykes together was not enough. We were different . . . It was a while before we came to realize that our place was the very house of difference rather than the security of any one particular difference. (Lorde, 1982, p. 226)

This concept of difference grounded much US multi-cultural feminist theorizing on gender in the late 1980s.

There have been many uses and criticisms of Rubin's sex-gender system. In an article at the centre of much Euro-American Marxist and socialist-feminist debate, Hartmann (1981) insisted that patriarchy was not simply an ideology, as Juliet Mitchell seemed to argue in her seminal 'Women: the Longest Revolution' (1966) and its expansion in *Women's Estate* (1971), but a material system that could be defined 'as a set of social relations between men, which have a material base, and which, though hierarchical, establish or create interdependence and solidarity among men that enable them to dominate women' (Hartmann, 1981, p. 14). Within this frame, Hartmann attempted to explain the partnership of patriarchy and capital and the failure of male-dominated socialist labour movements to prioritize sexism. Hartmann used Rubin's concept of the sex-gender system to call for an understanding of the mode of production of human beings in patriarchal social relations through male control of women's labour power.

In the debate stimulated by Hartmann's thesis, Iris Young (1981) criticized the 'dual systems' approach to capital and patriarchy, which were then allied in the oppressions of class and gender. Note how race, including an interrogation of white racial positioning, remained an unexplored system in these formulations. Young argued that 'patriarchal relations are internally related to production relations as a whole' (1981, p. 49), such that a focus on the gender division of labour could reveal the dynamics of a single system of oppression. In addition to waged labour, the gender division of labour also included the excluded and unhistoricized labour categories in Marx and Engels, that is, bearing and rearing children, caring for the sick, cooking, housework, and sex-work like prostitution, in order to bring gender and women's specific situation to the centre of historical materialist analysis. In this theory, since the gender division of labour was also the first division of labour, one must give an account of the emergence of class society out of changes in the gender division of labour. Such an analysis does not posit that all women have a common, unified situation; but it makes the historically differentiated positions of women central. If capitalism and patriarchy are a single system, called capitalist patriarchy, then the struggle against class and gender oppressions must be unified. The struggle is the obligation of men and women, although autonomous women's organization would remain a practical necessity. This theory is a good example of strongly rationalist, modernist approaches, for which the 'postmodern' moves of the disaggregation of metaphors of single systems in favour of complex open fields of criss-crossing plays of domination, privilege, and difference appeared very threatening. Young's 1981 work was also a good example of the power of modernist approaches in specific circumstances to provide political direction.

In exploring the epistemological consequences of a feminist historical materialism, Nancy Hartsock (1983a,b) also concentrated on the categories that Marxism had been unable to historicize: (1) women's sensuous labour in the making of human beings through child-bearing and raising; and (2) women's nurturing and subsistence labour of all kinds. But Hartsock rejected the terminology of the *gender* division of labour in favour of the *sexual* division of labour, in order to emphasize the bodily dimensions of women's activity. Hartsock was also critical of Rubin's formulation of the sex-gender system because it emphasized the exchange system of kinship at the expense of a materialist analysis of the labour process that grounded women's potential construction of a revolutionary standpoint. Hartsock relied on versions of Marxist humanism embedded in the story of human self-formation in the sensuous mediations of nature and humanity through labour. In showing how women's lives differed systematically from men's, she aimed to establish the ground for a feminist materialist standpoint, which would be an engaged position and vision, from which the real relations of domination could be unmasked and a liberatory reality struggled for. She called for exploration of the relations between the exchange abstraction and abstract masculinity in the hostile systems of power characterizing phallocratic worlds. Several other Marxist feminists have contributed to intertwined and independent versions of feminist standpoint theory, where the debate on the sex/gender division of labour is a central issue. Fundamental to the debate is a progressive problematization of the *category* labour, or its extensions in Marxist-feminist meanings of reproduction, for efforts to theorize women's active agency and status as subjects in history.[10] Collins (1989a) adapted standpoint theory to characterize the foundations of black feminist thought in the self-defined perspective of black women on their own oppression.

Sandra Harding (1983) took account of the feminist theoretical flowering as a reflection of a heightening of lived contradictions in the sex-gender system, such that fundamental change can now be struggled for. In extending her approach to the sex-gender system to *The Science Question in Feminism* (1986), Harding stressed three variously interrelated elements of gender: (1) a fundamental category through which meaning is ascribed to everything, (2) a way of organizing social relations, and (3) a structure of personal identity. Disaggregating these three elements has been part of coming to understand the complexity and problematic value of politics based on gender identities. Using the sex-gender system to explore post-Second World War politics of sexual identity in gay movements, Jeffrey Escoffier (1985) argued for a need to theorize the emergence and limitations of new forms of political subjectivity, in order to develop a committed, positioned politics without metaphysical identity closures. Haraway's (1985) 'Manifesto for Cyborgs' (see this volume, pp. 149–81) developed similar arguments in order to explore Marxist-feminist politics addressed to women's positionings in multi-national science- and technology-mediated social, cultural, and technical systems.

In another theoretical development indebted to Marxism, while critical of both it and of the language of gender, Catherine MacKinnon (1982, p. 515) argued that

> Sexuality is to feminism what work is to marxism: that which is most one's own, yet most taken away ... Sexuality is that social process which creates, organizes, expresses, and directs desire, creating the social beings we know as women and men, as their relations create society ... As the organized expropriation of the work of some for the benefit of others defines a class – workers – the organized expropriation of the sexuality of some for the use of other defines the sex, woman.

MacKinnon's position has been central to controversial approaches to political action in much of the US movement against pornography, defined as violence against women and/or as a violation of women's civil rights; that is, a refusal to women, via their construction as woman, of the status of citizen. MacKinnon saw the construction of woman as the material and ideological construction of the object of another's desire. Thus women are not simply alienated from the product of their labour; in so far as they exist as 'woman', that is to say, sex objects, they are not even potentially historical subjects. 'For women, there is no distinction between objectification and alienation because women have not authored objectifications, we have been them' (1982, pp. 253–4). The epistemological and political consequences of this position are far reaching and have been extremely controversial. For MacKinnon, the production of women is the production of a very material illusion, 'woman'. Unpacking this material illusion, which is women's lived reality, requires a politics of consciousness-raising, the specific form of feminist politics in MacKinnon's frame. 'Sexuality determines gender', and 'women's sexuality is its use, just as our femaleness *is* its alterity' (p. 243). Like independent formulations in Lacanian feminisms, MacKinnon's position has been fruitful in theorizing processes of representation, in which 'power to create the world from one's point of view is power in its male form' (p. 249).

In an analysis of the gendering of violence sympathetic to MacKinnon's, but drawing on different theoretical and political resources, Teresa de Lauretis's (1984, 1985) approaches to representation led her to view gender as the unexamined tragic flaw of modern and postmodern theories of culture, whose faultline is the heterosexual contract. De Lauretis defined gender as the social construction of 'woman' and 'man' and the semiotic production of subjectivity; gender has to do with 'the history, practices, and imbrication of meaning and experience'; that is, with the 'mutually constitutive effects in semiosis of the outer world of social reality with the inner world of subjectivity' (1984, pp. 158–86). De Lauretis drew on Charles Peirce's theories of semiosis to develop an approach to 'experience', one of the most problematic notions in modern feminism, that takes account both of experience's intimate embodiment and its mediation through signifying practices. Experience is never *im*-mediately accessible. Her efforts have been particularly helpful in understanding and contesting inscriptions of gender in cinema and other areas where the idea that gender is an embodied semiotic difference is crucial and empowering. Differentiating technologies of gender from Foucault's formulation of technologies of sex, de Lauretis identified a specific feminist gendered subject position within sex/gender systems. Her formulation echoed Lorde's understanding of the inhabitant of the house of difference: 'The female subject of feminism is one constructed across a multiplicity of discourses, positions, and meanings, which are often in conflict with one another and inherently (historically) contradictory' (de Lauretis, 1987, pp. ix–x).

Offering a very different theory of consciousness and the production of meanings from MacKinnon or de Lauretis, Hartsock's (1983a) exploration of the sexual division of labour drew on anglophone versions of psychoanalysis that were particularly important in US feminist theory, that is, object relations theory as developed especially by Nancy Chodorow (1978). Without adopting Rubin's Lacanian theories of always fragmentary sexed subjectivity, Chodorow adopted the concept of the sex-gender system in her study of the social organization of parenting, which produced women more capable of non-hostile relationality than men, but which also perpetuated the subordinate position of women through their production as people who are structured for mothering in patriarchy. Preferring an object relations psychoanalysis over a Lacanian version is related to neighbouring concepts like 'gender identity', with its empirical social science web of meanings, over 'acquisition of positions of sexed subjectivity', with this concept's immersion in Continental cultural/textual theory. Although criticized as an essentializing of woman-as-relational, Chodorow's feminist object relations theory has been immensely influential, having been adapted to explore a wide range of social phenomena. Drawing on and criticizing Lawrence Kohlberg's neo-

Kantian theories, Gilligan (1982) also argued for women's greater contextual consciousness and resistance to universalizing abstractions, for example in moral reasoning.

Evelyn Keller developed a version of object relations theory to theorize systematic epistemological, psychic, and organizational masculine domin- ance of natural science (Keller, 1985). Keller foregrounded the logical mistake of equating *women* with *gender*.[11] Gender is a system of social, symbolic, and psychic relations, in which men and women are differentially positioned. Looking at the expression of gender as a cognitive experience, in which masculine psychic individuation produces an investment in imperson- ality, objectification, and domination, Keller described her project as an effort to understand the 'science-gender system' (p. 8). Emphasizing social construction and concentrating on psychodynamic aspects of that construc- tion, Keller took as her subject 'not women *per se*, or even women and science: it is the making of men, women, and science, or, more precisely, how the making of men and women has affected the making of science' (p. 4). Her goal was to work for science as a human project, not a masculine one. She phrased her question as, 'Is sex to gender as nature is to science?' (Keller, 1987).

Chodorow's early work was developed in the context of a related series of sociological and anthropological papers theorizing a key role for the public/private division in the subordination of women (Rosaldo and Lam- phere, 1974). In that collection, Rosaldo argued the universal salience of the limitation of women to the domestic realm, while power was vested in the space men inhabit, called public. Sherry Ortner connected that approach to her structuralist analysis of the proposition that women are to nature as men are to culture. Many Euro-American feminist efforts to articulate the social positioning of women that followed *Woman, Culture, and Society* and *Toward an Anthropology of Women* (Reiter, 1975), both strategically published in the mid-1970s, were deeply influenced by the universalizing and powerful theories of sex and gender of those early collections. In anthropology as a discipline, criticisms and other outgrowths of the early formulations were rich, leading both to extensive cross-cultural study of gender symbolisms and to fundamental rejection of the universal applicability of the nature/ culture pair. Within the disciplines, there was growing criticism of universal- izing explanations as an instance of mistaking the analytical tool for the reality (MacCormack and Strathern, 1980; Rosaldo, 1980; Ortner and Whitehead 1981; Rubin, 1984). As feminist anthropology moved away from its early formulations, they none the less persisted in much feminist discourse outside anthropological disciplinary circles, as if the mid-1970s positions were permanently authoritative feminist anthropological theory, rather than a discursive node in a specific political-historical-disciplinary moment.

The universalizing power of the sex-gender system and the analytical split between public and private were also sharply criticized politically, especially by women of colour, as part of the ethnocentric and imperializing tendencies of European and Euro-American feminisms. The category of gender obscured or subordinated all the other 'others'. Efforts to use Western or 'white' concepts of gender to characterize a 'Third World Woman' often resulted in reproducing orientalist, racist, and colonialist discourse (Mohanty, 1984; Amos et al., 1984). Furthermore, US 'women of colour', itself a complex and contested political construction of sexed identities, produced critical theory about the production of systems of hierarchical differences, in which race, nationality, sex, and class were intertwined, both in the nineteenth and early twentieth centuries and from the earliest days of the women's movements that emerged from the 1960s civil rights and anti-war movements.[12] These theories of the social positioning of women ground and organize 'generic' feminist theory, in which concepts like 'the house of difference' (Lorde), 'oppositional consciousness' (Sandoval), 'womanism' (Walker), 'shuttle from center to margin' (Spivak), 'Third World feminism' (Moraga and Smith), 'el mundo zurdo' (Anzaldúa and Moraga), 'la mestiza' (Anzaldúa), 'racially-structured patriarchal capitalism' (Bhavnani and Coulson, 1986), and 'inappropriate/d other' (Trinh, 1986–7, 1989) structure the field of feminist discourse, as it decodes what counts as a 'woman' within as well as outside 'feminism'. Complexly related figures have emerged also in feminist writing by 'white' women: 'sex-political classes' (Sofoulis, 1987); 'cyborg' (Haraway, 1985 and this vol. pp. 149–81); the female subject of feminism (de Lauretis, 1987).

In the early 1980s, Kitchen Table: Women of Color Press was established in New York and began to publish the critical theoretical and other writings of radical women of colour. This development must be seen in the context of international publishing in many genres by women writing into consciousness the stories of their constructions, and thereby destabilizing the canons of Western feminism, as well as those of many other discourses. As the heterogeneous and critical subject positions of 'women of colour' were progressively elaborated in diverse publishing practices, the status of 'white' or 'Western' also was more readily seen as a contestable location and not as a given ethnicity, race, or inescapable destiny. Thus, 'white' women could be called to account for their active positioning.

Rubin's 1975 theory of the sex/gender system explained the complementarity of the sexes (obligatory heterosexuality) and the oppression of women by men through the central premise of the exchange of women in the founding of culture through kinship. But what happens to this approach when women are not positioned in similar ways in the institution of kinship? In particular, what happens to the idea of gender if whole groups of women and men are positioned *outside* the *institution* of kinship altogether, but in relation to the kinship systems of another, dominant group? Carby (1987), Spillers (1987), and Hurtado (1989) interrogated the concept of gender through an exploration of the history and consequences of these matters.

Carby clarified how in the New World, and specifically in the United States, black women were not constituted as 'woman', as white women were. Instead, black women were constituted simultaneously racially and sexually – as marked female (animal, sexualized and without rights), but not as woman (human, potential wife, conduit for the name of the father) – in a specific institution, slavery, that excluded them from 'culture' defined as the circulation of signs through the system of marriage. If kinship vested men with rights in women that they did not have in themselves, slavery abolished kinship for one group in a legal discourse that produced whole groups of people as alienable property (Spillers, 1987). MacKinnon (1982, 1987) defined woman as an imaginary figure, the object of another's desire, made real. The 'imaginary' figures made real in slave discourse were objects in another sense that made them different from either the Marxist figure of the alienated labourer or the 'unmodified' feminist figure of the object of desire. Free women in US white patriarchy were exchanged in a system that oppressed them, but white women *inherited* black women and men. As Hurtado (1989, p. 841) noted, in the nineteenth century prominent white feminists were *married* to white men, while black feminists were *owned* by white men. In a racist patriarchy, white men's 'need' for racially pure offspring positioned free and unfree women in incompatible, asymmetrical symbolic and social spaces.

The female slave was marked with these differences in a most literal fashion – the flesh was turned inside out, 'add[ing] a lexical dimension to the narratives of woman in culture and society' (Spillers, 1987, pp. 67–8). These differences did not end with formal emancipation; they have had definitive consequences into the late twentieth century and will continue to do so until racism as a founding institution of the New World is ended. Spillers called these founding relations of captivity and literal mutilation 'an American grammar' (p. 68). Under conditions of the New World conquest, of slavery, and of their consequences up to the present, 'the lexis of reproduction, desire, naming, mothering, fathering, etc. [are] all thrown into extreme crisis' (p. 76). 'Gendering, in its coeval reference to African-American women, *insinuates* an implicit and unresolved puzzle both within currrent feminist discourse *and* within those discursive communities that investigate the problematics of culture' (p. 78).

Spillers foregrounded the point that free men and women inherited their *name* from the father, who in turn had rights in his minor children and wife that they did not have in themselves, but he did not own them in the full sense of alienable property. Unfree men and women inherited their *condition* from their mother, who in turn specifically did not control their children. They had no *name* in the sense theorized by Lévi-Strauss or Lacan. Slave mothers could not transmit a name; they could not be wives; they were outside the system of marriage exchange. Slaves were unpositioned, unfixed, in a system of names; they were, specifically, unlocated and so disposable. In these discursive frames, white women were not legally or symbolically *fully* human; slaves were not legally or symbolically human *at all*. 'In this absence from a subject position, the captured sexualities provide a physical and biological expression of "otherness"' (Spillers, 1987, p. 67). To give birth (unfreely) to the heirs of property is not the same thing as to give birth (unfreely) to property (Carby, 1987, p. 53).

This little difference is part of the reason that 'reproductive rights' for women of colour in the US prominently hinge on comprehensive control of children – for example, their freedom from destruction through lynching, imprisonment, infant mortality, forced pregnancy, coercive sterilization, inadequate housing, racist education, or drug addiction (Hurtado, 1989, p. 853). For white women the concept of property in the self, the ownership of one's own body, in relation to reproductive freedom has more readily focused on the field of events around conception, pregnancy, abortion, and birth, because the system of white patriarchy turned on the control of legitimate children and the consequent constitution of white females as woman. To have or not have children then becomes literally a subject-defining choice for women. Black women specifically – and the women subjected to the conquest of the New World in general – faced a broader social field of reproductive unfreedom, in which their children did not inherit the status of human in the founding hegemonic discourses of US society. The problem of the black mother in this context is not simply her own status as subject, but also the status of her children and her sexual partners, male and female. Small wonder that the image of uplifting the race and the refusal of the categorical separation of men and women – without flinching from an analysis of coloured and white sexist oppression – have been prominent in New World black feminist discourse (Carby, 1987, pp. 6–7; hooks, 1981, 1984).

The positionings of African-American women are not the same as those of other women of colour; each condition of oppression requires specific analysis that refuses the separations but insists on the non-identities of race, sex, and class. These matters make starkly clear why an adequate feminist theory of gender must *simultaneously* be a theory of racial difference in specific historical conditions of production and reproduction. They also make clear why a theory and practice of sisterhood cannot be grounded in shared positionings in a system of sexual difference and the cross-cultural structural antagonism between coherent categories called women and men. Finally, they make clear why feminist theory produced by women of colour has constructed alternative discourses of womanhood that disrupt the humanisms of many Western discursive traditions.

> [I]t is our task to make a place for this different social subject. In so doing we are less interested in joining the ranks of gendered femaleness than gaining the *insurgent* ground as female social subject. Actually *claiming* the monstrosity of a female with the potential to 'name' . . . 'Sapphire' might rewrite after all a radically different text of female empowerment. (Spillers, 1987, p. 80)

While contributing fundamentally to the breakup of any master subject location, the politics of 'difference' emerging from this and other complex reconstructings of concepts of social subjectivity and their associated writing practices is deeply opposed to levelling relativisms. Non-feminist theory in the human sciences has tended to identify the breakup of 'coherent' or masterful subjectivity as the 'death of the subject'. Like others in newly *unstably* subjugated positions, many feminists resist this formulation of the project and question its emergence at just the moment when raced/sexed/ colonized speakers begin 'for the first time', that is, they claim an originary authority to represent themselves in institutionalized publishing practices and other kinds of self-constituting practice. Feminist deconstructions of the 'subject' have been fundamental, and they are not nostalgic for masterful coherence. Instead, necessarily political accounts of constructed embodiments, like feminist theories of gendered racial subjectivities, have to take affirmative *and* critical account of emergent, differentiating, self-representing, contradictory social subjectivities, with their claims on action, knowledge, and belief. The point involves the commitment to transformative social change, the moment of hope embedded in feminist theories of gender and other emergent discourses about the breakup of masterful subjectivity and the emergence of inappropriate/d others (Trinh, 1986–7, 1989).

The multiple academic and other institutional roots of the literal (written) category 'gender', feminist and otherwise, sketched in this entry have been part of the race-hierarchical system of relations that obscures the publications by women of colour because of their origin, language, genre – in short, 'marginality', 'alterity', and 'difference' as seen from the 'unmarked' positions of hegemonic and imperializing ('white') theory. But 'alterity' and 'difference' are precisely what 'gender' is 'grammatically' about, a fact that constitutes feminism as a politics defined by its fields of contestation and repeated refusals of master theories. 'Gender' was developed as a category to explore what counts as a 'woman', to problematize the previously taken-for-granted. If feminist theories of gender followed from Simone de Beauvoir's thesis that one is not born a woman, with all the consequences of that insight, in the light of Marxism and psychoanalysis, for understanding that any finally coherent subject is a fantasy, and that personal and collective identity is precariously and constantly socially reconstituted (Coward, 1983, p. 265), then the title of bell hooks's provocative book, echoing the great nineteenth-century black feminist and abolitionist, Sojourner Truth, *Ain't I a Woman* (1981), bristles with irony, as the identity of 'woman' is both claimed and deconstructed simultaneously. Struggle over the agents, memories, and terms of these reconstitutions is at the heart of feminist sex/gender politics.

The refusal to become or to remain a 'gendered' man or a woman, then, is an eminently political insistence on emerging from the nightmare of the all-too-real, imaginary narrative of sex and race. Finally and ironically, the political and explanatory power of the 'social' category of gender depends upon historicizing the categories of sex, flesh, body, biology, race, and nature in such a way that the binary, universalizing opposition that spawned the concept of the sex/gender system at a particular time and place in feminist theory implodes into articulated, differentiated, accountable, located, and consequential theories of embodiment, where nature is no longer imagined and enacted as resource to culture or sex to gender. Here is my location for a utopian intersection of heterogeneous, multi-cultural, 'Western' (coloured, white, European, American, Asian, African, Pacific) feminist theories of gender hatched in odd siblingship with contradictory, hostile, fruitful, inherited binary dualisms. Phallogocentrism was the egg ovulated by the master subject, the brooding hen to the permanent chickens of history. But into the nest with that literal-minded egg has been placed the germ of a phoenix that will speak in all the tongues of a world turned upside down.

Chapter Eight

A Cyborg Manifesto: Science, Technology, and Socialist-Feminism in the Late Twentieth Century[1]

AN IRONIC DREAM OF A COMMON LANGUAGE FOR WOMEN IN THE INTEGRATED CIRCUIT

This chapter is an effort to build an ironic political myth faithful to feminism, socialism, and materialism. Perhaps more faithful as blasphemy is faithful, than as reverent worship and identification. Blasphemy has always seemed to require taking things very seriously. I know no better stance to adopt from within the secular-religious, evangelical traditions of United States politics, including the politics of socialist feminism. Blasphemy protects one from the moral majority within, while still insisting on the need for community. Blasphemy is not apostasy. Irony is about contradictions that do not resolve into larger wholes, even dialectically, about the tension of holding incompatible things together because both or all are necessary and true. Irony is about humour and serious play. It is also a rhetorical strategy and a political method, one I would like to see more honoured within socialist-feminism. At the centre of my ironic faith, my blasphemy, is the image of the cyborg.

A cyborg is a cybernetic organism, a hybrid of machine and organism, a creature of social reality as well as a creature of fiction. Social reality is lived social relations, our most important political construction, a world-changing fiction. The international women's movements have constructed 'women's experience', as well as uncovered or discovered this crucial collective object. This experience is a fiction and fact of the most crucial, political kind. Liberation rests on the construction of the consciousness, the imaginative apprehension, of oppression, and so of possibility. The cyborg is a matter of fiction and lived experience that changes what counts as women's experience in the late twentieth century. This is a struggle over life and death, but the boundary between science fiction and social reality is an optical illusion.

Contemporary science fiction is full of cyborgs – creatures simultaneously animal and machine, who populate worlds ambiguously natural and crafted.

Modern medicine is also full of cyborgs, of couplings between organism and machine, each conceived as coded devices, in an intimacy and with a power that was not generated in the history of sexuality. Cyborg 'sex' restores some of the lovely replicative baroque of ferns and invertebrates (such nice organic prophylactics against heterosexism). Cyborg replication is uncoupled from organic reproduction. Modern production seems like a dream of cyborg colonization work, a dream that makes the nightmare of Taylorism seem idyllic. And modern war is a cyborg orgy, coded by C^3I, command-control-communication-intelligence, an \$84 billion item in 1984's US defence budget. I am making an argument for the cyborg as a fiction mapping our social and bodily reality and as an imaginative resource suggesting some very fruitful couplings. Michael Foucault's biopolitics is a flaccid premonition of cyborg politics, a very open field.

By the late twentieth century, our time, a mythic time, we are all chimeras, theorized and fabricated hybrids of machine and organism; in short, we are cyborgs. The cyborg is our ontology; it gives us our politics. The cyborg is a condensed image of both imagination and material reality, the two joined centres structuring any possibility of historical transformation. In the traditions of 'Western' science and politics – the tradition of racist, male-dominant capitalism; the tradition of progress; the tradition of the appropriation of nature as resource for the productions of culture; the tradition of reproduction of the self from the reflections of the other – the relation between organism and machine has been a border war. The stakes in the border war have been the territories of production, reproduction, and imagination. This chapter is an argument for *pleasure* in the confusion of boundaries and for *responsibility* in their construction. It is also an effort to contribute to socialist-feminist culture and theory in a postmodernist, non-naturalist mode and in the utopian tradition of imagining a world without gender, which is perhaps a world without genesis, but maybe also a world without end. The cyborg incarnation is outside salvation history. Nor does it mark time on an oedipal calendar, attempting to heal the terrible cleavages of gender in an oral symbiotic utopia or post-oedipal apocalypse. As Zoe Sofoulis argues in her unpublished manuscript on Jacques Lacan, Melanie Klein, and nuclear culture, *Lacklein*, the most terrible and perhaps the most promising monsters in cyborg worlds are embodied in non-oedipal narratives with a different logic of repression, which we need to understand for our survival.

The cyborg is a creature in a post-gender world; it has no truck with bisexuality, pre-oedipal symbiosis, unalienated labour, or other seductions to organic wholeness through a final appropriation of all the powers of the parts into a higher unity. In a sense, the cyborg has no origin story in the Western sense – a 'final' irony since the cyborg is also the awful apocalyptic *telos* of the

'West's' escalating dominations of abstract individuation, an ultimate self untied at last from all dependency, a man in space. An origin story in the 'Western', humanist sense depends on the myth of original unity, fullness, bliss and terror, represented by the phallic mother from whom all humans must separate, the task of individual development and of history, the twin potent myths inscribed most powerfully for us in psychoanalysis and Marxism. Hilary Klein has argued that both Marxism and psychoanalysis, in their concepts of labour and of individuation and gender formation, depend on the plot of original unity out of which difference must be produced and enlisted in a drama of escalating domination of woman/nature. The cyborg skips the step of original unity, of identification with nature in the Western sense. This is its illegitimate promise that might lead to subversion of its teleology as star wars.

The cyborg is resolutely committed to partiality, irony, intimacy, and perversity. It is oppositional, utopian, and completely without innocence. No longer structured by the polarity of public and private, the cyborg defines a technological polis based partly on a revolution of social relations in the *oikos*, the household. Nature and culture are reworked; the one can no longer be the resource for appropriation or incorporation by the other. The relationships for forming wholes from parts, including those of polarity and hierarchical domination, are at issue in the cyborg world. Unlike the hopes of Frankenstein's monster, the cyborg does not expect its father to save it through a restoration of the garden; that is, through the fabrication of a heterosexual mate, through its completion in a finished whole, a city and cosmos. The cyborg does not dream of community on the model of the organic family, this time without the oedipal project. The cyborg would not recognize the Garden of Eden; it is not made of mud and cannot dream of returning to dust. Perhaps that is why I want to see if cyborgs can subvert the apocalypse of returning to nuclear dust in the manic compulsion to name the Enemy. Cyborgs are not reverent; they do not re-member the cosmos. They are wary of holism, but needy for connection– they seem to have a natural feel for united front politics, but without the vanguard party. The main trouble with cyborgs, of course, is that they are the illegitimate offspring of militarism and patriarchal capitalism, not to mention state socialism. But illegitimate offspring are often exceedingly unfaithful to their origins. Their fathers, after all, are inessential.

I will return to the science fiction of cyborgs at the end of this chapter, but now I want to signal three crucial boundary breakdowns that make the following political-fictional (political-scientific) analysis possible. By the late twentieth century in United States scientific culture, the boundary between human and animal is thoroughly breached. The last beachheads of uniqueness have been polluted if not turned into amusement parks – language, tool use, social behaviour, mental events, nothing really convincingly settles the separation of human and animal. And many people no longer feel the need for such a separation; indeed, many branches of feminist culture affirm the pleasure of connection of human and other living creatures. Movements for animal rights are not irrational denials of human uniqueness; they are a clear-sighted recognition of connection across the discredited breach of nature and culture. Biology and evolutionary theory over the last two centuries have simultaneously produced modern organisms as objects of knowledge and reduced the line between humans and animals to a faint trace re-etched in ideological struggle or professional disputes between life and social science. Within this framework, teaching modern Christian creationism should be fought as a form of child abuse.

Biological-determinist ideology is only one position opened up in scientific culture for arguing the meanings of human animality. There is much room for radical political people to contest the meanings of the breached boundary.[2] The cyborg appears in myth precisely where the boundary between human and animal is transgressed. Far from signalling a walling off of people from other living beings, cyborgs signal disturbingly and pleasurably tight coupling. Bestiality has a new status in this cycle of marriage exchange.

The second leaky distinction is between animal-human (organism) and machine. Pre-cybernetic machines could be haunted; there was always the spectre of the ghost in the machine. This dualism structured the dialogue between materialism and idealism that was settled by a dialectical progeny, called spirit or history, according to taste. But basically machines were not self-moving, self-designing, autonomous. They could not achieve man's dream, only mock it. They were not man, an author to himself, but only a caricature of that masculinist reproductive dream. To think they were otherwise was paranoid. Now we are not so sure. Late twentieth-century machines have made thoroughly ambiguous the difference between natural and artificial, mind and body, self-developing and externally designed, and many other distinctions that used to apply to organisms and machines. Our machines are disturbingly lively, and we ourselves frighteningly inert.

Technological determination is only one ideological space opened up by the reconceptions of machine and organism as coded texts through which we engage in the play of writing and reading the world.[3] 'Textualization' of everything in poststructuralist, postmodernist theory has been damned by Marxists and socialist feminists for its utopian disregard for the lived relations of domination that ground the 'play' of arbitrary reading.[4] It is certainly true that postmodernist strategies, like my cyborg myth, subvert myriad organic wholes (for example, the poem, the primitive culture, the biological organism). In short, the certainty of what counts as nature – a source of insight and promise of innocence – is undermined, probably fatally. The transcendent authorization of interpretation is lost, and with it the ontology grounding 'Western' epistemology. But the alternative is not cynicism or faithlessness, that is, some version of abstract existence, like the accounts of technological determinism destroying 'man' by the 'machine' or 'meaningful political action' by the 'text'. Who cyborgs will be is a radical question; the answers are a matter of survival. Both chimpanzees and artefacts have politics, so why shouldn't we (de Waal, 1982; Winner, 1980)?

The third distinction is a subset of the second: the boundary between physical and non-physical is very imprecise for us. Pop physics books on the consequences of quantum theory and the indeterminacy principle are a kind of popular scientific equivalent to Harlequin romances* as a marker of radical change in American white heterosexuality: they get it wrong, but they are on the right subject. Modern machines are quintessentially microelectronic devices: they are everywhere and they are invisible. Modern machinery is an irreverent upstart god, mocking the Father's ubiquity and spirituality. The silicon chip is a surface for writing; it is etched in molecular scales disturbed only by atomic noise, the ultimate interference for nuclear scores. Writing, power, and technology are old partners in Western stories of the origin of civilization, but miniaturization has changed our experience of mechanism. Miniaturization has turned out to be about power; small is not so much beautiful as pre-eminently dangerous, as in cruise missiles. Contrast the TV sets of the 1950s or the news cameras of the 1970s with the TV wrist bands or hand-sized video cameras now advertised. Our best machines are made of sunshine; they are all light and clean because they are nothing but signals, electromagnetic waves, a section of a spectrum, and these machines are eminently portable, mobile – a matter of immense human pain in Detroit and Singapore. People are nowhere near so fluid, being both material and opaque. Cyborgs are ether, quintessence.

The ubiquity and invisibility of cyborgs is precisely why these sunshine-belt machines are so deadly. They are as hard to see politically as materially. They are about consciousness – or its simulation.[5] They are floating signifiers moving in pickup trucks across Europe, blocked more effectively by the witch-weavings of the displaced and so unnatural Greenham women, who read the cyborg webs of power so very well, than by the militant labour of older masculinist politics, whose natural constituency needs defence jobs. Ultimately the 'hardest' science is about the realm of greatest boundary confusion, the realm of pure number, pure spirit, C^3I, cryptography, and the preservation of potent secrets. The new machines are so clean and light. Their engineers are sun-worshippers mediating a new scientific revolution

* The US equivalent of Mills & Boon.

associated with the night dream of post-industrial society. The diseases evoked by these clean machines are 'no more' than the minuscule coding changes of an antigen in the immune system, 'no more' than the experience of stress. The nimble fingers of 'Oriental' women, the old fascination of little Anglo-Saxon Victorian girls with doll's houses, women's enforced attention to the small take on quite new dimensions in this world. There might be a cyborg Alice taking account of these new dimensions. Ironically, it might be the unnatural cyborg women making chips in Asia and spiral dancing in Santa Rita jail* whose constructed unities will guide effective oppositional strategies.

So my cyborg myth is about transgressed boundaries, potent fusions, and dangerous possibilities which progressive people might explore as one part of needed political work. One of my premises is that most American socialists and feminists see deepened dualisms of mind and body, animal and machine, idealism and materialism in the social practices, symbolic formulations, and physical artefacts associated with 'high technology' and scientific culture. From *One-Dimensional Man* (Marcuse, 1964) to *The Death of Nature* (Merchant, 1980), the analytic resources developed by progressives have insisted on the necessary domination of technics and recalled us to an imagined organic body to integrate our resistance. Another of my premises is that the need for unity of people trying to resist world-wide intensification of domination has never been more acute. But a slightly perverse shift of perspective might better enable us to contest for meanings, as well as for other forms of power and pleasure in technologically mediated societies.

From one perspective, a cyborg world is about the final imposition of a grid of control on the planet, about the final abstraction embodied in a Star Wars apocalypse waged in the name of defence, about the final appropriation of women's bodies in a masculinist orgy of war (Sofia, 1984). From another perspective, a cyborg world might be about lived social and bodily realities in which people are not afraid of their joint kinship with animals and machines, not afraid of permanently partial identities and contradictory standpoints. The political struggle is to see from both perspectives at once because each reveals both dominations and possibilities unimaginable from the other vantage point. Single vision produces worse illusions than double vision or many-headed monsters. Cyborg unities are monstrous and illegitimate; in our present political circumstances, we could hardly hope for more potent myths for resistance and recoupling. I like to imagine LAG, the Livermore Action Group, as a kind of cyborg society, dedicated to realistically converting the laboratories that most fiercely embody and spew out the tools

---

* A practice at once both spiritual and political that linked guards and arrested anti-nuclear demonstrators in the Alameda County jail in California in the early 1980s.

of technological apocalypse, and committed to building a political form that acutally manages to hold together witches, engineers, elders, perverts, Christians, mothers, and Leninists long enough to disarm the state. Fission Impossible is the name of the affinity group in my town .(Affinity: related not by blood but by choice, the appeal of one chemical nuclear group for another, avidity.)[6]

FRACTURED IDENTITIES

It has become difficult to name one's feminism by a single adjective – or even to insist in every circumstance upon the noun. Consciousness of exclusion through naming is acute. Identities seem contradictory, partial, and strategic. With the hard-won recognition of their social and historical constitution, gender, race, and class cannot provide the basis for belief in 'essential' unity. There is nothing about being 'female' that naturally binds women. There is not even such a state as 'being' female, itself a highly complex category constructed in contested sexual scientific discourses and other social practices. Gender, race, or class consciousness is an achievement forced on us by the terrible historical experience of the contradictory social realities of patriarchy, colonialism, and capitalism. And who counts as 'us' in my own rhetoric? Which identities are available to ground such a potent political myth called 'us', and what could motivate enlistment in this collectivity? Painful fragmentation among feminists (not to mention among women) along every possible fault line has made the concept of *woman* elusive, an excuse for the matrix of women's dominations of each other. For me – and for many who share a similar historical location in white, professional middle-class, female, radical, North American, mid-adult bodies – the sources of a crisis in political identity are legion. The recent history for much of the US left and US feminism has been a response to this kind of crisis by endless splitting and searches for a new essential unity. But there has also been a growing recognition of another response through coalition – affinity, not identity.[7]

Chela Sandoval (n.d., 1984), from a consideration of specific historical moments in the formation of the new political voice called women of colour, has theorized a hopeful model of political identity called 'oppositional consciousness', born of the skills for reading webs of power by those refused stable membership in the social categories of race, sex, or class. 'Women of color', a name contested at its origins by those whom it would incorporate, as well as a historical consciousness marking systematic breakdown of all the signs of Man in 'Western' traditions, constructs a kind of postmodernist identity out of otherness, difference, and specificity. This postmodernist identity is fully political, whatever might be said about other possible postmodernisms. Sandoval's oppositional consciousness is about contradictory locations and heterochronic calendars, not about relativisms and pluralisms.

Sandoval emphasizes the lack of any essential criterion for identifying who is a woman of colour. She notes that the definition of the group has been by conscious appropriation of negation. For example, a Chicana or US black woman has not been able to speak as a woman or as a black person or as a Chicano. Thus, she was at the bottom of a cascade of negative identities, left out of even the privileged oppressed authorial categories called 'women and blacks', who claimed to make the important revolutions. The category 'woman' negated all non-white women; 'black' negated all non-black people, as well as all black women. But there was also no 'she', no singularity, but a sea of differences among US women who have affirmed their historical identity as US women of colour. This identity marks out a self-consciously constructed space that cannot affirm the capacity to act on the basis of natural identification, but only on the basis of conscious coalition, of affinity, of political kinship.[8] Unlike the 'woman' of some streams of the white women's movement in the United States, there is no naturalization of the matrix, or at least this is what Sandoval argues is uniquely available through the power of oppositional consciousness.

Sandoval's argument has to be seen as one potent formulation for feminists out of the world-wide development of anti-colonialist discourse; that is to say, discourse dissolving the 'West' and its highest product – the one who is not animal, barbarian, or woman; man, that is, the author of a cosmos called history. As orientalism is deconstructed politically and semiotically, the identities of the occident destabilize, including those of feminists.[9] Sandoval argues that 'women of colour' have a chance to build an effective unity that does not replicate the imperializing, totalizing revolutionary subjects of previous Marxisms and feminisms which had not faced the consequences of the disorderly polyphony emerging from decolonization.

Katie King has emphasized the limits of identification and the political/poetic mechanics of identification built into reading 'the poem', that generative core of cultural feminism. King criticizes the persistent tendency among contemporary feminists from different 'moments' or 'conversations' in feminist practice to taxonomize the women's movement to make one's own political tendencies appear to be the *telos* of the whole. These taxonomies tend to remake feminist history so that it appears to be an ideological struggle among coherent types persisting over time, especially those typical units called radical, liberal, and socialist-feminism. Literally, all other feminisms are either incorporated or marginalized, usually by building an explicit ontology and epistemology.[10] Taxonomies of feminism produce epistemologies to police deviation from official women's experience. And of course, 'women's culture', like women of colour, is consciously created by mechanisms inducing affinity. The rituals of poetry, music, and certain forms of academic practice have been pre-eminent. The politics of race and culture in the US women's movements are intimately interwoven. The common achievement of King and Sandoval is learning how to craft a poetic/political unity without relying on a logic of appropriation, incorporation, and taxonomic identification.

The theoretical and practical struggle against unity-through-domination or unity-through-incorporation ironically not only undermines the justifications for patriarchy, colonialism, humanism, positivism, essentialism, scientism, and other unlamented -isms, but *all* claims for an organic or natural standpoint. I think that radical and socialist/Marxist-feminisms have also undermined their/our own epistemological strategies and that this is a crucially valuable step in imagining possible unities. It remains to be seen whether all 'epistemologies' as Western political people have known them fail us in the task to build effective affinities.

It is important to note that the effort to construct revolutionary standpoints, epistemologies as achievements of people committed to changing the world, has been part of the process showing the limits of identification. The acid tools of postmodernist theory and the constructive tools of ontological discourse about revolutionary subjects might be seen as ironic allies in dissolving Western selves in the interests of survival. We are excruciatingly conscious of what it means to have a historically constituted body. But with the loss of innocence in our origin, there is no expulsion from the Garden either. Our politics lose the indulgence of guilt with the *naïveté* of innocence. But what would another political myth for socialist-feminism look like? What kind of politics could embrace partial, contradictory, permanently unclosed constructions of personal and collective selves and still be faithful, effective – and, ironically, socialist-feminist?

I do not know of any other time in history when there was greater need for political unity to confront effectively the dominations of 'race', 'gender', 'sexuality', and 'class'. I also do not know of any other time when the kind of unity we might help build could have been possible. None of 'us' have any longer the symbolic or material capability of dictating the shape of reality to any of 'them'. Or at least 'we' cannot claim innocence from practising such dominations. White women, including socialist feminists, discovered (that is, were forced kicking and screaming to notice) the non-innocence of the category 'woman'. That consciousness changes the geography of all previous categories; it denatures them as heat denatures a fragile protein. Cyborg feminists have to argue that 'we' do not want any more natural matrix of unity and that no construction is whole. Innocence, and the corollary insistence on victimhood as the only ground for insight, has done enough damage. But the constructed revolutionary subject must give late-twentieth-century people pause as well. In the fraying of identities and in the reflexive strategies for constructing them, the possibility opens up for weaving something other than a shroud for the day after the apocalypse that so prophetically ends salvation history.

Both Marxist/socialist-feminisms and radical feminisms have simultaneously naturalized and denatured the category 'woman' and consciousness of the social lives of 'women'. Perhaps a schematic caricature can highlight both kinds of moves. Marxian socialism is rooted in an analysis of wage labour which reveals class structure. The consequence of the wage relationship is systematic alienation, as the worker is dissociated from his (sic) product. Abstraction and illusion rule in knowledge, domination rules in practice. Labour is the pre-eminently privileged category enabling the Marxist to overcome illusion and find that point of view which is necessary for changing the world. Labour is the humanizing activity that makes man; labour is an ontological category permitting the knowledge of a subject, and so the knowledge of subjugation and alienation.

In faithful filiation, socialist-feminism advanced by allying itself with the basic analytic strategies of Marxism. The main achievement of both Marxist feminists and socialist feminists was to expand the category of labour to accommodate what (some) women did, even when the wage relation was subordinated to a more comprehensive view of labour under capitalist patriarchy. In particular, women's labour in the household and women's activity as mothers generally (that is, reproduction in the socialist-feminist sense), entered theory on the authority of analogy to the Marxian concept of labour. The unity of women here rests on an epistemology based on the ontological structure of 'labour'. Marxist/socialist-feminism does not 'naturalize' unity; it is a possible achievement based on a possible standpoint rooted in social relations. The essentializing move is in the ontological structure of labour or of its analogue, women's activity.[11] The inheritance of Marxian humanism, with its pre-eminently Western self, is the difficulty for me. The contribution from these formulations has been the emphasis on the daily responsibility of real women to build unities, rather than to naturalize them.

Catherine MacKinnon's (1982, 1987) version of radical feminism is itself a caricature of the appropriating, incorporating, totalizing tendencies of Western theories of identity grounding action.[12] It is factually and politically wrong to assimilate all of the diverse 'moments' or 'conversations' in recent women's politics named radical feminism to MacKinnon's version. But the teleological logic of her theory shows how an epistemology and ontology – including their negations – erase or police difference. Only one of the effects of MacKinnon's theory is the rewriting of the history of the polymorphous field called radical feminism. The major effect is the production of a theory of experience, of women's identity, that is a kind of apocalypse for all revolutionary standpoints. That is, the totalization built into this tale of radical feminism achieves its end – the unity of women – by enforcing the experience of and testimony to radical non-being. As for the Marxist/ socialist feminist, consciousness is an achievement, not a natural fact. And MacKinnon's theory eliminates some of the difficulties built into humanist revolutionary subjects, but at the cost of radical reductionism.

MacKinnon argues that feminism necessarily adopted a different analytical strategy from Marxism, looking first not at the structure of class, but at the structure of sex/gender and its generative relationship, men's constitution and appropriation of women sexually. Ironically, MacKinnon's 'ontology' constructs a non-subject, a non-being. Another's desire, not the self's labour, is the origin of 'woman'. She therefore develops a theory of consciousness that enforces what can count as 'women's' experience – anything that names sexual violation, indeed, sex itself as far as 'women' can be concerned. Feminist practice is the construction of this form of consciousness; that is, the self-knowledge of a self-who-is-not.

Perversely, sexual appropriation in this feminism still has the epistemological status of labour; that is to say, the point from which an analysis able to contribute to changing the world must flow. But sexual objectification, not alienation, is the consequence of the structure of sex/gender. In the realm of knowledge, the result of sexual objectification is illusion and abstraction. However, a woman is not simply alienated from her product, but in a deep sense does not exist as a subject, or even potential subject, since she owes her existence as a woman to sexual appropriation. To be constituted by another's desire is not the same thing as to be alienated in the violent separation of the labourer from his product.

MacKinnon's radical theory of experience is totalizing in the extreme; it does not so much marginalize as obliterate the authority of any other women's political speech and action. It is a totalization producing what Western patriarchy itself never succeeded in doing – feminists' consciousness of the non-existence of women, except as products of men's desire. I think MacKinnon correctly argues that no Marxian version of identity can firmly ground women's unity. But in solving the problem of the contradictions of any Western revolutionary subject for feminist purposes, she develops an even more authoritarian doctrine of experience. If my complaint about socialist/Marxian standpoints is their unintended erasure of polyvocal, unassimilable, radical difference made visible in anti-colonial discourse and practice, MacKinnon's intentional erasure of all difference through the device of the 'essential' non-existence of women is not reassuring.

In my taxonomy, which like any other taxonomy is a re-inscription of history, radical feminism can accommodate all the activities of women named by socialist feminists as forms of labour only if the activity can somehow be sexualized. Reproduction had different tones of meanings for the two tendencies, one rooted in labour, one in sex, both calling the consequences of domination and ignorance of social and personal reality 'false consciousness'.

Beyond either the difficulties or the contributions in the argument of any one author, neither Marxist nor radical feminist points of view have tended to embrace the status of a partial explanation; both were regularly constituted as totalities. Western explanation has demanded as much; how else could the 'Western' author incorporate its others? Each tried to annex other forms of domination by expanding its basic categories through analogy, simple listing, or addition. Embarrassed silence about race among white radical and socialist feminists was one major, devastating political consequence. History and polyvocality disappear into political taxonomies that try to establish genealogies. There was no structural room for race (or for much else) in theory claiming to reveal the construction of the category woman and social group women as a unified or totalizable whole. The structure of my caricature looks like this:

socialist feminism – structure of class // wage labour // alienation
labour, by analogy reproduction, by extension sex, by addition race
radical feminism – structure of gender // sexual appropriation // objectification
sex, by analogy labour, by extension reproduction, by addition race

In another context, the French theorist, Julia Kristeva, claimed women appeared as a historical group after the Second World War, along with groups like youth. Her dates are doubtful; but we are now accustomed to remembering that as objects of knowledge and as historical actors, 'race' did not always exist, 'class' has a historical genesis, and 'homosexuals' are quite junior. It is no accident that the symbolic system of the family of man – and so the essence of woman – breaks up at the same moment that networks of connection among people on the planet are unprecedentedly multiple, pregnant, and complex. 'Advanced capitalism' is inadequate to convey the structure of this historical moment. In the 'Western' sense, the end of man is at stake. It is no accident that woman disintegrates into women in our time. Perhaps socialist feminists were not substantially guilty of producing essentialist theory that suppressed women's particularity and contradictory interests. I think we have been, at least through unreflective participation in the logics, languages, and practices of white humanism and through searching for a single ground of domination to secure our revolutionary voice. Now we have less excuse. But in the consciousness of our failures, we risk lapsing into boundless difference and giving up on the confusing task of making partial, real connection. Some differences are playful; some are poles of world historical systems of domination. 'Epistemology' is about knowing the difference.

THE INFORMATICS OF DOMINATION

In this attempt at an epistemological and political position, I would like to sketch a picture of possible unity, a picture indebted to socialist and feminist principles of design. The frame for my sketch is set by the extent and importance of rearrangements in world-wide social relations tied to science and technology. I argue for a politics rooted in claims about fundamental changes in the nature of class, race, and gender in an emerging system of world order analogous in its novelty and scope to that created by industrial capitalism; we are living through a movement from an organic, industrial society to a polymorphous, information system – from all work to all play, a deadly game. Simultaneously material and ideological, the dichotomies may be expressed in the following chart of transitions from the comfortable old hierarchical dominations to the scary new networks I have called the informatics of domination:

Representation	Simulation
Bourgeois novel, realism	Science fiction, postmodernism
Organism	Biotic component
Depth, integrity	Surface, boundary
Heat	Noise
Biology as clinical practice	Biology as inscription
Physiology	Communications engineering
Small group	Subsystem
Perfection	Optimization
Eugenics	Population Control
Decadence, *Magic Mountain*	Obsolescence, *Future Shock*
Hygiene	Stress Management
Microbiology, tuberculosis	Immunology, AIDS
Organic division of labour	Ergonomics / cybernetics of labour
Functional specialization	Modular construction
Reproduction	Replication
Organic sex role specialization	Optimal genetic strategies
Biological determinism	Evolutionary inertia, constraints
Community ecology	Ecosystem
Racial chain of being	Neo-imperialism, United Nations humanism

Scientific management in home / factory	Global factory / Electronic cottage
Family / Market / Factory	Women in the Integrated Circuit
Family wage	Comparable worth
Public / Private	Cyborg citizenship
Nature / Culture	Fields of difference
Co-operation	Communications enhancement
Freud	Lacan
Sex	Genetic engineering
Labour	Robotics
Mind	Artificial Intelligence
Second World War	Star Wars
White Capitalist Patriarchy	Informatics of Domination

This list suggests several interesting things.[13] First, the objects on the right-hand side cannot be coded as 'natural', a realization that subverts naturalistic coding for the left-hand side as well. We cannot go back ideologically or materially. It's not just that 'god' is dead; so is the 'goddess'. Or both are revivified in the worlds charged with microelectronic and biotechnological politics. In relation to objects like biotic components, one must think not in terms of essential properties, but in terms of design, boundary constraints, rates of flows, systems logics, costs of lowering constraints. Sexual reproduction is one kind of reproductive strategy among many, with costs and benefits as a function of the system environment. Ideologies of sexual reproduction can no longer reasonably call on notions of sex and sex role as organic aspects in natural objects like organisms and families. Such reasoning will be unmasked as irrational, and ironically corporate executives reading *Playboy* and anti-porn radical feminists will make strange bedfellows in jointly unmasking the irrationalism.

Likewise for race, ideologies about human diversity have to be formulated in terms of frequencies of parameters, like blood groups or intelligence scores. It is 'irrational' to invoke concepts like primitive and civilized. For liberals and radicals, the search for integrated social systems gives way to a new practice called 'experimental ethnography' in which an organic object dissipates in attention to the play of writing. At the level of ideology, we see translations of racism and colonialism into languages of development and under-development, rates and constraints of modernization. Any objects or persons can be reasonably thought of in terms of disassembly and reassembly; no 'natural' architectures constrain system design. The financial districts in all the world's cities, as well as the export-processing and free-trade zones, proclaim this elementary fact of 'late capitalism'. The entire universe of objects that can be known scientifically must be formulated as problems in communications engineering (for the managers) or theories of the text (for those who would resist). Both are cyborg semiologies.

One should expect control strategies to concentrate on boundary conditions and interfaces, on rates of flow across boundaries – and not on the integrity of natural objects. 'Integrity' or 'sincerity' of the Western self gives way to decision procedures and expert systems. For example, control strategies applied to women's capacities to give birth to new human beings will be developed in the languages of population control and maximization of goal achievement for individual decision-makers. Control strategies will be formulated in terms of rates, costs of constraints, degrees of freedom. Human beings, like any other component or subsystem, must be localized in a system architecture whose basic modes of operation are probabilistic, statistical. No objects, spaces, or bodies are sacred in themselves; any component can be interfaced with any other if the proper standard, the proper code, can be constructed for processing signals in a common language. Exchange in this world transcends the universal translation effected by capitalist markets that Marx analysed so well. The privileged pathology affecting all kinds of components in this universe is stress – communications breakdown (Hogness, 1983). The cyborg is not subject to Foucault's biopolitics; the cyborg simulates politics, a much more potent field of operations.

This kind of analysis of scientific and cultural objects of knowledge which have appeared historically since the Second World War prepares us to notice some important inadequacies in feminist analysis which has proceeded as if the organic, hierarchical dualisms ordering discourse in 'the West' since Aristotle still ruled. They have been cannibalized, or as Zoe Sofia (Sofoulis) might put it, they have been 'techno-digested'. The dichotomies between mind and body, animal and human, organism and machine, public and private, nature and culture, men and women, primitive and civilized are all in question ideologically. The actual situation of women is their integration/ exploitation into a world system of production/reproduction and communication called the informatics of domination. The home, workplace, market, public arena, the body itself – all can be dispersed and interfaced in nearly infinite, polymorphous ways, with large consequences for women and others – consequences that themselves are very different for different people and which make potent oppositional international movements difficult to imagine and essential for survival. One important route for reconstructing socialist-feminist politics is through theory and practice addressed to the social relations of science and technology, including crucially the systems of myth and meanings structuring our imaginations. The cyborg is a kind of disassembled and reassembled, postmodern collective and personal self. This is the self feminists must code.

Communications technologies and biotechnologies are the crucial tools recrafting our bodies. These tools embody and enforce new social relations for women world-wide. Technologies and scientific discourses can be partially understood as formalizations, i.e., as frozen moments, of the fluid social interactions constituting them, but they should also be viewed as instruments for enforcing meanings. The boundary is permeable between tool and myth, instrument and concept, historical systems of social relations and historical anatomies of possible bodies, including objects of knowledge. Indeed, myth and tool mutually constitute each other.

Furthermore, communications sciences and modern biologies are constructed by a common move – *the translation of the world into a problem of coding,* a search for a common language in which all resistance to instrumental control disappears and all heterogeneity can be submitted to disassembly, reassembly, investment, and exchange.

In communications sciences, the translation of the world into a problem in coding can be illustrated by looking at cybernetic (feedback-controlled) systems theories applied to telephone technology, computer design, weapons deployment, or data base construction and maintenance. In each case, solution to the key questions rests on a theory of language and control; the key operation is determining the rates, directions, and probabilities of flow of a quantity called information. The world is subdivided by boundaries differentially permeable to information. Information is just that kind of quantifiable element (unit, basis of unity) which allows universal translation, and so unhindered instrumental power (called effective communication). The biggest threat to such power is interruption of communication. Any system breakdown is a function of stress. The fundamentals of this technology can be condensed into the metaphor C^3I, command-control-communication-intelligence, the military's symbol for its operations theory.

In modern biologies, the translation of the world into a problem in coding can be illustrated by molecular genetics, ecology, sociobiological evolutionary theory, and immunobiology. The organism has been translated into problems of genetic coding and read-out. Biotechnology, a writing technology, informs research broadly.[14] In a sense, organisms have ceased to exist as objects of knowledge, giving way to biotic components, i.e., special kinds of information-processing devices. The analogous moves in ecology could be examined by probing the history and utility of the concept of the ecosystem. Immunobiology and associated medical practices are rich exemplars of the privilege of coding and recognition systems as objects of knowledge, as constructions of bodily reality for us. Biology here is a kind of cryptography. Research is necessarily a kind of intelligence activity. Ironies abound. A stressed system goes awry; its communication processes break down; it fails to recognize the difference between self and other. Human babies with baboon hearts evoke national ethical perplexity – for animal rights activists at least as much as for the guardians of human purity. In the US gay men and intravenous drug users are the 'privileged' victims of an awful immune system disease that marks (inscribes on the body) confusion of boundaries and moral pollution (Treichler, 1987).

But these excursions into communications sciences and biology have been at a rarefied level; there is a mundane, largely economic reality to support my claim that these sciences and technologies indicate fundamental transformations in the structure of the world for us. Communications technologies depend on electronics. Modern states, multinational corporations, military power, welfare state apparatuses, satellite systems, political processes, fabrication of our imaginations, labour-control systems, medical constructions of our bodies, commercial pornography, the international division of labour, and religious evangelism depend intimately upon electronics. Microelectronics is the technical basis of simulacra; that is, of copies without originals.

Microelectronics mediates the translations of labour into robotics and word processing, sex into genetic engineering and reproductive technologies, and mind into artificial intelligence and decision procedures. The new biotechnologies concern more than human reproduction. Biology as a powerful engineering science for redesigning materials and processes has revolutionary implications for industry, perhaps most obvious today in areas of fermentation, agriculture, and energy. Communications sciences and biology are constructions of natural-technical objects of knowledge in which the difference between machine and organism is thoroughly blurred; mind, body, and tool are on very intimate terms. The 'multinational' material organization of the production and reproduction of daily life and the symbolic organization of the production and reproduction of culture and imagination seem equally implicated. The boundary-maintaining images of base and superstructure, public and private, or material and ideal never seemed more feeble.

I have used Rachel Grossman's (1980) image of women in the integrated circuit to name the situation of women in a world so intimately restructured through the social relations of science and technology.[15] I used the odd circumlocution, 'the social relations of science and technology', to indicate that we are not dealing with a technological determinism, but with a historical system depending upon structured relations among people. But the phrase should also indicate that science and technology provide fresh sources of power, that we need fresh sources of analysis and political action (Latour, 1984). Some of the rearrangements of race, sex, and class rooted in high-tech-facilitated social relations can make socialist-feminism more relevant to effective progressive politics.

THE 'HOMEWORK ECONOMY' OUTSIDE 'THE HOME'

The 'New Industrial Revolution' is producing a new world-wide working class, as well as new sexualities and ethnicities. The extreme mobility of capital and the emerging international division of labour are intertwined with the emergence of new collectivities, and the weakening of familiar groupings. These developments are neither gender- nor race-neutral. White men in advanced industrial societies have become newly vulnerable to permanent job loss, and women are not disappearing from the job rolls at the same rates as men. It is not simply that women in Third World countries are the preferred labour force for the science-based multinationals in the export-processing sectors, particularly in electronics. The picture is more systematic and involves reproduction, sexuality, culture, consumption, and production. In the prototypical Silicon Valley, many women's lives have been structured around employment in electronics-dependent jobs, and their intimate realities include serial heterosexual monogamy, negotiating childcare, distance from extended kin or most other forms of traditional community, a high likelihood of loneliness and extreme economic vulnerability as they age. The ethnic and racial diversity of women in Silicon Valley structures a microcosm of conflicting differences in culture, family, religion, education, and language.

Richard Gordon has called this new situation the 'homework economy'.[16] Although he includes the phenomenon of literal homework emerging in connection with electronics assembly, Gordon intends 'homework economy' to name a restructuring of work that broadly has the characteristics formerly ascribed to female jobs, jobs literally done only by women. Work is being redefined as both literally female and feminized, whether performed by men or women. To be feminized means to be made extremely vulnerable; able to be disassembled, reassembled, exploited as a reserve labour force; seen less as workers than as servers; subjected to time arrangements on and off the paid job that make a mockery of a limited work day; leading an existence that always borders on being obscene, out of place, and reducible to sex. Deskilling is an old strategy newly applicable to formerly privileged workers. However, the homework economy does not refer only to large-scale deskilling, nor does it deny that new areas of high skill are emerging, even for women and men previously excluded from skilled employment. Rather, the concept indicates that factory, home, and market are integrated on a new scale and that the places of women are crucial – and need to be analysed for differences among women and for meanings for relations between men and women in various situations.

The homework economy as a world capitalist organizational structure is made possible by (not caused by) the new technologies. The success of the attack on relatively privileged, mostly white, men's unionized jobs is tied to the power of the new communications technologies to integrate and control labour despite extensive dispersion and decentralization. The consequences of the new technologies are felt by women both in the loss of the family (male) wage (if they ever had access to this white privilege) and in the character of their own jobs, which are becoming capital-intensive; for example, office work and nursing.

The new economic and technological arrangements are also related to the collapsing welfare state and the ensuing intensification of demands on women to sustain daily life for themselves as well as for men, children, and old people. The feminization of poverty – generated by dismantling the welfare state, by the homework economy where stable jobs become the exception, and sustained by the expectation that women's wages will not be matched by a male income for the support of children – has become an urgent focus. The causes of various women-headed households are a function of race, class, or sexuality; but their increasing generality is a ground for coalitions of women on many issues. That women regularly sustain daily life partly as a function of their enforced status as mothers is hardly new; the kind of integration with the overall capitalist and progressively war-based economy is new. The particular pressure, for example, on US black women, who have achieved an escape from (barely) paid domestic service and who now hold clerical and similar jobs in large numbers, has large implications for continued enforced black poverty *with* employment. Teenage women in industrializing areas of the Third World increasingly find themselves the sole or major source of a cash wage for their families, while access to land is ever more problematic. These developments must have major consequences in the psychodynamics and politics of gender and race.

Within the framework of three major stages of capitalism (commercial/ early industrial, monopoly, multinational) – tied to nationalism, imperialism, and multinationalism, and related to Jameson's three dominant aesthetic periods of realism, modernism, and postmodernism – I would argue that specific forms of families dialectically relate to forms of capital and to its political and cultural concomitants. Although lived problematically and unequally, ideal forms of these families might be schematized as (1) the patriarchal nuclear family, structured by the dichotomy between public and private and accompanied by the white bourgeois ideology of separate spheres and nineteenth-century Anglo-American bourgeois feminism; (2) the modern family mediated (or enforced) by the welfare state and institutions like the family wage, with a flowering of a-feminist heterosexual ideologies, including their radical versions represented in Greenwich Village around the First World War; and (3) the 'family' of the homework economy with its oxymoronic structure of women-headed households and its explosion of feminisms and the paradoxical intensification and erosion of gender itself.

This is the context in which the projections for world-wide structural unemployment stemming from the new technologies are part of the picture of the homework economy. As robotics and related technologies put men out of work in 'developed' countries and exacerbate failure to generate male jobs in Third World 'development', and as the automated office becomes the rule even in labour-surplus countries, the feminization of work intensifies. Black women in the United States have long known what it looks like to face the structural underemployment ('feminization') of black men, as well as their own highly vulnerable position in the wage economy. It is no longer a secret that sexuality, reproduction, family, and community life are interwoven with this economic structure in myriad ways which have also differentiated the situations of white and black women. Many more women and men will contend with similar situations, which will make cross-gender and race alliances on issues of basic life support (with or without jobs) necessary, not just nice.

The new technologies also have a profound effect on hunger and on food production for subsistence world-wide. Rae Lessor Blumberg (1983) estimates that women produce about 50 per cent of the world's subsistence food.[17] Women are excluded generally from benefiting from the increased high-tech commodification of food and energy crops, their days are made more arduous because their responsibilities to provide food do not diminish, and their reproductive situations are made more complex. Green Revolution technologies interact with other high-tech industrial production to alter gender divisions of labour and differential gender migration patterns.

The new technologies seem deeply involved in the forms of 'privatization' that Ros Petchesky (1981) has analysed, in which militarization, right-wing family ideologies and policies, and intensified definitions of corporate (and state) property as private synergistically interact.[18] The new communications technologies are fundamental to the eradication of 'public life' for everyone. This facilitates the mushrooming of a permanent high-tech military establishment at the cultural and economic expense of most people, but especially of women. Technologies like video games and highly miniaturized televisions seem crucial to production of modern forms of 'private life'. The culture of video games is heavily orientated to individual competition and extraterrestrial warfare. High-tech, gendered imaginations are produced here, imaginations that can contemplate destruction of the planet and a sci-fi escape from its consequences. More than our imaginations is militarized; and the other realities of electronic and nuclear warfare are inescapable. These are the technologies that promise ultimate mobility and perfect exchange – and incidentally enable tourism, that perfect practice of mobility and exchange, to emerge as one of the world's largest single industries.

The new technologies affect the social relations of both sexuality and of reproduction, and not always in the same ways. The close ties of sexuality and instrumentality, of views of the body as a kind of private satisfaction- and utility-maximizing machine, are described nicely in sociobiological origin stories that stress a genetic calculus and explain the inevitable dialectic of domination of male and female gender roles.[19] These sociobiological stories depend on a high-tech view of the body as a biotic component or cybernetic communications system. Among the many transformations of reproductive situations is the medical one, where women's bodies have boundaries newly permeable to both 'visualization' and 'intervention'. Of course, who controls the interpretation of bodily boundaries in medical hermeneutics is a major feminist issue. The speculum served as an icon of women's claiming their bodies in the 1970s; that handcraft tool is inadequate to express our needed body politics in the negotiation of reality in the practices of cyborg reproduction. Self-help is not enough. The technologies of visualization recall the important cultural practice of hunting with the camera and the deeply predatory nature of a photographic consciousness.[20] Sex, sexuality, and reproduction are central actors in high-tech myth systems structuring our imaginations of personal and social possibility.

Another critical aspect of the social relations of the new technologies is the reformulation of expectations, culture, work, and reproduction for the large scientific and technical work-force. A major social and political danger is the formation of a strongly bimodal social structure, with the masses of women and men of all ethnic groups, but especially people of colour, confined to a homework economy, illiteracy of several varieties, and general redundancy and impotence, controlled by high-tech repressive apparatuses ranging from entertainment to surveillance and disappearance. An adequate socialist-feminist politics should address women in the privileged occupational categories, and particularly in the production of science and technology that constructs scientific-technical discourses, processes, and objects.[21]

This issue is only one aspect of enquiry into the possibility of a feminist science, but it is important. What kind of constitutive role in the production of knowledge, imagination, and practice can new groups doing science have? How can these groups be allied with progressive social and political movements? What kind of political accountability can be constructed to tie women together across the scientific-technical hierarchies separating us? Might there be ways of developing feminist science/technology politics in alliance with anti-military science facility conversion action groups? Many scientific and technical workers in Silicon Valley, the high-tech cowboys included, do not want to work on military science.[22] Can these personal preferences and cultural tendencies be welded into progressive politics among this professional middle class in which women, including women of colour, are coming to be fairly numerous?

WOMEN IN THE INTEGRATED CIRCUIT

Let me summarize the picture of women's historical locations in advanced industrial societies, as these positions have been restructured partly through the social relations of science and technology. If it was ever possible ideologically to characterize women's lives by the distinction of public and private domains – suggested by images of the division of working-class life into factory and home, of bourgeois life into market and home, and of gender existence into personal and political realms – it is now a totally misleading ideology, even to show how both terms of these dichotomies construct each other in practice and in theory. I prefer a network ideological image, suggesting the profusion of spaces and identities and the permeability of boundaries in the personal body and in the body politic. 'Networking' is both a feminist practice and a multinational corporate strategy – weaving is for oppositional cyborgs.

So let me return to the earlier image of the informatics of domination and trace one vision of women's 'place' in the integrated circuit, touching only a few idealized social locations seen primarily from the point of view of advanced capitalist societies: Home, Market, Paid Work Place, State, School, Clinic-Hospital, and Church. Each of these idealized spaces is logically and practically implied in every other locus, perhaps analogous to a holographic photograph. I want to suggest the impact of the social relations mediated and enforced by the new technologies in order to help formulate needed analysis and practical work. However, there is no 'place' for women in these networks, only geometrics of difference and contradiction crucial to women's cyborg identities. If we learn how to read these webs of power and social life, we might learn new couplings, new coalitions. There is no way to read the following list from a standpoint of 'identification', of a unitary self. The issue is dispersion. The task is to survive in the diaspora.

Home: Women-headed households, serial monogamy, flight of men, old women alone, technology of domestic work, paid homework, re-emergence of home sweat-shops, home-based businesses and telecommuting, electronic cottage, urban homelessness, migration, module architecture, reinforced (simulated) nuclear family, intense domestic violence.

Market: Women's continuing consumption work, newly targeted to buy the profusion of new production from the new technologies (especially as the competitive race among industrialized and industrializing nations to avoid dangerous mass unemployment necessitates finding ever bigger new markets for ever less clearly needed commodities); bimodal buying power, coupled with advertising targeting of the numerous affluent groups and neglect of the previous mass markets; growing importance of informal markets in labour and commodities parallel to high-tech, affluent market structures; surveillance systems through electronic funds transfer; intensified market abstraction (commodification) of experience, resulting in ineffective utopian or equivalent cynical theories of community; extreme mobility (abstraction) of marketing/financing systems; interpenetration of sexual and labour markets; intensified sexualization of abstracted and alienated consumption.

Paid Work Place: Continued intense sexual and racial division of labour, but considerable growth of membership in privileged occupational categories for many white women and people of colour; impact of new technologies on women's work in clerical, service, manufacturing (especially textiles), agriculture, electronics; international restructuring of the working classes; development of new time arrangements to facilitate the homework economy (flex time, part time, over time, no time); homework and out work; increased pressures for two-tiered wage structures; significant numbers of people in cash-dependent populations world-wide with no experience or no further hope of stable employment; most labour 'marginal' or 'feminized'.

State: Continued erosion of the welfare state; decentralizations with increased surveillance and control; citizenship by telematics; imperialism and political power broadly in the form of information rich/information poor differentiation; increased high-tech militarization increasingly opposed by many social groups; reduction of civil service jobs as a result of the growing capital intensification of office work, with implications for occupational mobility for women of colour; growing privatization of material and ideological life and culture; close integration of privatization and militarization, the high-tech forms of bourgeois capitalist personal and public life; invisibility of different social groups to each other, linked to psychological mechanisms of belief in abstract enemies.

School: Deepening coupling of high-tech capital needs and public education at all levels, differentiated by race, class, and gender; managerial classes involved in educational reform and refunding at the cost of remaining progressive educational democratic structures for children and teachers; education for mass ignorance and repression in technocratic and militarized culture; growing anti-science mystery cults in dissenting and radical political movements; continued relative scientific illiteracy among white women and people of colour; growing industrial direction of education (especially higher education) by science-based multinationals (particularly in electronics- and biotechnology-dependent companies); highly educated, numerous élites in a progressively bimodal society.

Clinic-hospital: Intensified machine–body relations; renegotiations of public metaphors which channel personal experience of the body, particularly in relation to reproduction, immune system functions, and 'stress' phenomena; intensification of reproductive politics in response to world historical implications of women's unrealized, potential control of their relation to reproduction; emergence of new, historically specific diseases; struggles over meanings and means of health in environments pervaded by high technology products and processes; continuing feminization of health work; intensified struggle over state responsibility for health; continued ideological role of popular health movements as a major form of American politics.

Church: Electronic fundamentalist 'super-saver' preachers solemnizing the union of electronic capital and automated fetish gods; intensified importance of churches in resisting the militarized state; central struggle over women's meanings and authority in religion; continued relevance of spirituality, intertwined with sex and health, in political struggle.

The only way to characterize the informatics of domination is as a massive intensification of insecurity and cultural impoverishment, with common failure of subsistence networks for the most vulnerable. Since much of this picture interweaves with the social relations of science and technology, the urgency of a socialist-feminist politics addressed to science and technology is plain. There is much now being done, and the grounds for political work are rich. For example, the efforts to develop forms of collective struggle for women in paid work, like SEIU's District 925,* should be a high priority for all of us. These efforts are profoundly tied to technical restructuring of labour processes and reformations of working classes. These efforts also are providing understanding of a more comprehensive kind of labour organization, involving community, sexuality, and family issues never privileged in the largely white male industrial unions.

The structural rearrangements related to the social relations of science and technology evoke strong ambivalence. But it is not necessary to be ultimately depressed by the implications of late twentieth-century women's relation to all aspects of work, culture, production of knowledge, sexuality, and reproduction. For excellent reasons, most Marxisms see domination best and have trouble understanding what can only look like false consciousness and people's complicity in their own domination in late capitalism. It is crucial to remember that what is lost, perhaps especially from women's points of view, is often virulent forms of oppression, nostalgically naturalized in the face of current violation. Ambivalence towards the disrupted unities mediated by high-tech culture requires not sorting consciousness into categories of 'clear-sighted critique grounding a solid political epistemology'

* Service Employees International Union's office workers' organization in the US.

versus 'manipulated false consciousness', but subtle understanding of emerging pleasures, experiences, and powers with serious potential for changing the rules of the game.

There are grounds for hope in the emerging bases for new kinds of unity across race, gender, and class, as these elementary units of socialist-feminist analysis themselves suffer protean transformations. Intensifications of hardship experienced world-wide in connection with the social relations of science and technology are severe. But what people are experiencing is not transparently clear, and we lack sufficiently subtle connections for collectively building effective theories of experience. Present efforts – Marxist, psychoanalytic, feminist, anthropological – to clarify even 'our' experience are rudimentary.

I am conscious of the odd perspective provided by my historical position – a PhD in biology for an Irish Catholic girl was made possible by Sputnik's impact on US national science-education policy. I have a body and mind as much constructed by the post-Second World War arms race and cold war as by the women's movements. There are more grounds for hope in focusing on the contradictory effects of politics designed to produce loyal American technocrats, which also produced large numbers of dissidents, than in focusing on the present defeats.

The permanent partiality of feminist points of view has consequences for our expectations of forms of political organization and participation. We do not need a totality in order to work well. The feminist dream of a common language, like all dreams for a perfectly true language, of perfectly faithful naming of experience, is a totalizing and imperialist one. In that sense, dialectics too is a dream language, longing to resolve contradiction. Perhaps, ironically, we can learn from our fusions with animals and machines how not to be Man, the embodiment of Western logos. From the point of view of pleasure in these potent and taboo fusions, made inevitable by the social relations of science and technology, there might indeed be a feminist science.

CYBORGS: A MYTH OF POLITICAL IDENTITY

I want to conclude with a myth about identity and boundaries which might inform late twentieth-century political imaginations (Plate 1). I am indebted in this story to writers like Joanna Russ, Samuel R. Delany, John Varley, James Tiptree, Jr, Octavia Butler, Monique Wittig, and Vonda McIntyre.[23] These are our story-tellers exploring what it means to be embodied in high-tech worlds. They are theorists for cyborgs. Exploring conceptions of bodily boundaries and social order, the anthropologist Mary Douglas (1966, 1970) should be credited with helping us to consciousness about how fundamental body imagery is to world view, and so to political language.

French feminists like Luce Irigaray and Monique Wittig, for all their differences, know how to write the body; how to weave eroticism, cosmology, and politics from imagery of embodiment, and especially for Wittig, from imagery of fragmentation and reconstitution of bodies.[24]

American radical feminists like Susan Griffin, Audre Lorde, and Adrienne Rich have profoundly affected our political imaginations – and perhaps restricted too much what we allow as a friendly body and political language.[25] They insist on the organic, opposing it to the technological. But their symbolic systems and the related positions of ecofeminism and feminist paganism, replete with organicisms, can only be understood in Sandoval's terms as oppositional ideologies fitting the late twentieth century. They would simply bewilder anyone not preoccupied with the machines and consciousness of late capitalism. In that sense they are part of the cyborg world. But there are also great riches for feminists in explicitly embracing the possibilities inherent in the breakdown of clean distinctions between organism and machine and similar distinctions structuring the Western self. It is the simultaneity of breakdowns that cracks the matrices of domination and opens geometric possibilities. What might be learned from personal and political 'technological' pollution? I look briefly at two overlapping groups of texts for their insight into the construction of a potentially helpful cyborg myth: constructions of women of colour and monstrous selves in feminist science fiction.

Earlier I suggested that 'women of colour' might be understood as a cyborg identity, a potent subjectivity synthesized from fusions of outsider identities and in the complex political-historical layerings of her 'biomythography', *Zami* (Lorde, 1982; King, 1987a, 1987b). There are material and cultural grids mapping this potential, Audre Lorde (1984) captures the tone in the title of her *Sister Outsider*. In my political myth, Sister Outsider is the offshore woman, whom US workers, female and feminized, are supposed to regard as the enemy preventing their solidarity, threatening their security. Onshore, inside the boundary of the United States, Sister Outsider is a potential amidst the races and ethnic identities of women manipulated for division, competition, and exploitation in the same industries. 'Women of colour' are the preferred labour force for the science-based industries, the real women for whom the world-wide sexual market, labour market, and politics of reproduction kaleidoscope into daily life. Young Korean women hired in the sex industry and in electronics assembly are recruited from high schools, educated for the integrated circuit. Literacy, especially in English, distinguishes the 'cheap' female labour so attractive to the multinationals.

Contrary to orientalist stereotypes of the 'oral primitive', literacy is a special mark of women of colour, acquired by US black women as well as men through a history of risking death to learn and to teach reading and writing. Writing has a special significance for all colonized groups. Writing has been crucial to the Western myth of the distinction between oral and written cultures, primitive and civilized mentalities, and more recently to the erosion of that distinction in 'postmodernist' theories attacking the phallogo-centrism of the West, with its worship of the monotheistic, phallic, authoritative, and singular work, the unique and perfect name.[26] Contests for the meanings of writing are a major form of contemporary political struggle. Releasing the play of writing is deadly serious. The poetry and stories of US women of colour are repeatedly about writing, about access to the power to signify; but this time that power must be neither phallic nor innocent. Cyborg writing must not be about the Fall, the imagination of a once-upon-a-time wholeness before language, before writing, before Man. Cyborg writing is about the power to survive, not on the basis of original innocence, but on the basis of seizing the tools to mark the world that marked them as other.

The tools are often stories, retold stories, versions that reverse and displace the hierarchical dualisms of naturalized identities. In retelling origin stories, cyborg authors subvert the central myths of origin of Western culture. We have all been colonized by those origin myths, with their longing for fulfilment in apocalypse. The phallogocentric origin stories most crucial for feminist cyborgs are built into the literal technologies – technologies that write the world, biotechnology and microelectronics – that have recently textualized our bodies as code problems on the grid of C^3I. Feminist cyborg stories have the task of recoding communication and intelligence to subvert command and control.

Figuratively and literally, language politics pervade the struggles of women of colour; and stories about language have a special power in the rich contemporary writing by US women of colour. For example, retellings of the story of the indigenous woman Malinche, mother of the mestizo 'bastard' race of the new world, master of languages, and mistress of Cortés, carry special meaning for Chicana constructions of identity. Cherríe Moraga (1983) in *Loving in the War Years* explores the themes of identity when one never possessed the original language, never told the original story, never resided in the harmony of legitimate heterosexuality in the garden of culture, and so cannot base identity on a myth or a fall from innocence and right to natural names, mother's or father's.[27] Moraga's writing, her superb literacy, is presented in her poetry as the same kind of violation as Malinche's mastery of the conqueror's language – a violation, an illegitimate production, that allows survival. Moraga's language is not 'whole'; it is self-consciously spliced, a chimera of English and Spanish, both conqueror's languages. But it is this chimeric monster, without claim to an original language before violation, that crafts the erotic, competent, potent identities of women of colour. Sister Outsider hints at the possibility of world survival not because of her innocence, but because of her ability to live on the boundaries, to write without the founding myth of original wholeness, with its inescapable apocalypse of final return to a deathly oneness that Man has imagined to be the innocent and all-powerful Mother, freed at the End from another spiral of appropriation by her son. Writing marks Moraga's body, affirms it as the body of a woman of colour, against the possibility of passing into the unmarked category of the Anglo father or into the orientalist myth of 'original illiteracy' of a mother that never was. Malinche was mother here, not Eve before eating the forbidden fruit. Writing affirms Sister Outsider, not the Woman-before-the-Fall-into-Writing needed by the phallogocentric Family of Man.

Writing is pre-eminently the technology of cyborgs, etched surfaces of the late twentieth century. Cyborg politics is the struggle for language and the struggle against perfect communication, against the one code that translates all meaning perfectly, the central dogma of phallogocentrism. That is why cyborg politics insist on noise and advocate pollution, rejoicing in the illegitimate fusions of animal and machine. These are the couplings which make Man and Woman so problematic, subverting the structure of desire, the force imagined to generate language and gender, and so subverting the structure and modes of reproduction of 'Western' identity, of nature and culture, of mirror and eye, slave and master, body and mind. 'We' did not originally choose to be cyborgs, but choice grounds a liberal politics and epistemology that imagines the reproduction of individuals before the wider replications of 'texts'.

From the perspective of cyborgs, freed of the need to ground politics in 'our' privileged position of the oppression that incorporates all other dominations, the innocence of the merely violated, the ground of those closer to nature, we can see powerful possibilities. Feminisms and Marxisms have run aground on Western epistemological imperatives to construct a revolutionary subject from the perspective of a hierarchy of oppressions and/or a latent position of moral superiority, innocence, and greater closeness to nature. With no available original dream of a common language or original symbiosis promising protection from hostile 'masculine' separation, but written into the play of a text that has no finally privileged reading or salvation history, to recognize 'oneself' as fully implicated in the world, frees us of the need to root politics in identification, vanguard parties, purity, and mothering. Stripped of identity, the bastard race teaches about the power of the margins and the importance of a mother like Malinche. Women of colour have transformed her from the evil mother of masculinist fear into the originally literate mother who teaches survival.

This is not just literary deconstruction, but liminal transformation. Every story that begins with original innocence and privileges the return to wholeness imagines the drama of life to be individuation, separation, the birth of the self, the tragedy of autonomy, the fall into writing, alienation; that is, war, tempered by imaginary respite in the bosom of the Other. These plots are ruled by a reproductive politics – rebirth without flaw, perfection, abstraction. In this plot women are imagined either better or worse off, but all agree they have less selfhood, weaker individuation, more fusion to the oral, to Mother, less at stake in masculine autonomy. But there is another route to having less at stake in masculine autonomy, a route that does not pass through Woman, Primitive, Zero, the Mirror Stage and its imaginary. It passes through women and other present-tense, illegitimate cyborgs, not of Woman born, who refuse the ideological resources of victimization so as to have a real life. These cyborgs are the people who refuse to disappear on cue, no matter how many times a 'Western' commentator remarks on the sad passing of another primitive, another organic group done in by 'Western' technology, by writing.[28] These real-life cyborgs (for example, the Southeast Asian village women workers in Japanese and US electronics firms described by Aihwa Ong) are actively rewriting the texts of their bodies and societies. Survival is the stakes in this play of readings.

To recapitulate, certain dualisms have been persistent in Western traditions; they have all been systemic to the logics and practices of domination of women, people of colour, nature, workers, animals – in short, domination of all constituted as others, whose task is to mirror the self. Chief among these troubling dualisms are self/other, mind/body, culture/nature, male/female, civilized/primitive, reality/appearance, whole/part, agent/resource, maker/made, active/passive, right/wrong, truth/illusion, total/partial, God/man. The self is the One who is not dominated, who knows that by the service of the other, the other is the one who holds the future, who knows that by the experience of domination, which gives the lie to the autonomy of the self. To be One is to be autonomous, to be powerful, to be God; but to be One is to be an illusion, and so to be involved in a dialectic of apocalypse with the other. Yet to be other is to be multiple, without clear boundary, frayed, insubstantial. One is too few, but two are too many.

High-tech culture challenges these dualisms in intriguing ways. It is not clear who makes and who is made in the relation between human and machine. It is not clear what is mind and what body in machines that resolve into coding practices. In so far as we know ourselves in both formal discourse (for example, biology) and in daily practice (for example, the homework economy in the integrated circuit), we find ourselves to be cyborgs, hybrids, mosaics, chimeras. Biological organisms have become biotic systems, communications devices like others. There is no fundamental, ontological separation in our formal knowledge of machine and organism, of technical and organic. The replicant Rachel in the Ridley Scott film *Blade Runner* stands as the image of a cyborg culture's fear, love, and confusion.

One consequence is that our sense of connection to our tools is heightened. The trance state experienced by many computer users has become a staple of science-fiction film and cultural jokes. Perhaps paraplegics and other severely handicapped people can (and sometimes do) have the most intense experiences of complex hybridization with other communication devices.[29] Anne McCaffrey's pre-feminist *The Ship Who Sang* (1969) explored the consciousness of a cyborg, hybrid of girl's brain and complex machinery, formed after the birth of a severely handicapped child. Gender, sexuality, embodiment, skill: all were reconstituted in the story. Why should our bodies end at the skin, or include at best other beings encapsulated by skin? From the seventeenth century till now, machines could be animated – given ghostly souls to make them speak or move or to account for their orderly development and mental capacities. Or organisms could be mechanized – reduced to body understood as resource of mind. These machine/organism relationships are obsolete, unnecessary. For us, in imagination and in other practice, machines can be prosthetic devices, intimate components, friendly selves. We don't need organic holism to give impermeable wholeness, the total woman and her feminist variants (mutants?). Let me conclude this point by a very partial reading of the logic of the cyborg monsters of my second group of texts, feminist science fiction.

The cyborgs populating feminist science fiction make very problematic the statuses of man or woman, human, artefact, member of a race, individual entity, or body. Katie King clarifies how pleasure in reading these fictions is not largely based on identification. Students facing Joanna Russ for the first time, students who have learned to take modernist writers like James Joyce or Virginia Woolf without flinching, do not know what to make of *The Adventures of Alyx* or *The Female Man*, where characters refuse the reader's search for innocent wholeness while granting the wish for heroic quests, exuberant eroticism, and serious politics. *The Female Man* is the story of four versions of one genotype, all of whom meet, but even taken together do not make a whole, resolve the dilemmas of violent moral action, or remove the growing scandal of gender. The feminist science fiction of Samuel R. Delany, especially *Tales of Nevèrÿon*, mocks stories of origin by redoing the neolithic revolution, replaying the founding moves of Western civilization to subvert their plausibility. James Tiptree, Jr, an author whose fiction was regarded as particularly manly until her 'true' gender was revealed, tells tales of reproduction based on non-mammalian technologies like alternation of generations of male brood pouches and male nurturing. John Varley constructs a supreme cyborg in his arch-feminist exploration of Gaea, a mad goddess-planet-trickster-old woman-technological device on whose surface an extraordinary array of post-cyborg symbioses are spawned. Octavia Butler writes of an African sorceress pitting her powers of transformation against the genetic manipulations of her rival (*Wild Seed*), of time warps that bring a modern US black woman into slavery where her actions in relation to her white master-ancestor determine the possibility of her own birth (*Kindred*), and of the illegitimate insights into identity and community of an adopted cross-species child who came to know the enemy as self (*Survivor*). In *Dawn* (1987), the first instalment of a series called *Xenogenesis*, Butler tells the story of Lilith Iyapo, whose personal name recalls Adam's first and repudiated wife and whose family name marks her status as the widow of the son of Nigerian immigrants to the US. A black woman and a mother whose child is dead, Lilith mediates the transformation of humanity through genetic exchange with extra-terrestrial lovers/rescuers/destroyers/genetic engineers, who reform earth's habitats after the nuclear holocaust and coerce surviving humans into intimate fusion with them. It is a novel that interrogates reproductive, linguistic, and nuclear politics in a mythic field structured by late twentieth-century race and gender.

Because it is particularly rich in boundary transgressions, Vonda McIntyre's *Superluminal* can close this truncated catalogue of promising and dangerous monsters who help redefine the pleasures and politics of embodiment and feminist writing. In a fiction where no character is 'simply' human, human status is highly problematic. Orca, a genetically altered diver, can speak with killer whales and survive deep ocean conditions, but she longs to explore space as a pilot, necessitating bionic implants jeopardizing her kinship with the divers and cetaceans. Transformations are effected by virus vectors carrying a new developmental code, by transplant surgery, by implants of microelectronic devices, by analogue doubles, and other means. Laenea becomes a pilot by accepting a heart implant and a host of other alterations allowing survival in transit at speeds exceeding that of light. Radu Dracul survives a virus-caused plague in his outerworld planet to find himself with a time sense that changes the boundaries of spatial perception for the whole species. All the characters explore the limits of language; the dream of communicating experience; and the necessity of limitation, partiality, and intimacy even in this world of protean transformation and connection. *Superluminal* stands also for the defining contradictions of a cyborg world in another sense; it embodies textually the intersection of feminist theory and colonial discourse in the science fiction I have alluded to in this chapter. This is a conjunction with a long history that many 'First World' feminists have tried to repress, including myself in my readings of *Superluminal* before being called to account by Zoe Sofoulis, whose different location in the world system's informatics of domination made her acutely alert to the imperialist moment of all science fiction cultures, including women's science fiction. From an Australian feminist sensitivity, Sofoulis remembered more readily McIntyre's role as writer of the adventures of Captain Kirk and Spock in TV's *Star Trek* series than her rewriting the romance in *Superluminal*.

Monsters have always defined the limits of community in Western imaginations. The Centaurs and Amazons of ancient Greece established the limits of the centred polis of the Greek male human by their disruption of marriage and boundary pollutions of the warrior with animality and woman. Unseparated twins and hermaphrodites were the confused human material in early modern France who grounded discourse on the natural and supernatural, medical and legal, portents and diseases – all crucial to establishing modern identity.[30] The evolutionary and behavioural sciences of monkeys and apes have marked the multiple boundaries of late twentieth-century industrial identities. Cyborg monsters in feminist science fiction define quite different political possibilities and limits from those proposed by the mundane fiction of Man and Woman.

There are several consequences to taking seriously the imagery of cyborgs as other than our enemies. Our bodies, ourselves; bodies are maps of power and identity. Cyborgs are no exception. A cyborg body is not innocent; it was not born in a garden; it does not seek unitary identity and so generate antagonistic dualisms without end (or until the world ends); it takes irony for granted. One is too few, and two is only one possibility. Intense pleasure in skill, machine skill, ceases to be a sin, but an aspect of embodiment. The machine is not an *it* to be animated, worshipped, and dominated. The machine is us, our processes, an aspect of our embodiment. We can be responsible for machines; *they* do not dominate or threaten us. We are responsible for boundaries; we are they. Up till now (once upon a time), female embodiment seemed to be given, organic, necessary; and female embodiment seemed to mean skill in mothering and its metaphoric extensions. Only by being out of place could we take intense pleasure in machines, and then with excuses that this was organic activity after all, appropriate to females. Cyborgs might consider more seriously the partial, fluid, sometimes aspect of sex and sexual embodiment. Gender might not be global identity after all, even if it has profound historical breadth and depth.

The ideologically charged question of what counts as daily activity, as experience, can be approached by exploiting the cyborg image. Feminists have recently claimed that women are given to dailiness, that women more than men somehow sustain daily life, and so have a privileged epistemological position potentially. There is a compelling aspect to this claim, one that makes visible unvalued female activity and names it as the ground of life.

But *the* ground of life? What about all the ignorance of women, all the exclusions and failures of knowledge and skill? What about men's access to daily competence, to knowing how to build things, to take them apart, to play? What about other embodiments? Cyborg gender is a local possibility taking a global vengeance. Race, gender, and capital require a cyborg theory of wholes and parts. There is no drive in cyborgs to produce total theory, but there is an intimate experience of boundaries, their construction and deconstruction. There is a myth system waiting to become a political language to ground one way of looking at science and technology and challenging the informatics of domination – in order to act potently.

One last image: organisms and organismic, holistic politics depend on metaphors of rebirth and invariably call on the resources of reproductive sex. I would suggest that cyborgs have more to do with regeneration and are suspicious of the reproductive matrix and of most birthing. For salamanders, regeneration after injury, such as the loss of a limb, involves regrowth of structure and restoration of function with the constant possibility of twinning or other odd topographical productions at the site of former injury. The regrown limb can be monstrous, duplicated, potent. We have all been injured, profoundly. We require regeneration, not rebirth, and the possibilities for our reconstitution include the utopian dream of the hope for a monstrous world without gender.

Cyborg imagery can help express two crucial arguments in this essay: first, the production of universal, totalizing theory is a major mistake that misses most of reality, probably always, but certainly now; and second, taking responsibility for the social relations of science and technology means refusing an anti-science metaphysics, a demonology of technology, and so means embracing the skilful task of reconstructing the boundaries of daily life, in partial connection with others, in communication with all of our parts. It is not just that science and technology are possible means of great human satisfaction, as well as a matrix of complex dominations. Cyborg imagery can suggest a way out of the maze of dualisms in which we have explained our bodies and our tools to ourselves. This is a dream not of a common language, but of a powerful infidel heteroglossia. It is an imagination of a feminist speaking in tongues to strike fear into the circuits of the super-savers of the new right. It means both building and destroying machines, identities, categories, relationships, space stories. Though both are bound in the spiral dance, I would rather be a cyborg than a goddess.

Chapter Nine

Situated Knowledges: The Science Question in Feminism and the Privilege of Partial Perspective[1]

A cademic and activist feminist enquiry has repeatedly tried to come to terms with the question of what *we* might mean by the curious and inescapable term 'objectivity'. We have used a lot of toxic ink and trees processed into paper decrying what *they* have meant and how it hurts *us*. The imagined 'they' constitute a kind of invisible conspiracy of masculinist scientists and philosophers replete with grants and laboratories; and the imagined 'we' are the embodied others, who are not allowed *not* to have a body, a finite point of view, and so an inevitably disqualifying and polluting bias in any discussion of consequence outside our own little circles, where a 'mass'-subscription journal might reach a few thousand readers composed mostly of science-haters. At least, I confess to these paranoid fantasies and academic resentments lurking underneath some convoluted reflections in print under my name in the feminist literature in the history and philosophy of science. We, the feminists in the debates about science and technology, are the Reagan era's 'special interest groups' in the rarefied realm of epistemology, where traditionally what can count as knowledge is policed by philosophers codifying cognitive canon law. Of course, a special interest group is, by Reaganoid definition, any collective historical subject which dares to resist the stripped-down atomism of Star Wars, hypermarket, postmodern, media-simulated citizenship. Max Headroom doesn't have a body; therefore, he alone *sees* everything in the great communicator's empire of the Global Network. No wonder Max gets to have a naïve sense of humour and a kind of happily regressive, pre-oedipal sexuality, a sexuality which we ambivalently – and dangerously incorrectly – had imagined was reserved for lifelong inmates of female and colonized bodies, and maybe also white male computer hackers in solitary electronic confinement.

It has seemed to me that feminists have both selectively and flexibly used and been trapped by two poles of a tempting dichotomy on the question of objectivity. Certainly I speak for myself here, and I offer the speculation that there is a collective discourse on these matters. On the one hand, recent social studies of science and technology have made available a very strong social constructionist argument for *all* forms of knowledge claims, most certainly and especially scientific ones.[2] In these tempting views, no insider's perspective is privileged, because all drawings of inside–outside boundaries in knowledge are theorized as power moves, not moves towards truth. So, from the strong social constructionist perspective, why should we be cowed by scientists' descriptions of their activity and accomplishments; they and their patrons have stakes in throwing sand in our eyes. They tell parables about objectivity and scientific method to students in the first years of their initiation, but no practitioner of the high scientific arts would be caught dead *acting on* the textbook versions. Social constructionists make clear that official ideologies about objectivity and scientific method are particularly bad guides to how scientific knowledge is actually *made*. Just as for the rest of us, what scientists believe or say they do and what they really do have a very loose fit.

The only people who end up actually *believing* and, goddess forbid, acting on the ideological doctrines of disembodied scientific objectivity enshrined in elementary textbooks and technoscience booster literature are non-scientists, including a few very trusting philosophers. Of course, my designation of this last group is probably just a reflection of residual disciplinary chauvinism from identifying with historians of science and too much time spent with a microscope in early adulthood in a kind of disciplinary pre-oedipal and modernist poetic moment when cells seemed to be cells and organisms, organisms. *Pace*, Gertrude Stein. But then came the law of the father and its resolution of the problem of objectivity, solved by always already absent referents, deferred signifieds, split subjects, and the endless play of signifiers. Who wouldn't grow up warped? Gender, race, the world itself – all seem just effects of warp speeds in the play of signifiers in a cosmic force field. All truths become warp speed effects in a hyper-real space of simulations. But we cannot afford these particular plays on words – the projects of crafting reliable knowledge about the 'natural' world cannot be given over to the genre of paranoid or cynical science fiction. For political people, social constructionism cannot be allowed to decay into the radiant emanations of cynicism.

In any case, social constructionists could maintain that the ideological doctrine of scientific method and all the philosophical verbiage about epistemology were cooked up to distract our attention from getting to know the world *effectively* by practising the sciences. From this point of view, science – the real game in town, the one we must play – is rhetoric, the persuasion of the relevant social actors that one's manufactured knowledge is a route to a desired form of very objective power. Such persuasions must take account of the structure of facts and artefacts, as well as of language-mediated actors in the knowledge game. Here, artefacts and facts are parts of the powerful art of rhetoric. Practice is persuasion, and the focus is very much on practice. All knowledge is a condensed node in an agonistic power field. The strong programme in the sociology of knowledge joins with the lovely and nasty tools of semiology and deconstruction to insist on the rhetorical nature of truth, including scientific truth. History is a story Western culture buffs tell each other; science is a contestable text and a power field; the content is the form.[3] Period. The form in science is the artefactual-social rhetoric of crafting the world into effective objects. This is a practice of world-changing persuasions that take the shape of amazing new objects – like microbes, quarks, and genes.

But whether or not they have the structure and properties of rhetorical objects, late twentieth-century scientific entities – infective vectors (microbes), elementary particles (quarks), and biomolecular codes (genes) – are not Romantic or modernist objects with internal laws of coherence.[4] They are momentary traces focused by force fields, or they are information vectors in a barely embodied and highly mutable semiosis ordered by acts of recognition and misrecognition. Human nature, encoded in its genome and its other writing practices, is a vast library worthy of Umberto Eco's imagined secret labyrinth in *The Name of the Rose* (1980). The stabilization and storage of this text of human nature promise to cost more than its writing. This is a terrifying view of the relationship of body and language for those of us who would still like to talk about *reality* with more confidence than we allow the Christian right's discussion of the Second Coming and their being raptured out of the final destruction of the world. We would like to think our appeals to real worlds are more than a desperate lurch away from cynicism and an act of faith like any other cult's, no matter how much space we generously give to all the rich and always historically specific mediations through which we and everybody else must know the world.

So, the further I get with the description of the radical social constructionist programme and a particular version of postmodernism, coupled to the acid tools of critical discourse in the human sciences, the more nervous I get. Like all neuroses, mine is rooted in the problem of metaphor, that is, the problem of the relation of bodies and language. For example, the force field imagery of moves in the fully textualized and coded world is the matrix for many arguments about socially negotiated reality for the postmodern subject. This world-as-code is, just for starters, a high-tech military field, a kind of automated academic battlefield, where blips of light called players disintegrate (what a metaphor!) each other in order to stay in the knowledge and power game. Technoscience and science fiction collapse into the sun of their radiant (ir)reality – war.[5] It shouldn't take decades of feminist theory to sense the enemy here. Nancy Hartsock (1983b) got all this crystal clear in her concept of abstract masculinity.

I, and others, started out wanting a strong tool for deconstructing the truth claims of hostile science by showing the radical historical specificity, and so contestability, of *every* layer of the onion of scientific and technological constructions, and we end up with a kind of epistemological electro-shock therapy, which far from ushering us into the high stakes tables of the game of contesting public truths, lays us out on the table with self-induced multiple personality disorder. We wanted a way to go beyond showing bias in science (that proved too easy anyhow), and beyond separating the good scientific sheep from the bad goats of bias and misuse. It seemed promising to do this by the strongest possible constructionist argument that left no cracks for reducing the issues to bias versus objectivity, use versus misuse, science versus pseudo-science. We unmasked the doctrines of objectivity because they threatened our budding sense of collective historical subjectivity and agency and our 'embodied' accounts of the truth, and we ended up with one more excuse for not learning any post-Newtonian physics and one more reason to drop the old feminist self-help practices of repairing our own cars. They're just texts anyway, so let the boys have them back. Besides these textualized postmodern worlds are scary, and we prefer our science fiction to be a bit more utopic, maybe like *Woman on the Edge of Time* or even *Wanderground*.

Some of us tried to stay sane in these disassembled and dissembling times by holding out for a feminist version of objectivity. Here, motivated by many of the same political desires, is the other seductive end of the duplicitous objectivity problem. Humanistic Marxism was polluted at the source by its structuring ontological theory of the domination of nature in the self-construction of man and by its closely related impotence to historicize anything women did that didn't qualify for a wage. But Marxism was still a promising resource in the form of epistemological feminist mental hygiene that sought our own doctrines of objective vision. Marxist starting points offered tools to get to our versions of standpoint theories, insistent embodiment, a rich tradition of critiques of hegemony without disempowering positivisms and relativisms, and nuanced theories of mediation. Some versions of psychoanalysis aided this approach immensely, especially anglophone object relations theory, which maybe did more for US socialist-feminism for a time than anything from the pen of Marx or Engels, much less Althusser or any of the late pretenders to sonship treating the subject of ideology and science.[6]

Another approach, 'feminist empiricism', also converges with feminist uses of Marxian resources to get a theory of science which continues to insist on legitimate meanings of objectivity and which remains leery of a radical constructivism conjugated with semiology and narratology (Harding, 1986, pp. 24–6, 161–2). Feminists have to insist on a better account of the world; it is not enough to show radical historical contingency and modes of construction for everything. Here, we, as feminists, find ourselves perversely conjoined with the discourse of many practising scientists, who, when all is said and done, mostly believe they are describing and discovering things *by means of* all their constructing and arguing. Evelyn Keller has been particularly insistent on this fundamental matter, and Harding calls the goal of these approaches a 'successor science'. Feminists have stakes in a successor science project that offers a more adequate, richer, better account of a world, in order to live in it well and in critical, reflexive relation to our own as well as others' practices of domination and the unequal parts of privilege and oppression that make up all positions. In traditional philosophical categories, the issue is ethics and politics perhaps more than epistemology.

So, I think my problem and 'our' problem is how to have *simultaneously* an account of radical historical contingency for all knowledge claims and knowing subjects, a critical practice for recognizing our own 'semiotic technologies' for making meanings, *and* a no-nonsense commitment to faithful accounts of a 'real' world, one that can be partially shared and friendly to earth-wide projects of finite freedom, adequate material abundance, modest meaning in suffering, and limited happiness. Harding calls this necessary multiple desire a need for a successor science project and a postmodern insistence on irreducible difference and radical multiplicity of local knowledges. *All* components of the desire are paradoxical and dangerous, and their combination is both contradictory and necessary. Feminists don't need a doctrine of objectivity that promises transcendence, a story that loses track of its mediations just where someone might be held responsible for something, and unlimited instrumental power. We don't want a theory of innocent powers to represent the world, where language and bodies both fall into the bliss of organic symbiosis. We also don't want to theorize the world, much less act within it, in terms of Global Systems, but we do need an earth-wide network of connections, including the ability partially to translate knowledges among very different – and power-differentiated – communities. We need the power of modern critical theories of how meanings and bodies get made, not in order to deny meaning and bodies, but in order to live in meanings and bodies that have a chance for a future.

Natural, social, and human sciences have always been implicated in hopes like these. Science has been about a search for translation, convertibility, mobility of meanings, and universality – which I call reductionism, when one language (guess whose) must be enforced as the standard for all the translations and conversions. What money does in the exchange orders of capitalism, reductionism does in the powerful mental orders of global sciences: there is finally only one equation. That is the deadly fantasy that feminists and others have identified in some versions of objectivity doctrines in the service of hierarchical and positivist orderings of what can count as knowledge. That is one of the reasons the debates about objectivity matter, metaphorically and otherwise. Immortality and omnipotence are not our goals. But we could use some enforceable, reliable accounts of things not reducible to power moves and agonistic, high status games of rhetoric or to scientistic, positivist arrogance. This point applies whether we are talking about genes, social classes, elementary particles, genders, races, or texts; the point applies to the exact, natural, social, and human sciences, despite the slippery ambiguities of the words *objectivity* and *science* as we slide around the discursive terrain. In our efforts to climb the greased pole leading to a usable doctrine of objectivity, I and most other feminists in the objectivity debates have alternatively, or even simultaneously, held on to both ends of the dichotomy, which Harding describes in terms of successor science projects versus postmodernist accounts of difference and I have sketched in this chapter as radical constructivism versus feminist critical empiricism. It is, of course, hard to climb when you are holding on to both ends of a pole, simultaneously or alternately. It is, therefore, time to switch metaphors.

THE PERSISTENCE OF VISION[7]

I would like to proceed by placing metaphorical reliance on a much maligned sensory system in feminist discourse: vision. Vision can be good for avoiding binary oppositions. I would like to insist on the embodied nature of all vision, and so reclaim the sensory system that has been used to signify a leap out of the marked body and into a conquering gaze from nowhere. This is the gaze that mythically inscribes all the marked bodies, that makes the unmarked category claim the power to see and not be seen, to represent while escaping representation. This gaze signifies the unmarked positions of Man and White, one of the many nasty tones of the world *objectivity* to feminist ears in scientific and technological, late industrial, militarized, racist and male dominant societies, that is, here, in the belly of the monster, in the United States in the late 1980s. I would like a doctrine of embodied objectivity that accommodates paradoxical and critical feminist science projects: feminist objectivity means quite simply *situated knowledges*.

The eyes have been used to signify a perverse capacity – honed to perfection in the history of science tied to militarism, capitalism, colonialism, and male supremacy – to distance the knowing subject from everybody and everything in the interests of unfettered power. The instruments of visualization in multinationalist, postmodernist culture have compounded these meanings of dis-embodiment. The visualizing technologies are without apparent limit; the eye of any ordinary primate like us can be endlessly enhanced by sonography systems, magnetic resonance imaging, artificial intelligence-linked graphic manipulation systems, scanning electron microscopes, computer-aided tomography scanners, colour enhancement techniques, satellite surveillance systems, home and office VDTs, cameras for every purpose from filming the mucous membrane lining the gut cavity of a marine worm living in the vent gases on a fault between continental plates to mapping a planetary hemisphere elsewhere in the solar system. Vision in this technological feast becomes unregulated gluttony; all perspective gives way to infinitely mobile vision, which no longer seems just mythically about the god-trick of seeing everything from nowhere, but to have put the myth into ordinary practice. And like the god-trick, this eye fucks the world to make techno-monsters. Zoe Sofoulis (1988) calls this the cannibal-eye of masculinist extra-terrestrial projects for excremental second birthing.

A tribute to this ideology of direct, devouring, generative, and unrestricted vision, whose technological mediations are simultaneously celebrated and presented as utterly transparent, the volume celebrating the 100th anniversary of the National Geographic Society closes its survey of the magazine's quest literature, effected through its amazing photography, with two juxtaposed chapters. The first is on 'Space', introduced by the epigraph, 'The choice is the universe – or nothing' (Bryan, 1987, p. 352). Indeed. This chapter recounts the exploits of the space race and displays the colour-enhanced 'snapshots' of the outer planets reassembled from digitalized signals transmitted across vast space to let the viewer 'experience' the moment of discovery in immediate vision of the 'object'.[8] These fabulous objects come to us simultaneously as indubitable recordings of what is simply there and as heroic feats of techno-scientific production. The next chapter is the twin of outer space: 'Inner Space', introduced by the epigraph, 'The stuff of stars has come alive' (Bryan, 1987, p. 454). Here, the reader is brought into the realm of the infinitesimal, objectified by means of radiation outside the wave lengths that 'normally' are perceived by hominid primates, i.e., the beams of lasers and scanning electron microscopes, whose signals are processed into the wonderful full-colour snapshots of defending T cells and invading viruses.

But of course that view of infinite vision is an illusion, a god-trick. I would like to suggest how our insisting metaphorically on the particularity and embodiment of all vision (though not necessarily organic embodiment and including technological mediation), and not giving in to the tempting myths of vision as a route to disembodiment and second-birthing, allows us to construct a usable, but not an innocent, doctrine of objectivity. I want a feminist writing of the body that metaphorically emphasizes vision again, because we need to reclaim that sense to find our way through all the visualizing tricks and powers of modern sciences and technologies that have transformed the objectivity debates. We need to learn in our bodies, endowed with primate colour and stereoscopic vision, how to attach the objective to our theoretical and political scanners in order to name where we are and are not, in dimensions of mental and physical space we hardly know how to name. So, not so perversely, objectivity turns out to be about particular and specific embodiment, and definitely not about the false vision promising transcendence of all limits and responsibility. The moral is simple: only partial perspective promises objective vision. This is an objective vision that initiates, rather than closes off, the problem of responsibility for the generativity of all visual practices. Partial perspective can be held accountable for both its promising and its destructive monsters. All Western cultural narratives about objectivity are allegories of the ideologies of the relations of what we call mind and body, of distance and responsibility, embedded in the science question in feminism. Feminist objectivity is about limited location and situated knowledge, not about transcendence and splitting of subject and object. In this way we might become answerable for what we learn how to see.

These are lessons which I learned in part walking with my dogs and wondering how the world looks without a fovea and very few retinal cells for colour vision, but with a huge neural processing and sensory area for smells. It is a lesson available from photographs of how the world looks to the compound eyes of an insect, or even from the camera eye of a spy satellite or the digitally transmitted signals of space probe-perceived differences 'near' Jupiter that have been transformed into coffee table colour photographs. The 'eyes' made available in modern technological sciences shatter any idea of passive vision; these prosthetic devices show us that all eyes, including our own organic ones, are active perceptual systems, building in translations and specific *ways* of seeing, that is, ways of life. There is no unmediated photograph or passive camera obscura in scientific accounts of bodies and machines; there are only highly specific visual possibilities, each with a wonderfully detailed, active, partial way of organizing worlds. All these pictures of the world should not be allegories of infinite mobility and interchangeability, but of elaborate specificity and difference and the loving care people might take to learn how to see faithfully from another's point of view, even when the other is our own machine. That's not alienating distance; that's a *possible* allegory for feminist versions of objectivity. Understanding how these visual systems work, technically, socially, and psychically ought to be a way of embodying feminist objectivity.

Many currents in feminism attempt to theorize grounds for trusting especially the vantage points of the subjugated; there is good reason to believe vision is better from below the brilliant space platforms of the powerful (Hartsock, 1983a; Sandoval, n.d.; Harding, 1986; Anzaldúa, 1987). Linked to this suspicion, this chapter is an argument for situated and embodied knowledges and against various forms of unlocatable, and so irresponsible, knowledge claims. Irresponsible means unable to be called into account. There is a premium on establishing the capacity to see from the peripheries and the depths. But here lies a serious danger of romaticizing and/or appropriating the vision of the less powerful while claiming to see from their positions. To see from below is neither easily learned nor unproblematic, even if 'we' 'naturally' inhabit the great underground terrain of subjugated knowledges. The positionings of the subjugated are not exempt from critical re-examination, decoding, deconstruction, and inter-pretation; that is, from both semiological and hermeneutic modes of critical enquiry. The standpoints of the subjugated are not 'innocent' positions. On the contrary, they are preferred because in principle they are least likely to allow denial of the critical and interpretative core of all knowledge. They are savvy to modes of denial through repression, forgetting, and disappearing acts – ways of being nowhere while claiming to see comprehensively. The subjugated have a decent chance to be on to the god-trick and all its dazzling – and, therefore, blinding – illuminations. 'Subjugated' standpoints are preferred because they seem to promise more adequate, sustained, objective, transforming accounts of the world. But *how* to see from below is a problem requiring at least as much skill with bodies and language, with the mediations of vision, as the 'highest' techno-scientific visualizations.

Such preferred positioning is as hostile to various forms of relativism as to the most explicitly totalizing versions of claims to scientific authority. But the alternative to relativism is not totalization and single vision, which is always finally the unmarked category whose power depends on systematic narrow-ing and obscuring. The alternative to relativism is partial, locatable, critical knowledges sustaining the possibility of webs of connections called solidarity in politics and shared conversations in epistemology. Relativism is a way of being nowhere while claiming to be everywhere equally. The 'equality' of positioning is a denial of responsibility and critical enquiry. Relativism is the perfect mirror twin of totalization in the ideologies of objectivity; both deny the stakes in location, embodiment, and partial perspective; both make it impossible to see well. Relativism and totalization are both 'god-tricks' promising vision from everywhere and nowhere equally and fully, common myths in rhetorics surrounding Science. But it is precisely in the politics and epistemology of partial perspectives that the possibility of sustained, rational, objective enquiry rests.

So, with many other feminists, I want to argue for a doctrine and practice of objectivity that privileges contestation, deconstruction, passionate con-struction, webbed connections, and hope for transformation of systems of knowledge and ways of seeing. But not just any partial perspective will do; we must be hostile to easy relativisms and holisms built out of summing and subsuming parts. 'Passionate detachment' (Kuhn, 1982) requires more than acknowledged and self-critical partiality. We are also bound to seek perspective from those points of view, which can never be known in advance, which promise something quite extraordinary, that is, knowledge potent for constructing worlds less organized by axes of domination. In such a viewpoint, the unmarked category would *really* disappear – quite a difference from simply repeating a disappearing act. The imaginary and the rational – the visionary and objective vision – hover close together. I think Harding's plea for a successor science and for postmodern sensibilities must be read to argue that this close touch of the fantastic element of hope for transformative knowledge and the severe check and stimulus of sustained critical enquiry are jointly the ground of any believable claim to objectivity or rationality not riddled with breath-taking denials and repressions. It is even possible to read the record of scientific revolutions in terms of this feminist doctrine of rationality and objectivity. Science has been utopian and visionary from the start; that is one reason 'we' need it.

A commitment to mobile positioning and to passionate detachment is dependent on the impossibility of innocent 'identity' politics and epistemologies as strategies for seeing from the standpoints of the subjugated in order to see well. One cannot 'be' either a cell or molecule – or a woman, colonized person, labourer, and so on – if one intends to see and see from these positions critically. 'Being' is much more problematic and contingent. Also, one cannot relocate in any possible vantage point without being accountable for that movement. Vision is *always* a question of the power to see – and perhaps of the violence implicit in our visualizing practices. With whose blood were my eyes crafted? These points also apply to testimony from the position of 'oneself'. We are not immediately present to ourselves. Self-knowledge requires a semiotic-material technology linking meanings and bodies. Self-identity is a bad visual system. Fusion is a bad strategy of positioning. The boys in the human sciences have called this doubt about self-presence the 'death of the subject', that single ordering point of will and consciousness. That judgement seems bizarre to me. I prefer to call this generative doubt the opening of non-isomorphic subjects, agents, and territories of stories unimaginable from the vantage point of the cyclopian, self-satiated eye of the master subject. The Western eye has fundamentally been a wandering eye, a travelling lens. These peregrinations have often been violent and insistent on mirrors for a conquering self – but not always. Western feminists also *inherit* some skill in learning to participate in revisualizing worlds turned upside down in earth-transforming challenges to the views of the masters. All is not to be done from scratch.

The split and contradictory self is the one who can interrogate positionings and be accountable, the one who can construct and join rational
conversations and fantastic imaginings that change history.[9] Splitting, not
being, is the privileged image for feminist epistemologies of scientific
knowledge. 'Splitting' in this context should be about heterogeneous
multiplicities that are simultaneously necessary and incapable of being
squashed into isomorphic slots or cumulative lists. This geometry pertains
within and among subjects. The topography of subjectivity is multi-
dimensional; so, therefore, is vision. The knowing self is partial in all its
guises, never finished, whole, simply there and original; it is always
constructed and stitched together imperfectly, and *therefore* able to join with
another, to see together without claiming to be another. Here is the promise
of objectivity: a scientific knower seeks the subject position not of identity,
but of objectivity; that is, partial connection. There is no way to 'be'
simultaneously in all, or wholly in any, of the privileged (subjugated)
positions structured by gender, race, nation, and class. And that is a short list
of critical positions. The search for such a 'full' and total position is the
search for the fetishized perfect subject of oppositional history, sometimes
appearing in feminist theory as the essentialized Third World Woman
(Mohanty, 1984). Subjugation is not grounds for an ontology; it might be a
visual clue. Vision requires instruments of vision; an optics is a politics of
positioning. Instruments of vision mediate standpoints; there is no immediate vision from the standpoints of the subjugated. Identity, including
self-identity, does not produce science; critical positioning does, that is,
objectivity. Only those occupying the positions of the dominators are
self-identical, unmarked, disembodied, unmediated, transcendent, born
again. It is unfortunately possible for the subjugated to lust for and even
scramble into that subject position – and then disappear from view.
Knowledge from the point of view of the unmarked is truly fantastic,
distorted, and so irrational. The only position from which objectivity could
not possibly be practised and honoured is the standpoint of the master, the
Man, the One God, whose Eye produces, appropriates, and orders all
difference. No one ever accused the God of monotheism of objectivity, only
of indifference. The god-trick is self-identical, and we have mistaken that
for creativity and knowledge, omniscience even.

Positioning is, therefore, the key practice grounding knowledge organized
around the imagery of vision, as so much Western scientific and philosophic
discourse is organized. Positioning implies responsibility for our enabling
practices. It follows that politics and ethics ground struggles for the contests
over what may count as rational knowledge. That is, admitted or not, politics
and ethics ground struggles over knowledge projects in the exact, natural,
social, and human sciences. Otherwise, rationality is simply impossible, an

optical illusion projected from nowhere comprehensively. Histories of science may be powerfully told as histories of the technologies. These technologies are ways of life, social orders, practices of visualization. Technologies are skilled practices. How to see? Where to see from? What limits to vision? What to see for? Whom to see with? Who gets to have more than one point of view? Who gets blinkered? Who wears blinkers? Who interprets the visual field? What other sensory powers do we wish to cultivate besides vision? Moral and political discourse should be the paradigm of rational discourse in the imagery and technologies of vision. Sandra Harding's claim, or observation, that movements of social revolution have most contributed to improvements in science might be read as a claim about the knowledge consequences of new technologies of positioning. But I wish Harding had spent more time remembering that social and scientific revolutions have not always been liberatory, even if they have always been visionary. Perhaps this point could be captured in another phrase: the science question in the military. Struggles over what will count as rational accounts of the world are struggles over *how* to see. The terms of vision: the science question in colonialism; the science question in exterminism (Sofoulis, 1988); the science question in feminism.

The issue in politically engaged attacks on various empiricisms, reductionisms, or other versions of scientific authority should not be relativism, but location. A dichotomous chart expressing this point might look like this:

universal rationality	ethnophilosophies
common language	heteroglossia
new organon	deconstruction
unified field theory	oppositional positioning
world system	local knowledges
master theory	webbed accounts

But a dichotomous chart misrepresents in a critical way the positions of embodied objectivity which I am trying to sketch. The primary distortion is the illusion of symmetry in the chart's dichotomy, making any position appear, first, simply alternative and, second, mutually exclusive. A map of tensions and resonances between the fixed ends of a charged dichotomy better represents the potent politics and epistemologies of embodied, therefore accountable, objectivity. For example, local knowledges have also to be in tension with the productive structurings that force unequal translations and exchanges – material and semiotic – within the webs of knowledge and power. Webs *can* have the property of systematicity, even of centrally structured global systems with deep filaments and tenacious tendrils into time, space and consciousness, the dimensions of world history. Feminist accountability requires a knowledge tuned to resonance, not to dichotomy. Gender is a field of structured and structuring difference, where the tones of extreme localization, of the intimately personal and individualized body, vibrate in the same field with global high tension emissions. Feminist embodiment, then, is not about fixed location in a reified body, female or otherwise, but about nodes in fields, inflections in orientations, and responsibility for difference in material-semiotic fields of meaning. Embodiment is significant prosthesis; objectivity cannot be about fixed vision when what counts as an object is precisely what world history turns out to be about.

How should one be positioned in order to see in this situation of tensions, resonances, transformations, resistances, and complicities? Here, primate vision is not immediately a very powerful metaphor or technology for feminist political-epistemological clarification, since it seems to present to consciousness already processed and objectified fields; things seem already fixed and distanced. But the visual metaphor allows one to go beyond fixed appearances, which are only the end products. The metaphor invites us to investigate the varied apparatuses of visual production, including the prosthetic technologies interfaced with our biological eyes and brains. And here we find highly particular machineries for processing regions of the electro-magnetic spectrum into our pictures of the world. It is in the intricacies of these visualization technologies in which we are embedded that we will find metaphors and means for understanding and intervening in the patterns of objectification in the world, that is, the patterns of reality for which we must be accountable. In these metaphors, we find means for appreciating simultaneously *both* the concrete, 'real' aspect and the aspect of semiosis and production in what we call scientific knowledge.

I am arguing for politics and epistemologies of location, positioning, and situating, where partiality and not universality is the condition of being heard to make rational knowledge claims. These are claims on people's lives; the view from a body, always a complex, contradictory, structuring and structured body, versus the view from above, from nowhere, from simplicity. Only the god-trick is forbidden. Here is a criterion for deciding the science question in militarism, that dream science/technology of perfect language, perfect communication, final order.

Feminism loves another science: the sciences and politics of interpretation, translation, stuttering, and the partly understood. Feminism is about the sciences of the multiple subject with (at least) double vision. Feminism is about a critical vision consequent upon a critical positioning in in-homogeneous gendered social space.[10] Translation is always interpretative, critical, and partial. Here is a ground for conversation, rationality, and objectivity – which is power-sensitive, not pluralist, 'conversation'. It is not even the mythic cartoons of physics and mathematics – incorrectly caricatured in anti-science ideology as exact, hyper-simple knowledges – that have come to represent the hostile other to feminist paradigmatic models of scientific knowledge, but the dreams of the perfectly known in high-technology, permanently militarized scientific productions and positionings, the god-trick of a Star Wars paradigm of rational knowledge. So location is about vulnerability; location resists the politics of closure, finality, or, to borrow from Althusser, feminist objectivity resists 'simplification in the last instance'. That is because feminist embodiment resists fixation and is insatiably curious about the webs of differential positioning. There is no single feminist standpoint because our maps require too many dimensions for that metaphor to ground our visions. But the feminist standpoint theorists' goal of an epistemology and politics of engaged, accountable positioning remains eminently potent. The goal is better accounts of the world, that is, 'science'.

Above all, rational knowledge does not pretend to disengagement: to be from everywhere and so nowhere, to be free from interpretation, from being represented, to be fully self-contained or fully formalizable. Rational knowledge is a process of ongoing critical interpretation among 'fields' of interpreters and decoders. Rational knowledge is power-sensitive conversation (King, 1987a):

knowledge:community::knowledge:power
hermeneutics:semiology::critical interpretation:codes.

Decoding and transcoding plus translation and criticism; all are necessary. So science becomes the paradigmatic model not of closure, but of that which is contestable and contested. Science becomes the myth not of what escapes human agency and responsibility in a realm above the fray, but rather of accountability and responsibility for translations and solidarities linking the cacophonous visions and visionary voices that characterize the knowledges of the subjugated. A splitting of senses, a confusion of voice and sight, rather than clear and distinct ideas, becomes the metaphor for the ground of the rational. We seek not the knowledges ruled by phallogocentrism (nostalgia for the presence of the one true Word) and disembodied vision, but those ruled by partial sight and limited voice. We do not seek partiality for its own sake, but for the sake of the connections and unexpected openings situated knowledges make possible. The only way to find a larger vision is to be somewhere in particular. The science question in feminism is about objectivity as positioned rationality. Its images are not the products of escape and transcendence of limits, i.e., the view from above, but the joining of partial views and halting voices into a collective subject position that promises a vision of the means of ongoing finite embodiment, of living within limits and contradictions, i.e., of views from somewhere.

OBJECTS AS ACTORS: THE APPARATUS OF BODILY PRODUCTION

Throughout this reflection on 'objectivity', I have refused to resolve the ambiguities built into referring to science without differentiating its extraordinary range of contexts. Through the insistent ambiguity, I have foregrounded a field of commonalities binding exact, physical, natural, social, political, biological, and human sciences; and I have tied this whole heterogeneous field of academically (and industrially, for example, in publishing, the weapons trade, and pharmaceuticals) institutionalized knowledge production to a meaning of science that insists on its potency in ideological struggles. But, partly in order to give play to both the specificities and the highly permeable boundaries of meanings in discourse on science, I would like to suggest a resolution to one ambiguity. Throughout the field of meanings constituting science, one of the commonalities concerns the status of any object of knowledge and of related claims about the faithfulness of our accounts to a 'real world', no matter how mediated for us and no matter how complex and contradictory these worlds may be. Feminists, and others who have been most active as critics of the sciences and their claims or associated ideologies, have shied away from doctrines of scientific objectivity in part because of the suspicion that an 'object' of knowledge is a passive and inert thing. Accounts of such objects can seem to be either appropriations of a fixed and determined world reduced to resource for the instrumentalist projects of destructive Western societies, or they can be seen as masks for interests, usually dominating interests.

For example, 'sex' as an object of biological knowledge appears regularly in the guise of biological determinism, threatening the fragile space for social constructionism and critical theory, with their attendant possibilities for active and transformative intervention, called into being by feminist concepts of gender as socially, historically, and semiotically positioned difference. And yet, to lose authoritative biological accounts of sex, which set up productive tensions with its binary pair, gender, seems to be to lose too much; it seems to be to lose not just analytic power within a particular Western tradition, but the body itself as anything but a blank page for social inscriptions, including those of biological discourse. The same problem of loss attends a radical 'reduction' of the objects of physics or of any other sciences to the ephemera of discursive production and social construction.[11]

But the difficulty and loss are not necessary. They derive partly from the analytical tradition, deeply indebted to Aristotle and to the transformative history of 'White Capitalist Patriarchy' (how may we name this scandalous Thing?) that turns everything into a resource for appropriation, in which an object of knowledge is finally itself only matter for the seminal power, the act, of the knower. Here, the object both guarantees and refreshes the power of the knower, but any status as *agent* in the productions of knowledge must be denied the object. It – the world – must, in short, be objectified as thing, not as an agent; it must be matter for the self-formation of the only social being in the productions of knowledge, the human knower. Zoe Sofoulis (1988) identified the structure of this mode of knowing in technoscience as 'resourcing' – the second-birthing of Man through the homogenizing of all the world's body into resource for his perverse projects. Nature is only the raw material of culture, appropriated, preserved, enslaved, exalted, or otherwise made flexible for disposal by culture in the logic of capitalist colonialism. Similarly, sex is only the matter to the act of gender; the productionist logic seems inescapable in traditions of Western binarisms. This analytical and historical narrative logic accounts for my nervousness about the sex/gender distinction in the recent history of feminist theory. Sex is 'resourced' for its re-presentation as gender, which 'we' can control. It has seemed all but impossible to avoid the trap of an appropriationist logic of domination built into the nature/culture binarism and its generative lineage, including the sex/gender distinction.

It seems clear that feminist accounts of objectivity and embodiment – that is, of a world – of the kind sketched in this chapter require a deceptively simple manoeuvre within inherited Western analytical traditions, a man-oeuvre begun in dialectics, but stopping short of the needed revisions. Situated knowledges require that the object of knowledge be pictured as an actor and agent, not a screen or a ground or a resource, never finally as slave to the master that closes off the dialectic in his unique agency and authorship of 'objective' knowledge. The point is paradigmatically clear in critical approaches to the social and human sciences, where the agency of people studied itself transforms the entire project of producing social theory. Indeed, coming to terms with the agency of the 'objects' studied is the only way to avoid gross error and false knowledge of many kinds in these sciences. But the same point must apply to the other knowledge projects called sciences. A corollary of the insistence that ethics and politics covertly or overtly provide the bases for objectivity in the sciences as a heterogeneous whole, and not just in the social sciences, is granting the status of agent/actor to the 'objects' of the world. Actors come in many and wonderful forms. Accounts of a 'real' world do not, then, depend on a logic of 'discovery', but on a power-charged social relation of 'conversation'. The world neither speaks itself nor disappears in favour of a master decoder. The codes of the world are not still, waiting only to be read. The world is not raw material for humanization; the thorough attacks on humanism, another branch of 'death of the subject' discourse, have made this point quite clear. In some critical sense that is crudely hinted at by the clumsy category of the social or of agency, the world encountered in knowledge projects is an active entity. In so far as a scientific account has been able to engage this dimension of the world as object of knowledge, faithful knowledge can be imagined and can make claims on us. But no particular doctrine of representation or decoding or discovery guarantees anything. The approach I am recommending is not a version of 'realism', which has proved a rather poor way of engaging with the world's active agency.

My simple, perhaps simple-minded, manoeuvre is obviously not new in Western philosophy, but it has a special feminist edge to it in relation to the science question in feminism and to the linked questions of gender as situated difference and of female embodiment. Ecofeminists have perhaps been most insistent on some version of the world as active subject, not as resource to be mapped and appropriated in bourgeois, Marxist, or masculinist projects. Acknowledging the agency of the world in knowledge makes room for some unsettling possibilities, including a sense of the world's independent sense of humour. Such a sense of humour is not comfortable for humanists and others committed to the world as resource. Richly evocative figures exist for feminist visualizations of the world as witty agent. We need not lapse into an appeal to a primal mother resisting becoming resource. The Coyote or Trickster, embodied in American Southwest Indian accounts, suggests our situation when we give up mastery but keep searching for fidelity, knowing all the while we will be hoodwinked. I think these are useful myths for scientists who might be our allies. Feminist objectivity makes room for surprises and ironies at the heart of all knowledge production; we are not in charge of the world. We just live here and try to strike up non-innocent conversations by means of our prosthetic devices, including our visualization technologies. No wonder science fiction has been such a rich writing practice in recent feminist theory. I like to see feminist theory as a reinvented coyote discourse obligated to its enabling sources in many kinds of heterogeneous accounts of the world.

Another rich feminist practice in science in the last couple of decades illustrates particularly well the 'activation' of the previously passive categories of objects of knowledge. The activation permanently problematizes binary distinctions like sex and gender, without however eliminating their strategic utility. I refer to the reconstructions in primatology, especially but not only women's practice as primatologists, evolutionary biologists, and behavioural ecologists, of what may count as sex, especially as female sex, in scientific accounts (Haraway, 1989b). The *body*, the object of biological discourse, itself becomes a most engaging being. Claims of biological determinism can never be the same again. When female 'sex' has been so thoroughly re-theorized and revisualized that it emerges as practically indistinguishable from 'mind', something basic has happened to the categories of biology. The biological female peopling current biological behavioural accounts has almost no passive properties left. She is structuring and active in every respect; the 'body' is an agent, not a resource. Difference is theorized *biologically* as situational, not intrinsic, at every level from gene to foraging pattern, thereby fundamentally changing the biological politics of the body. The relations between sex and gender have to be categorically reworked within these frames of knowledge. I would like to suggest this trend in explanatory strategies in biology as an allegory for interventions faithful to projects of feminist objectivity. The point is not that these new pictures of the biological female are simply true or not open to contestation and conversation. Quite the opposite. But these pictures foreground knowledge as situated conversation at every level of its articulation. The boundary between animal and human is one of the stakes in this allegory, as well as that between machine and organism.

So I will close with a final category useful to a feminist theory of situated knowledges: the apparatus of bodily production. In her analysis of the production of the poem as an object of literary value, Katie King offers tools that clarify matters in the objectivity debates among feminists. King suggests the term 'apparatus of literary production' to highlight the emergence of what is embodied as literature at the intersection of art, business, and technology. The apparatus of literary production is a matrix from which 'literature' is born. Focusing on the potent object of value called the 'poem', King applies her analytic frame to the relation of women and writing technologies (King, 1987b). I would like to adapt her work to understanding the generation – the actual production and reproduction – of bodies and other objects of value in scientific knowledge projects. At first glance, there is a limitation to using King's scheme inherent in the 'facticity' of biological discourse that is absent from literary discourse and its knowledge claims. Are biological bodies 'produced' or 'generated' in the same strong sense as poems? From the early stirrings of Romanticism in the late eighteenth century, many poets and biologists have believed that poetry and organisms are siblings. *Frankenstein* may be read as a meditation on this proposition. I continue to believe in this potent proposition, but in a postmodern and not a Romantic manner of belief. I wish to translate the ideological dimensions of 'facticity' and 'the organic' into a cumbersome entity called a 'material-semiotic actor'. This unwieldy term is intended to highlight the object of knowledge as an active, meaning-generating axis of the apparatus of bodily production, without *ever* implying immediate presence of such objects or, what is the same thing, their final or unique determination of what can count as objective knowledge at a particular historical juncture. Like King's objects called 'poems', which are sites of literary production where language also is an actor independent of intentions and authors, bodies as objects of knowledge are material-semiotic generative nodes. Their *boundaries* materialize in social interaction. Boundaries are drawn by mapping practices; 'objects' do not pre-exist as such. Objects are boundary projects. But boundaries shift from within; boundaries are very tricky. What boundaries provisionally contain remains generative, productive of meanings and bodies. Siting (sighting) boundaries is a risky practice.

Objectivity is not about dis-engagement, but about mutual *and* usually unequal structuring, about taking risks in a world where 'we' are permanently mortal, that is, not in 'final' control. We have, finally, no clear and distinct ideas. The various contending biological bodies emerge at the intersection of biological research and writing, medical and other business practices, and technology, such as the visualization technologies enlisted as metaphors in this chapter. But also invited into that node of intersection is the analogue to the lively languages that actively intertwine in the production of literary value: the coyote and protean embodiments of a world as witty agent and actor. Perhaps the world resists being reduced to mere resource because it is – not mother/matter/mutter – but coyote, a figure for the always problematic, always potent tie of meaning and bodies. Feminist embodiment, feminist hopes for partiality, objectivity and situated knowledges, turn on conversations and codes at this potent node in fields of possible bodies and meanings. Here is where science, science fantasy, and science fiction converge in the objectivity question in feminism. Perhaps our hopes for accountability, for politics, for ecofeminism, turn on revisioning the world as coding trickster with whom we must learn to converse.

Chapter Ten

The Biopolitics of Postmodern Bodies: Constitutions of Self in Immune System Discourse[1]

for Robert Filomeno (1949–86),
who loved peace and died of AIDS
(Plate 2)

If Koch's postulates must be fulfilled to identify a given microbe with a given disease, perhaps it would be helpful, in rewriting the AIDS text, to take 'Turner's postulates' into account (1984, p. 209): 1) disease is a language; 2) the body is a representation; and 3) medicine is a political practice. (Treichler, 1987, p. 27)

Non-self: A term covering everything which is detectably different from an animal's own constituents. (Playfair, 1984, p. 1)

[T]he immune system must *recognize* self in some manner in order to react to something foreign. (Golub, 1987, p. 484)

LUMPY DISCOURSES AND THE DENATURED BODIES OF BIOLOGY AND MEDICINE

It has become commonplace to emphasize the multiple and specific cultural dialects interlaced in any social negotiation of disease and sickness in the contemporary worlds marked by biological research, biotechnology, and scientific medicine. The language of biomedicine is never alone in the field of empowering meanings, and its power does not flow from a consensus about symbols and actions in the face of suffering. Paula Treichler's (1987) excellent phrase in the title of her essay on the constantly contested meanings of AIDS as an 'epidemic of signification' could be applied widely to the social text of sickness. The power of biomedical language – with its stunning artefacts, images, architectures, social forms, and technologies – for shaping the unequal experience of sickness and death for millions is a social fact deriving from ongoing heterogeneous social processes. The power of biomedicine and biotechnology is constantly re-produced, or it would cease. This power is not a thing fixed and permanent, embedded in plastic and ready to section for microscopic observation by the historian or critic. The cultural and material authority of biomedicine's productions of bodies and selves is more vulnerable, more dynamic, more elusive, and more powerful than that.

But if there has been recognition of the many non-, para-, anti-, or extra-scientific languages in company with biomedicine that structure the embodied semiosis of mortality in the industrialized world, it is much less common to find emphasis on the multiple languages *within* the territory that is often so glibly marked scientific. 'Science says' is represented as a univocal language. Yet even the spliced character of the potent words in 'science' hints at a barely contained and inharmonious heterogeneity. The words for the overlapping discourses and their objects of knowledge, and for the abstract corporate names for the concrete places where the discourse-building work is done, suggest both the blunt foreshortening of technicist approaches to communication and the uncontainable pressures and confusions at the boundaries of meanings within 'science' – biotechnology, biomedicine, psychoneuroimmunology, immunogenetics, immunoendocrinology, neuroendocrinology, monoclonal antibodies, hybridomas, interleukines, Genentech, Embrex, Immunetech, Biogen.

This chapter explores some of the contending popular and technical languages constructing biomedical, biotechnical bodies and selves in postmodern scientific culture in the United States in the 1980s. Scientific discourses are 'lumpy'; they contain and enact condensed contestations for meanings and practices. The chief object of my attention will be the potent and polymorphous object of belief, knowledge, and practice called the immune system. My thesis is that the immune system is an elaborate icon for principal systems of symbolic and material 'difference' in late capitalism. Pre-eminently a twentieth-century object, the immune system is a map drawn to guide recognition and misrecognition of self and other in the dialectics of Western biopolitics. That is, the immune system is a plan for meaningful action to construct and maintain the boundaries for what may count as self and other in the crucial realms of the normal and the pathological. The immune system is a historically specific terrain, where global and local politics; Nobel Prize-winning research; heteroglossic cultural productions, from popular dietary practices, feminist science fiction, religious imagery, and children's games, to photographic techniques and military strategic theory; clinical medical practice; venture capital investment strategies; world-changing developments in business and technology; and the deepest personal and collective experiences of embodiment, vulnerability, power, and mortality interact with an intensity matched perhaps only in the biopolitics of sex and reproduction.[2]

The immune system is both an iconic mythic object in high-technology culture and a subject of research and clinical practice of the first importance. Myth, laboratory, and clinic are intimately interwoven. This mundane point was fortuitously captured in the title listings in the 1986–87 *Books in Print*, where I was searching for a particular undergraduate textbook on immunology. The several pages of entries beginning with the prefix 'immuno-' were bounded, according to the English rules of alphabetical listing, by a volume called *Immortals of Science Fiction*, near one end, and by *The Immutability of God*, at the other. Examining the last section of the textbook to which *Books in Print* led me, *Immunology: A Synthesis* (Golub, 1987), I found what I was looking for: a historical progression of diagrams of theories of immunological regulation and an obituary for their draftsman, an important immunologist, Richard K. Gershon, who 'discovered' the suppressor T cell. The standard obituary tropes for the scientist, who 'must have had what the earliest explorers had, an insatiable desire to be the first person to see something, to know that you are where no man has been before', set the tone. The hero-scientist 'gloried in the layer upon interconnected layer of [the immune response's] complexity. He thrilled at seeing a layer of that complexity which no one had seen before' (Golub, 1987, pp. 531–2). It is reasonable to suppose that all the likely readers of this textbook have been reared within hearing range of the ringing tones of the introduction to the voyages of the federation starship *Enterprise* in *Star Trek* – to boldly go where no man has gone before. Science remains an important genre of Western exploration and travel literature. Similarly, no reader, no matter how literal-minded, could be innocent of the gendered erotic trope that figures the hero's probing into nature's laminated secrets, glorying simultaneously in the layered complexity and in his own techno-erotic touch that goes ever deeper. Science as heroic quest and as erotic technique applied to the body of nature are utterly conventional figures. They take on a particular edge in late twentieth-century immune system discourse, where themes of nuclear exterminism, space adventure, extra-terrestrialism, exotic invaders, and military high-technology are pervasive.

But Golub's and Gershon's intended and explicit text is not about space invaders and the immune system as a Star Wars prototype. Their theme is the love of complexity and the intimate natural bodily technologies for generating the harmonies of organic life. In four illustrations – dated 1968, 1974, 1977, and 1982 – Gershon sketched his conception of 'the immunological orchestra' (Golub, 1987, pp. 533–6). This orchestra is a wonderful picture of the mythic and technical dimensions of the immune system (Plates 3–6). All the illustrations are about co-operation and control, the major themes of organismic biology since the late eighteenth century. From his commanding position in the root of a lymph node, the G.O.D. of the first illustration conducts the orchestra of T and B cells and macrophages as they march about the body and play their specific parts (Plate 3). The lymphocytes all look like Casper the ghost with the appropriate distinguishing nuclear morphologies drawn in the centre of their shapeless bodies. Baton in hand, G.O.D.'s arms are raised in quotation of a symphonic conductor. G.O.D. recalls the other 1960s bioreligious, Nobel Prize-winning 'joke' about the coded bodily text of post-DNA biology and medicine – the Central Dogma of molecular biology, specifying that 'information' flows only from DNA to RNA to protein. These three were called the Blessed Trinity of the secularized sacred body, and histories of the great adventures of molecular biology could be titled *The Eighth Day of Creation* (Judson, 1979), an image that takes on a certain irony in the venture capital and political environments of current biotechnology companies, like Genentech. In the technical-mythic systems of molecular biology, code rules embodied structure and function, never the reverse. Genesis is a serious joke, when the body is theorized as a coded text whose secrets yield only to the proper reading conventions, and when the laboratory seems best characterized as a vast assemblage of technological and organic inscription devices. The Central Dogma was about a master control system for information flow in the codes that determine meaning in the great technological communication systems that organisms progressively have become after the Second World War. The body is an artificial intelligence system, and the relation of copy and original is reversed and then exploded.

G.O.D. is the Generator of Diversity, the source of the awe-inspiring multiple specificities of the polymorphous system of recognition and mis-recognition we call the immune system. By the second illustration (1974), G.O.D. is no longer in front of the immune orchestra, but is standing, arms folded, looking authoritative but not very busy, at the top of the lymph node, surrounded by the musical lymphocytes (Plate 4). A special cell, the T suppressor cell, has taken over the role of conductor. By 1977, the illustration (Plate 5) no longer has a single conductor, but is 'led' by three mysterious subsets of T cells, who hold a total of twelve batons signifying their direction-giving surface identity markers; and G.O.D. scratches his head in patent confusion. But the immune band plays on. In the final illustration, from 1982, (Plate 6) 'the generator of diversity seems resigned to the conflicting calls of the angels of help and suppression', who perch above his left and right shoulders (Golub, 1987, p. 536). Besides G.O.D. and the two angels, there is a T cell conductor and two conflicting prompters, 'each urging its own interpretation'. The joke of single masterly control of organismic harmony in the symphonic system responsible for the integrity of 'self' has become a kind of postmodern pastiche of multiple centres and peripheries, where the immune music that the page suggests would surely sound like nursery school space music. All the actors that used to be on the stage-set for the unambiguous and coherent biopolitical subject are still present, but their harmonies are definitely a bit problematic.

By the 1980s, the immune system is unambiguously a postmodern object – symbolically, technically, and politically. Katherine Hayles (1987b) characterizes postmodernism in terms of 'three waves of developments occurring at multiple sites within the culture, including literature and science'. Her archaeology begins with Saussurean linguistics, through which symbol systems were 'denaturalized'. Internally generated relational difference, rather than mimesis, ruled signification. Hayles sees the culmination of this approach in Claude Shannon's mid-century statistical theory of information, developed for packing the largest number of signals on a transmission line for the Bell Telephone Company and extended to cover communication acts in general, including those directed by the codes of bodily semiosis in ethology or molecular biology. 'Information' generating and processing systems, therefore, are postmodern objects, embedded in a theory of internally differentiated signifiers and remote from doctrines of representation as mimesis. A history-changing artefact, 'information' exists only in very specific kinds of universes.[3] Progressively, the world and the sign seemed to exist in incommensurable universes – there was literally no *measure* linking them, and the reading conventions for all texts came to resemble those required for science fiction. What emerged was a global technology that 'made the separation of text from context an everyday experience'. Hayles's second wave, 'energized by the rapid development of information technology, made the disappearance of stable, reproducible context an international phenomenon . . . Context was no longer a natural part of every experience, but an artifact that could be altered at will.' Hayles's third wave of denaturalization concerned time. 'Beginning with the Special Theory of Relativity, time increasingly came to be seen not as an inevitable progression along a linear scale to which all humans were subject, but as a construct that could be conceived in different ways.'

Language is no longer an echo of the *verbum dei*, but a technical construct working on principles of internally generated difference. If the early modern natural philosopher or Renaissance physician conducted an exegesis of the text of nature written in the language of geometry or of cosmic correspondences, the postmodern scientist still reads for a living, but has as a text the coded systems of recognition – prone to the pathologies of mis-recognition – embodied in objects like computer networks and immune systems. The extraordinarily close tie of language and technology could hardly be overstressed in postmodernism. The 'construct' is at the centre of attention; making, reading, writing, and meaning seem to be very close to the same thing. This near-identity between technology, body, and semiosis suggests a particular edge to the mutually constitutive relations of political economy, symbol, and science that 'inform' contemporary research trends in medical anthropology.

THE APPARATUS OF BODILY PRODUCTION:
THE TECHNO-BIOPOLITICS OF ENGAGEMENT

Bodies, then, are not born; they are made (Plate 7). Bodies have been as thoroughly denaturalized as sign, context, and time. Late twentieth-century bodies do not grow from internal harmonic principles theorized within Romanticism. Neither are they discovered in the domains of realism and modernism. One is not born a woman, Simone de Beauvoir correctly insisted. It took the political-epistemological terrain of postmodernism to be able to insist on a co-text to de Beauvoir's: one is not born an organism. Organisms are made; they are constructs of a world-changing kind. The constructions of an organism's boundaries, the job of the discourses of immunology, are particularly potent mediators of the experiences of sickness and death for industrial and post-industrial people.

In this over-determined context, I will ironically – and inescapably – invoke a constructionist concept as an analytic device to pursue an under-standing of what kinds of units, selves, and individuals inhabit the universe structured by immune system discourse: This conceptual tool, 'the apparatus of bodily production', was discussed earlier on pp. 197–201 (King, 1987b). Scientific bodies are not *ideological* constructions. Always radically historically specific, bodies have a different kind of specificity and effectivity, and so they invite a different kind of engagement and intervention. The notion of a 'material-semiotic actor' is intended to highlight the object of knowledge as an active part of the apparatus of bodily production, without *ever* implying immediate presence of such objects or, what is the same thing, their final or unique determination of what can count as objective knowledge of a biomedical body at a particular historical juncture. Bodies as objects of knowledge are material-semiotic generative nodes. Their boundaries materialize in social interaction; 'objects' like bodies do not pre-exist as such. Scientific objectivity (the siting/sighting of objects) is not about dis-engaged discovery, but about mutual and usually unequal structuring, about taking risks. The various contending biological bodies emerge at the intersection of biological research, writing, and publishing; medical and other business practices; cultural productions of all kinds, including available metaphors and narratives; and technology, such as the visualization technologies that bring colour-enhanced killer T cells and intimate photographs of the developing foetus into high-gloss art books for every middle-class home (Nilsson, 1977, 1987).

But also invited into that node of intersection is the analogue to the lively languages that actively intertwine in the production of literary value: the coyote and protean embodiments of a world as witty agent and actor. Perhaps our hopes for accountability in the techno-biopolitics in postmodern frames turn on revisioning the world as coding trickster with whom we must learn to converse. Like a protein subjected to stress, the world for us may be thoroughly denatured, but it is not any less consequential. So while the late twentieth-century immune system is a construct of an elaborate apparatus of bodily production, neither the immune system nor any other of bio-medicine's world-changing bodies – like a virus – is a ghostly fantasy. Coyote is not a ghost, merely a protean trickster.

The following chart abstracts and dichotomizes two historical moments in the biomedical production of bodies from the late nineteenth century to the 1980s. The chart highlights epistemological, cultural, and political aspects of possible contestations for constructions of scientific bodies in this century. The chart itself is a traditional little machine for making particular meanings. Not a description, it must be read as an argument, and one which relies on a suspect technology for the production of meanings – binary dichotomization.

Representation	Simulation
Bourgeois novel	Science fiction
Realism and modernism	Postmodernism
Organism	Biotic component, code
Work	Text
Mimesis	Play of signifiers
Depth, integrity	Surface, boundary
Heat	Noise
Biology as clinical practice	Biology as inscription
Physiology	Communications engineering
Microbiology, tuberculosis	Immunology, AIDS
Magic bullet	Immunomodulation
Small group	Subsystem
Perfection	Optimization
Eugenics	Genetic engineering
Decadence	Obsolescence
Hygiene	Stress management
Organic division of labour	Ergonomics, cybernetics
Functional specialization	Modular construction
Biological determinism	System constraints

Reproduction	Replication
Individual	Replicon
Community ecology	Ecosystem
Racial chain of being	United Nations humanism
Colonialism	Transnational capitalism
Nature/culture	Fields of difference
Co-operation	Communications enhancement
Freud	Lacan
Sex	Surrogacy
Labour	Robotics
Mind	Artificial intelligence
Second World War	Star Wars
White capitalist patriarchy	Informatics of domination

It is impossible to see the entries in the right-hand column as 'natural', a realization that subverts naturalistic status for the left-hand column as well. From the eighteenth to the mid-twentieth centuries, the great historical constructions of gender, race, and class were embedded in the organically marked bodies of woman, the colonized or enslaved, and the worker. Those inhabiting these marked bodies have been symbolically other to the fictive rational self of universal, and so unmarked, species man, a coherent subject. The marked organic body has been a critical locus of cultural and political contestation, crucial both to the language of the liberatory politics of identity and to systems of domination drawing on widely shared languages of nature as resource for the appropriations of culture. For example, the sexualized bodies of nineteenth-century middle-class medical advice literature in England and the United States, in their female form organized around the maternal function and the physical site of the uterus and in their male form ordered by the spermatic economy tied closely to the nervous system, were part of an elaborate discourse of organic economy. The narrative field in which these bodies moved generated accounts of rational citizenship, bourgeois family life, and prophylaxis against sexual pollution and ineffici- ency, such as prostitution, criminality, or race suicide. Some feminist politics argued for the full inclusion of women in the body politic on grounds of maternal functions in the domestic economy extended to a public world. Late into the twentieth century, gay and lesbian politics have ironically and critically embraced the marked bodies constructed in nineteenth- and twentieth-century sexologies and gender identity medicines to create a complex humanist discourse of sexual liberation. Negritude, feminine writing, various separatisms, and other recent cultural movements have both drawn on and subverted the logics of naturalization central to biomedical discourse on race and gender in the histories of colonization and male supremacy. In all of these various, oppositionally interlinked, political and biomedical accounts, the body remained a relatively unambiguous locus of identity, agency, labour, and hierarchicalized function. Both scientific humanisms and biological determinisms could be authorized and contested in terms of the biological organism crafted in post-eighteenth-century life sciences.

But how do narratives of the normal and the pathological work when the biological and medical body is symbolized and operated upon, not as a system of work, organized by the hierarchical division of labour, ordered by a privileged dialectic between highly localized nervous and reproductive functions, but instead as a coded text, organized as an engineered communications system, ordered by a fluid and dispersed command-control-intelligence network? From the mid-twentieth century, biomedical discourses have been progressively organized around a very different set of technologies and practices, which have destabilized the symbolic privilege of the hierarchical, localized, organic body. Concurrently – and out of some of the same historical matrices of decolonization, multinational capitalism, world-wide high-tech militarization, and the emergence of new collective political actors in local and global politics from among those persons previously consigned to labour in silence – the question of 'differences' has destabilized humanist discourses of liberation based on a politics of identity and substantive unity. Feminist theory as a self-conscious discursive practice has been generated in this post-Second World War period characterized by the translation of Western scientific and political languages of nature from those based on work, localization, and the marked body to those based on codes, dispersal and networking, and the fragmented postmodern subject. An account of the biomedical, biotechnical body must start from the multiple molecular interfacings of genetic, nervous, endocrine, and immune systems. Biology is about recognition and misrecognition, coding errors, the body's reading practices (for example, frameshift mutations), and billion-dollar projects to sequence the human genome to be published and stored in a national genetic 'library'. The body is conceived as a strategic system, highly militarized in key arenas of imagery and practice. Sex, sexuality, and reproduction are theorized in terms of local investment strategies; the body ceases to be a stable spatial map of normalized functions and instead emerges as a highly mobile field of strategic differences. The biomedical-biotechnical body is a semiotic system, a complex meaning-producing field, for which the discourse of immunology, that is, the central biomedical discourse on recognition/misrecognition, has become a high-stakes practice in many senses.

In relation to objects like biotic components and codes, one must think, not in terms of laws of growth and essential properties, but rather in terms of strategies of design, boundary constraints, rates of flows, system logics, and costs of lowering constraints. Sexual reproduction becomes one possible strategy among many, with costs and benefits theorized as a function of the system environment. Disease is a subspecies of information malfunction or communications pathology; disease is a process of misrecognition or transgression of the boundaries of a strategic assemblage called self. Ideologies of sexual reproduction can no longer easily call upon the notions of unproblematic sex and sex role as organic aspects in 'healthy' natural objects like organisms and families. Likewise for race, ideologies of human diversity have to be developed in terms of frequencies of parameters and fields of power-charged differences, not essences and natural origins or homes. Race and sex, like individuals, are artefacts sustained or undermined by the discursive nexus of knowledge and power. Any objects or persons can be reasonably thought of in terms of disassembly and reassembly; no 'natural' architectures constrain system design. Design is none the less highly constrained. What counts as a 'unit', a one, is highly problematic, not a permanent given. Individuality is a strategic defence problem.

One should expect control strategies to concentrate on boundary conditions and interfaces, on rates of flow across boundaries, not on the integrity of natural objects. 'Integrity' or 'sincerity' of the Western self gives way to decision procedures, expert systems, and resource investment strategies. 'Degrees of freedom' becomes a very powerful metaphor for politics. Human beings, like any other component or subsystem, must be localized in a system architecture whose basic modes of operation are probabilistic. No objects, spaces, or bodies are sacred in themselves; any component can be interfaced with any other if the proper standard, the proper code, can be constructed for processing signals in a common language. In particular, there is no ground for ontologically opposing the organic, the technical, and the textual.[4] But neither is there any ground for opposing the *mythical* to the organic, textual, and technical. Their convergences are more important than their residual oppositions. The privileged pathology affecting all kinds of components in this universe is stress – communications breakdown. In the body stress is theorized to operate by 'depressing' the immune system. Bodies have become cyborgs – cybernetic organisms – compounds of hybrid techno-organic embodiment and textuality (Haraway, 1985 [this vol. pp. 149–81]). The cyborg is text, machine, body, and metaphor – all theorized and engaged in practice in terms of communications.

CYBORGS FOR EARTHLY SURVIVAL[5]
However, just as the nineteenth- and twentieth-century organism accommodated a diverse field of cultural, political, financial, theoretic and technical contestation, so also the cyborg is a contested and heterogeneous construct.

It is capable of sustaining oppositional and liberatory projects at the levels of research practice, cultural productions, and political intervention. This large theme may be introduced by examining contrasting constructions of the late twentieth-century biotechnical body, or of other contemporary postmodern communications systems. These constructs may be conceived and built in at least two opposed modes: (1) in terms of master control principles, articulated within a rationalist paradigm of language and embodiment; or (2) in terms of complex, structurally embedded semiosis with many 'generators of diversity' within a counter-rationalist (*not* irrationalist) or hermeneutic/situationist/constructivist discourse readily available within Western science and philosophy. Terry Winograd and Fernando Flores' (1986) joint work on *Understanding Computers and Cognition* is particularly suggestive for thinking about the potentials for cultural/scientific/political contestation over the technologies of representation and embodiment of 'difference' within immunological discourse, whose object of knowledge is a kind of 'artificial intelligence/language/communication system of the biological body'.[6]

Winograd and Flores conduct a detailed critique of the rationalist paradigm for understanding embodied (or 'structure-determined') perceptual and language systems and for designing computers that can function as prostheses in human projects. In the simple form of the rationalist model of cognition,

> One takes for granted the existence of an objective reality made up of things bearing properties and entering into relations. A cognitive being gathers 'information' about those things and builds up a mental 'model' which will be in some respects correct (a faithful representation of reality) and in other respects incorrect. Knowledge is a storehouse of representations that can be called upon to do reasoning and that can be translated into language. Thinking is a process of manipulating those representations'. (Winograd, in Edwards and Gordon, forthcoming)

It is this doctrine of representation that Winograd finds wrong in many senses, including on the plane of political and moral discourse usually suppressed in scientific writing. The doctrine, he continues, is also technically wrong for further guiding research in software design: 'Contrary to common consensus, the "commonsense" understanding of language, thought, and rationality inherent in this tradition ultimately *hinders* the fruitful application of computer technology to human life and work'. Drawing on Heidegger, Gadamer, Maturana, and others, Winograd and Flores develop a doctrine of interdependence of interpreter and interpreted, which are not discrete and independent entities. Situated pre-understandings are critical to all communication and action. 'Structure-determined systems' with histories shaped through processes of 'structural-coupling' give a better approach to perception than doctrines of representation.

> Changes in the environment have the potential of changing the relative patterns of activity within the nervous system itself that in turn orient the organism's behavior, a perspective that invalidates the assumption that we acquire representations of our environment. Interpretation, that is, arises as a necessary consequence of the structure of biological beings. (Winograd, in Edwards and Gordon, forthcoming)

Winograd conceives the coupling of the inner and outer worlds of organisms and ecosystems, of organisms with each other, or of organic and technical structures in terms of metaphors of language, communication, and construction – but not in terms of a rationalist doctrine of mind and language or a disembodied instrumentalism. Linguistic acts involve shared acts of interpretation, and they are fundamentally tied to engaged location in a structured world. Context is a fundamental matter, not as surrounding 'information', but as co-structure or co-text. Cognition, engagement, and situation-dependence are linked concepts for Winograd, technically and philosophically. Language is not about description, but about commitment. The point applies to 'natural' language and to 'built' language.

How would such a way of theorizing the technics and biologics of communication affect immune system discourse about the body's 'technology' for recognizing self and other and for mediating between 'mind' and 'body' in postmodern culture? Just as computer design is a map of and for ways of living, the immune system is in some sense a diagram of relationships and a guide for action in the face of questions about the boundaries of the self and about mortality. Immune system discourse is about constraint and possibility for engaging in a world of full of 'difference', replete with non-self. Winograd and Flores' approach contains a way to contest for notions of pathology, or 'breakdown', without militarizing the terrain of the body.

> Breakdowns play a central role in human understanding. A breakdown is not a negative situation to be avoided, but a situation of non-obviousness, in which some aspect of the network of tools that we are engaged in using is brought forth to visibility ... A breakdown reveals the nexus of relations necessary for us to accomplish our task ... This creates a clear objective for design – to anticipate the form of breakdowns and provide a space of possibilities for action when they occur. (Winograd, in Edwards and Gordon, forthcoming)

This is not a Star Wars or Strategic Computing Initiative relation to vulnerability, but neither does it deny therapeutic action. It insists on locating therapeutic, reconstructive action (and so theoretic understanding) in terms of situated purposes, not fantasies of the utterly defended self in a body as automated militarized factory, a kind of ultimate self as Robotic Battle Manager meeting the enemy (not-self) as it invades in the form of bits of foreign information threatening to take over the master control codes.

Situated purposes are necessarily finite, rooted in partiality and a subtle play of same and different, maintenance and dissolution. Winograd and Flores' linguistic systems are 'denaturalized', fully constructivist entities; and in that sense they are postmodern cyborgs that do not rely on impermeable boundaries between the organic, technical, and textual. But their linguistic/ communication systems are distinctly oppositional to the AI cyborgs of an 'information society', with its exterminist pathologies of final abstraction from vulnerability, and so from embodiment.[7]

THE ONE AND THE MANY:
SELVES, INDIVIDUALS, UNITS, AND SUBJECTS

What is constituted as an individual within postmodern biotechnical, biomedical discourse? There is no easy answer to this question, for even the most reliable Western individuated bodies, the mice and men of a well-equipped laboratory, neither stop nor start at the skin, which is itself something of a teeming jungle threatening illicit fusions, especially from the perspective of a scanning electron microscope. The multi-billion-dollar project to sequence 'the human genome' in a definitive genetic library might be seen as one practical answer to the construction of 'man' as 'subject' of science. The genome project is a kind of technology of postmodern humanism, defining 'the' genome by reading and writing it. The technology required for this particular kind of literacy is suggested by the advertisment for MacroGene Workstation. The ad ties the mythical, organic, technical, and textual together in its graphic invocation of the 'missing link' crawling from the water on to the land, while the text reads, 'In the LKB MacroGene Workstation [for sequencing nucleic acids], there are no "missing links".' (See Plate 8.) The monster *Ichthyostega* crawling out of the deep in one of earth's great transitions is a perfect figure for late twentieth-century bodily and technical metamorphoses. An act of canonization to make the theorists of the humanities pause, the standard reference work called the human genome would be the means through which human diversity and its pathologies could be tamed in the exhaustive code kept by a national or international genetic bureau of standards. Costs of storage of the giant dictionary will probably exceed costs of its production, but this is a mundane matter to any librarian (Roberts, 1987a,b,c; Kanigel, 1987). Access to this standard for 'man' will be a matter of international financial, patent, and similar struggles. The Peoples of the Book will finally have a standard genesis story. In the beginning was the copy.

The Human Genome Project might define postmodern species being (*pace* the philosophers), but what of *individual* being? Richard Dawkins raised this knotty problem in *The Extended Phenotype*. He noted that in 1912, Julian Huxley defined individuality in biological terms as 'literally indivisibility – the quality of being sufficiently heterogeneous in form to be rendered non-functional if cut in half' (Dawkins, 1982, p. 250). That seems a promising start. In Huxley's terms, surely you or I would count as an individual, while many worms would not. The individuality of worms was not achieved even at the height of bourgeois liberalism, so no cause to worry there. But Huxley's definition does not answer *which function* is at issue. Nothing answers that in the abstract; it depends on what is to be done.[8] You or I (whatever problematic address these pronouns have) might be an individual for some purposes, but not for others. This is a normal ontological state for cyborgs and women, if not for Aristotelians and men. Function is about action. Here is where Dawkins has a radical solution, as he proposes a view of individuality that is strategic at every level of meaning. There are many kinds of individuals for Dawkins, but one kind has primacy. 'The whole purpose of our search for a "unit of selection" is to discover a suitable actor to play the leading role in our metaphors of purpose' (1982, p. 91). The 'metaphors of purpose' come down to a single bottom line: replication. 'A successful replicator is one that succeeds in lasting, in the form of copies, for a very long time measured in generations, and succeeds in propogating many copies of itself' (1982, pp. 87–8).

The replicator fragment whose individuality finally matters most, in the constructed time of evolutionary theory, is not particularly 'unitary'. For all that it serves, for Dawkins, as the 'unit' of natural selection, the replicator's boundaries are not fixed and its inner reaches remain mutable. But still, these units must be a bit smaller than a 'single' gene coding for a protein. Units are only good enough to sustain the technology of copying. Like the replicons' borders, the boundaries of other strategic assemblages are not fixed either – it all has to do with the broad net cast by strategies of replication in a world where self and other are very much at stake.

> The integrated multi-cellular organism is a phenomenon which has emerged as a result of natural selection on primitively selfish replicators. It has paid replicators to behave gregariously [so much for 'harmony', in the short run]. The phenotypic power by which they ensure their survival is in principle extended and unbounded. In practice the organism has arisen as a partially bounded local concentration, a shared knot of replicator power. (Dawkins, 1982, p. 264)

'In principle extended and unbounded' – this is a remarkable statement of interconnectedness, but of a very particular kind, one that leads to theorizing the living world as one vast arms race. '[P]henotypes that extend outside the body do not have to be inanimate artefacts: they themselves can be built of living tissue . . . I shall show that it is logically sensible to regard parasite genes as having phenotypic expression in host bodies *and behaviour*' (1982, p. 210, emphasis mine). But the being who serves as another's phenotype is itself populated by propagules with their own replicative ends. '[A]n animal will not necessarily submit passively to being manipulated, and an evolution-ary "arms race" is expected to develop' (1982, p. 39). This is an arms race that must take account of the stage of the development of the means of bodily production and the costs of maintaining it:

> The many-celled body is a machine for the production of single-celled propagules. Large bodies, like elephants, are best seen as heavy plant and machinery, a temporary resource drain, invested so as to improve later propagule production. In a sense the germ-line would 'like' to reduce capital investment in heavy machinery . . . (1982, p. 254)

Large capital is indeed a drain; small is beautiful. But you and I have required large capital investments, in more than genetic terms. Perhaps we should keep an eye on the germ-line, especially since 'we' – the non-germ-line components of adult mammals (unless you identify with your haploid gametes and their contents, and some do) – cannot be copy units. 'We' can only aim for a defended self, not copy fidelity, the property of other sorts of units. Within 'us' is the most threatening other – the propagules, whose phenotype we, temporarily, are.

What does all this have to do with the discourse of immunology as a map of systems of 'difference' in late capitalism? Let me attempt to convey the flavour of representations of the curious bodily object called the human immune system, culled from textbooks and research reports published in the 1980s. The IS is composed of about 10 to the 12th cells, two orders of magnitude more cells than the nervous system has. These cells are regenerated throughout life from pluripotent stem cells that themselves remain undifferentiated. From embryonic life through adulthood, the immune system is sited in several relatively amorphous tissues and organs, including the thymus, bone marrow, spleen, and lymph nodes; but a large fraction of its cells are in the blood and lymph circulatory systems and in body fluids and spaces. There are two major cell lineages to the system. The first is the *lymphocytes*, which include the several types of T cells (helper, suppressor, killer, and variations of all these) and the B cells (each type of which can produce only one sort of the vast array of potential circulating antibodies). T and B cells have particular specificities capable of recognizing almost any molecular array of the right size that can ever exist, no matter how clever industrial chemistry gets. This specificity is enabled by a baroque somatic mutation mechanism, clonal selection, and a polygenic receptor or marker system. The second immune cell lineage is the *mononuclear phagocyte system*, including the multi-talented macrophages, which, in addition to their other recognition skills and connections, also appear to share receptors and some hormonal peptide products with neural cells. Besides the cellular compartment, the immune system comprises a vast array of circulating acellular products, such as antibodies, lymphokines, and complement components. These molecules mediate communication among components of the immune system, but also between the immune system and the nervous and endocrine systems, thus linking the body's multiple control and co-ordination sites and functions. The genetics of the immune system cells, with their high rates of somatic mutation and gene product splicings and rearrangings to make finished surface receptors and antibodies, makes a mockery of the notion of a constant genome even within 'one' body. The hierarchical body of old has given way to a network-body of truly amazing complexity and specificity. The immune system is everywhere and nowhere. Its specificities are indefinite if not infinite, and they arise randomly; yet these extraordinary variations are the critical means of maintaining individual bodily coherence.

In the early 1970s, the Nobel Prize-winning immunologist, Niels Jerne, proposed a theory of immune system self-regulation, called the network theory, that must complete this minimalist account (Jerne, 1985; Golub, 1987, pp. 379–92). 'The network theory differs from other immunological thinking because it endows the immune system with the ability to regulate itself using only itself' (Golub, 1987, p. 379). Jerne's basic idea was that any antibody molecule must be able to act functionally as both antibody to some antigen *and* as antigen for the production of an antibody to itself, albeit at another region of 'itself'. All these sites have acquired a nomenclature sufficiently daunting to keep popular understanding of the theory at bay indefinitely, but the basic conception is simple. The concatenation of internal recognitions and responses would go on indefinitely, in a series of interior mirrorings of sites on immunoglobulin molecules, such that the immune system would always be in a state of dynamic internal responding. It would never be passive, 'at rest', awaiting an activating stimulus from a hostile outside. In a sense, there could be no *exterior* antigenic structure, no 'invader', that the immune system had not already 'seen' and mirrored internally. 'Self' and 'other' lose their rationalistic oppositional quality and become subtle plays of partially mirrored readings and responses. The notion of the *internal image* is the key to the theory, and it entails the premise that every member of the immune system is capable of interacting with every other member. As with Dawkins's extended phenotype, a radical conception of *connection* emerges unexpectedly at the heart of postmodern moves.

> This is a unique idea, which if correct means that all possible reactions
> that the immune system can carry out with epitopes in the world outside
> of the animal are already accounted for in the internal system of paratopes
> and idiotopes already present inside the animal. (Golub, 1987, pp. 382–3)

Jerne's conception recalls Winograd and Flores' insistence on structural
coupling and structure-determined systems in their approach to perception.
The internal, structured activity of the system is the crucial issue, not formal
representations of the 'outer' world within the 'inner' world of the communications system that is the organism. Both Jerne's and Winograd's
formulations resist the means of conceptualization facilitated most readily by
a rationalist theory of recognition or representation. In discussing what he
called the deep structure and generative grammar of the immune system,
Jerne argued that 'an identical structure can appear on many structures in
many contexts and be reacted to by the reader or by the immune system'
(quoted in Golub, 1987, p. 384).[9]

Does the immune system – the fluid, dispersed, networking techno-
organic-textual-mythic system that ties together the more stodgy and
localized centres of the body through its acts of recognition – represent the
ultimate sign of altruistic evolution towards wholeness, in the form of the
means of co-ordination of a coherent biological self? In a word, no, at least
not in Leo Buss's (1987) persuasive postmodern theoretic scheme of *The
Evolution of Individuality*.

Constituting a kind of technological holism, the earliest cybernetic
communications systems theoretic approaches to the biological body from
the late 1940s through the 1960s privileged co-ordination, effected by
'circular causal feedback mechanisms'. In the 1950s, biological bodies
became technological communications systems, but they were not quite fully
reconstituted as sites of 'difference' in its postmodern sense – the play of
signifiers and replicators in a strategic field whose significance depended
problematically, at best, on a world outside itself. Even the first synthetic
proclamations of sociobiology, particularly E.O. Wilson's *Sociobiology: The
New Synthesis* (1975), maintained a fundamentally techno-organicist or holist
ontology of the cybernetic organism, or cyborg, repositioned in evolutionary
theory by post-Second World War extensions and revisions of the principle
of natural selection. This 'conservative' dimension of Wilson and of several
other sociobiologists has been roundly criticized by evolutionary theorists
who have gone much further in denaturing the co-ordinating principles of
organismic biology at every level of biotic organization, from gene fragments
through ecosystems. The sociobiological theory of inclusive fitness maintained a kind of envelope around the organism and its kin, but that envelope

has been opened repeatedly in late 1970s' and 1980s' evolutionary theory.

Dawkins (1976, 1982) has been among the most radical disrupters of cyborg biological holism, and in that sense he is most deeply informed by a postmodern consciousness, in which the logic of the permeability among the textual, the technic, and the biotic and of the deep theorization of all possible texts and bodies as strategic assemblages has made the notions of 'organism' or 'individual' extremely problematic. He ignores the mythic, but it pervades his texts. 'Organism' and 'individual' have not disappeared; rather, they have been fully denaturalized. That is, they are ontologically contingent constructs from the point of view of the biologist, not just in the loose ravings of a cultural critic or feminist historian of science.

Leo Buss reinterpreted two important remaining processes or objects that had continued to resist such denaturing: (1) embryonic development, the very process of the construction of an individual; and (2) immune system interactions, the iconic means for maintaining the integrity of the one in the face of the many. His basic argument for the immune system is that it is made up of several variant cell lineages, each engaged in its own replicative 'ends'. The contending cell lineages serve somatic function because

> the receptors that ensure delivery of growth-enhancing mitogens also compel somatic function. The cytotoxic T-cell recognizes its target with the same receptor arrangement used by the macrophage to activate that cell lineage. It is compelled to attack the infected cell by the same receptor required for it to obtain mitogens from helper cells ... The immune system works by exploiting the inherent propensity of cells to further their own rate of replication. (Buss, 1987, p. 87)

The individual is a constrained accident, not the highest fruit of earth history's labours. In metazoan organisms, at least two units of selection, cellular and individual, pertain; and their 'harmony' is highly contingent. The parts are not *for* the whole. There is no part/whole relation at all, in any sense Aristotle would recognize. Pathology results from a conflict of interests between the cellular and organismic units of selection. Buss has thereby recast the multi-cellular organism's means of self-recognition, of the maintenance of 'wholes', from an illustration of the priority of co-ordination in biology's and medicine's ontology to a chief witness for the irreducible vulnerability, multiplicity, and contingency of every construct of individuality.

The potential meanings of such a move for conceptualizations of pathology and therapeutics within Western biomedicine are, to say the least, intriguing. Is there a way to turn the discourse suggested by Jerne, Dawkins, and Buss into an oppositional/alternative/liberatory approach analogous to that of Winograd and Flores in cognition and computer research? Is this postmodern body, this construct of always vulnerable and contingent individuality, *necessarily* an automated Star Wars battlefield in the now extra-terrestrial space of the late twentieth-century Western scientific body's intimate interior? What might we learn about this question by attending to the many contemporary representations of the immune system, in visualization practices, self-help doctrines, biologists' metaphors, discussions of immune system diseases, and science fiction? This is a large enquiry, and in the paragraphs that follow I only begin to sketch a few of the sometimes promising but more often profoundly disturbing recent cultural productions of the postmodern immune system-mediated body.[10] At this stage, the analysis can only serve to sharpen, not to answer, the question.

IMMUNE POWER: IMAGES, FICTIONS, AND FIXATIONS

This chapter opened with a reminder that science has been a travel discourse, intimately implicated in the other great colonizing and liberatory readings and writings so basic to modern constitutions and dissolutions of the marked bodies of race, sex, and class. The colonizing and the liberatory, and the constituting and the dissolving, are related as internal images. So I continue this tour through the science museum of immunology's cultures with the 'land, ho!' effect described by my colleague, James Clifford, as we waited in our university chancellor's office for a meeting in 1986. The chancellor's office walls featured beautiful colour-enhanced photographic portraits of the outer planets of earth's solar system. Each 'photograph' created the effect for the viewer of having been there. It seemed some other observer must have been there, with a perceptual system like ours and a good camera; somehow it must have been possible to *see* the land masses of Jupiter and Saturn coming into view of the great ships of *Voyager* as they crossed the empty reaches of space. Twentieth-century people are used to the idea that all photographs are constructs in some sense, and that the appearance that a photograph gives of being a 'message without a code', that is, what is pictured being simply *there*, is an effect of many layers of history, including prominently, technology (Barthes, 1982; Haraway, 1984–5; Petchesky, 1987). But the photographs of the outer planets up the ante on this issue by orders of magnitude. The wonderful pictures have gone through processes of construction that make the metaphor of the 'eye of the camera' completely misleading. The chancellor's snapshot of Jupiter is a postmodern photographic portrait – a denatured construct of the first order, which has the effect of utter naturalistic realism. *Someone* was there. Land, ho! But that some*one* was a spaceship that sent back digitalized signals to a whole world of transformers and imagers on a distant place called 'earth', where art photographs could be produced to give a reassuring sense of the *thereness* of Jupiter, and, not incidentally, of *spacemen*, or at least virtual spacemen, whose eyes would see in the same colour spectrum as an earthly primate's.

The same analysis must accompany any viewing of the wonderful photographs and other imaging precipitates of the components of the immune system. The cover of *Immunology: A Synthesis* (Golub, 1987) features an iconic replication of its title's allusion to synthesis: a multi-coloured computer graphic of the three-dimensional structure of insulin showing its antigenic determinants clustered in particular regions. Golub elicits consciousness of the *constructed* quality of such images in his credit: 'Image created by John A. Tainer and Elizabeth D. Getzoff'. Indeed, the conventional trope of scientist as artist runs throughout Golub's text, such that scientific construction takes on the particular resonances of high art and genius, more than of critical theories of productions of the postmodern body. But the publications of Lennart Nilsson's photographs, in the coffee table art book *The Body Victorious* (Nilsson, 1987) and in the *National Geographic* (Jaret, 1986), allow the 'land, ho!' effect unmediated scope (Plates 9 and 10). The blasted scenes, sumptuous textures, evocative colours, and ET monsters of the immune landscape are simply *there*, inside *us*. A white extruding tendril of a pseudopodinous macrophage ensnares a bacterium; the hillocks of chromosomes lie flattened on a blue-hued moonscape of some other planet; an infected cell buds myriads of deadly virus particles into the reaches of inner space where more cells will be victimized; the auto-immune-disease-ravaged head of a femur glows in a kind of sunset on a non-living world; cancer cells are surrounded by the lethal mobil squads of killer T cells that throw chemical poisons into the self's malignant traitor cells.

The equation of Outer Space and Inner Space, and of their conjoined discourses of extra-terrestrialism, ultimate frontiers, and high technology war, is quite literal in the official history celebrating 100 years of the National Geographic Society (Bryan, 1987). The chapter that recounts the *National Geographic*'s coverage of the Mercury, Gemini, Apollo, and Mariner voyages is called 'Space' and introduced with the epigraph, 'The Choice Is the Universe – or Nothing'. The final chapter, full of Nilsson's and other biomedical images, is entitled 'Inner Space' and introduced with the epigraph, 'The Stuff of the Stars Has Come Alive' (Bryan, 1987, pp. 454, 352). It is photography that convinces the viewer of the fraternal relation of inner and outer space. But curiously, in outer space, we see spacemen fitted into explorer craft or floating about as individuated cosmic foetuses, while in the supposed earthy space of our own interiors, we see non-humanoid strangers who are supposed to be the means by which our bodies sustain our integrity and individuality, indeed our humanity in the face of a world of others. We seem invaded not just by the threatening 'non-selves' that the immune system guards against, but more fundamentally by our own strange parts. No wonder auto-immune disease carries such awful significance, marked from the first suspicion of its existence in 1901 by Morgenroth and Ehrlich's term, *horror autotoxicus*.

The trope of space invaders evokes a particular question about directionality of travel: in which direction is there an invasion? From space to earth? From outside to inside? The reverse? Are boundaries defended symmetrically? Is inner/outer a hierarchicalized opposition? Expansionist Western medical discourse in colonizing contexts has been obsessed with the notion of contagion and hostile penetration of the healthy body, as well as of terrorism and mutiny from within. This approach to disease involved a stunning reversal: the colonized was perceived as the invader. In the face of the disease genocides accompanying European 'penetration' of the globe, the 'coloured' body of the colonized was constructed as the dark source of infection, pollution, disorder, and so on, that threatened to overwhelm white manhood (cities, civilization, the family, the white personal body) with its decadent emanations. In establishing the game parks of Africa, European law turned indigenous human inhabitants of the 'nature reserves' into poachers, invaders in their own terrain, or into part of the wildlife. The residue of the history of colonial tropical medicine and natural history in late twentiety-century immune discourse should not be underestimated. Discourses on parasitic diseases and AIDS provide a surfeit of examples.

The tones of colonial discourse are also audible in the opening paragraphs of *Immunology: The Science of Non-Self Discrimination*, where the dangers to individuality are almost lasciviously recounted. The first danger is 'fusion of individuals':

> In a jungle or at the bottom of the sea, organisms – especially plants, but also all kinds of sessile animals – are often in such close proximity that they are in constant danger of losing their individuality by fusion . . . But only in the imagination of an artist does all-out fusion occur; in reality, organisms keep pretty much separate, no matter how near to one another they live and grow. (Klein, 1982, p. 3)

In those exotic, allotropic places, any manner of contact might occur to threaten proper mammalian self-definition. Harmony of the organism, that favourite theme of biologists, is explained in terms of the aggressive defence of individuality; and Klein advocates devoting as much time in the undergraduate biology curriculum to defence as to genetics and evolution. It reads a bit like the defence department fighting the social services budget for federal funds. Immunology for Klein is 'intraorganismic defense reaction', proceding by '*recognition, processing,* and *response*'. Klein defines '*self*' as 'everything constituting an integral part of a given individual' (1982, p. 5; emphasis in original). What counts as an individual, then, is the nub of the matter. Everything else is '*not-self*' and elicits a defence reaction if boundaries are crossed. But this chapter has repeatedly tried to make problematic just what does count as self, within the discourses of biology and medicine, much less in the postmodern world at large.

A diagram of the 'Evolution of Recognition Systems' in a recent immunology textbook makes clear the intersection of the themes of literally 'wonderful' diversity, escalating complexity, the self as a defended stronghold, and extra-terrestrialism (Plate 11). Under a diagram culminating in the evolution of the mammals, represented without comment by a mouse and a *fully-suited spaceman*,[11] who appears to be stepping out, perhaps on the surface of the moon, is this explanation:

> From the humble amoeba searching for food (top left) to the mammal with its sophisticated humoral and cellular immune mechanisms (bottom right), the process of **'self versus non-self recognition'** shows a steady development, keeping pace with the increasing need of animals to maintain their integrity in a hostile environment. The decision at which point 'immunity' appeared is thus a purely semantic one'. (Playfair, 1984, p. 3; emphasis in original)

These are the semantics of defence and invasion. When is a self enough of a self that its boundaries become central to entire institutionalized discourses in medicine, war, and business? Immunity and invulnerability are intersecting concepts, a matter of consequence in a nuclear culture unable to accommodate the experience of death and finitude within available liberal discourse on the collective and personal individual. Life is a window of vulnerability. It seems a mistake to close it. The perfection of the fully defended, 'victorious' self is a chilling fantasy, linking phagocytotic amoeba and moon-voyaging man cannibalizing the earth in an evolutionary teleology of post-apocalypse extra-terrestrialism. It is a chilling fantasy, whether located in the abstract spaces of national discourse, or in the equally abstract spaces of our interior bodies.

Images of the immune system as battlefield abound in science sections of daily newspapers and in popular magazines, for example, *Time* magazine's 1984 graphic for the AIDS virus's 'invasion' of the cell-as-factory. The virus is imaged as a tank, and the viruses ready for export from the expropriated cells are lined up as tanks ready to continue their advance on the body as a productive force. The *National Geographic* explicitly punned on Star Wars in its graphic entitled 'Cell Wars' in Jaret's 'The Wars Within' (1986, pp. 708–9). The battle imagery is conventional, not unique to a nuclear and Cold War era, but it has taken on all the specific markings of those particular historical crises. The militarized, automated factory is a favourite convention among immune system illustrators and photographic processors. The specific historical markings of a Star Wars-maintained individuality[12] are enabled in large measure by high-technology visualization technologies, which are also critical to the material means of conducting postmodern war, science, and business, such as computer-aided graphics, artificial intelligence software, and many kinds of scanning systems.

'Imaging' or 'visualization' has also become part of therapeutic practice in both self-help and clinical settings, and here the contradictory possibilities and potent ambiguities over biomedical technology, body, self, and other emerge poignantly. The immune system has become a lucrative terrain of self-development practices, a scene where contending forms of power are evoked and practised. In *Dr. Berger's Immune Power Diet*, the 'invincible you' is urged to 'put immune power to work for you' by using your 'IQ (Immune Quotient)' (Berger, 1985, p. 186). In the great tradition of evangelical preaching, the reader is asked if 'You are ready to make the immune power commitment?' (1985, p. 4). In visualization self-help, the sufferer learns in a state of deep relaxation to image the processes of disease and healing, in order both to gain more control in many senses and to engage in a kind of meditation on the meanings of living and dying from an embodied vantage point in the microplaces of the postmodern body. These visualization exercises need not be prototypes for Star Wars, but they often are in the advice literature. The *National Geographic* endorses this approach in its description of one such effort: 'Combining fun and therapy, a young cancer patient at the M. D. Anderson Hospital in Houston, Texas, zaps cancer cells in the "Killer T Cell" video game' (Jaret, 1987, p. 705). Other researchers have designed protocols to determine if aggressive imagery is effective in mediating the healing work of visualization therapies, or if the relaxation techniques and non-aggressive imagery would 'work'. As with any function, 'work' for *what* cannot remain unexamined, and not just in terms of the statistics of cancer survival. Imaging is one of the vectors in the 'epidemics of signification' spreading in the cultures of postmodern therapeutics. What is at stake is the kind of collective and personal selves that will be constructed in this organic-technical-mythic-textual semiosis. As cyborgs in this field of meanings, how can 'we', late-twentieth-century Westerners, image our vulnerability as a window on to life?

Immunity can also be conceived in terms of shared specificities; of the semi-permeable self able to engage with others (human and non-human, inner and outer), but always with finite consequences; of situated possibilities and impossibilities of individuation and identification; and of partial fusions and dangers. The problematic multiplicities of postmodern selves, so potently figured *and* repressed in the lumpy discourses of immunology, must be brought into other emerging Western and multi-cultural discourses on health, sickness, individuality, humanity, and death.

The science fictions of the black American writer, Octavia Butler, invite both sobering and hopeful reflections on this large cultural project. Drawing on the resources of black and women's histories and liberatory movements, Butler has been consumed with an interrogation into the boundaries of what counts as human and into the limits of the concept and practices of claiming 'property in the self' as the ground of 'human' individuality and selfhood. In *Clay's Ark* (1984) Butler explores the consequences of an extra-terrestrial disease invading earth in the bodies of returned spacemen. The invaders have become an intimate part of all the cells of the infected bodies, changing human beings at the level of their most basic selves. The invaders have a single imperative that they enforce on their hosts: replication. Indeed, *Clay's Ark* reads like *The Extended Phenotype*; the invaders seem disturbingly like the 'ultimate' unit of selection that haunts the biopolitical imaginations of postmodern evolutionary theorists and economic planners. The humans in Butler's profoundly dystopic story struggle to maintain their own areas of choice and self-definition in the face of the disease they have become. Part of their task is to craft a transformed relation to the 'other' within themselves and to the children born to infected parents. The offsprings' quadruped form archetypically marks them as the Beast itself, but they are also the future of what it will mean to be human. The disease will be global. The task of the multi-racial women and men of *Clay's Ark* comes to be to reinvent the dialectics of self and other within the emerging epidemics of signification signalled by extra-terrestrialism in inner and outer space. Success is not judged in this book; only the naming of the task is broached.

In *Dawn*, the first novel of Butler's series on *Xenogenesis*, the themes of global holocaust and the threateningly intimate other as self emerge again. Butler's is a fiction predicated on the natural status of adoption and the unnatural violence of kin. Butler explores the interdigitations of human, machine, non-human animal or alien, and their mutants, especially in relation to the intimacies of bodily exchange and mental communication. Her fiction in the opening novel of *Xenogenesis* is about the monstrous fear and hope that the child will not, after all, be like the parent. There is never one parent. Monsters share more than the word's root with the verb 'to demonstrate'; monsters signify. Butler's fiction is about resistance to the imperative to recreate the sacred image of the same (Butler, 1978). Butler is like 'Doris Lessing, Marge Piercy, Joanna Russ, Ursula LeGuin, Margaret Atwood, and Christa Wolf, [for whom] reinscribing the narrative of catastrophe engages them in the invention of an alternate fictional world in which the other (gender, race, species) is no longer subordinated to the same' (Brewer, 1987, p. 46).

Catastrophe, survival, and metamorphosis are Butler's constant themes. From the perspective of an ontology based on mutation, metamorphosis, and the diaspora, restoring an original sacred image can be a bad joke. Origins are precisely that to which Butler's people do not have access. But patterns are another matter. At the end of *Dawn*, Butler has Lilith – whose name recalls her original unfaithful double, the repudiated wife of Adam – pregnant with the child of five progenitors, who come from two species, at least three genders, two sexes, and an indeterminate number of races. Preoccupied with marked bodies, Butler writes not of Cain or Ham, but of Lilith, the woman of colour whose confrontations with the terms of selfhood, survival, and reproduction in the face of repeated ultimate catastrophe presage an ironic salvation history, with a salutary twist on the promise of a woman who will crush the head of the serpent. Butler's salvation history is not utopian, but remains deeply furrowed by the contradictions and questions of power within all communication. Therefore, her narrative has the possibility of figuring something other than the Second Coming of the sacred image. Some other order of difference might be possible in *Xenogenesis* – and in immunology.

In the story, Lilith Iyapo is a young American black woman rescued with a motley assortment of remnants of humanity from an earth in the grip of nuclear war. Like all the surviving humans, Lilith has lost everything. Her son and her second-generation Nigerian-American husband had died in an accident before the war. She had gone back to school, vaguely thinking she might become an anthropologist. But nuclear catastrophe, even more radically and comprehensively than the slave trade and history's other great genocides, ripped all rational and natural connections with past and future from her and everyone else. Except for intermittent periods of questioning, the human remnant is kept in suspended animation for 250 years by the Oankali, the alien species that originally believed humanity was intent on committing suicide and so would be far too dangerous to try to save. Without human sensory organs, the Oankali are primatoid Medusa figures, their heads and bodies covered with multi-talented tentacles like a terran marine invertebrate's. These humanoid serpent people speak to the woman and urge her to touch them in an intimacy that would lead humanity to a monstrous metamorphosis. Multiply stripped, Lilith fights for survival, agency, and choice on the shifting boundaries that shape the possibility of meaning.

The Oankali do not rescue human beings only to return them unchanged to a restored earth. Their own origins lost to them through an infinitely long series of mergings and exchanges reaching deep into time and space, the Oankali *are* gene traders. Their essence is embodied commerce, conversation, communication – with a vengeance. Their nature is always to be midwife to themselves as other. Their bodies themselves are immune and genetic technologies, driven to exchange, replication, dangerous intimacy across the boundaries of self and other, and the power of images. Not unlike us. But unlike us, the hydra-headed Oankali do not build non-living technologies to mediate their self-formations and reformations. Rather, they are complexly webbed into a universe of living machines, all of which are partners in their apparatus of bodily production, including the ship on which the action of *Dawn* takes place. But deracinated captive fragments of humanity packed into the body of the aliens' ship inescapably evoke the terrible Middle Passage of the Atlantic slave trade that brought Lilith's ancestors to a 'New World'. There also the terms of survival were premised on an unfree 'gene trade' that permanently altered meanings of self and other for all the 'partners' in the exchange. In Butler's science fictional 'middle passage' the resting humans sleep in tamed carnivorous plant-like pods, while the Oankali do what they can to heal the ruined earth. Much is lost for ever, but the fragile layer of life able to sustain other life is restored, making earth ready for recolonization by large animals. The Oankali are intensely interested in humans as potential exchange partners partly because humans are built from such beautiful and dangerous genetic structures. The Oankali believe humans to be fatally, but reparably, flawed by their genetic nature as simultaneously intelligent and hierarchical. Instead, the aliens live in the postmodern geometries of vast webs and networks, in which the nodal points of individuals are still intensely important. These webs are hardly innocent of power and violence; hierarchy is not power's only shape – for aliens or humans. The Oankali make 'prints' of all their refugees, and they can print out replicas of the humans from these mental-organic-technical images. The replicas allow a great deal of gene trading. The Oankali are also fascinated with Lilith's 'talent' for cancer, which killed several of her relatives, but which in Oankali 'hands' would become a technology for regeneration and metamorphoses. But the Oankali want more from human-ity; they want a full trade, which will require the intimacies of sexual mingling and embodied pregnancy in a shared colonial venture in, of all places, the Amazon valley. Human individuality will be challenged by more than the Oankali communication technology that translates other beings into themselves as signs, images, and memories. Pregnancy raises the tricky question of consent, property in the self, and the humans' love of themselves as the sacred image, the sign of the same. The Oankali intend to return to earth as trading partners with humanity's remnants. In difference is the irretrievable loss of the illusion of the one.

Lilith is chosen to train and lead the first party of awakened humans. She will be a kind of midwife/mother for these radically atomized peoples' emergence from their cocoons. Their task will be to form a community. But first Lilith is paired in an Oankali family with the just pre-metamorphic youngster, Nikanj, an ooloi. She is to learn from Nikanj, who alters her mind and body subtly so that she can live more freely among the Oankali; and she is to protect it during its metamorphosis, from which they both emerge deeply bonded to each other. Endowed with a second pair of arms, an adult ooloi is the third gender of the Oankali, a neuter beeing who uses its special appendages to mediate and engineer the gene trading of the species and of each family. Each child among the Oankali has a male and female parent, usually sister and brother to each other, and an ooloi from another group, race, or moitié. One translation in Oankali languages for ooloi is 'treasured strangers'. The ooloi will be the mediators among the four other parents of the planned cross-species children. Heterosexuality remains unquestioned, if more complexly mediated. The different social subjects, the different genders that could emerge from another embodiment of resistance to compulsory heterosexual reproductive politics, do not inhabit this *Dawn*.

The treasured strangers can give intense pleasure across the boundaries of group, sex, gender, and species. It is a fatal pleasure that marks Lilith for the other awakened humans, even though she has not yet consented to a pregnancy. Faced with her bodily and mental alterations and her bonding with Nikanj, the other humans do not trust that she is still human, whether or not she bears a human-alien child. Neither does Lilith. Worrying that she is none the less a Judas-goat, she undertakes to train the humans with the intention that they will survive and run as soon as they return to earth, keeping their humanity as people before them kept theirs. In the training period, each female human pairs with a male human, and then each pair, willing or not, is adopted by an adult ooloi. Lilith loses her Chinese-American lover, Joseph, who is murdered by the suspicious and enraged humans. At the end, the first group of humans, estranged from their ooloi and hoping to escape, are ready to leave for earth. Whether they can still be fertile without their ooloi is doubtful. Perhaps it is more than the individual of a sexually reproducing species who always has more than one parent; the species too might require multiple mediation of its replicative biopolitics. Lilith finds she must remain behind to train another group, her return to earth indefinitely deferred. But Nikanj has made her pregnant with Joseph's sperm and the genes of its own mates. Lilith has not consented, and the first book of *Xenogenesis* leaves her with the ooloi's uncomprehending comfort that 'The differences will be hidden until metamorphosis' (Butler, 1987, p. 263). Lilith remains unreconciled: 'But they won't be human. That's what matters. You can't understand, but that is what matters.' The treasured stranger responds, 'The child inside you matters' (p. 263). Butler does not resolve this dilemma. The contending shapes of sameness and difference in any possible future are at stake in the unfinished narrative of traffic across the specific cultural, biotechnical, and political boundaries that separate and link animal, human, and machine in a contemporary global world where survival is at stake. Finally, this is the contested world where, with or without our consent, we are located. '[Lilith] laughed bitterly. "I suppose I could think of this as fieldwork – but how the hell do I get out of the field?"' (1987, p. 91).

From this field of differences, replete with the promises and terrors of cyborg embodiments and situated knowledges, there is no exit. Anthropologists of possible selves, we are technicians of realizable futures. Science *is* culture.

Notes

1 Animal Sociology and a Natural Economy of the Body Politic: A Political Physiology of Dominance

1 Young (1977), which also has an excellent bibliography of radical critique of science. See also Burtt (1952), Marcuse (1964), Marx and Engels (1970).

2 Braverman (1974). Albeit without a feminist perspective, Braverman situates the female work-force in the centre of his Marxist analysis of modern labour, scientific management, and the deskilling of working people in a period of increasing scientific and technical expertise.

3 See Ortner (1974) and de Beauvoir (1952). Both Ortner, from structuralist anthropology, and de Beauvoir, from existentialism, allow the ideology of the nature–culture split to dominate their feminist analyses. MacCormack (1977) draws on Mary Douglas's (1966, 1973) anthropological theories to challenge the nature–culture distinction. MacCormack analyses the female Sande sodality of Sierra Leone to stress women's collective construction of their own bodies for assuming active roles in the body politic. MacCormack's organicist and functionalist framework needs critical attention.

4 Nancy Hartsock's unpublished papers 'Objectivity and revolution: problems of knowledge in Marxist theory' and 'Social science, praxis, and political action' were crucial to me when I wrote this essay in 1978. For slightly later formulations, see Hartsock (1983a, 1983b). These papers are more useful for a feminist critique of the theory and practice of scientific objectivity than those of Habermas (1970) or Marcuse (1964).

5 See the University of Chicago 50th anniversary celebration symposium jointly produced by the biological and social sciences divisions (Redfield, 1942).

6 For early anarchist and Marxist socialisms on the meaning of nature for the body politic, see Kropotkin (1902) and Engels (1940).

7 See also Haraway (1989b). Yerkes links foundations, universities, neurophysiology and endocrinology, personnel management, psychopathology, educational testing, personality studies, social and sexual hygiene.

8 Yerkes and his peers were not using 'human engineering' simply as a metaphor. They explicitly saw physiological, biopsychological, and social sciences as key parts of rational management in advanced monopoly capitalism. The sciences inventoried raw materials, and the laboratory functioned as a pilot plant for human engineering (Yerkes, 1922). For a history of the project of human engineering, see Noble (1977), especially ch. 10.

9 See Emma Goldman (1931) for her keen analysis of the effects of sexual ignorance on working-class women. See Hall (1974) for background on the political context of sex research. For an insider's discussion, see Aberle and Corner (1953). The complicated network of scientific communities emerges clearly from Diana Long Hall's work.

10 Carpenter (1964) is a collection of his major papers. Carpenter moved from primate studies to concern with educational television in American rural and Third World contexts. Carpenter (1972) brought into communications systems work the same functionalist, hierarchical conceptions of organization he used in analysing primates (1945).

11   C.M. Child's (1928) gradient field theories entered social theory.

12   Baritz (1960) discusses Mayo's industrial mythology in the context of a general criticism of the subservient role to established power played by American social science. See also Heyl (1968), Henderson (1935), Parsons (1970). Stephen Cross, then a graduate student at Johns Hopkins, was my mentor for thinking about these issues. The theme of co-operation and competition in the anthropological focus on personality and culture in the 1930s was pervasive (e.g., Mead, 1937). Under Social Science Research Council auspices, May and Doob (1937) published a bibliography on the competition–co-operation theme.

2   The Past Is the Contested Zone: Human Nature and Theories of Production and Reproduction in Primate Behaviour Studies

1   Rayna Rapp helped construct this analysis when she was an anonymous reviewer for the original publication.

2   A powerful figure in British science politics since the Second World War, Zuckerman (1972, 1978) provided his own view of his science career. On a Rockefeller Research Fellowship, Zuckerman spent 1933–34 affiliated with Robert Yerkes' new Yale primate laboratories. Yerkes' and Zuckerman's correspondence in the Yerkes papers at Yale University archives shows their disenchantment with each other's approach to primate science.

3   For a critical history of functionalist explanation from the early nineteenth century in the mystification of capitalist class relations, see Young (1985).

4   Lancaster and Lee (1965). Based on the 1962–63 Primate Project at the Center for Advanced Study in the Behavioral Sciences, *Primate Behavior* represents Sherwood Washburn's and David Hamburg's entrepreneurial effort to refound primate studies within the frameworks of medical, evolutionary, and social functionalism.

5   Documentation to reconstruct his career, grants, students, and projects was courteously provided by Washburn from his files.

6   Part II of their argument appeared as Zihlman (1978a).

7   For the nineteenth-century context of the relation of political and natural economy, see Young (1973, pp. 164–248).

8   Compare the role of physiology in the nineteenth century in the theoretical production of nature in terms of hierarchically organized, differentiated organisms (Cooter, 1979).

3   The Biological Enterprise: Sex, Mind, and Profit from Human Engineering to Sociobiology

1   Thanks to members of the Baltimore Science for the People for helpful discussion of the ideas of this chapter. Useful work on ideological issues has been done by Science for the People, but they have tended to exempt from analysis the history and structure of biology, citing mainly illicit extensions into political or social areas. See Ann Arbor Science for the People (1977) and Chasin (1977). Sahlins (1976) and, with attention to the history of animal behaviour studies, Washburn (1978) defend the autonomy of the social sciences. More theoretical analysis has been undertaken by *Radical Science Journal* in London.

2   My method is analogous to Marx's reading of classical political economy and to the approach of Foucault (1970) and Jacob (1974).

3   Yerkes (1927a, 1932, 1943); Yerkes and Yerkes (1929).

4   Kohler (1976). On the general role of foundations in science, see Cohen (1976) and Fosdick (1952).

5   On systems, see Mesarovic (1968), von Bertalanffy (1968), Emery (1969), Pugh (1971), Lilienfeld (1978). On evolutionary strategy, see Dawkins (1976), Hamilton (1964). Stressing some of the non-oppressive potential of such forms of thought, Hutchinson (1978) provides an elegant explanation of history and basic ideas in systems-based ecology. See also MacArthur and Wilson (1967). Basic sociobiological reading includes Barash (1977), Wilson (1971, 1975, 1978), Caplan (1978).

6   Yerkes (1900, 1907, 1919); Yerkes et al. (1915); Yerkes, 'Testament', unpublished autobiography, in the R.M. Yerkes papers of the Yale library (RMY).

7   Yerkes (1935–6). The project was related to sex research on animals, 'primitive' people, and New Yorkers with marital problems (Hamilton, 1929; archives of the Committee for Research in Problems of Sex [CRPS], National Academy of Sciences, Washington, DC, especially files on Clark Wissler, 1928–31, and on Research Centers, Marital Research, 1923ff).

8   The organism–superorganism problem may be followed in Wheeler (1939), Emerson (1954), Kroeber (1917), Redfield (1942), Wilson (1971, pp. 12n, 282, 317–19; 1975, pp. 383–86).

9   CRPS ('Formulation of Program', 1922ff); Aberle and Corner (1953); Mead (1935); Gordon (1976); Miles and Terman (1929).

10 For example, CRPS (1921: Beginning of Program: Presentations of Project to NRC Divisions; 1921: Conference on Sex Problems).

11 CRPS (1923–37: Grantees: Declined). This folder includes an application from Margaret Sanger. Earl Zinn to Sanger, 23 April 1928, pleaded inadequate resources of the CRPS.

12 For critique of the idea of sexual repression as the form of the relation of capitalism and sex, see Foucault (1976).

13 RMY: Angell correspondence, 1923ff; Annual Reports of the Institute of Psychology, 1924–29; Testament, pp. 221–7.

14 RMY: Annual Reports of the Anthropoid Experiment Station of the Laboratories of Comparative Psychobiology (1930–35); later the Yale Laboratories of Primate Biology (1935–42); Angell correspondence. Fosdick (1952).

15 Yerkes, with colleagues like Fulton, established a new discipline within biology, primatology. See Ruch (1941).

16 Cybernetic systems are automated technological devices based on principles of internal regulation (such as feedback circuits). See especially Optner (1973), Singh (1966), Buckley (1968), Weiner (1954), Ashby (1961).

17 For example, see Weaver (1948); Gray (1963); Lettvin et al. (1959).

18 Cowdry (1930), Redfield (1942), Mesarovic (1968), Wilson et al. (1978).

19 Two fictional works develop the consequences of the new systems approach for human former-organisms: Pynchon (1974), Piercy (1976).

20 For texts illustrating this thesis: for molecular biology, Jacob (1974); for neural and behavioural sciences, Angyal (1941), Peterfreund and Schwartz (1966), Altmann (1967); for ecology, Odum (1955, 1959, 1971, 1977), Farley (1977); for political science, Lasswell and Kaplan (1950), Somit (1976), Eastman (1958); for ethics as quality control, Potter (1971), Stanley (1978).

21 Young (1985, pp. 164–248). Kropotkin (1902) proposed an anarchist natural economy. For a pacifist version see Allee (1938), and for comment, Caron (1977). Ghiselin (1974) provides a capitalist natural history.

22   On the disappearance of superorganisms, see Wilson (1971, pp. 317–19, and 1975, pp. 383–6).

23   Crook (1970), Ellis (1965); for extension to primates, Crook and Gartlan (1966).

24   The principal linguist drawn upon by Wilson is Thomas A. Sebeok, who in turn built on the language phiolsophy of Charles Morris. See Sebeok (1968), Morris (1938).

25   Wilson (1963, 1968). The human sociology source Wilson cites is Murrell (1965).

26   Throughout *On Human Nature*, Wilson uses the technological metaphors of the developmental geneticist, C.H. Waddington (1957).

27   Transcending a critique of sexism as explicit justification of sex role differentiation, a feminist theory of knowledge addressing the fundamental dualism of man and nature, mind and body, controller and controlled, has begun to appear in many disciplinary and practical contexts. See Hartsock (1983a, 1983b), Harding (1978), Merchant (1980), Griffin (1978), all of which construct a kind of feminist humanism. The most important non-feminist critique of humanism as a logic of domination is Foucault (1970).

4   In the Beginning Was the Word: The Genesis of Biological Theory

1   Merchant (1980) analyses the metaphors of female Nature in her transformation from nurturing mother to patient resource in Europe from the fifteenth to the eighteenth century. Dominating nature was possible within *both* metaphor (and social) systems, but all limits seem to disappear in the capitalist form of patriarchy. Merchant helps in seeing this scientific-humanistic dialectic of apocalypse.

2   This language is Barash's: on knowing the self and free will (1979, pp. 90, 233–4); on biogrammar (p. 10); on the variable icing/constant cake theory of culture and biology (pp. 10–11). While claiming that he, speaking for science, is giving 'plain facts' (pp. 25, 29, 44, 112, 126), Barash uses insistently phallic language throughout the book: pollination becomes floral 'rape' in which male flowers 'bombard female flowers' and grow a pollen tube which 'forces its way to the ovary' (p. 30). Harem masters abound, and Barash savours the language of LeBoeuf, who studied nursing elephant seal puppies in sociobiological terms of 'double mother-suckers', 'super weaners', and, now in Barash's phrase, 'evolutionary stars'. Barash's lesson from these patriarchal puns is that males take evolutionary risks and win big when they 'strike it rich'. Be a female only if you have no choice; females must be content with 'modest evolutionary success' (p. 59).

3   In the 'Acknowledgments', Barash recognizes his lover as his 'co-shareholder in my fitness'.

4   'Marxists' seem to be chief among these comfortable weaklings (Barash, 1979, ch. 8).

5   The funniest extended example of Barash's rhetoric of persuasion by patrilineal naming is his introduction of Robert Trivers's theory of parental investment – as if cost-benefit analysis would startle anyone since at least the early nineteenth century.

> Truly new and exciting ideas come along only rarely, even in science. I was privileged to be at the public unveiling of one of these ideas. It was December 1972, and the occasion was the annual meeting of the American Association for the Advancement of Science in Washington, D.C. The featured symposium on the 'ecology and evolution of social behavior' was nearly completed when Harvard sociobiologist Robert Trivers began speaking. He used no notes, seeming to figure it all out as he went along, but I'm sure he wasn't doing anything of the sort. In any event, it was arresting – and brilliant. When the young Huxley first read Darwin, he is said to have exclaimed, 'How stupid of me not to have thought of this!' The ideas Bob Trivers presented that day had much the same appeal as Darwin's work – simple, elegant, important, and almost incontrovertibly true'. (Barash, 1979, p. 125)

Then follows the 'pure, unadulterated biology' (p. 126) of parental investment theory – all about inheritance.

6   Ch. 8. Barash disavows seeking moral dictation from his science but enthusiastically endorses sociobiology's medical voice – especially in assessing mental health in terms of fitness-maximization behaviour (1979, pp. 214–15). The collapsing of morality into health is an old rhetorical strategy.

7   Washburn's opposition to sociobiology is an example of his complexity and of the inadequacy of some feminist critiques of his role as the chief author of the man-the-hunter theory in the history of physical anthropology.

8   Lila Leibowitz and Ruth Bleier highlight illogical evidence and special pleading in animal model research. Freda Salzman criticizes Maccoby and Jacklin on the relation of aggression and gender. Marian Lowe and Ruth Hubbard show the deep and shoddy similarities in E.O. Wilson's sociobiology and Alice Rossi's biosociology. Susan Leigh Star explores lateralization research in neurophysiology, and Janice Raymond argues the medicalization of moral-political issues through transexual surgery. Hubbard and Lowe provide the project's summary and theoretical framing.

9   Latour and Woolgar (1979) provide a comprehensive analysis of the epistemological and material factors involved in the production of facts packaged in objects solid enough to weigh and mail to colleagues. They calculated the cost per published paper from a Nobel Prize-winning research project in a productive Salk Institute laboratory. The word is not cheap.

10 Philosopher Noretta Koertge made the same point at the 1980 National Women's Studies Association meetings when she described a memory of herself at four years old being scolded by her mother for masturbating. Her mother claimed the act was naughty and would make her nervous. Little Noretta knew that she could never win on the naughty issue but that her mother might be wrong about the nervous part. Moral: science is a feminist resource; falsifiability is a feminist issue.

11 For example, Bleier, writing in Hubbard and Lowe (1979) on animal studies applied to humans, tried to have all arguments all ways as long as they come out right for feminists. Beginning with the premise that '[S]cience is a cultural institution', she still posited that 'the structure of science has its edges pure and probing into the knowable unknown'. But pollution results from the 'massive core' which perpetuates dominant social values (p. 49). Later she argues: (1) there is a real science with unclouded vision, feminist science, for example, Jane Lancaster's conclusions (p. 57) on primate behaviour are 'more rational', though why Lancaster can engage in a science of sex differences and escape male clouded vision is unexplained; (2) real science of sex differences is impossible for historical reasons; (3) such a science does exist and has yielded feminist facts and conclusions (pp. 58, 63–4); and (4) drawing on French feminist standpoints, 'All that remains to do is to write and speak ourselves into being; to construct a new language, a new scholarship, a new knowledge that is whole' (p. 66). Pure edges, massive cores, degrees of rationality, and French feminist theories that language constitutes reality imply mutually inconsistent epistemologies. They might all somehow be necessary, but the contradictions should be analysed.

12 The other essays include Barbara Fried on the language of sex and gender, Susan Leigh Star on sex differences and brain asymmetry, Datha Clapper Brack on physicians' displacing midwives, Martha Roth Walsh on women physicians, Vicki Druss and Mary Sue Henifin on anorexia, Emily Culpepper on menstrual attitudes among the ancient Hebrews and within a women's community in a possible future, Marilyn Grossman and Pauline Bart on male control of interpretations of the menopause and female reappropriation, Naomi Weisstein on sexist barriers to womens practising science, and a useful

extended bibliography provided by Henifin on women, science, and health. Various articles note that women producing current science have had the social role of subordinates in the scientific-technical work-force. We have not been so much absent in making scientific knowledge as we have been serviceable. The collaborative and collective, largely non-hierarchical, social structure supporting both Hubbard and Lowe's book and Hubbard *et al.*'s book contrasts sharply with the official 'debate' of the NEXA volume and with the heavy hero's burden of telling the hard truth that makes up Barash's persona. The writers in both feminist books are also explicit about their own class and race privilege and *their own* impediments to telling full, new stories (see, for example, Hubbard *et al.*, 1979, p. 32).

13   This is a central feminist criticism of Foucault's work: by highlighting the ubiquitous microcirculations of domination in his masterful analysis of the capillarity of power relations – that is, the constitution of resistance by power in a never-ending dialectic, and the demonstration of the impossibility of acquiring space without reproducing the domination named – he threatens to make the grand circulations of domination invisible.

14   This position is a non-guilt-ridden way of baking, having, sharing, and eating cake; it is a welcome pleasure after slicing Barash's iced torte. This rather free reading of Harding and Hartsock is based on Harding's unpublished essay, 'Philosophy and history of science as patriarchal oral history' (University of Delaware, 1980), and on Hartsock's unpublished manuscript, 'Money, sex, and power' (Johns Hopkins University, 1980). Harding believes the humanist and scientific approaches, at least in the social sciences, have really been opposed to each other; I disagree. In Foucault's terms there is a shared *episteme*.

5   The Contest for Primate Nature: Daughters of Man-the-Hunter in the Field, 1960–80

1   Aristotle (*Generatione animalium*), Lloyd (1968), Bacon (1893, 1942), Linnaeus (1758 – this edition added humans to the Order, Primates; 1972).

2   See, for example, Barash (1979), Wilson (1975, 1978), Fox (1967), Ardrey (1966, 1970), Dawkins (1976), Morgan (1972), Goodall (1971).

3   Kummer (1968), Altmann (1980), Altmann (1967), Hrdy (1977), Bogess (1979), Chevalier-Skolnikoff (1974), Lindberg (1967), Sugiyama (1967, pp. 221–36), Rowell (1972), Lancaster (1975). (Haraway [1989b] examines these issues more fully).

4   Langurs are highly adaptable monkeys from a group, colobines, specialized to eat mature leaves. They spend time on the ground and in trees, can be found in bisexual multi- or single-male troops, all-male groups and groups composed of adult females, juveniles, and infants. Troop size is highly variable. Adult males weigh about 18 kg, adult females about 11 kg. Langurs occur in remote areas and in semi-urban temple settings close to people. They range from arid lowlands to mountains (Hrdy, 1977, pp. 72–6).

5   Papers important to this essay include: Washburn (1951a, 1951b, 1978), Washburn and Avis (1958), Washburn and DeVore (1961), Washburn and Hamburg (1965), Washburn and Lancaster (1968).

6   Cravens (1978), Zacharias (1980), Haraway (1981–2, 1983), Frisch (1959).

7   Haller (1971), Hooton (1931, 1942). In correspondence in 1959, Washburn and Julian Steward agreed that use of Hooton's book for teaching was impossible because of its racism (Washburn personal papers). Washburn (1963) delivered an anti-racist presidential address to the 1962 meeting of the American Anthropological Association. See also Washburn's letters to the editor (*Newsweek*, 28 April 1969) in the race–IQ debate around Arthur Jensen's *Harvard Educational Review* paper.

8   This summary was compiled from Washburn's *curriculum vitae*, annual supplements to his University of California biobibliography, copies of grant proposals, and personal interviews. Professor Washburn's generous co-operation in providing these materials is greatly appreciated.

9   These rough figures were compiled from the International Primatological Society, Members' Handbook, 1977–78; the American Society of Primatologists, Directory, 1980; and the membership list in the *American Journal of Physical Anthropology* 51 (September 1979): 481–504. I divided professional locations into anthropology, medicine, regional primate research centre (specialty not otherwise determined), psychology (including neuropsychology), zoology, wildlife conservation, psychiatry, other. Women were identified conservatively; in case only initials were used, the person was ascribed masculine gender unless counterindicated by specific knowledge. Thanks to Rusten Hogness for help in obtaining these figures.

The following is an incomplete listing of women who earned PhDs through the 1970s in the direct Washburn and Jay/Dolhinow lineage and who have been important in major debates in their areas. The students often worked with both mentors, but Dolhinow's role in producing these students from her senior faculty position at UC Berkeley should be emphasized. Students of students, except Dolhinow's at Berkeley, are not included here. A lineage does not demonstrate what kind of importance such social links might have – or not have. Virginia Avis, 1958; Phyllis Jay, 1963; Suzanne Ripley, 1965; Jane Lancaster, 1967; Adrienne Zihlman, 1967; Judith Shirek (Ellefson), 1967; Suzanne Chevalier-Skolnikoff, 1971; Shirley Strum, 1976; Naomi Bishop, 1975; Elizabeth McCown, 1977; Jane Bogess, 1976; Sheila Curtain, 1976; Mary Ellen Morbeck, 1972. Jay, Ripley, Bisihp, Bogess, and Curtain studied langurs.

10   Speakers, titles, and drafts were obtained from Washburn's personal files. Other speakers in 1963 were: Ralph Holloway, Theodore Grand, Richard Lee, Peter Marler, Paul Simonds, and Washburn. Other speakers in 1966 were psychiatrist David Hamburg and student Richard van Horn. For the work of women, linked to Washburn, writing on themes relevant here, see: Zihlman (1967, 1978a, 1978b, 1978c), Tanner (1981), Jay (1963a, 1963b), Chevalier-Skolnikoff (1971, 1974), Chevalier-Skolnikoff and Poirier (1977), Ripley (1965), Lancaster (1967, 1968, 1971, 1973, 1975, 1978, 1979), Lancaster and Lee (1965).

11   An incomplete list of authors in the 1970s on langurs besides Dolhinow, Ripley, Bogess, and Hrdy is: Frank Poirier, Naomi Bishop, Richard Curtain, Sheila Curtain, S.M. Mohnot, R.P. Mukherjee, S.S. Saha, J.R. Oppenheimer, H. Rahaman, M.D. Parthasarathy, Y. Sugiyama, K. Yoshiba, Y. Furuya, C. Vogel, A. Hladik, and C.M. Hladik. Note the signs of primatology's collective and international structure.

12   For the famous picture of troop progression, see Hall and DeVore (1972, p. 141). A Time-Life book is the most available popular source propagating this baboon mythology (Eimerl and DeVore, 1965).

13   Principal people here are Adrienne Zihlman, Jane Lancaster, and Shirley Strum. For a popularization of what is mostly Strum's baboon narrative, see Moss (1975, pp. 193–230). A crucial part of this later story is the emergence of the chimpanzee as the most formidable candidate for modelling hominid evolution. But, not focusing on the chimpanzee, Strum, Lancaster, and Thelma Rowell told markedly different stories about the meanings of baboons, vervets, and patas monkeys. I think they de-emphasize *DeVore*'s baboons in part because a widespread women's movement altered what both male and female primatologists heard, saw, and believed. Jay never indicated that she thought langurs ought to be privileged models for hominid evolution. She had a different story to tell about *langurs*, which could not at that time command similar public interest.

That attention erupted later, for reasons at least as political as those sustaining the early baboon model.

14   Sugiyama (1967, p. 227). Caution is necessary in interpreting the language of papers translated, often badly, from Japanese.

15   Hrdy (1981) develops her arguments about the biological inheritance of human primate females in comparison with other living primate females in *The Woman That Never Evolved*. The females populating her book are assertive, competitive, various, independent – but not necessarily dominant. Hrdy regards human females to be in one of the worst positions *vis-à-vis* their male conspecifics, partly as a function of human male control of property. Harvard University Press again outdid itself in advertising strategies: in 1981 issues of the *New York Review of Books*, the press pictured a piece of stitchery, drawing on prominent contemporary feminist metaphors of quilting and stitchery and on both feminist and anti-feminist rhetorics for valuing women's traditional work positively. The Harvard sociobiological stitchery says, 'A woman's place is in the jungle.' Hrdy stresses that feminism and its product, human female equality, are a fragile historical-political achievement, not a biological inheritance. That the reviewer (Henry, 1982) in the influential radical feminist publication, *Off Our Backs*, enthusiastically endorsed *The Woman That Never Evolved* indicates the complexity of ideological alignments over sociobiological claims. Henry argued that 'Every aspect of [Hrdy's] book reflects a feminist perspective . . . I find it amazing that she could survive Harvard to write this . . . If Harvard University Press gets this important book out in paperback, maybe Hrdy can reach those to whom it is dedicated: "the liberated woman who never evolved . . ."' (pp. 18–19). Of course, Hrdy 'survived' Harvard with the patrilineal connection to the major male sociobiologists, who have been condemned by *Off Our Backs*, among other feminist publications, as the embodiment of scientific patriarchal purveyors of the biological determinism of female inferiority. Hrdy was a research associate; DeVore and Wilson were full professors. Hrdy was a mentor for Harvard physical anthropology women graduate students. Further, her explicit self-identification as a feminist was important in her view of the history of evolutionary theory (Hrdy and Williams, 1983). Obviously, the situation is more complex than 'simple' doctrinal alignments around sociobiology indicate.

16   Zuckerman (1933), Lindberg (1967), Tanner and Zihlman (1976), Zihlman (1978a, 1978b, 1978c).

17   Although Lancaster and Zihlman were not close collaborators, they shared the excitement of their new ideas and exchanged letters and manuscripts during the mid-1970s when so many women were using inherited tools to craft new stories. Lancaster to Zihlman (23 August 1976) expresses her pleasure at Zihlman's twist on the oestrus, sexual selection, and female choice tale. Thanks to Adrienne Zihlman for access to her correspondence file.

Sexual reproduction and female sexuality continue to figure in opposing new hypotheses for reconstructing hominid evolution, and tales of the past continue to be pregnant with the structure of possibilities for the future. For a blatant rejuvenation of male control of female sexuality (the pair bond) as the key to most aspects of hominid life, see Lovejoy (1981). That this paper was able to be published in a major journal without citing crucial evidence and publications on its major points is itself the subject for analysis on the establishment of scientific authority. What may count as crucial evidence about human evolution? That is the heart of the contest for human nature.

6   Reading Buchi Emecheta: Contests for 'Women's Experience' in Women's Studies

1   This chapter has been revised from a talk presented as part of the conference on Feminism and the Critical Study of Colonial Discourse at UCSC in the spring of 1987. Proceedings were published in *Inscriptions* 3/4 (1988), the journal of the Group for the Critical Study of Colonial Discourse. Thanks especially to the organizers of the conference (Deborah Gordon, Lisa Bloom, Vivek Dareshawar) and co-member of the panel (Teresa de Lauretis).

2   Feminist theorist, bell hooks, emphasized the difference between the noun, as in 'the women's movement', with the potential for pernicious taxonomies and vanguardism inherent in this curious substantive, contrasted to the more active verb-like form, as in 'women's movement', that resists reification and claims to special political correctness (hooks, 1981, 1984). Avoiding the pitfalls of liberal definitions emphasizing 'equality of rights', hooks argued, 'Feminism is the struggle to end sexist oppression. Its aim is not to benefit solely any specific group of women, any particular race or class of women. It does not privilege women over men. It has the power to transform in a meaningful way all our lives' (hooks, 1984, p. 26). Feminist movement is thus directed at the 'cultural basis of group oppression ... This would mean that race and class oppression would be recognized as feminist issues with as much relevance as sexism' (p. 25). Thanks to Katie King for reminding me of hooks's usage, and also for much else in my understanding of the detailed apparatuses of production of women's culture and women's experience (King, 1986, 1988, forthcoming).

3   At the heart of US feminist theory in the 1980s has been an effort to articulate the specificity of location from which politics and knowledge must be built. The earlier formulation that 'the personal is political' intersected with and has been transformed by representations of the webs of women's local and global positionings, resulting in a major transformation of the forms and contents of feminist movement. One of the written traces is a large network of implicit intertextuality and explicit citation in feminist publishing. See, for example, Mohanty's (1988, p. 43) citation of Adrienne Rich's (1986) 'Notes toward a politics of location' and Bernice Johnson Reagon's (1983) originary 'Coalition politics'. Mohanty repeats, as I do, Rich's line from 'North American tunnel vision,' published first in 1983: 'It was not enough to say "As a woman I have no country; as a woman my country is the whole world" ... Magnificent as that vision may be, we cannot explode into breadth without a conscious grasp on the particular and concrete meaning of our location here and now, in the United States of America' (Rich, 1986, p. 162). Neither Rich, Reagon, Mohanty, nor I disavow the hope of world-wide feminist connection, which, located within the established disorder of the United States, I call the hope for an 'elsewhere' in an appropriation of SF tropes. This kind of 'elsewhere' is brought into being out of feminist movement rooted in specification and articulation, not out of common 'identities' nor assumption of the right or ability of any particular to 'represent' the general. The 'particular' in feminist movement is not about liberal individualism nor a despairing isolation of endless differences, much less about rejecting the hope for collective movement. But the means and processes of collective movement must be imagined and acted out in new geometries. That is why I find the reading and writing strategies of SF (speculative fiction, science fiction, science fantasy, speculative feminism) so useful for feminist theorizing.

4   Trinh T. Minh-ha (1986–7, pp. 3–38; 1988, pp. 71–7; 1989) discusses this ungraspable middle space and develops her theory of the 'inappropriate/d other' as a figure for post-colonial women. Theorizing this materially real space – which is also simultaneously an

SF (speculative fiction) space – inhabited by inappropriate/d others intersects with the enquiry into 'home', the 'politics of location', the 'politics of experience', and 'situated knowledges' suggested by Reagon, Rich, Mohanty, myself, and others.

5   The practices of consciousness-raising literally produced women's experience as a politically potent – and potentially imperializing – feminist discursive object. Examining another practice, Mohanty (1984) pointed out how feminist publishing, for example, many of London's Zed Press books on Third World women, were part of the apparatus of production of the 'Third World Woman' as an essentialized icon of super-oppression. This woman, at the bottom of cascades of oppression, then became the privileged potentially revolutionary subject in feminist discourses on 'liberation'. Her condition represented allegorically the state of Woman as victim coming to consciousness. See the Zed Books catalogue, Spring 1988/Spring 1989, for a complete list. There are many ways of reading these Zed books, many of which do not fit Mohanty's analysis. But these books collectively have been part of a feminist apparatus of production of the Third World Woman as a site of discourse for many agendas. This is one concrete example of a feminist constitution of experience as a discursive object and its appropriation in international networks. In the words of the Zed catalogue, 'For more than a decade Zed Books has been publishing outstanding writing by and about women of the Third World ... Widely read throughout the world, many are now used in educational institutions and as an essential reference in libraries.' There is nothing innocent (nor inherently evil) about such a process; the political and epistemological problems centre around accountability and the power-charged technologies of representation, including 'self'-representation. Ong (1987) describes how young Malay women factory workers are contested sites of discourse, where others struggle to set the terms for religious authority, national identity, and family honour. Corporations, state official and oppositional Islamic organizations, the national mass media, and popular street discourse all compete to represent the sexuality of the women. Ong also discursively constructs the women – in her narrative as complex historical actors affirming their humanity in multiply constrained frameworks where gender, age, region, ethnicity, nation, and class are especially salient (Haraway, 1989a). All constructions of women as sites of discourse are not equal; to point out their circuits of production and distribution is not to forbid the process, but to attempt to engage it with deliberate accountability. Both Ong and Mani (1987) are excellent examples of feminist efforts to do just that. What they never claim is that their representations – even or especially of women representing themselves – precipitate out of the solution of discourse and give the 'experience', 'voice', or 'empirical reality' of women im-mediately to the reader. This entire issue is strongly analogous to the impossibility of representations of nature precipitating out of scientific discourses to reveal 'nature herself'.

6   On Emecheta see Schipper (1985, pp. 44–6), Bruner (1983, pp. 49–50). For the changing book jacket copy see Emecheta (1972, 1975, 1976, 1977, 1979, 1982, 1983a, b, 1985). See also Brown (1981), Taiwo (1984), Davies and Graves (1986), Jameson (1986).

7   Caren Kaplan (1986–7, 1987b) movingly and incisively theorized the 'deterritorializations' in feminist discourse and the importance of displacement in the fictions constructing post-colonial subjectivity. Writing of Alicia Dujovne Ortiz's novel *Buenos Aires*, Kaplan formulated a reading practice that might also be engaged from Emecheta's novels: '*Buenos Aires* reinvents identity as a form of selfconscious cultural criticism. Displacement is a force in the modern world which can be reckoned with, not to heal splits but to explore them, to acknowledge the politics and limits of cultural processes' (Kaplan 1986–7, p. 98).

8   *The Nation* for 24–31 July 1989, edited and written by black women, examines 'The
scapegoating of the black family'. See especially Jewell Handy Gresham, 'The politics of
family in America', pp. 116–22. See also Collins (1989a, 1989b) for an analysis of the
attacks on black mothers and families in the last twenty years in the US and the use of
gender to demonstrate racial inferiority. Carby (1987) analyses black women's discourse
on mothering and racial uplift in the late nineteenth and early twentieth centuries in
terms of a specific non-racist and non-patriarchal reconstruction of womanhood. A
major intervention in feminist literary theory, Carby's book develops a 'feminist critical
practice that pays particular attention to the articulation of gender, race, and class' (p.
17). She argues that 'Black feminist criticism be regarded critically as a problem, not a
solution, as a sign that should be interrogated, a locus of contradictions' (p. 15). Thus,
Carby is suspicious of Christian's – and, by my extension, of Ogunyemi's – historical
narrative of the literary progression of black women writers and her method of
constructing a maturing tradition, which Carby sees as highly problematic (p. 14). Carby
disagrees with the frequent dismissal by critics of nineteenth- and twentieth-century
black fiction, including Christian, of the mulatta figure as an attempt to counter white
audiences' negative images of black people. Carby argues that the mulatto/a as a
narrative figure works as a 'vehicle for an exploration of relation between the races and,
at the same time, an expression of the relationship between the races. The figure of the
mulatto should be understood and analyzed as a narrative device of mediation' (p. 89).
Carby also foregrounds the black as well as white readership for black writing before the
last twenty years and insists that the writing by black women in the late nineteenth and
early twentieth centuries represents 'an earlier and perhaps more politically resonant
renaissance [than the "black women's renaissance" conditionally certified by Hollywood,
academia, and big publishing houses in the 1980s] so we may rethink the cultural politics
of black women' (p. 7). These debates over the narratives of black literary and political
history – cast in the figures of decades, traditions, pivotal writers, and literary
characterizations – are pre-eminently debates about contemporary politics. They are
also methodological debates over how to do cultural studies. Carby drinks deeply from
the work in England associated with Stuart Hall. The contested and heterogeneous
discourse of US 'black feminist criticism' could be traced from Smith (1977).

7   'Gender' for a Marxist Dictionary: The Sexual Politics of a Word

1   The project proved so daunting that the 'supplement' split off from the translation
project and is underway as a two-volume work of its own, the *Marxistisches Wörterbuch*,
under the general editorship of Wolfgang F. Haug of the Institut für Philosophie, Freie
Universität, Berlin. There are hundreds of contributors from Germany and many other
countries. Taken from a list compiled in 1985, some of the planned keywords of
particular interest to feminists include: *Diskurs, Dritte Welt, Familie, Feminismus,
feministische Theologie, Frauen, Frauenbewegung, Geschlecht, Homosexualität, Kulturarbeit,
Kybernetik, Luxemburgismus, Marxismus-Feminismus, Natur, Ökologie, Patriarchat, Post-
modernismus, Rasse, Rassismus, Repräsentation, Sex/gender system, Sexismus, Sexpol, Sisterhood, technologische Rationalität, weibliche Ästhetik*, and *weibliche Bildung*. This was, indeed,
not the daily vocabulary of Marx and Engels. But they do, emphatically, belong in a late
twentieth-century Marxist dictionary.

2   A curious linguistic point shows itself here: there is no marker to distinguish (biological)
race and (cultural) race, as there is for (biological) sex and (cultural) gender, even though
the nature/culture and biology/society binarisms pervade Western race discourse. The
linguistic situation highlights the very recent and uneven entry of gender into the

political, as opposed to the grammatical, lexicon. The non-naturalness of race – it is always and totally an arbitrary, cultural construction – can be emphasized from the lack of a linguistic marker. But, as easily, the total collapse of the category of race into biologism is linguistically invited. All these matters continue to hinge on unexamined functioning of the productionist, Aristotelian logic fundamental to so much Western discourse. In this linguistic, political, and historical matrix, matter and form, act and potency, raw material and achieved product play out their escalating dramas of production and appropriation. Here is where subjects and objects get born and endlessly reincarnated.

3   Although not mutually exclusive, the language of 'gender' in Euro-American feminist discourse usually is the language of 'sexed subject position' and 'sexual difference' in European writing. For British Marxist feminism on the 'sexed subject in patriarchy', see Kuhn and Wolpe (1978), Marxist-Feminist Literature Collective (1978), Brown and Adams (1979), the journal *m/f*, Barrett (1980). German socialist-feminist positions on sexualization have stressed the dialectic of women's self-constructing agency, already structured social determinations, and partial restructurings. This literature examines how women construct themselves into existing structures, in order to find the point where change might be possible. If women are theorized as passive victims of sex and gender as a system of domination, no theory of liberation will be possible. So social constructionism on the question of gender must not be allowed to become a theory of closed determinism (Haug, 1980, 1982; Haug *et al.*, 1983, 1987; Mouffe, 1983). Looking for a theory of experience, of how women actively embody themselves, the women in the collective writing the *Frauenformen* publications insisted on a descriptive/theoretical practice showing 'the ways we live ourselves in bodily terms' (Haug *et al.*, 1987, p. 30). They evolved a method called 'memory work' that emphasizes collectively criticized, written narratives about 'a stranger', a past 'remembered' self, while problematizing the self-deluding assumptions of autobiography and other causal accounts. The problem is to account for the emergence of 'the sexual itself as the process that produces the insertion of women into, and their subordination within, determinate social practices' (p. 33). Ironically, self-constituted as sexualized, as woman, women cannot be accountable for themselves or society (p. 27). Like all the theories of sex, sexuality, and gender surveyed in this effort to write for a standard reference work that inevitably functions to canonize some meanings over others, the *Frauenformen* versions insist on gender as a gerund or a verb, rather than a finished noun, a substantive. For feminists, gender means making and unmaking 'bodies' in a contestable world; an account of gender is a theory of experience as signifying and significant embodiment.

4   Joan Scott (1988, pp. 28–50) wrote an incisive treatment of the development of gender as a theoretical category in the discipline of history. She noted the long history of play on the grammatical gender difference for making figurative allusions to sex or character (p. 28). Scott quoted as her epigram *Fowler's Dictionary of Modern English Usage*'s insistence that to use gender to mean the male or female sex was either a mistake or a joke. The ironies in this injunction abound. One benefit of the inheritance of feminist uses of gender from grammar is that, in that domain, 'gender is understood to be a way of classifying phenomena, a socially agreed-upon system of distinctions, rather than an objective description of inherent traits' (p. 29).

5   See Coward (1983, chs 5 and 6) for a thorough discussion of the concepts of the family and the woman question in Marxist thought from 1848 to about 1930.

6   Rubin (1975), Young and Levidow (1981), Harding (1983, 1986), Hartsock (1983 a, b), Hartmann (1981), O'Brien (1981), Chodorow (1978), Jaggar (1983).

7   See *The Woman Question* (1951); Marx and Aveling (1885-6); Kollontai (1977).

8   To sample the uses and criticisms, see Sayers (1982), Hubbard *et al.* (1982), Bleier (1984, 1986), Fausto-Sterling (1985), Kessler and McKenna (1978), Thorne and Henley (1975), West and Zimmermann (1987), Morawski (1987), Brighton Women and Science Group (1980), Lowe and Hubbard (1983), Lewontin *et al.* (1984).

9   Several streams of European feminisms (some disavowing the name) were born after the events of May '68. The stream drawing from Simone de Beauvoir's formulations, especially work by Monique Wittig, Monique Plaza, Colette Guillaumin, and Christine Delphy, published in *Questions féministes*, *Nouvelles questions féministes*, and *Feminist Issues*, and the stream associated complexly with the group 'Psychanalyse et Politique' and/or with Julia Kristeva, Luce Irigaray, Sarah Kofman, and Hélène Cixous have been particularly influential in international feminist development on issues of sexual difference. (For introductory summaries, see Marks and de Courtivron, 1980; Gallop, 1982; Moi, 1985; Duchen, 1986). These streams deserve large, separate treatments; but in the context of this entry two contributions to theories of 'gender' from these writers, who are deeply opposed among themselves on precisely these issues, must be signalled. First, there are Wittig's and Delphy's arguments for a materialist feminism, which insist that the issue is 'domination', not 'difference'. Second, there are Irigaray's, Kristeva's, and Cixous's various ways (intertextually positioned in relation to Derrida, Lacan and others) of insisting that the subject, which is perhaps best approached through writing and textuality, is always in process, always disrupted, that the idea of woman remains finally unclosed and multiple. Despite their important opposition between and within the francophone streams, all these theorists are possessed with flawed, contradictory, and critical projects of denaturalization of 'woman'.

10 Smith (1974), Flax (1983), O'Brien (1981), Rose, H. (1983, 1986), Harding (1983).

11 Similarly, it is an error to equate 'race' with people of colour; whiteness is a racial construction as well, invisible as such because of its (like man's) occupation of the unmarked category (Frankenberg, 1988; Carby, 1987, p. 18; Haraway, 1989b, pp. 152, 401-2).

12 See, for example, Ware (1970); Combahee River Collective (1979); Bethel and Smith (1979); Joseph and Lewis (1981); hooks (1981, 1984); Moraga and Anzaldúa (1981); Davis (1982); Hull *et al.* (1982); Lorde (1982, 1984); Aptheker (1982); Moraga (1983); Walker (1983); Smith (1983); Bulkin *et al.* (1984); Sandoval (n.d.); Christian (1985); Giddings (1985); Anzaldúa (1987); Carby (1987); Spillers (1987); Collins (1989a), 1989b); Hurtado (1989).

8   A Cyborg Manifesto: Science, Technology, and Socialist-Feminism in the Late Twentieth Century

1   Research was funded by an Academic Senate Faculty Research Grant from the University of California, Santa Cruz. An earlier version of the paper on genetic engineering appeared as 'Lieber Kyborg als Göttin: für eine sozialistisch-feministische Unterwanderung der Gentechnologie', in Bernd-Peter Lange and Anna Marie Stuby, eds, Berlin: Argument-Sonderband 105, 1984, pp 66–84. The cyborg manifesto grew from my 'New machines, new bodies, new communities: political dilemmas of a cyborg feminist', 'The Scholar and the Feminist X: The Question of Technology', Conference, Barnard College, April 1983.

The people associated with the History of Consciousness Board of UCSC have had an enormous influence on this paper, so that it feels collectively authored more than most, although those I cite may not recognize their ideas. In particular, members of graduate and undergraduate feminist theory, science, and politics, and theory and methods courses contributed to the cyborg manifesto. Particular debts here are due Hilary Klein (1989), Paul Edwards (1985), Lisa Lowe (1986), and James Clifford (1985).

Parts of the paper were my contribution to a collectively developed session, 'Poetic Tools and Political Bodies: Feminist Approaches to High Technology Culture', 1984 California American Studies Association, with History of Consciousness graduate students Zoe Sofoulis, 'Jupiter space'; Katie King, 'The pleasures of repetition and the limits of identification in feminist science fiction: reimaginations of the body after the cyborg'; and Chela Sandoval, 'The construction of subjectivity and oppositional consciousness in feminist film and video'. Sandoval's (n.d.) theory of oppositional consciousness was published as 'Women respond to racism: A Report on the National Women's Studies Association Conference'. For Sofoulis's semiotic-psychoanalytic readings of nuclear culture, see Sofia (1984). King's unpublished papers ('Questioning tradition: canon formation and the veiling of power'; 'Gender and genre: reading the science fiction of Joanna Russ'; 'Varley's *Titan* and *Wizard*: feminist parodies of nature, culture, and hardware') deeply informed the cyborg manifesto.

Barbara Epstein, Jeff Escoffier, Rusten Hogness, and Jaye Miler gave extensive discussion and editorial help. Members of the Silicon Valley Research Project of UCSC and participants in SVRP conferences and workshops were very important, especially Rick Gordon, Linda Kimball, Nancy Snyder, Langdon Winner, Judith Stacey, Linda Lim, Patricia Fernandez-Kelly, and Judith Gregory. Finally, I want to thank Nancy Hartsock for years of friendship and discussion on feminist theory and feminst science fiction. I also thank Elizabeth Bird for my favourite political button: 'Cyborgs for Earthly Survival'.

2   Useful references to left and/or feminist radical science movements and theory and to biological/biotechnical issues include: Bleier (1984, 1986), Harding (1986), Fausto-Sterling (1985), Gould (1981), Hubbard *et al.* (1982), Keller (1985), Lewontin *et al.* (1984), *Radical Science Journal* (became *Science as Culture* in 1987), 26 Freegrove Road, London N7 9RQ; *Science for the People*, 897 Main St, Cambridge, MA 02139.

3   Starting points for left and/or feminist approaches to technology and politics include: Cowan (1983), Rothschild (1983), Traweek (1988), Young and Levidow (1981, 1985), Weizenbaum (1976), Winner (1977, 1986), Zimmerman (1983), Athanasiou (1987), Cohn (1987a, 1987b), Winograd and Flores (1986), Edwards (1985). *Global Electronics Newsletter*, 867 West Dana St, #204, Mountain View, CA 94041; *Processed World*, 55 Sutter St, San Francisco, CA 94104; ISIS, Women's International Information and Communication Service, PO Box 50 (Cornavin), 1211 Geneva 2, Switzerland, and Via Santa Maria Dell'Anima 30, 00186 Rome, Italy. Fundamental approaches to modern social studies of science that do not continue the liberal mystification that it all started with Thomas Kuhn, include: Knorr-Cetina (1981), Knorr-Cetina and Mulkay (1983), Latour and Woolgar (1979), Young (1979). The 1984 Directory of the Network for the Ethnographic Study of Science, Technology, and Organizations lists a wide range of people and projects crucial to better radical analysis; available from NESSTO, PO Box 11442, Stanford, CA 94305.

4   A provocative, comprehensive argument about the politics and theories of 'postmodernism' is made by Fredric Jameson (1984), who argues that postmodernism is not an option, a style among others, but a cultural dominant requiring radical reinvention of left politics from within; there is no longer any place from without that gives meaning to the comforting fiction of critical distance. Jameson also makes clear why one cannot be for or against postmodernism, an essentially moralist move. My position is that feminists (and

others) need continuous cultural reinvention, postmodernist critique, and historical materialism; only a cyborg would have a chance. The old dominations of white capitalist patriarchy seem nostalgically innocent now: they normalized heterogeneity, into man and woman, white and black, for example. 'Advanced capitalism' and postmodernism release heterogeneity without a norm, and we are flattened, without subjectivity, which requires depth, even unfriendly and drowning depths. It is time to write *The Death of the Clinic*. The clinic's methods required bodies and works; we have texts and surfaces. Our dominations don't work by medicalization and normalization any more; they work by networking, communications redesign, stress management. Normalization gives way to automation, utter redundancy. Michel Foucault's *Birth of the Clinic* (1963), *History of Sexuality* (1976), and *Discipline and Punish* (1975) name a form of power at its moment of implosion. The discourse of biopolitics gives way to technobabble, the language of the spliced substantive; no noun is left whole by the multinationals. These are their names, listed from one issue of *Science*: Tech-Knowledge, Genentech, Allergen, Hybritech, Compupro, Genen-cor, Syntex, Allelix, Agrigenetics Corp., Syntro, Codon, Repligen, MicroAngelo from Scion Corp., Percom Data, Inter Systems, Cyborg Corp., Statcom Corp., Intertec. If we are imprisoned by language, then escape from that prison-house requires language poets, a kind of cultural restriction enzyme to cut the code; cyborg heteroglossia is one form of radical cultural politics. For cyborg poetry, see Perloff (1984); Fraser (1984). For feminist modernist/postmodernist 'cyborg' writing, see HOW(ever), 871 Corbett Ave, San Francisco, CA 94131.

5   Baudrillard (1983). Jameson (1984, p. 66) points out that Plato's definition of the simulacrum is the copy for which there is no original, i.e., the world of advanced capitalism, of pure exchange. See *Discourse* 9 (Spring/Summer 1987) for a special issue on technology (cybernetics, ecology, and the postmodern imagination).

6   For ethnographic accounts and political evaluations, see Epstein (forthcoming), Sturgeon (1986). Without explicit irony, adopting the spaceship earth/whole earth logo of the planet photographed from space, set off by the slogan 'Love Your Mother', the May 1987 Mothers and Others Day action at the nuclear weapons testing facility in Nevada none the less took account of the tragic contradictions of views of the earth. Demonstrators applied for official permits to be on the land from officers of the Western Shoshone tribe, whose territory was invaded by the US government when it built the nuclear weapons test ground in the 1950s. Arrested for trespassing, the demonstrators argued that the police and weapons facility personnel, without authorization from the proper officials, were the trespassers. One affinity group at the women's action called themselves the Surrogate Others; and in solidarity with the creatures forced to tunnel in the same ground with the bomb, they enacted a cyborgian emergence from the constructed body of a large, non-heterosexual desert worm.

7   Powerful developments of coalition politics emerge from 'Third World' speakers, speaking from nowhere, the displaced centre of the universe, earth: 'We live on the third planet from the sun' – *Sun Poem* by Jamaican writer, Edward Kamau Braithwaite, review by Mackey (1984). Contributors to Smith (1983) ironically subvert naturalized identities precisely while constructing a place from which to speak called home. See especially Reagon (in Smith, 1983, pp. 356–68). Trinh T. Minh-ha (1986–87).

8   hooks (1981, 1984); Hull *et al.* (1982). Bambara (1981) wrote an extraordinary novel in which the women of colour theatre group, The Seven Sisters, explores a form of unity. See analysis by Butler-Evans (1987).

9   On orientalism in feminist works and elsewhere, see Lowe (1986); Said (1978); Mohanty (1984); *Many Voices, One Chant: Black Feminist Perspectives* (1984).

10 Katie King (1986, 1987a) has developed a theoretically sensitive treatment of the

workings of feminist taxonomies as genealogies of power in feminist ideology and polemic. King examines Jaggar's (1983) problematic example of taxonomizing feminisms to make a little machine producing the desired final position. My caricature here of socialist and radical feminism is also an example.

11   The central role of object relations versions of psychoanalysis and related strong universalizing moves in discussing reproduction, caring work, and mothering in many approaches to epistemology underline their authors' resistance to what I am calling postmodernism. For me, both the universalizing moves and these versions of psychoanalysis make analysis of 'women's place in the integrated circuit' difficult and lead to systematic difficulties in accounting for or even seeing major aspects of the construction of gender and gendered social life. The feminist standpoint argument has been developed by: Flax (1983), Harding (1986), Harding and Hintikka (1983), Hartsock (1983a, b), O'Brien (1981), Rose (1983), Smith (1974, 1979). For rethinking theories of feminist materialism and feminist standpoints in response to criticism, see Harding (1986, pp. 163–96), Hartsock (1987), and H. Rose (1986).

12   I make an argumentative category error in 'modifying' MacKinnon's positions with the qualifier 'radical', thereby generating my own reductive critique of extremely heterogeneous writing, which does explicitly use that label, by my taxonomically interested argument about writing which does not use the modifier and which brooks no limits and thereby adds to the various dreams of a common, in the sense of univocal, language for feminism. My category error was occasioned by an assignment to write from a particular taxonomic position which itself has a heterogeneous history, socialist-feminism, for *Socialist Review*. A critique indebted to MacKinnon, but without the reductionism and with an elegant feminist account of Foucault's paradoxical conservatism on sexual violence (rape), is de Lauretis (1985; see also 1986, pp. 1–19). A theoretically elegant feminist social-historical examination of family violence, that insists on women's, men's, and children's complex agency without losing sight of the material structures of male domination, race, and class, is Gordon (1988).

13   This chart was published in 1985. My previous efforts to understand biology as a cybernetic command-control discourse and organisms as 'natural-technical objects of knowledge' were Haraway (1979, 1983, 1984). The 1979 version of this dichotomous chart appears in this vol., ch. 3; for a 1989 version, see ch. 10. The differences indicate shifts in argument.

14   For progressive analyses and action on the biotechnology debates: *GeneWatch, a Bulletin of the Committee for Responsible Genetics*, 5 Doane St, 4th Floor, Boston, MA 02109; Genetic Screening Study Group (formerly the Sociobiology Study Group of Science for the People), Cambridge, MA; Wright (1982, 1986); Yoxen (1983).

15   Starting references for 'women in the integrated circuit': D'Onofrio-Flores and Pfafflin (1982), Fernandez-Kelly (1983), Fuentes and Ehrenreich (1983), Grossman (1980), Nash and Fernandez-Kelly (1983), Ong (1987), Science Policy Research Unit (1982).

16   For the 'homework economy outside the home' and related arguments: Gordon (1983); Gordon and Kimball (1985); Stacey (1987); Reskin and Hartmann (1986); *Women and Poverty* (1984); S. Rose (1986); Collins (1982); Burr (1982); Gregory and Nussbaum (1982); Piven and Coward (1982); Microelectronics Group (1980); Stallard *et al.* (1983) which includes a useful organization and resource list.

17   The conjunction of the Green Revolution's social relations with biotechnologies like plant genetic engineering makes the pressures on land in the Third World increasingly intense. AID's estimates (*New York Times*, 14 October 1984) used at the 1984 World Food Day are that in Africa, women produce about 90 per cent of rural food supplies, about 60–80 per cent in Asia, and provide 40 per cent of agricultural labour in the Near

East and Latin America. Blumberg charges that world organizations' agricultural politics, as well as those of multinationals and national governments in the Third World, generally ignore fundamental issues in the sexual division of labour. The present tragedy of famine in Africa might owe as much to male supremacy as to capitalism, colonialism, and rain patterns. More accurately, capitalism and racism are usually structurally male dominant. See also Blumberg (1981); Hacker (1984); Hacker and Bovit (1981); Busch and Lacy (1983); Wilfred (1982); Sachs (1983); International Fund for Agricultural Development (1985); Bird (1984).

18   See also Enloe (1983a, b).

19   For a feminist version of this logic, see Hrdy (1981). For an analysis of scientific women's story-telling practices, especially in relation to sociobiology in evolutionary debates around child abuse and infanticide, see this vol., ch. 5.

20   For the moment of transition of hunting with guns to hunting with cameras in the construction of popular meanings of nature for an American urban immigrant public, see Haraway (1984–5, 1989b), Nash (1979), Sontag (1977), Preston (1984).

21   For guidance for thinking about the political/cultural/racial implications of the history of women doing science in the United States see: Haas and Perucci (1984); Hacker (1981); Keller (1983); National Science Foundation (1988); Rossiter (1982); Schiebinger (1987); Haraway (1989b).

22   Markoff and Siegel (1983). High Technology Professionals for Peace and Computer Professionals for Social Responsibility are promising organizations.

23   King (1984). An abbreviated list of feminist science fiction underlying themes of this essay: Octavia Butler, *Wild Seed, Mind of My Mind, Kindred, Survivor*; Suzy McKee Charnas, *Motherliness*; Samuel R. Delany, the Neverÿon series; Anne McCaffery, *The Ship Who Sang, Dinosaur Planet*; Vonda McIntyre, *Superluminal, Dreamsnake*; Joanna Russ, *Adventures of Alix, The Female Man*; James Tiptree, Jr, *Star Songs of an Old Primate, Up the Walls of the World*; John Varley, *Titan, Wizard, Demon*.

24   French feminisms contribute to cyborg heteroglossia. Burke (1981); Irigaray (1977, 1979); Marks and de Courtivron (1980); *Signs* (Autumn 1981); Wittig (1973); Duchen (1986). For English translation of some currents of francophone feminism see *Feminist Issues: A Journal of Feminist Social and Political Theory*, 1980.

25   But all these poets are very complex, not least in their treatment of themes of lying and erotic, decentred collective and personal identities. Griffin (1978), Lorde (1984), Rich (1978).

26   Derrida (1976, especially part II); Lévi-Strauss (1961, especially 'The Writing Lesson'); Gates (1985); Kahn and Neumaier (1985); Ong (1982); Kramarae and Treichler (1985).

27   The sharp relation of women of colour to writing as theme and politics can be approached through: Program for 'The Black Woman and the Diaspora: Hidden Connections and Extended Acknowledgments', An International Literary Conference, Michigan State University, October 1985; Evans (1984); Christian (1985); Carby (1987); Fisher (1980); *Frontiers* (1980, 1983); Kingston (1977); Lerner (1973); Giddings (1985); Moraga and Anzaldúa (1981); Morgan (1984). Anglophone European and Euro-American women have also crafted special relations to their writing as a potent sign: Gilbert and Gubar (1979), Russ (1983).

28   The convention of ideologically taming militarized high technology by publicizing its applications to speech and motion problems of the disabled/differently abled takes on a special irony in monotheistic, patriarchal, and frequently anti-semitic culture when computer-generated speech allows a boy with no voice to chant the Haftorah at his bar mitzvah. See Sussman (1986). Making the always context-relative social definitions of

'ableness' particularly clear, military high-tech has a way of making human beings disabled by definition, a perverse aspect of much automated battlefield and Star Wars R&D. See Welford (1 July 1986).

29   James Clifford (1985, 1988) argues persuasively for recognition of continuous cultural reinvention, the stubborn non-disappearance of those 'marked' by Western imperializing practices.

30   DuBois (1982), Daston and Park (n.d.), Park and Daston (1981). The noun *monster* shares its root with the verb *to demonstrate*.

9   Situated Knowledges: The Science Question in Feminism and the Privilege of Partial Perspective

1   This chapter originated as a commentary on Harding (1986), at the Western Division meetings of the American Philosophical Association, San Francisco, March 1987. Support during the writing of this paper was generously provided by the Alpha Fund of the Institute for Advanced Study, Princeton, New Jersey. Thanks especially to Joan Scott, Rayna Rapp, Judy Newton, Judy Butler, Lila Abu-Lughod, and Dorinne Kondo.

2   For example, see Knorr-Cetina and Mulkay (1983); Bijker *et al.* (1987); and especially, Latour (1984, 1988). Borrowing from Michel Tournier's *Vendredi* (1967), Latour's brilliant and maddening aphoristic polemic against all forms of reductionism makes the essential point for feminists: 'Méfiez-vous de la pureté; c'est le vitriol de l'âme' (Latour, 1984, p. 171). Latour is not otherwise a notable feminist theorist, but he might be made into one by readings as perverse as those he makes of the laboratory, that great machine for making significant mistakes faster than anyone else can, and so gaining world-changing power. The laboratory for Latour is the railroad industry of epistemology, where facts can only be made to run on the tracks laid down from the laboratory out. Those who control the railroads control the surrounding territory. How could we have forgotten? But now it's not so much the bankrupt railroads we need as the satellite network. Facts run on lightbeams these days.

3   For an elegant and very helpful elucidation of a non-cartoon version of this argument, see White (1987). I still want more; and unfulfilled desire can be a powerful seed for changing the stories.

4   In her analysis exploring the fault line between modernism and postmodernism in ethnography and anthropology – in which the high stakes are the authorization or prohibition to craft *comparative* knowledge across 'cultures', from some epistemologically grounded vantage point *either* inside, outside, or in dialogical relation with any unit of analysis – Marilyn Strathern (1987a) made the crucial observation that it is not the written ethnography that is parallel to the work of art as object-of-knowledge, but the *culture*. The Romantic and modernist natural-technical objects of knowledge, in science and in other cultural practice, stand on one side of this divide. The postmodernist formation stands on the other side, with its 'anti-aesthetic' of permanently split, problematized, always receding and deferred 'objects' of knowledge and practice, including signs, organisms, systems, selves, and cultures. 'Objectivity' in a postmodern frame cannot be about unproblematic objects; it must be about specific prosthesis and translation. Objectivity, which at root has been about crafting *comparative* knowledge (how to name things to be stable and to be like each other), becomes a question of the politics of redrawing of boundaries in order to have non-innocent conversations and connections. What is at stake in the debates about modernism and postmodernism is the pattern of relationships between and within bodies and language.

5   Zoe Sofoulis (1988) has produced a dazzlingly (she will forgive me the metaphor) theoretical treatment of technoscience, the psychoanalysis of science fiction culture, and the metaphorics of extra-terrestrialism, including a wonderful focus on the ideologies and philosophies of light, illumination, and discovery in Western mythics of science and technology. My essay was revised in dialogue with Sofoulis's arguments and metaphors in her PhD dissertation.

6   Crucial to this discussion are Harding (1986), Keller (1985), Hartsock (1983a, 1983b), Flax (1983, 1987), Keller and Grontkowski (1983), H. Rose (1986), Haraway (1985; this vol. pp. 149–81), and Petchesky (1987).

7   John Varley's science fiction short story called 'The Persistence of Vision' is part of the inspiration for this section. In the story, Varley constructs a utopian community designed and built by the deaf-blind. He then explores these people's technologies and other mediations of communication and their relations to sighted children and visitors (Varley, 1978). In 'Blue Champagne', Varley (1986) transmutes the theme to interrogate the politics of intimacy and technology for a paraplegic young woman whose prosthetic device, the golden gypsy, allows her full mobility. But since the infinitely costly device is owned by an intergalactic communications and entertainment empire for which she works as a media star making 'feelies', she may keep her technological, intimate, enabling, other self only in exchange for her complicity in the commodification of all experience. What are her limits to the reinvention of experience for sale? Is the personal political under the sign of simulation? One way to read Varley's repeated investigations of finally always limited embodiments, differently abled beings, prosthetic technologies, and cyborgian encounters with their finitude despite their extraordinary transcendence of 'organic' orders is to find an allegory for the personal and political in the historical mythic time of the late twentieth century, the era of techno-biopolitics. Prosthesis becomes a fundamental category for understanding our most intimate selves. Prosthesis is semiosis, the making of meanings and bodies, not for transcendence but for power-charged communication.

8   I owe my understanding of the experience of these photographs to Jim Clifford, University of California at Santa Cruz, who identified their 'land ho!' effect on the reader.

9   Joan Scott reminded me that Teresa de Lauretis (1986a, pp. 14–15) put it like this:

> Differences among women may be better understood as differences within women ... But once understood in their constitutive power – once it is understood, that is, that these differences not only constitute each woman's consciousness and subjective limits but all together define the *female subject of feminism* in its very specificity, its inherent and at least for now irreconcilable contradiction – these differences, then, cannot be again collapsed into a fixed identity, a sameness of all women as Woman, or a representation of Feminism as a coherent and available image.

10 Harding (1986, p. 18) suggested that gender has three dimensions, each historically specific: gender symbolism, the social-sexual division of labour, and processes of constructing individual gendered identity. I would enlarge her point to note that there is no reason to expect the three dimensions to co-vary or co-determine each other, at least not directly. That is, extremely steep gradients between contrasting terms in gender symbolism may very well not correlate with sharp social-sexual divisions of labour or social power, but may be closely related to sharp racial stratification or something else. Similarly, the processes of gendered subject formation may not be directly illuminated by knowledge of the sexual division of labour or the gender symbolism in the particular historical situation under examination. On the other hand, we should expect mediated

relations among the dimensions. The mediations might move through quite different social axes of organization of both symbols, practice, and identity, such as race. And vice versa. I would suggest also that science, as well as gender or race, might usefully be broken up into such a multi-part scheme of symbolism, social practice, and subject position. More than three dimensions suggest themselves when the parallels are drawn. The different dimensions of, for example, gender, race, and science might mediate relations among dimensions on a parallel chart. That is, racial divisions of labour might mediate the patterns of connection between symbolic connections and formation of individual subject positions on the science or gender chart. Or formations of gendered or racial subjectivity might mediate the relations between scientific social division of labour and scientific symbolic patterns.

The chart below begins an analysis by parallel dissections. In the chart (and in reality?), both gender and science are analytically asymmetrical; i.e., each term contains and obscures a structuring hierarchicalized binarism, sex/gender and nature/science. Each binarism orders the silent term by a logic of appropriation, as resource to product, nature to culture, potential to actual. Both poles of the binarism are constructed and structure each other dialectically. Within each voiced or explicit term, further asymmetrical splittings can be excavated, as from gender, masculine to feminine, and from science, hard sciences to soft sciences. This is a point about remembering how a particular analytical tool works, willy nilly, intended or not. The chart reflects common ideological aspects of discourse on science and gender and may help as an analytical tool to crack open mystified units like Science or Woman.

Gender	Science
symbolic system	symbolic system
social division of labour (by sex, by race, etc.)	social division of labour (by craft, industrial, or post-industrial logics)
individual identity/subject position (desiring/desired; autonomous/relational)	individual identity/subject position (knower/known; scientist/other)
material culture (gender paraphernalia and daily gender technologies: the narrow tracks on which sexual difference runs)	material culture (laboratories: the narrow tracks on which facts run)
dialectic of construction and discovery	dialectic of construction and discovery

11   Evelyn Keller (1987) insists on the important possibilities opened up by the construction of the intersection of the distinction between sex and gender, on the one hand, and nature and science, on the other. She also insists on the need to hold to some non-discursive grounding in 'sex' and 'nature', perhaps what I am calling the 'body' and 'world'.

10 The Biopolitics of Postmodern Bodies: Constitutions of Self in Immune System Discourse

1 Special thanks to Scott Gilbert, Rusten Hogness, Jaye Miller, Rayna Rapp, and Joan Scott. Research and writing for this project were supported by the Alpha Fund and the Institute for Advanced Study, Princeton, NJ; Academic Senate Faculty Research Grants of the University of California Santa Cruz; and the Silicon Valley Research Project, UCSC. Crystal Gray was an excellent research assistant. Benefiting from many people's comments, this paper was first presented at the Wenner Gren Foundation's Conference on Medical Anthropology, Lisbon, Portugal, 5–13 March 1988.

2 Even without taking much account of questions of consciousness and culture, the extensive importance of immunological discourse and artefacts has many diagnostic signs: (1) The first Nobel Prize in medicine in 1901 was given for an originary development, namely, the use of diphtheria anti-toxin. With many intervening awards, the pace of Nobel awards in immunology since 1970 is stunning, covering work on the generation of antibody diversity, the histocompatibility system, monoclonal antibodies and hybridomas, the network hypothesis of immune regulation, and development of the radioimmunoassay system. (2) The products and processes of immunology enter into present and projected medical, pharmaceutical, and other industrial practices. This situation is exemplified by monoclonal antibodies, which can be used as extremely specific tools to identify, isolate, and manipulate components of production at a molecular scale and then gear up to an industrial scale with unheard-of specificity and purity, for a wide array of enterprises – from food flavouring technology, to design and manufacture of industrial chemicals, to delivery systems in chemotherapy (see figure on 'Applications of monoclonal antibodies in immunology and related disciplines', Nicholas, 1985, p. 12). The *Research Briefings* for 1983 for the federal Office of Science and Technology Policy and various other federal departments and agencies identified immunology, along with artificial intelligence and cognitive science, solid earth sciences, computer design and manufacture, and regions of chemistry, as research areas 'that were likely to return the highest scientific dividends as a result of incremental federal investment' (Committee on Science, Engineering, and Public Policy, 1983). The dividends in such fields are hardly expected to be simply 'scientific'. 'In these terms the major money spinner undoubtedly is hybridoma technology, and its chief product the monoclonal antibody' (Nicholas, 1985, Preface). (3) The field of immunology is itself an interational growth industry. The First International Congress of Immunology was held in 1971 in Washington, DC, attended by most of the world's leading researchers in the field, about 3500 people from 45 countries. Over 8000 people attended the Fourth Interational Congress in 1980 (Klein, 1982, p. 623). The number of journals in the field has been expanding since 1970 from around twelve to over eighty by 1984. The total of books and monographs on the subject reached well over 1000 by 1980. The industrial-university collaborations characteristic of the new biotechnology pervade research arrangements in immunology, as in molecular biology, with which it cross-reacts extensively, for example, the Basel Institute for Immunology, entirely financed by Hoffman-La Roche but featuring all the benefits of academic practice, including publishing freedoms. The International Union of Immunological Societies began in 1969 with ten national societies, increased to thirty-three by 1984 (Nicholas, 1985). Immunology will be at the heart of global biotechnological inequality and 'technology transfer' struggles. Its importance approaches that of information technologies in global science politics. (4) Ways of writing about the immune system are also ways of determining which diseases – and which interpretations of them – will prevail in courts,

hospitals, international funding agencies, national policies, memories and treatment of war veterans and civilian populations, and so on. See for example the efforts of oppositional people, like labour and consumer advocates, to establish a category called 'chemical AIDS' to call attention to widespread and unnamed ('amorphous') sickness in late industrial societies putatively associated with its products and environments and to link this sickness with infectious AIDS as a political strategy (Hayes, 1987; Marshall, 1986). Discourse on infectious AIDS is part of mechanisms that determine what counts as 'the general population', such that over a million infected people in the US alone, not to mention the global dimensions of infection, can be named in terms that make them *not* part of the general population, with important national medical, insurance, and legal policy implications. Many leading textbooks of immunology in the United States give considerably more space to allergies or auto-immune diseases than to parasitic diseases, an allocation that might lead future Nobel Prize-winners into some areas of research rather than others and that certainly does nothing to lead undergraduates or medical students to take responsibility for the differences and inequalities of sickness globally. (Contrast Golub [1987] with Desowitz [1987] for the sensitivities of a cellular immunology researcher and a parasitologist.) Who counts as an individual is not unrelated to who counts as the general population.

3   Like the universe inhabited by readers and writer of this essay.

4   This ontological continuity enables the discussion of the growing practical problem of 'virus' programs infecting computer software (McLellan, 1988). The infective, invading information fragments that parasitize their host code in favour of their own replication and their own program commands are more than metaphorically like biological viruses. And like the body's unwelcome invaders, the software viruses are discussed in terms of pathology as communications terrorism, requiring therapy in the form of strategic security measures. There is a kind of epidemiology of virus infections of artificial intelligence systems, and neither the large corporate or military systems nor the personal computers have good immune defences. Both are extremely vulnerable to terrorism and rapid proliferation of the foreign code that multiplies silently and subverts their normal functions. Immunity programs to kill the viruses, like Data Physician sold by Digital Dispatch, Inc., are being marketed. More than half the buyers of Data Physician in 1985 were military. Every time I start up my Macintosh, it shows the icon for its vaccine program – a hypodermic needle.

5   Thanks to Elizabeth Bird for creating a political button with this slogan, which I wore as a member of an affinity group called Surrogate Others at the Mothers and Others Day Action at the Nevada Nuclear Test Site in May 1987.

6   The relation of the immune and nervous systems conceived within contemporary neuroimmunology or psychoneuroimmunology would be the ideal place to locate a fuller argument here. With the discovery of receptors and products shared by cells of the neural, endocrine, and immune systems, positing the dispersed and networking immune system as the mediator between mind and body began to make sense to 'hard' scientists. The implications for popular and official therapeutics are legion, for example, in relation to the polysemic entity called 'stress'. See Barnes (1986, 1987); Wechsler (1987); Kanigel (1986). The biological metaphors invoked to name the immune system also facilitate or inhibit notions of the IS as a potent mediator, rather than a master control system or hyper-armed defence department. For example, developmental biologist and immunologist, Scott Gilbert, refers in his teaching to the immune system as an ecosystem and neuroimmunology researcher, Edwin Blalock, calls the immune system a sensory organ. These metaphors can be oppositional to the hyper-rationalistic AI

immune body in Star Wars imagery. They can also have multiple effects in research design, as well as teaching and therapeutics.

7 When I begin to think I am paranoid for thinking anyone *really* dreams of transcendent disembodiment as the telos of life and mind, I find such things as the following quote by the computer designer W. Daniel Hillis in the Winter 1988 issue of *Daedalus* on artificial intelligence:

> Of course, I understand that this is just a dream, and I will admit that I am propelled more by hope than by the probability of success. But if this artificial mind can sustain itself and grow of its own accord, then for the first time human thought will live free of bones and flesh, giving this child of mind an earthly immortality denied to us. (Hillis, 1988, p. 189)

Thanks to Evelyn Keller for pointing me to the quote. See her 'From secrets of life, secrets of death', (1990). I am indebted to Zoe Sofia (1984; Sofoulis, 1988) for analysis of the iconography and mythology of nuclear exterminism, extra-terrestrialism, and cannibalism.

8 That, of course, is why women have had so much trouble counting as individuals in modern Western discourses. Their personal, bounded individuality is compromised by their bodies' troubling talent for making other bodies, whose individuality can take precedence over their own, even while the little bodies are fully contained and invisible without major optical technologies (Petchesky, 1987). Women can, in a sense, be cut in half and retain their maternal function – witness their bodies maintained after death to sustain the life of another individual. The special ambiguity of female individuality – perhaps more resistant, finally, than worms to full liberal personhood – extends into accounts of immune function during pregnancy. The old biomedical question has been, why does the mother not reject the little invader within as foreign? After all, the embryo and foetus are quite well marked as 'other' by all the ordinary immunological criteria; and there is intimate contact between foetal and maternal tissue at the site of certain cells of the placenta, called trophoblasts. Counter-intuitively, it turns out that it is women with 'underactive immune systems' who end up rejecting their foetuses immunologically by forming antibodies against their tissues. Normally, women make special antibodies that mask the tell-tale foreign signals on the foetal trophoblasts, so that the mother's immune surveillance system remains blind to the foetus's presence. By immunizing the 'rejecting' women with cells taken from their 'husbands' or other genetically unrelated donors, the women's immune systems can be induced to make blocking antibodies. It appears that most women are induced to make this sort of antibody as a result of 'immunization' from their 'husband's' sperm during intercourse. But if the 'husband' is too genetically close to the potential mother, some women won't recognize the sperm as foreign, and their immune systems won't make blocking antibodies. So the baby gets recognized as foreign. But even this hostile act doesn't make the female a good invidivual, since it resulted from her failure to respond properly to the original breach of her boundaries in intercourse (Kolata, 1988a, b). It seems pretty clear that the biopolitical discourses of individuation have their limits for feminist purposes!

9 Jerne's debt to Chomsky's structuralism is obvious, as are the difficulties that pertain to any such version of structuralist internal totality. My argument is that there is more to see here than a too rapid criticism would allow. Jerne's and Chomsky's internal image of each other does not constitute the first time theories of the living animal and of language have occupied the same epistemic terrain. See Foucault, *The Order of Things* (1970). Remember that Foucault in *Archaeology of Knowledge* defined discourses as 'practices that

systematically form the objects of which they speak' (Foucault, 1972, p. 49). The family relation between structuralism and rationalism is something I will avoid for now.

10   Emily Martin has begun a three-year fieldwork project on networks of immunological discourse in laboratories, the media, and among people with and without AIDS.

11   Mice and 'men' are constantly associated in immune discourse because these sibling animal bodies have been best characterized in the immunological laboratory. For example, the Major Histocompatibility Complex (MHC), a complex of genes that encodes a critical array of surface markers involved in almost all of the key immune response recognition events, is well characterized for each species. The complex is called the H_2 locus in the mouse and the HLA locus in humans. The MHC codes for what will be recognized as 'self'. The locus is critically involved in 'restriction' of specificities. Highly polygenic and polyallelic, the MHC may be the main system allowing discrimination between self and non-self. 'Non-self' must be presented to an immune system cell 'in the context of self'; that is, associated with the surface markers coded by the MHC. Comparative studies of the antigens of the MHC with the molecular structures of other key actors in the immune response (antibodies, T cell differentiation antigens) have led to the concept of the 'immunoglobulin superfamily', characterized by its extensive sequence homologies that suggest an evolutionary elaboration from a common genic ancestor (Golub, 1987, pp. 202–33). The conceptual and laboratory tools developed to construct knowledge of the MHC are a microcosm for understanding the apparatus of production of the bodies of the immune system. Various antigens coded by the MHC confer 'public' or 'private' specificities, terms which designate degrees of shared versus differentiating antigens against a background of close genetic similarity, but not identity. Immunology could be approached as the science constructing such language-like 'distinguishing features' of the organic communications system. Current research on 'tolerance' and the ways thymic cells (T cells) 'educate' other cells about what is and is not 'self' led the biologist, Scott Gilbert, to ask if that is immunology's equivalent of the injunction to know 'thy-self' (personal communication). Reading immunological language requires both extreme literal-mindedness and a taste for troping. Jennifer Terry examined AIDS as a 'trop(olog)ical pandemic' (unpublished paper, UCSC).

12   It is not just imagers of the immune system who learn from military cultures; military cultures draw symbiotically on immune system discourse, just as strategic planners draw directly from and contribute to video game practices and science fiction. For example, in *Military Review* Colonel Frederick Timmerman argued for an élite corps of special strike force soldiers in the army of the future in these terms:

> The most appropriate example to describe how this system would work is the most complex biological model we know – the body's immune system. Within the body there exists a remarkably complex corps of internal bodyguards. In absolute numbers they are small – only about one percent of the body's cells. Yet they consist of reconnaissance specialists, killers, reconstitution specialists, and communicators that can seek out invaders, sound the alarm, reproduce rapidly, and swarm to the attack to repel the enemy ... In this regard, the June 1986 issue of *National Geographic* contains a detailed account of how the body's immune system functions. (Timmerman, 1987, p. 52)

Bibliography

A

Aberle, Sophie and Corner, George W. (1953) *Twenty-five Years of Sex Research: History of the National Research Council Committee for Research on Problems of Sex, 1922–47*. Philadelphia: Saunders.

Allee, W.C. (1938) *The Social Life of Animals*. New York: Norton.

Allen, Paula Gunn (1986) *The Sacred Hoop: Recovering the Feminine in American Indian Traditions*. Boston: Beacon.

Altmann, Jeanne (1980) *Baboon Mothers and Infants*. Cambridge, MA: Harvard University Press.

Altmann, S.A., ed. (1967) *Social Communication among Primates*. Chicago: University of Chicago Press.

Amos, Valerie, Lewis, Gail, Mama, Amina, and Parmar, Pratibha, eds (1984) *Many Voices, One Chant: Black Feminist Perspectives, Feminist Review* 17, 118 pp.

Angyal, Andras (1941) *Foundations of a Science of Personality*. Cambridge, MA: Harvard University Press.

Ann Arbor Science for the People (1977) *Biology as a Social Weapon*. Minneapolis: Burgess.

Anzaldúa, Gloria (1987) *Borderlands/La Frontera*. San Francisco: Spinsters/Aunt Lute.

Aptheker, Betina (1982) *Woman's Legacy: Essays on Race, Sex, and Class in American History*. Amherst: University of Massachusetts Press.

Ardrey, Robert (1966) *Territorial Imperative*. New York: Atheneum.

—— (1970) *The Social Contract*. New York: Atheneum.

Aristotle (1979) *Generation of Animals*, A.L. Peck, trans. Loeb Classical Library, XIII. London: Heinemann.

Ashby, W. Ross (1961) *An Introduction to Cybernetics*. London: Chapman and Hall.

Athanasiou, Tom (1987) 'High-tech politics: the case of artificial intelligence', *Socialist Review* 92: 7–35.

B

Bacon, Francis (1893) *Novum Organum*, J. Spedding, trans. London: G. Routledge.

—— (1942) *Essays and New Atlantis*. London: Walter J. Black.

Bambara, Toni Cade (1981) *The Salt Eaters*. New York: Vintage/Random House.

Barash, D.P. (1977) *Sociobiology and Behavior*. New York: Elsevier North Holland.

—— (1979) *The Whisperings Within: Evolution and the Origin of Human Nature*. New York: Harper & Row.

Baritz, Leon (1960) *Servants of Power*. Middletown: Wesleyan University Press.

Barnes, Deborah M. (1986) 'Nervous and immune system disorders linked in a variety of diseases', *Science* 232: 160–1.

—— (1987) 'Neuroimmunology sits on broad research base', *Science* 237: 1568–9.

Barrett, Michèle (1980) *Women's Oppression Today*. London: Verso.

Barthes, Roland (1982) 'The photographic message', in Susan Sontag, ed. *A Barthes Reader*. New York: Hill & Wang.

Baudrillard, Jean (1983) *Simulations*, P. Foss, P. Patton, P. Beitchman, trans. New York: Semiotext[e].

Bebel, August (1883) *Woman under Socialism*, D. De Leon, trans. New York: Shocken, 1971; (orig. *Women in the Past, Present and Future*, 1878).

Berger, Stewart (1985) *Dr. Berger's Immune Power Diet*. New York: New American Library.

Bethel, Lorraine and Smith, Barbara, eds (1979) *The Black Women's Issue, Conditions* 5.

Bhavnani, Kum-Kum and Coulson, Margaret (1986) 'Transforming socialist-feminism: the challenge of racism', *Feminist Review* 23: 81–92.

Bijker, Wiebe E., Hughes, Thomas, P., and Pinch, Trevor, eds (1987) *The Social Construction of Technological Systems*. Cambridge, MA: MIT Press.

Bingham, Harold C. (1928) 'Sex Development in Apes', *Comparative Psychology Monographs* 5: 1–165.

Bird, Elizabeth (1984) 'Green Revolution imperialism, I & II', papers delivered at the University of California, Santa Cruz.

Blalock, J. Edwin (1984) 'The immune system as a sensory organ', *Journal of Immunology* 132(3): 1067–70.

Bleier, Ruth (1984) *Science and Gender: A Critique of Biology and Its Themes on Women*. New York: Pergamon.

——, ed. (1986) *Feminist Approaches to Science*. New York: Pergamon.

Blumberg, Rae Lessor (1981) *Stratification: Socioeconomic and Sexual Inequality*. Boston: Brown.

—— (1983) 'A general theory of sex stratification and its application to the positions of women in today's world economy', paper delivered to Sociology Board, University of California at Santa Cruz.

Bogess, Jane (1976) 'The social behavior of the Himalayan langur (*Presbytis entellus*) in eastern Nepal', University of California, Berkeley, PhD thesis.

—— (1979) 'Troop male membership changes and infant killing in langurs (*Presbytis entellus*)', *Folia Primatologica* 32: 65–107.

—— (1980) 'Intermale relations and troop male membership changes in langurs (*Presbytis entellus*) in Nepal', *International Journal of Primatology* 1(2): 233–74.

Braverman, Harry (1974) *Labor and Monopoly Capital: The Degradation of Work in the Twentieth Century*. New York: Monthly Review.

Brewer, Mária Minich (1987) 'Surviving fictions: gender and difference in postmodern and postnuclear narrative', *Discourse* 9: 37–52.

Brighton Women and Science Group (1980) *Alice through the Microscope*. London: Virago.

Brown, Beverley and Adams, Parveen (1979) 'The feminine body and feminist politics', *m/f* 3: 35–57.

Brown, Lloyd, ed. (1981) *Women Writers of Black Africa*. Westport, CT: Greenwood Press.

Brown, Norman O. (1966) *Love's Body*. New York: Random House.

Bruner, Charlotte H., ed. (1983) *Unwinding Threads: Writing by Women in Africa*. London and Ibadan: Heinemann.

Bryan, C.D.B. (1987) *The National Geographic Society: 100 Years of Adventure and Discovery*. New York: Abrams.

Buckley, Walter, ed. (1968) *Modern Systems Research for the Behavioral Scientist*. Chicago: Aldine.

Bulkin, Elly, Pratt, Minnie Bruce, and Smith, Barbara (1984) *Yours in Struggle: Three Feminist Perspectives on Racism and Anti-Semitism*. New York: Long Haul.

Burke, Carolyn (1981) 'Irigaray through the looking glass', *Feminist Studies* 7(2): 288–306.

Burr, Sara G. (1982) 'Women and work', in Barbara K. Haber, ed. *The Women's Annual, 1981*. Boston: G.K. Hall.

Burtt, E.A. (1952) *The Metaphysical Foundations of Modern Science*. New York: Humanities.

Busch, Lawrence and Lacy, William (1983) *Science, Agriculture, and the Politics of Research*. Boulder, CO: Westview

Buss, Leo (1987) *The Evolution of Individuality*. Princeton: Princeton University Press.

Butler, Judith (1989) *Gender Trouble: Feminism and the Subversion of Identity*. New York: Routledge.

Butler, Octavia (1984) *Clay's Ark*. New York: St Martin's.

—— (1987) *Dawn*. New York: Warner.

Butler-Evans, Elliott (1987) 'Race, gender and desire: narrative strategies and the production of ideology in the fiction of Toni Cade Bambara, Toni Morrison and Alice Walker', University of California at Santa Cruz, PhD thesis.

C

Caplan, Arthur L. (1978) *The Sociobiology Debate*. New York: Harper & Row.

Carby, Hazel (1987) *Reconstructing Womanhood: The Emergence of the Afro-American Woman Novelist*. New York: Oxford University Press.

Caron, Joseph (1977) 'Animal cooperation in the ecology of W.C. Allee', paper delivered at the Joint Atlantic Seminar in the History of Biology, Montreal.

Carpenter, Clarence R. (1945) 'Concepts and problems of primate sociometry', *Sociometry* 8: 56–61.

—— (1964) *Naturalistic Behavior of Nonhuman Primates*. University Park: Pennsylvania State University Press.

—— (1972) 'The applications of less complex instructional technologies', in W. Schramm, ed. *Quality Instructional Television*. Honolulu: East–West Center, pp. 191–205.

Chasin, Barbara (1977) 'Sociobiology: a sexist synthesis', *Science for the People* 9: 27–31.

Chevalier-Skolnikoff, Suzanne (1971) 'The female sexual response in stumptail monkeys (*Macaca speciosa*), and its broad implications for female mammalian sexuality'. Paper presented at the American Anthropological Association meetings, New York City.

—— (1974) 'Male–female, female–female, and male–male sexual behavior in the stumptail monkey, with special attention to the female orgasm', *Archives of Sexual Behavior* 3: 96–116.

—— and Poirier, F.E., eds (1977) *Primate Bio-Social Development*. New York: Garland Press.

Chicanas en el ambiente nacional (1980) *Frontiers* 5(2).

Child, Charles Manning (1928) 'Biological foundations of social integration', *Publications of the American Sociological Society* 22: 26–42.

Chodorow, Nancy (1978) *The Reproduction of Mothering: Psychoanalysis and the Sociology of Gender*. Los Angeles: University of California Press.

Christian, Barbara (1985) *Black Feminist Criticism: Perspectives on Black Women Writers*. New York: Pergamon.

Clifford, James (1985) 'On ethnographic allegory', in James Clifford and George Marcus, eds *Writing Culture: The Poetics and Politics of Ethnography*. Berkeley: University of California Press.

—— (1988) *The Predicament of Culture: Twentieth-Century Ethnography, Literature, and Art*. Cambridge, MA: Harvard University Press.

Clyne, N. and Klynes, M. (1961) *Drugs, Space and Cybernetics. Evolution to Cyborg*. New York: Columbia University Press.

Cohen, Stanley (1976) 'Foundation officials and fellowships: innovation in the patronage of science', *Minerva* 14: 225–40.

Cohn, Carol (1987a) 'Nuclear language and how we learned to pat the bomb', *Bulletin of Atomic Scientists*, pp. 17–24.

—— (1987b) 'Sex and death in the rational world of defense intellectuals', *Signs* 12(4): 687–718.

Collingwood, R.G. (1945) *The Idea of Nature*. Oxford: Clarendon Press.

Collins, Patricia Hill (1982) 'Third World women in America', in Barbara K. Haber, ed. *The Women's Annual, 1981*. Boston: G.K. Hall.

—— (1989a) 'The social construction of Black feminist thought', *Signs* 14(4): 745–73.

—— (1989b) 'A comparison of two works on Black family life', *Signs* 14(4): 875–84.

Combaheee River Collective (1979) 'A Black feminist statement', in Zillah Eisenstein, ed. *Capitalist Patriarchy and the Case for Socialist Feminism*. New York: Monthly Review.

Committee on Science, Engineering, and Public Policy of the National Academy of Sciences, the National Academy of Medicine, and the Institute of Medicine (1983) *Research Briefings 1983*. Washington: National Academy Press.

Cooter, Roger (1979) 'The power of the body: the early nineteenth century', in Barry Barnes and Stephen Shapin, eds *Natural Order: Historical Studies of Scientific Culture*. Beverly Hills: Sage, pp. 73–96.

Cowan, Ruth Schwartz (1983) *More Work for Mother: The Ironies of Household Technology from the Open Hearth to the Microwave*. New York: Basic.

Coward, Rosalind (1983) *Patriarchal Precedents: Sexuality and Social Relations*. London: Routledge & Kegan Paul.

Cowdry, E.V., ed. (1930) *Human Biology and Racial Welfare*. New York: Hoeber.

Cravens, Hamilton (1978) *Triumph of Evolution*. Philadelphia: University of Pennsylvania Press.

Crook, J.H., ed. (1970) *Social Behavior in Birds and Mammals*. New York: Academic Press.

—— and Gartlan, J.S. (1966) 'Evolution of Primate Societies', *Nature* 210(5042): 1200–3.

D

Daston, Lorraine and Park, Katherine (n.d.) 'Hermaphrodites in Renaissance France', unpublished paper.

Davies, Carole Boyce and Graves, Anne Adams, eds (1986) *Ngambika: Studies of Women in African Literature*. Trenton: Africa World.

Davis, Angela (1982) *Women, Race, and Class*. London: Women's Press.

Dawkins, Richard (1976) *The Selfish Gene*. Oxford: Oxford University Press.

—— (1982) *The Extended Phenotype: The Gene as the Unit of Selection*. Oxford: Oxford University Press.

de Beauvoir, Simone (1949) *Le deuxième sexe*. Paris: Gallimard.

—— (1952) *The Second Sex*, H.M. Parshley, trans. New York: Bantam.

de Lauretis, Teresa (1984) *Alice Doesn't: Feminism, Semiotics, Cinema*. Bloomington: Indiana University Press.

—— (1985) 'The violence of rhetoric: considerations on representation and gender', *Semiotica* 54: 11–31.

—— (1986a) 'Feminist studies/critical studies: issues, terms, and contexts', in de Lauretis (1986b), pp. 1–19.

——, ed. (1986b) *Feminist Studies/Critical Studies*. Bloomington: Indiana University Press.

—— (1987) *Technologies of Gender: Essays on Theory, Film, and Fiction*. Bloomington: Indiana University Press.

—— Huyssen, Andreas, and Woodward, Kathleen, eds (1980) *The Technological Imagination: Theories and Fictions*. Madison: Coda.

de Waal, Frans (1982) *Chimpanzee Politics: Power and Sex among the Apes*. New York: Harper & Row.

Derrida, Jacques (1976) *Of Grammatology*, G.C. Spivak, trans. and introd. Baltimore: Johns Hopkins University Press.

Desowitz, Robert S. (1987) *The Immune System and How It Works*. New York: Norton.

DeVore, Irven (1962) 'The social behavior and organization of baboon troops', University of Chicago, PhD thesis.

——, ed. (1965) *Primate Behavior: Field Studies of Monkeys and Apes*. New York: Holt, Rinehart & Winston.

Dillard, Annie (1975) *Pilgrim at Tinker Creek*. New York: Bantam.

Dinnerstein, Dorothy (1977) *The Mermaid and the Minotaur: Sexual Arrangements and Human Malaise*. New York: Harper & Row.

Dolhinow, Phyllis (1972) 'The North Indian langur', in Dolhinow (1972), pp. 181–238.

——, ed. (1972) *Primate Patterns*. New York: Holt, Rinehart & Winston.

D'Onofrio-Flores, Pamela and Pfafflin, Sheila M., eds (1982) *Scientific-Technological Change and the Role of Women in Development*. Boulder: Westview.

Douglas, Mary (1966) *Purity and Danger*. London: Routledge & Kegan Paul.

—— (1970) *Natural Symbols*. London: Cresset Press.

—— (1973) *Rules and Meanings*. Harmondsworth: Penguin.

—— (1989) 'A gentle deconstruction', *London Review of Books*, 4 May, pp. 17–18.

DuBois, Page (1982) *Centaurs and Amazons*. Ann Arbor: University of Michigan Press.

Duchen, Claire (1986) *Feminism in France from May '68 to Mitterrand*. London: Routledge & Kegan Paul.

Du Plessis, Rachel Blau (1985) *Writing beyond the Ending: Narrative Strategies of Twentieth Century Women Writers*. Bloomington: Indiana University Press.

E

Eastman, David (1958) *A Systems Analysis of Political Life*. New York: Wiley.

Eco, Umberto (1980) *Il nome della rosa*. Milano: Bompiani.

—— (1983) *The Name of the Rose*, William Weaver, trans. New York: Harcourt Brace Jovanovich.

Editors of *Questions féministes* (1980) 'Variations on some common themes', *Feminist Issues* 1(1): 3–22.

Edwards, Paul (1985) 'Border wars: the science and politics of artificial intelligence', *Radical America* 19(6): 39–52.

Eimerl, Sarel and DeVore, Irven (1965) *The Primates*. New York: Time-Life Nature Library.

Eisenstein, Zillah, ed. (1979) *Capitalist Patriarchy and the Case for Socialist Feminism*. New York: Monthly Review.

Ellis, P.E., ed. (1965) 'Social organization of animal communities', *Symposium of the Zoological Society of London* 14.

Emecheta, Buchi (1972) *In the Ditch*. London: Allison & Busby, 1979

—— (1975) *Second Class Citizen*. New York: Braziller.

—— (1976) *The Bride Price*. New York: Braziller.

—— (1977) *The Slave Girl*. New York: Braziller.

—— (1979) *The Joys of Motherhood*. New York: Braziller.

—— (1982) *Destination Biafra*. London: Allison & Busby, 1982; Glasgow: William Collins & Sons, Fontana African Fiction, 1983.

—— (1983a) *Double Yoke*. New York: Braziller; London and Ibuza: Ogwugwu Afor.

—— (1983b) *The Rape of Shavi*. London and Ibuza: Ogwugwu Afor, 1983; New York: Braziller, 1985.

Emerson, A.E. (1954) 'Dynamic homeostasis, a unifying principle in organic, social, and ethical evolution', *Scientific Monthly* 78: 67–85.

Emery, F.E., ed. (1969) *Systems Thinking*. New York: Penguin.

Engels, Frederick (1884) *The Origins of the Family, Private Property and the State*, Eleanor B.

Leacock, trans. New York: International, 1972.

—— (1940) *Dialectics of Nature*, Clemens Dutt, trans. and ed. New York: International.

Enloe, Cynthia (1983a) 'Women textile workers in the militarization of Southeast Asia', in Nash and Fernandez-Kelly (1983), pp. 407–25.

—— (1983b) *Does Khaki Become You? The Militarization of Women's Lives*. Boston: South End.

Epstein, Barbara (forthcoming) *Political Protest and Cultural Revolution: Nonviolent Direct Action in the Seventies and Eighties*. Berkeley: University of California Press.

Escoffier, Jeffrey (1985) 'Sexual revolution and the politics of gay identity', *Socialist Review* 82/83: 119–53.

Evans, Mari, ed. (1984) *Black Women Writers: A Critical Evaluation*. Garden City, NY: Doubleday/Anchor.

F

Farley, Michael (1977) 'Formations et transformations de la synthèse écologique aux États-Unis, 1949–1971', L'Institut d'Histoire et de Sociopolitique des Sciences, Université de Montréal, Master's thesis.

Fausto-Sterling, Anne (1985) *Myths of Gender: Biological Theories about Women and Men*. New York: Basic.

Fedigan, Linda Marie (1982) *Primate Paradigms: Sex Roles and Social Bonds*. Montreal: Eden Press.

Fee, Elizabeth (1986) 'Critiques of modern science: the relationship of feminism to other radical epistemologies', in Ruth Bleier, ed. *Feminist Approaches to Science*. New York: Pergamon, pp. 42–56.

Feminisms in the Non-Western World (1983) *Frontiers* 7.

Fernandez-Kelly, Maria Patricia (1983) *For We Are Sold, I and My People*. Albany: State University of New York Press.

Firestone, Shulamith (1970) *Dialectic of Sex*. New York: Morrow.

Fisher, Dexter, ed. (1980) *The Third Woman: Minority Women Writers of the United States*. Boston: Houghton Mifflin.

Flax, Jane (1983) 'Political philosophy and the patriarchal unconscious: a psychoanalytic perspective on epistemology and metaphysics', in Harding and Hintikka (1983), pp. 245–82.

—— (1987) 'Postmodernism and gender relations in feminist theory', *Signs* 12(4): 621–43.

Ford, Barbara (1976, May) 'Murder and mothering among the sacred monkeys', *Science Digest*, pp. 23–32.

Fosdick, Raymond (1952) *The Story of the Rockefeller Foundation*. New York: Harper & Row.

Foucault, Michel (1963) *The Birth of the Clinic: An Archaeology of Medical Perception*, A.M. Smith, trans. New York: Vintage, 1975.

—— (1970) *The Order of Things*, New York: Random House.

—— (1972) *The Archaeology of Knowledge*, Alan Sheridan, trans. New York: Pantheon.

—— (1975) *Discipline and Punish: The Birth of the Prison*, Alan Sheridan, trans. New York: Vintage, 1979.

—— (1976) *The History of Sexuality*, Vol. 1: *An Introduction*, Robert Hurley, trans. New York: Pantheon, 1978.

Fox, Robin (1967) 'In the beginning', *Man* 2: 415–33.

Frankenberg, Ruth (1988) 'The social construction of whiteness', University of California at Santa Cruz, PhD thesis.

Fraser, Kathleen (1984) *Something. Even Human Voices. In the Foreground, a Lake*. Berkeley, CA: Kelsey St Press.

French Feminism, special issue (Autumn 1981) *Signs* 7(1).

Freud, Sigmund (1930) *Civilization and Its Discontents*. New York: Norton, 1962.

Frisch, J.E. (1959) 'Research on primate behavior in Japan', *American Anthropologist* 61: 584–96.

Fuentes, Annette and Ehrenreich, Barbara (1983) *Women in the Global Factory*. Boston: South End.

G

Gallop, Jane (1982) *The Daughter's Seduction: Feminism and Psychoanalysis*. New York: Macmillan.

Gates, Henry Louis (1985) 'Writing "race" and the difference it makes', in *'Race', Writing, and Difference*, special issue, *Critical Inquiry* 12(1): 1–20.

Ghiselin, Michael T. (1974) *The Economy of Nature and the Evolution of Sex*. Berkeley: University of California Press.

Giddings, Paula (1985) *When and Where I Enter: The Impact of Black Women on Race and Sex in America*. Toronto: Bantam.

Gilbert, Sandra M. and Gubar, Susan (1979) *The Madwoman in the Attic: The Woman Writer and the Nineteenth-Century Literary Imagination*. New Haven, CT: Yale University Press.

Gilligan, Carol (1982) *In a Different Voice*. Cambridge, MA: Harvard University Press.

Goldman, Emma (1931) *Living my Life*. New York: Knopf.

Goleman, Daniel (1987) 'The mind over the body', *New York Times Sunday Magazine*, 27 September, pp. 36–7, 59–60.

Golub, Edward S. (1987) *Immunology: A Synthesis*. Sunderland, MA: Sinauer Associates.

Goodall, Jane (1971) *In the Shadow of Man*. Boston: Houghton Mifflin.

Gordon, Linda (1976) *Woman's Body, Woman's Right: A Social History of Birth Control in America*. New York: Viking.

—— (1988) *Heroes of Their Own Lives. The Politics and History of Family Violence, Boston 1880–1960*. New York: Viking Penguin.

Gordon, Richard (1983) 'The computerization of daily life, the sexual division of labor, and the homework economy', Silicon Valley Workshop conference, University of California at Santa Cruz.

—— and Kimball, Linda (1985) 'High-technology, employment and the challenges of education', Silicon Valley Research Project, Working Paper, no. 1.

Gould, Stephen J. (1981) *Mismeasure of Man*. New York: Norton.

Gray, J.S. (1963) 'A physiologist looks at engineering', *Science* 140: 461–4.

Gregory, Judith and Nussbaum, Karen (1982) 'Race against time: automation of the office', *Office: Technology and People* 1: 197–236

Gregory, Michael, Silver, Anita, and Sutch, Diane, eds (1978) *Sociobiology and Human Nature: An Interdisciplinary Critique and Defense*. San Francisco: Jossey-Bass.

Gresham, Jewell Handy (1989) 'The scapegoating of the black family in America', *The Nation*, 24–31 July, pp. 116–22.

Griffin, Susan (1978) *Woman and Nature: The Roaring Inside Her*. New York: Harper & Row.

Grossman, Rachel (1980) 'Women's place in the integrated circuit', *Radical America* 14(1): 29–50.

H

Haas, Violet and Perucci, Carolyn, eds (1984) *Women in Scientific and Engineering Professions*. Ann Arbor: University of Michigan Press.

Habermas, Jürgen (1970) *Toward a Rational Society: Student Protest, Science, and Politics*. Boston: Beacon.

Hacker, Sally (1981) 'The culture of engineering: women, workplace, and machine', *Women's Studies International Quarterly* 4(3): 341–53.

—— (1984) 'Doing it the hard way: ethnographic studies in the agribusiness and engineering classroom', paper delivered at the California American Studies Association, Pomona.

—— and Bovit, Liza (1981) 'Agriculture to agribusiness: technical imperatives and changing roles', paper delivered at the Society for the History of Technology, Milwaukee.

Hall, Diana Long (1974) 'Biology, sex hormones and sexism in the 1920s', *Philosophical Forum* 5: 81–96.

Hall, K.R.L. and DeVore, Irven (1972) 'Baboon social behavior', in Dolhinow (1972), pp. 125–80.

Haller, J.S. (1971) *Outcasts from Evolution*. Urbana: Illinois University Press.

Hamilton, G.V. (1929) *A Research in Marriage*. New York: Boni.

Hamilton, W.D. (1964) 'The genetical theory of social behaviour, I, II', *Journal of Theoretical Biology* 7: 1–52.

Haraway, Donna J. (1978a) 'Animal sociology and a natural economy of the body politic, part I: a political physiology of dominance', *Signs* 4(1): 21–36. (This vol. pp. 7–20.)

—— (1978b) 'Animal sociology and a natural economy of the body politic, part II: the past is the contested zone: human nature and theories of production and reproduction in primate behavior studies', *Signs* 4(1): 37–60. (This vol. pp. 21–42.)

—— (1979) 'The biological enterprise: sex, mind, and profit from human engineering to sociobiology', *Radical History Review* 20: 206–37. (This vol. pp. 43–68.)

—— (1981–82) 'The high cost of information in post-World War II evolutionary biology', *Philosophical Forum* 13(2–3): 244–78.

—— (1983) 'Signs of dominance: from a physiology to a cybernetics of primate society', *Studies in History of Biology* 6: 129–219.

—— (1984) 'Class, race, sex, scientific objects of knowledge: a socialist-feminist perspective on the social construction of productive knowledge and some political consequences', in Violet Haas and Carolyn Perucci (1984), pp. 212–29.

—— (1984–5) 'Teddy bear patriarchy: taxidermy in the Garden of Eden, New York City, 1908–36', *Social Text* 11: 20–64.

—— (1985) 'Manifesto for cyborgs: science, technology, and socialist feminism in the 1980s', *Socialist Review* 80: 65–108. (This vol. pp. 149–81.)

—— (1989a) 'Review of A. Ong, *Spirits of Resistance and Capitalist Discipline*', *Signs* 14(4): 945–7.

—— (1989b) *Primate Visions: Gender, Race, and Nature in the World of Modern Science*. New York: Routledge.

Harding, Sandra (1978) 'What causes gender privilege and class privilege?', paper presented at the American Philosophical Association.

—— (1983) 'Why has the sex/gender system become visible only now?', in Harding and Hintikka (1983), pp. 311–24.

—— (1986) *The Science Question in Feminism*. Ithaca: Cornell University Press.

—— and Hintikka, Merill, eds (1983) *Discovering Reality: Feminist Perspectives on Epistemology, Metaphysics, Methodology, and Philosophy of Science*. Dordrecht: Reidel.

Hartmann, Heidi (1981) 'The unhappy marriage of marxism and feminism', in Sargent (1981), pp. 1–41.

Hartsock, Nancy (1983a) 'The feminist standpoint: developing the ground for a specifically feminist historical materialism', in Harding and Hintikka (1983), pp. 283–310.

—— (1983b) *Money, Sex, and Power*. New York: Longman; Boston: Northeastern University Press, 1984.

—— (1987) 'Rethinking modernism: minority and majority theories', *Cultural Critique* 7: 187–206.

Haug, Frigga, ed. (1980) *Frauenformen: Alltagsgeschichten und Entwurf einer Theorie weiblicher Sozialisation*. Berlin: Argument Sonderband 45.

—— (1982) 'Frauen und Theorie', *Das Argument* 136(11/12).

——, et al. (1983) *Sexualisierung: Frauenformen 2*. Berlin: Argument-Verlag.

——, et al. (1987) *Female Sexualization: A Collective Work of Memory*. London: Verso.

Haug, Wolfgang Fritz and others, eds (forthcoming) *Marxistisches Wörterbuch*. Berlin: Argument-Verlag.

Hayes, Dennis (1987) 'Making chips with dust-free poison', *Science as Culture* 1: 89–104.

Hayles, Katherine (1984) *The Cosmic Web: Scientific Field Models and Literary Strategies in the Twentieth Century*. Cornell University Press.

—— (1987a) 'Text out of context: situating postmodernism within an information society', *Discourse* 9: 24–36.

—— (1987b) 'Denaturalizing experience: postmodern literature and science', abstract, meetings of the Society for Literature and Science, 8–11 October, Worcester Polytechnic Institute.

Heidegger, Martin (1970) *The Question Concerning Technology and Other Essays*. New York: Harper & Row.

Henderson, Lawrence J. (1935) *Pareto's General Sociology: A Physiologist's Interpretation*. Cambridge, MA: Harvard University Press.

Henry, Alice (1982, January) 'Review of *The Woman That Never Evolved*', *Off Our Backs*, pp. 18–19.

Herschberger, Ruth (1948) *Adam's Rib*. New York: Pellegrine & Cudhay.

Heyl, Barbara (1968) 'The Harvard Pareto circle', *Journal of the History of Behavioral Sciences* 4: 316–34.

Hilgard, Ernest R. (1965) 'Robert Mearns Yerkes', *Biographical Memoirs of the National Academy of Sciences* 38: 384–425.

Hillis, W. Daniel (1988) 'Intelligence as an emergent behavior; or, the songs of Eden', *Daedalus*, winter, pp. 175–89.

Hogness, E. Rusten (1983) 'Why stress? A look at the making of stress, 1936–56', unpublished paper available from the author, 4437 Mill Creek Rd, Healdsburg, CA 95448.

hooks, bell (1981) *Ain't I a Woman*. Boston: South End.

—— (1984) *Feminist Theory: From Margin to Center*. Boston: South End.

Hooton, E.A. (1931) *Up from the Ape*. New York: Macmillan.

—— (1942) *Man's Poor Relations*. New York: Doubleday.

Hrdy, Sarah Blaffer (1975) 'Male and female strategies of reproduction among the langurs of Abu', Harvard University, PhD thesis.

—— (1977) *The Langurs of Abu: Female and Male Strategies of Reproduction*. Cambridge, MA: Harvard University Press.

—— (1981) *The Woman That Never Evolved*. Cambridge, MA: Harvard University Press.

—— and Williams, George C. (1983) 'Behavioral biology and the double standard', in Sam Wasser, ed. *Female Social Behavior*. New York: Academic Press, pp. 3–17.

Hubbard, Ruth and Lowe, Marian, eds (1979) *Genes and Gender*, vol. 2, *Pitfalls in Research on Sex and Gender*. Staten Island: Gordian Press.

Hubbard, Ruth, Henifin, Mary Sue, and Fried, Barbara, eds (1979) *Women Look at Biology Looking at Women: A Collection of Feminist Critiques*. Cambridge, MA: Schenkman.

——, eds (1982) *Biological Woman, the Convenient Myth*. Cambridge, MA: Schenkman.

Hull, Gloria, Scott, Patricia Bell, and Smith, Barbara, eds (1982) *All the Women Are White, All the Men Are Black, But Some of Us Are Brave*. Old Westbury: The Feminist Press.

Hurtado, Aida (1989) 'Relating to privilege: seduction and rejection in the subordination of white women and women of color', *Signs* 14(4): 833–55.

Hutchinson, G. Evelyn (1978) *An Introduction to Population Ecology*. New Haven: Yale Univesity Press.

I

Illich, Ivan (1982) *Gender*. New York: Pantheon.

International Fund for Agricultural Development (1985) *IFAD Experience Relating to Rural Women, 1977–84*. Rome: IFAD, 37.

Irigaray, Luce (1977) *Ce sexe qui n'en est pas un*. Paris: Minuit.

—— (1979) *Et l'une ne bouge pas sans l'autre*. Paris: Minuit.

J

Jacob, François (1974) *Logic of Life*, Betty Spillman, trans. New York: Pantheon.

Jaggar, Alison (1983) *Feminist Politics and Human Nature*. Totowa, NJ: Roman & Allenheld.

Jameson, Fredric (1984) 'Post-modernism, or the cultural logic of late capitalism', *New Left Review* 146: 53–92.

—— (1986) 'Third World literature in the era of multinational capitalism', *Social Text* 15: 65–88.

Jaret, Peter (1986) 'Our immune system: the wars within', *National Geographic* 169(6): 701–35.

—— and Mizel, Steven B. (1985) *In Self-Defense*. New York: Harcourt Brace Jovanovich.

Jay, Phyllis (1962) 'Aspects of maternal behavior among langurs', *Annals of the New York Academy of Sciences* 102: 468–76.

—— (1963a) 'The social behavior of the langur monkey', University of Chicago, PhD thesis.

—— (1963b) 'The Indian langur monkey (*Presbytis entellus*)', in C.H. Southwick, ed. *Primate Social Behavior*. Princeton: Van Nostrand, pp. 114–23.

—— (1965) 'The common langur of north India', in DeVore (1965), pp. 197–249.

Jerne, Niels K. (1985) 'The generative grammar of the immune system', *Science* 229: 1057–9.

Jordanova, Ludmilla, ed. (1987) *Languages of Nature*. London: Free Association Books.

Joseph, Gloria and Lewis, Jill (1981) *Common Differences*. New York: Anchor.

Judson, Horace Freeland (1979) *The Eighth Day of Creation*. New York: Simon & Schuster.

K

Kahn, Douglas and Neumaier, Diane, eds (1985) *Cultures in Contention*. Seattle: Real Comet.

Kanigel, Robert (1986) 'Where mind and body meet', *Mosaic* 17(2): 52–60.

—— (1987) 'The genome project', *New York Times Sunday Magazine* 13 December, pp. 44, 98–101, 106.

Kaplan, Caren (1986-7) 'The politics of displacement in *Buenos Aires*', *Discourse* 8: 84–100.

—— (1987a) 'The poetics of displacement: exile, immigration, and travel in contemporary autobiographical writing', University of California at Santa Cruz, PhD thesis.

—— (1987b) 'Deterritorializations: the rewriting of home and exile in Western feminist discourse', *Cultural Critique* 6: 187–98.

Keller, Evelyn Fox (1983) *A Feeling for the Organism*. San Francisco: Freeman.

—— (1985) *Reflections on Gender and Science*. New Haven: Yale University Press.

—— (1987) 'The gender/science system: or, is sex to gender as nature is to science?', *Hypatia* 2(3): 37–49.

—— (1990) 'From secrets of life to secrets of death', in M. Jacobus, E.F. Keller, and S. Shuttleworth, eds *Body/Politics: Women and the Discourses of Science*. New York: Routledge, pp. 177–91.

—— and Grontkowski, Christine (1983) 'The mind's eye', in Harding and Hintikka (1983), pp. 207–24.

Kessler, Suzanne and McKenna, Wendy (1978) *Gender: An Ethnomethodological Approach*. Chicago: University of Chicago Press.

Kevles, Daniel (1968) 'Testing the army's intelligence: psychologists and the military in World War I', *Journal of American History* 55: 565–81.

King, Katie (1984) 'The pleasure of repetition and the limits of identification in feminist science fiction: reimaginations of the body after the cyborg', paper delivered at the California American Studies Association, Pomona.

—— (1986) 'The situation of lesbianism as feminism's magical sign: contests for meaning and the U.S. women's movement, 1968–72', *Communication* 9(1): 65–92.

—— (1987a) 'Canons without innocence', University of California at Santa Cruz, PhD thesis.

—— (1987b) *The Passing Dreams of Choice ... Once Before and After: Audre Lorde and the Apparatus of Literary Production*, book prospectus, University of Maryland at College Park.

—— (1987c) 'Prospectus for research on feminism and writing technologies', University of Maryland at College Park.

—— (1988) 'Audre Lorde's lacquered layerings: the lesbian bar as a site of literary production', *Cultural Studies* 2(3): 321–42.

—— (forthcoming) 'Producing sex, theory, and culture: gay/straight remappings in contemporary feminism', in Marianne Hirsch and Evelyn Keller, eds, *Conflicts in Feminism*.

Kingston, Maxine Hong (1976) *The Woman Warrior*. New York: Knopf.

—— (1977) *China Men*. New York: Knopf.

Klein, Hilary (1989) 'Marxism, psychoanalysis, and mother nature', *Feminist Studies* 15(2): 255–78.

Klein, Jan (1982) *Immunology: The Science of Non-Self Discrimination*. New York: Wiley-Interscience.

Knorr-Cetina, Karin (1981) *The Manufacture of Knowledge*. Oxford: Pergamon.

—— and Mulkay, Michael, eds (1983) *Science Observed: Perspectives on the Social Study of Science*. Beverly Hills: Sage.

Kohler, Robert (1976) 'The management of science: the experience of Warren Weaver and the Rockefeller Foundation Programme in Molecular Biology', *Minerva* 14: 279–306.

Kolata, Gina (1988a) 'New treatments may aid women who have miscarriages', *The New York Times* 5 January, p. c3.

—— (1988b) 'New research yields clues in fight against autoimmune disease', *The New York Times*, 19 January, p. c3.

Kollontai, Alexandra (1977) *Selected Writings*. London: Allison & Busby.

Koshland, D.E., Jr, ed. (1986) *Biotechnology: The Renewable Frontier*. Washington: American Association for the Advancement of Science.

Kramarae, Cheris and Treichler, Paula (1985) *A Feminist Dictionary*. Boston: Pandora.

Kroeber, A.L. (1917) 'The super-organic', *American Anthropologist* 19: 163–213.

Kropotkin, Peter (1902) *Mutual Aid*. London: Heinemann.

Kuhn, Annette (1978) 'Structures of patriarchy and capital in the family', in Kuhn and Wolpe (1978), pp. 42–67.

—— (1982) *Women's Pictures: Feminism and Cinema*. London: Routledge & Kegan Paul.

—— and Wolpe, AnnMarie, eds (1978) *Feminism and Materialism*. London: Routledge & Kegan Paul.

Kummer, Hans (1968) *Social Organization of Hamadryas Baboons*. Chicago: University of Chicago Press.

L

Labica, Georges and Benussen, Gérard, eds (1985) *Dictionnaire Critique du Marxism*, 8 vols. Paris: Presses Universitaires de France.

Lancaster, Jane (1967) 'Primate communication systems and the emergence of human language', University of California at Berkeley, PhD thesis.

—— (1968) 'On the evolution of tool using behavior', *American Anthropologist* 70: 56–66.

—— (1971) 'Play mothering: the relations between juveniles and young infants among free-ranging vervet monkeys (*Cercopithecus aethiops*)', *Folia Primatoligica* 15: 161–82.

—— (1973) 'In praise of the achieving female monkey', *Psychology Today*, September, pp. 30–6, 90.

—— (1975) *Primate Behavior and the Emergence of Human Culture*. New York: Holt, Rinehart & Winston.

—— (1978) 'Carrying and sharing in human evolution', *Human Nature*, February, pp. 82–9.

—— (1979) 'Sex and gender in evolutionary perspective', in H.A. Katchadourian, ed. *Human Sexuality: A Comparative and Developmental Perspective*. Los Angeles: University of California Press, pp. 51–80.

—— and Lee, Richard (1965) 'The annual reproductive cycle in monkeys and apes', in DeVore (1965), pp. 486–513.

Lange, Bernd-Peter and Stuby, Anna Marie, eds (1984) *1984*. Berlin: Argument Sonderband 105.

Lasswell, H.D. and Kaplan, Abraham (1950) *Power and Society*. New Haven: Yale University Press.

Latour, Bruno (1984) *Les microbes, guerre et paix, suivi des irréductions*. Paris: Métailié.

—— (1988) *The Pasteurization of France, followed by Irreductions: A Politico-Scientific Essay*. Cambridge, MA: Harvard University Press.

—— and Woolgar, Steve (1979) *Laboratory Life: The Social Construction of Scientific Facts*. Beverly Hills: Sage.

Leacock, Eleanor (1972) 'Introduction', in Frederick Engels, *Origin of the Family, Private Property, and the State*. New York: International.

Lem, Stanislav (1964) *Summa technologiae*. Cracow: Wydawnictwo Literackie.

Lerner, Gerda, ed. (1973) *Black Women in White America: A Documentary History*. New York: Vintage.

Lettvin, J.Y., Maturana, H.R., McCulloch, W.S., and Pitts, W.H. (1959) 'What the frog's eye tells the frog's brain', *Proceedings of the Institute of Radio Engineers* 47: 1940–51.

Lévi-Strauss, Claude (1971) *Tristes Tropiques*, John Russell, trans. New York: Atheneum.

Lewontin, R.C., Rose, Steven, and Kamin, Leon J. (1984) *Not in Our Genes: Biology, Ideology, and Human Nature*. New York: Pantheon.

Lilienfeld, Robert (1978) *The Rise of Systems Theory*. New York: Wiley.

Lindberg, Donald (1967) 'A field study of the reproductive behavior of the rhesus monkey', University of California at Berkeley, PhD thesis.

Linden, Robin Ruth (1981) 'The social construction of gender: a methodological analysis of the gender identity paradigm', University of California at Santa Cruz, Sociology Board, Bachelor of Arts senior essay.

Linnaeus, Carl (1758) *Systema naturae per regna tria naturae, secundum classes, ordines, genera, species, cum characteribus, differentiis, synonymis, locis*, 10th edn. Holmiae: Laurentii Salvi.

—— (1972) *L'équilibre de la nature*, Bernard Jasmin, trans., Camille Limoges, intro. and notes. Paris: Librairie Philosophique J. Urin.

Lloyd, G.E.R. (1968) *Aristotle: The Growth of His Thought*. Cambridge: Cambridge University Press.

Locke, Steven E. and Hornig-Rohan, Mady (1983) *Mind and Immunity: Behavioral Immunology, An Annotated Bibliography, 1976–82*. New York: Institute for the Advancement of Health.

Lorde, Audre (1982) *Zami, a New Spelling of My Name*. Trumansberg, NY: Crossing, 1983.

—— (1984) *Sister Outsider*. Trumansberg, NY: Crossing.

Lovejoy, Owen (1981) 'The origin of man', *Science* 211: 341–50.

Lowe, Lisa (1986) 'French literary Orientalism: The representation of "others" in the texts of Montesquieu, Flaubert, and Kristeva', University of California at Santa Cruz, PhD thesis.

Lowe, Marian and Hubbard, Ruth, eds (1983) *Woman's Nature: Rationalizations of Inequality*. New York: Pergamon.

M

MacArthur, R.H. and Wilson, E.O. (1967) *The Theory of Island Biogeography*. Princeton: Princeton University Press.

McCaffrey, Anne (1969) *The Ship Who Sang*. New York: Ballantine.

MacCormack, Carol (1977) 'Biological events and cultural control', *Signs* 3: 93–100.

—— and Strathern, Marilyn, eds (1980) *Nature, Culture, Gender*. Cambridge; Cambridge University Press.

Mackey, Nathaniel (1984) 'Review', *Sulfur* 2: 200–5.

MacKinnon, Catherine (1982) 'Feminism, marxism, method, and the state: an agenda for theory', *Signs* 7(3): 515–44.

—— (1987) *Feminism Unmodified: Discourses on Life and Law*. Cambridge, MA: Harvard University Press.

McLellan, Vin (1988) 'Computer systems under siege', *New York Times* 31 January, Sec. 3: 1, 8.

Malamud, Bernard (1982) *God's Grace*. New York: Farrar Straus Giroux.

Malthus, Thomas Robert (1798) *An Essay on the Principle of Population*. New York: Norton, 1976.

Mani, Lata (1987) 'The construction of women as tradition in early nineteenth-century Bengal', *Cultural Critique* 7: 119–56.

Many Voices, One Chant: Black Feminist Perspectives (1984) *Feminist Review* 17, special issue.

Marcuse, Herbert (1964) *One-Dimensional Man: Studies in the Ideology of Advanced Industrial Society*. Boston: Beacon.

Markoff, John and Siegel, Lenny (1983) 'Military micros', paper presented at Silicon Valley Research Project conference, University of California at Santa Cruz.

Marks, Elaine and de Courtivron, Isabelle, eds (1980) *New French Feminisms*. Amherst: University of Massachusetts Press.

Marrack, Philippa and Kappler, John (1987) 'The T cell receptor', *Science* 238: 1073–9.

Marshall, Eliot (1986) 'Immune system theories on trial', *Science* 234: 1490–2.

Marx, Eleanor and Aveling, E. (1885–6) *The Woman Question*. London: Swann & Sonnenschein.

Marx, Karl (1964a) *Capital* vol. 1. New York: International.

—— (1964b) *The Economic and Philosophic Manuscripts of 1844*. New York: International.

—— (1972) *The Ethnological Notebooks of Karl Marx*, Laurence Krader, trans. and ed. Assen: Van Gorcum.

—— and Engels, Frederick (1970) *The German Ideology*. London: Lawrence & Wishart.

Marxist-Feminist Literature Collective (1978) 'Women's writing', *Ideology and Consciousness* 1(3): 27–48.

May, Mark A. and Doob, Leonard W. (1937) *Competition and Cooperation*. New York: Social Science Research Council.

Mayo, Elton (1933) *The Human Problems of Industrial Civilization*. New York: Macmillan.

Mead, Margaret (1935) *Sex and Temperament in Three Primitive Societies*. New York: Morrow.

—— (1937) *Cooperation and Competition among Primitive Peoples*. New York: McGraw-Hill.

Merchant, Carolyn (1980) *The Death of Nature: Women, Ecology, and the Scientific Revolution*. New York: Harper & Row.

Mesarovic, M.D., ed. (1968) *Systems Theory and Biology*. New York: Springer-Verlag.

Microelectronics Group (1980) *Microelectronics: Capitalist Technology and the Working Class*. London: CSE.

Miles, C.C. and Terman, Lewis (1929) 'Sex difference in association of ideas', *American Journal of Psychology* 41: 165–206.

Mitchell, Juliet (1966) 'Women: the longest revolution', *New Left Review* 40: 11–37.

—— (1971) *Women's Estate*. New York: Pantheon.

—— and Oakley, Ann, eds (1986) *What Is Feminism? A Re-examination*. New York: Pantheon.

Mohanty, Chandra Talpade (1984) 'Under western eyes: feminist scholarship and colonial discourse', *Boundary* 2, 3 (12/13): 333–58.

—— (1988) 'Feminist encounters: locating the politics of experience', *Copyright* 1: 30–44.

Moi, Toril (1985) *Sexual/Textual Politics*. New York: Methuen.

Money, John and Ehrhardt, Anke (1972) *Man and Woman, Boy and Girl*. New York: New American Library, 1974.

Moraga, Cherríe (1983) *Loving in the War Years: lo que nunca pasó por sus labios*. Boston: South End.

—— and Anzaldúa, Gloria, eds (1981) *This Bridge Called My Back: Writings by Radical Women of Color*. Watertown: Persephone.

Morawski, J.G. (1987) 'The troubled quest for masculinity, femininity and androgyny', *Review of Personality and Social Psychology* 7: 44–69.

Morgan, Elaine (1972) *The Descent of Woman*. New York: Stein & Day.

Morgan, Robin, ed. (1984) *Sisterhood Is Global*. Garden City, NY: Anchor/Doubleday.

Morris, C.W. (1938) *Foundation of the Theory of Signs*. Chicago: University of Chicago Press.

Moss, Cynthia (1975) *Portraits in the Wild*. Boston: Houghton Mifflin.

Mouffe, Chantal (1983) 'The sex-gender system and the discursive construction of women's subordination', *Rethinking Ideology*. Berlin: Argument Sonderband 84.

Murrell, K.F.H. (1965) *Ergonomics: Man in His Working Environment*. London: Chapman and Hall.

N

Nash, June and Fernandez-Kelly, Maria Patricia, eds (1983) *Women and Men and the International Division of Labor*. Albany: State University of New York Press.

Nash, Roderick (1979) 'The exporting and importing of nature: nature-appreciation as a commodity, 1850–1980', *Perspectives in American History* 3: 517–60.

National Science Foundation (1988) *Women and Minorities in Science and Engineering*. Washington: NSF.

Nicholas, Robin (1985) *Immunology: An Information Profile*. London: Mansell.

Nilsson, Lennart (1977) *A Child Is Born*. New York: Dell.

—— (1987) *The Body Victorious: The Illustrated Story of our Immune System and Other Defenses of the Human Body*. New York: Delacorte.

Noble, David F. (1977) *America by Design: Science, Technology and the Rise of Corporate Capitalism*. New York: Knopf.

O

O'Brien, Mary (1981) *The Politics of Reproduction*. New York: Routledge & Kegan Paul.

Odum, E.P. (1955, 1959, 1971) *Fundamentals of Ecology*, 3 edns. Philadelphia: Saunders.

—— (1977) 'The emergence of ecology as a new integrative discipline', *Science* 195: 1289–93.

Ogunyemi, Chickwenye Okonjo (1983) 'The shaping of a self: a study of Buchi Emecheta's novels', *Komparatistische Hefte* 8: 65–77.

—— (1985) 'Womanism: the dynamics of the contemporary Black female novel in English', *Signs* 11(1): 63–80.

On Technology (1987) *Discourse* 9, special issue on Cybernetics, Ecology and the Postmodern Imagination.

Ong, Aihwa (1987) *Spirits of Resistance and Capitalist Discipline: Factory Workers in Malaysia*. Albany: State University of New York Press.

—— (1988) 'Colonialism and modernity: feminist representations of women in non-western societies', *Inscriptions* 3/4: 79–93.

Ong, Walter (1982) *Orality and Literacy: The Technologizing of the Word*. New York: Methuen.

Optner, Stanford L., ed. (1973) *Systems Analysis*. Baltimore: Penguin.

Ortner, Sherry B. (1974) 'Is female to male as nature is to culture?', in Rosaldo and Lamphere (1974), pp. 67–87.

—— and Whitehead, Harriet, eds (1981) *Sexual Meanings: The Cultural Construction of Gender and Sexuality*. Cambridge: Cambridge University Press.

P

Park, Katherine and Daston, Lorraine J. (1981) 'Unnatural conceptions: the study of monsters in sixteenth- and seventeenth-century France and England', *Past and Present* 92: 20–54.

Parsons, Talcott (1970) 'On building social system theory: a personal history', *Daedalus* 99(4): 826–81.

Perloff, Marjorie (1984) 'Dirty language and scramble systems', *Sulfur* 11: 178–83.

Petchesky, Rosalind Pollack (1981) 'Abortion, anti-feminism and the rise of the New Right', *Feminist Studies* 7(2): 206–46.

—— (1987) 'Fetal images: the power of visual culture in the politics of reproduction', *Feminist Studies* 13(2): 263–92.

Peterfreund, Emanuel and Schwartz, J.T. (1966) *Information, Systems, and Psychoanalysis*. New York: McGraw-Hill.

Piercy, Marge (1976) *Woman on the Edge of Time*. New York: Knopf.

Piven, Frances Fox and Coward, Richard (1982) *The New Class War: Reagan's Attack on the Welfare State and Its Consequences*. New York: Pantheon.

Playfair, J.H.L. (1984) *Immunology at a Glance*, 3rd edn. Oxford: Blackwell.

Porush, David (1985) *The Soft Machine: Cybernetic Fiction*. New York: Methuen.

—— (1987) 'Reading in the servo-mechanical loop', *Discourse* 9: 53–62.

Potter, Van Rensselaer (1971) *Bioethics, Bridge to the Future*. Englewood Cliffs: Prentice-Hall.

Preston, Douglas (1984) 'Shooting in paradise', *Natural History* 93(12): 14–19.

Pugh, D.S., ed. (1971) *Organization Theory*. New York: Penguin.

Pynchon, Thomas (1974) *Gravity's Rainbow*. New York: Bantam.

R

Reagon, Bernice Johnson (1983) 'Coalition politics: turning the century', in Smith (1983) pp. 356–68.

Redfield, Robert, ed. (1942) *Levels of Integration in Biological and Social Systems*. Lancaster, PA: Cattell.

Reed, James (1978) *From Private Vice to Public Virtue: The Birth Control Movement and American Society since 1830*. New York: Basic.

Reiter, Rayna Rapp, ed. (1975) *Toward an Anthropology of Women*. New York: Monthly Review.

Reskin, Barbara F. and Hartmann, Heidi, eds (1986) *Women's Work, Men's Work*. Washington: National Academy of Sciences.

Rich, Adrienne (1978) *The Dream of a Common Language*. New York: Norton.

—— (1980) 'Compulsory heterosexuality and lesbian existence', *Signs* 5(4): 631–60.

—— (1986) 'Notes toward a politics of location', in *Blood, Bread, and Poetry: Selected Prose, 1979–85*, pp. 210–31. New York: Norton.

Ripley, Suzanne (1965) 'The ecology and social behavior of the Ceylon grey langur (*Presbytis entellus thersites*)', University of California, Berkeley, PhD thesis.

—— (1980) 'Infanticide in langurs and man: adaptive advantage or social pathology?', in M.N. Cohen, R.S. Malpass, and H.G. Klein, eds *Biosocial Mechanisms of Population Regulation*. New Haven: Yale University Press, pp. 349–90.

Roberts, Leslie (1987a) 'Who owns the human genome?', *Science* 237: 358–61.

—— (1987b) 'Human genome: questions of cost', *Science* 237: 1411–12.

—— (1987c) 'New sequencers take on the genome', *Science* 238: 271–3.

Rosaldo, Michelle (1980) 'The use and abuse of anthropology', *Signs* 5: 389–417.

—— and Lamphere, Louise, eds (1974) *Woman, Culture, and Society*. Palo Alto: Stanford University Press.

Rose, Hilary (1983) 'Hand, brain, and heart: a feminist epistemology for the natural sciences', *Signs* 9(1): 73–90.

—— (1986) 'Women's work: women's knowledge', in Juliet Mitchell and Ann Oakley, eds, *What Is Feminism? A Re-Examination*. New York: Pantheon, pp. 161–83.

Rose, Stephen (1986) *The American Profile Poster: Who Owns What, Who Makes How Much, Who Works Where, and Who Lives with Whom?* New York: Pantheon.

Rossiter, Margaret (1982) *Women Scientists in America*. Baltimore: Johns Hopkins University Press.

Rothschild, Joan, ed. (1983) *Machina ex Dea: Feminist Perspectives on Technology*. New York: Pergamon.

Rowell, Thelma E. (1966a) 'Forest-living baboons in Uganda', *Journal of Zoology* 149: 344–64.

—— (1966b) 'Hierarchy in the organization of a captive baboon group', *Animal Behaviour* 14: 430–43.

—— (1970) 'Baboon menstrual cycles affected by social environment', *Journal of Reproduction and Fertility* 21: 133–41.

—— (1972) *Social Behaviour of Monkeys*. Baltimore: Penguin.

—— (1974) 'The concept of social dominance', *Behavioral Biology* 11: 131–54.

Rubin, Gayle (1975) 'The traffic in women: notes on the political economy of sex', in Rayna Rapp Reiter (1975), pp. 157–210.

—— (1984) 'Thinking sex: notes for a radical theory of the politics of sexuality', in Carol Vance, ed. *Pleasure and Danger*. London: Routledge & Kegan Paul, pp. 267–319.

Ruch, Theodore (1941) *Bibliographia Primatologica*. Baltimore: Charles Thomas.

Russ, Joanna (1983) *How to Suppress Women's Writing*. Austin: University of Texas Press.

S

Sachs, Carolyn (1983) *The Invisible Farmers: Women in Agricultural Production*. Totowa: Rowman & Allenheld.

Sahlins, Marshall (1976) *The Use and Abuse of Biology*. Ann Arbor: University of Michigan Press.

Said, Edward (1978) *Orientalism*. New York: Pantheon.

Sandoval, Chela (1984) 'Dis-illusionment and the poetry of the future: the making of oppositional consciousness', University of California at Santa Cruz, PhD qualifying essay.

—— (n.d.) *Yours in Struggle: Women Respond to Racism, a Report on the National Women's Studies Association*. Oakland, CA: Center for Third World Organizing.

Sargent, Lydia, ed. (1981) *Women and Revolution*. Boston: South End.

Sayers, Janet (1982) *Biological Politics: Feminist and Anti-Feminist Perspectives*. London: Tavistock.

Schiebinger, Londa (1987) 'The history and philosophy of women in science: a review essay', *Signs* 12(2): 305–32.

Schipper, Mineke (1985) 'Women and literature in Africa', in Mineke Schipper, ed. *Unheard Words: Women and Literature in Africa, the Arab World, Asia, the Caribbean and Latin America*, Barbara Potter Fasting, trans. London: Allison & Busby, pp. 22–58.

Schjelderup-Ebbe, Thorlief (1935) 'Social behavior of birds', in Carl Murchison, ed. *Handbook of Social Psychology* 2: 947–72. Worcester, MA: Clark University Press.

Science Policy Research Unit (1982) *Microelectronics and Women's Employment in Britain*. University of Sussex.

Scott, Joan Wallach (1988) *Gender and the Politics of History*. New York: Columbia University Press.

Sebeok, T.A., ed. (1968) *Animal Communication: Techniques of Study and Results of Research*. Bloomington: Indiana University Press.

Shirek-Ellefson, Judith (1967) 'Visual communication in *Macaca irus*', University of California at Berkeley, PhD thesis.

Singh, Jagjit (1966) *Great Ideas in Information Theory, Language, and Cybernetics*. New York: Dover.

Smith, Barbara (1977) 'Toward a Black feminist criticism', in Elaine Showalter, ed. *The New Feminist Criticism: Essays on Women, Literature and Theory*. New York: Pantheon, 1985, pp. 168–85.

——, ed. (1983) *Home Girls: A Black Feminist Anthology*. New York: Kitchen Table, Women of Color Press.

Smith, Dorothy (1974) 'Women's perspective as a radical critique of sociology', *Sociological Inquiry* 44.

—— (1979) 'A sociology of women', in J. Sherman and E.T. Beck, eds *The Prism of Sex*. Madison: University of Wisconsin Press.

Sochurek, Howard (1987) 'Medicine's new vision', *National Geographic* 171(1): 2–41.

Sofia, Zoe (also Zoe Sofoulis) (1984) 'Exterminating fetuses: abortion, disarmament, and the sexo-semiotics of extra-terrestrialism', *Diacritics* 14(2): 47–59.

Sofoulis, Zoe (1984) 'Jupiter Space', paper delivered at the American Studies Association, Pomona, CA.

—— (1987) 'Lacklein', University of California at Santa Cruz, unpublished essay.

—— (1988) 'Through the lumen: Frankenstein and the optics of re-origination', University of California at Santa Cruz, PhD thesis.

Somit, Albert, ed. (1976) *Biology and Politics: Recent Explorations*. Paris and The Hague: Mouton.

Sontag, Susan (1977) *On Photography*. New York: Dell.

Spillers, Hortense (1987) 'Mama's baby, papa's maybe: an American grammar book', *Diacritics* 17(2): 65–81.

Spivak, Gayatri (1985) 'Three women's texts and a critique of imperialism', *Critical Inquiry* 12(1): 243–61.

Stacey, Judith (1987) 'Sexism by a subtler name? Postindustrial conditions and postfeminist consciousness', *Socialist Review* 96: 7–28.

Stallard, Karin, Ehrenreich, Barbara, and Sklar, Holly (1983) *Poverty in the American Dream*. Boston: South End.

Stanley, Manfred (1978) *The Technological Conscience*. New York: Free Press.

Stoller, Robert (1964) 'A contribution to the study of gender identity', *International Journal of Psychoanalysis* 45: 220–6.

—— (1968 and 1976) *Sex and Gender*, vol. I, New York: Science House; vol. II, New York: Jason Aronson.

Strathern, Marilyn (1987a) 'Out of context: the persuasive fictions of anthropology', *Current Anthropology* 28(3): 251–81.

—— (1987b) 'Partial connections', University of Edinburgh, Munro Lecture.

—— (1988) *The Gender of the Gift: Problems with Women and Problems with Society in Melanesia*. Berkeley: University of California Press.

Sturgeon, Noel (1986) 'Feminism, anarchism, and non-violent direct action politics', University of California at Santa Cruz, PhD qualifying essay.

Sugiyama, Yukimaru (1967) 'Social Organization of Hanuman langurs', in Altmann (1967), pp. 221–36.

Sussman, Vic (1986) 'Personal tech. Technology lends a hand', *The Washington Post Magazine*, 9 November, pp. 45–56.

T

Taiwo, Oladele (1984) *Female Novelists of Modern Africa*. New York: St Martin's.

Tanner, Nancy (1981) *On Becoming Human*. Cambridge: Cambridge University Press.

—— and Zihlman, Adrienne (1976) 'Women in evolution. Part I: innovation and selection in human origins', *Signs* 1(3): 585–608.

The Woman Question: Selected Writings of Marx, Engels, Lenin and Stalin (1951) New York: International.

Thorne, Barrie and Henley, Nancy, eds (1975) *Language and Sex: Difference and Dominance*. Rowley, MA: Newbury.

Timmerman, Colonel Frederick W., Jr (1987, September) 'Future warriors', *Military Review*, pp. 44–55.

Toulmin, Stephen (1982) *The Return of Cosmology: Postmodern Science and the Theology of Nature*. Berkeley: University of California Press.

Tournier, Michel (1967) *Vendredi*. Paris: Gallimard.

Traweek, Sharon (1988) *Beamtimes and Lifetimes: The World of High Energy Physics*. Cambridge, MA: Harvard University Press.

Treichler, Paula (1987) 'AIDS, homophobia, and biomedical discourse: an epidemic of signification', *October* 43: 31–70.

Trinh T. Minh-ha (1986–7) 'Introduction', and 'Difference: "a special third world women issue"', *Discourse: Journal for Theoretical Studies in Media and Culture* 8: 3–38.

——, ed. (1986–7) *She, the Inappropriate/d Other, Discourse* 8.

—— (1988) 'Not you/like you: post-colonial women and the interlocking questions of identity and difference', *Inscriptions* 3/4: 71–6.

—— (1989) *Woman, Native, Other: Writing Postcoloniality and Feminism*. Bloomington: Indiana University Press.

Trivers, R.L. (1971) 'The evolution of reciprocal altruism', *Quarterly Review of Biology* 46: 35–7.

—— (1972) 'Parental investment and sexual selection', in Bernard Campbell, ed. *Sexual Selection and the Descent of Man*. Chicago: Aldine, pp. 136–79.

Turner, Bryan S. (1984) *The Body and Society*. New York: Blackwell.

V

Varley, John (1978) 'The persistence of vision', in *The Persistence of Vision*. New York: Dell, pp. 263–316.

—— (1986) 'Blue champagne', in *Blue Champagne*. New York: Berkeley, pp. 17–79.

von Bertalanffy, Ludwig (1968) *General Systems Theory*. New York: Braziller.

W

Waddington, C.H. (1957) *The Strategy of the Gene*. London: Allen & Unwin.

Walker, Alice (1983) *In Search of Our Mothers' Gardens*. New York: Harcourt Brace Jovanovitch.

Ware, Celestine (1970) *Woman Power*. New York: Tower.

Washburn, Sherwood L. (1951a) 'The new physical anthropology', *Transactions of the New York Academy of Sciences*, series 2, 13(7): 298–304.

—— (1951b) 'The analysis of primate evolution with particular reference to man', *Cold Spring Harbor Symposium of Quantitative Biology* 15: 67–78.

—— (1963) 'The study of race', *American Anthropologist* 65: 521–32.

—— (1978) 'Human behavior and the behavior of other animals', *American Psychologist* 33: 405–18.

—— and Avis, Virginia (1958) 'The evolution of human behavior', in Anne Roe and George Gaylord Simpson, eds *Behavior and Evolution*. New Haven: Yale University Press, pp. 421–36.

—— and DeVore, Irven (1961) 'Social behavior of baboons and early man', in S.L. Washburn, ed. *Social Life of Early Man*, New York: Viking Fund Publications in Anthropology, pp. 91–105.

—— and Hamburg, David (1965) 'The implications of primate research', in DeVore (1965), pp. 607–22.

—— (1968) 'Aggressive behavior in Old World monkeys and apes', in Dolhinow (1972), pp. 276–96.

—— and Lancaster, C.S. (1968) 'The evolution of hunting', in Richard Lee and Irven DeVore, eds *Man the Hunter*. Chicago: Aldine, pp. 293–303.

Watson, J.D. (1976) *The Molecular Biology of the Gene*, 3rd edn. Menlo Park: Benjamin.

Weaver, Warren (1948) 'Science and Complexity', *American Scientist* 36: 536–44.

Wechsler, Rob (1987, February) 'A new prescription: mind over malady', *Discover*: 51–61.

Weill, Jean-Claude and Reynaud, Claude-Agnès (1987) 'The chicken B cell compartment', *Science* 238: 1094–8.

Weiner, Norbert (1954) *The Human Use of Human Beings*. New York: Avon, 1967.

Weinrich, James D. (1977) 'Human sociobiology: pair-bonding and resource predictability (effects of social class and race)', *Behavioral Ecology and Sociobiology* 2: 91–116.

Weizenbaum, Joseph (1976) *Computer Power and Human Reason*. San Francisco: Freeman.

Welford, John Noble (1 July, 1986) 'Pilot's helmet helps interpret high speed world', *New York Times*, pp. 21, 24.

West, Candance and Zimmermann, D.H. (1987) 'Doing gender', *Gender and Society* 1(2): 125–51.

Westinghouse Broadcasting Corporation (1987) 'The fighting edge', a television programme in the series, 'Life Quest'.

Wheeler, W.M. (1939) *Essays in Philosophical Biology*. Cambridge, MA: Harvard University Press.

White, Hayden (1987) *The Content of the Form: Narrative Discourse and Historical Representation*. Baltimore: Johns Hopkins University Press.

Wilfred, Denis (1982) 'Capital and agriculture, a review of Marxian problematics', *Studies in Political Economy* 7: 127–54.

Wilson, E.O. (1962) 'Chemical communication among workers of the fire ant, *Solemopsis saevissima* (Fr. Smith)', *Animal Behaviour* 10(1–2): 134–64.

—— (1963) 'The social biology of ants', *Annual Review of Entomology* 8: 345–68.

—— (1968) 'The ergonomics of caste in social insects', *American Naturalist* 102: 41–66.

—— (1971) *Insect Societies*. Cambridge, MA: Harvard University Press.

—— (1975) *Sociobiology: The New Synthesis*. Cambridge, MA: Harvard University Press.

—— (1978) *On Human Nature*. Cambridge, MA: Harvard University Press.

——, Eisner, T., Briggs, W.R., Dickerson, R.E., Metzenberg, R.L., O'Brien, R.D., Sussman, M. and Boggs, W.E. (1978) *Life on Earth*, 2nd edn. Sunderland, MA: Sinauer.

Winner, Langdon (1977) *Autonomous Technology: Technics out of Control as a Theme in Political Thought*. Cambridge, MA: MIT Press.

—— (1980) 'Do artifacts have politics?', *Daedalus* 109(1): 121–36.

—— (1986) *The Whale and the Reactor*. Chicago: University of Chicago Press.

Winograd, Terry (forthcoming) 'Computers and rationality: the myths and realities', in Paul N. Edwards and Richard Gordon, eds, *Strategic Computing: Defense Research and High Technology*.

—— and Flores, Fernando (1986) *Understanding Computers and Cognition: A New Foundation for Design*. Norwood, NJ; Ablex.

Wittig, Monique (1973) *The Lesbian Body*, David LeVay, trans. New York: Avon, 1975 (*Le corps lesbien*, 1973).

—— (1981) 'One is not born a woman', *Feminist Issues* 2: 47–54.

Women and Poverty, special issue (1984) *Signs* 10(2).

Woodward, Kathleen (1983) 'Cybernetic modeling in recent American writing', *North Dakota Quarterly* 51: 57–73.

—— ed. (1980) *The Myths of Information: Technology and Post-Industrial Culture*. London: Routledge & Kegan Paul.

Wright, Susan (1982, July/August) 'Recombinant DNA: the status of hazards and controls', *Environment* 24(6): 12–20, 51–53.

—— (1986) 'Recombinant DNA technology and its social transformation, 1972–82', *Osiris*, 2nd series, 2: 303–60.

Wynne-Edwards, V.C. (1962) *Animal Dispersion in Relation to Social Behaviour*. Edinburgh: Oliver & Boyd.

Y

Yerkes, R.M. (1900) 'Reaction of *Entomostraca* to stimulation by light,' Part II, 'Reactions of *Daphnia* and *Cypris*', *American Journal of Physiology* 4: 405–22.

—— (1907) *The Dancing Mouse*. New York: Macmillan.

—— (1913) 'Comparative psychology in relation to medicine', *Boston Medical Surgery Journal* 169: 779–81.

—— (1919) 'The measurement and utilization of brain power in the army', *Science* 44: 221–6, 251–9.

—— (1920) 'What psychology contributed to the war', in *The New World of Science*. New York: Century.

—— (1921) 'The relations of psychology to medicine', *Science* 53: 106–11.

—— (1922) 'What is personnel research?', *Journal Personnel Research* 1: 56–63.

—— (1927a) 'A program of anthropoid research', *American Journal of Psychology* 39: 181–99.

—— (1927b) 'The mind of a gorilla', Parts I, II, *Genetic Psychology Monographs* 2: 1–193, 375–551.

—— (1928) 'The mind of a gorilla', Part III, *Comparative Psychology Monographs* 5: 1–92.

—— (1932) 'Yale Laboratories of Comparative Psychobiology', *Comparative Psychology Monographs* 8: 1–33.

—— (1935–6) 'The significance of chimpanzee culture for biological research', *Harvey Lectures* 31: 57–73.

—— (1939) 'Social dominance and sexual status in the chimpanzee', *Quarterly Review of Biology* 14(2): 115–36.

—— (1943) *Chimpanzees, A Laboratory Colony*. New Haven: Yale University Press.

—— and Yerkes, A.W. (1929) *The Great Apes*. New Haven: Yale University Press.

——, Bridges, J.W., and Hardwick, R.S. (1915) *A Point Scale for Measuring Mental Ability*. Baltimore: Warwick & York.

Young, Iris (1981) 'Beyond the unhappy marriage: a critique of the dual systems theory', in Sargent (1981), pp. 44–69.

Young, Robert M. (1969) 'Malthus and the evolutionists: the common context of biological and social theory', *Past and Present* 43: 109–41.

—— (1973) 'The historiographic and ideological contexts of the nineteenth-century debate on man's place in nature', in Young (1985), pp. 164–248.

—— (1977) 'Science is social relations', *Radical Science Journal* 5: 65–129.

—— (1979, March) 'Interpreting the production of science', *New Scientist* 29: 1026–8.

—— (1985) *Darwin's Metaphor: Nature's Place in Victorian Culture*. London: Cambridge University Press.

—— and Levidow, Les, eds (1981, 1985) *Science, Technology and the Labour Process*, 2 vols. London: CSE and Free Association Books.

Yoxen, Edward (1983) *The Gene Business*. New York: Harper & Row.

Z

Zacharias, Kristin (1980) 'The construction of a primate order: taxonomy and comparative anatomy in establishing the human place in nature, 1735–1916', Johns Hopkins University, PhD thesis.

Zaki, Hoda M. (1988) 'Fantasies of difference', *Women's Review of Books* V(4): 13–14.

Zihlman, Adrienne (1967) 'Human locomotion: a reappraisal of functional and anatomical evidence', University of California, Berkeley, PhD thesis.

—— (1978a) 'Women in evolution, part II: subsistence and social organization among early hominids', *Signs* 4(1): 4–20.

—— (1978b) 'Motherhood in transition: from ape to human', in W. Miller and Lucille Newman, eds *First Child and Family Formation*. North Carolina: Carolina Population Center Publications.

—— (1978c) 'Gathering and the hominid adaptation', in Lionel Tiger and Heather Fowler, eds *Female Hierarchies*. Chicago: Beresford.

Zimmerman, Jan, ed. (1983) *The Technological Woman: Interfacing with Tomorrow*. New York: Praeger.

Zuckerman, Solly (1932) *The Social Life of Monkeys and Apes*. New York: Harcourt Brace.

—— (1933) *Functional Affinities of Man, Monkeys, and Apes: A Study of the Bearings of Physiology and Behavior on the Taxonomy and Phylogeny of Lemurs, Monkeys, Apes and Men*. New York: Harcourt Brace.

—— (1972) *Beyond the Ivory Tower: The Frontiers of Public and Private Science*. New York: Taplinger.

—— (1978) *From Apes to Warlords: The Autobiography of Solly Zuckerman*. New York: Harper & Row.

Index